MW00850912

DATE DUE

Quentin Burdick:
The Gentle Warrior

Quentin Burdick:
The Gentle Warrior

Dan Rylance

North Dakota Institute for Regional Studies
North Dakota State University

North Dakota Institute for Regional Studies
North Dakota State University

Printed in Canada.

International Standard Book Number (ISBN): 978-0-911042-68-9
Library of Congress Control Number: 2007921710

This book is dedicated to those who care the most:
Billie Jo, Keli, David, Alexander and Mecca.

Contents

Acknowledgments

Personal interviews with dozens of thoughtful and interesting people made this book possible. This is a book pruned almost exclusively from the memories of Burdick contemporaries. They include family, friends, political allies and adversaries, and Senate colleagues and staff. All interviews were recorded and deposited after each interviewee signed a legal release form agreeing to deposit his or her interview in the Elwyn B. Robinson Department of Special Collections in the Chester Fritz Library at the University of North Dakota. Those who requested to speak off the record were not interviewed and those who refused to sign the release form after being interviewed were excluded from the writing of this book. Fortunately, their numbers were few, although their contributions are missed. Some interviews were stronger than others, but every interview contains valuable information not found elsewhere. Some interviewees were missed because of their passing before I got to interview them; others have died since being interviewed. Living senators were the most difficult to interview and those deceased senators were impossible to interview. I will never forget my time with the late Senator Mike Mansfield, former Senate majority leader (D-MT), who began the interview by saying he did not have anything to say and then spent the next 30 minutes giving me insights into a friend he called "The Silent Senator."

Writing sources are not excluded. Newspapers and the personal letters of Usher Burdick were invaluable. I did not, however, spend a great deal of time researching the public papers of Senator Burdick. The reason was a simple and obvious one. The public papers of many contemporary public figures, such as Senator Burdick, are devoid of personal insights into the person. Senators do not convey these thoughts by letter anymore. They communicate by telephone and in closed meetings. Their public papers are extensive on issues, constituent requests and state initiatives, but they do not provide fertile kernels of historical information for a biography. For those in the future who seek to write an analysis of Burdick's voting record or his relationship to major North Dakota interests groups, his public papers offer a rich chronology. They were not, however, particularly helpful to me in this endeavor.

My support of oral history interviews are confirmed in this project. I marvel at the memories of Burdick's college roommates, Morteer Shewes and Ken Byerly; the sharp and vivid recall of Senator Burdick's younger sibling, Eugene, now deceased; and the insights of former Governor Art Link. All shared with me their stories and memories about Senator Burdick that simply cannot be found elsewhere. The historical knowledge about North Dakota is stronger and the life of Quentin Burdick much deeper because of these interviews.

This project chartered a course in some ways similar to Quentin Burdick's early political adventures. This is a polite way of stating there were many disappointments and delays before completion. Repeated attempts to secure funding often proved unsuccessful. I think everyone involved in the project soon realized how difficult it was to raise funds to research and write a biography of a deceased member of the United States Senate. Every potential donor recognized Senator Burdick's contributions, but few were keen about financially supporting a project to write his biography. I thought many times that securing funds to honor a standing senator, who still votes and exercises power, might have been easier. In American politics, a deceased politician quickly becomes a forgotten one.

In addition to disappointments in fundraising, the research and writing stages constantly were interrupted by three moves across the county. During the course of the project, I moved from North Dakota to Illinois, Illinois to Idaho and Idaho to Wisconsin. Every move postponed research and delayed writing. It became a standard joke among our family to treat the packing and transportation of the "Burdick stuff" as some sort of religious pilgrimage. The stuff never left our sight or the safety of our automobile whenever and wherever we moved.

Several individuals, however, deserve most of the credit for the success of this project. North Dakota Senator Kent Conrad and his able state coordinator, Lynn Clancy of Bismarck, launched the project. They obtained initial funding and the services of the Quentin Burdick Center for Cooperatives at North Dakota State University (NDSU) as the sponsor. Without Conrad's leadership and Clancy's hard work, there would be no biography of Quentin Burdick.

Two executive directors at the Quentin Burdick Center for Cooperatives administered the project from start to finish. David Cobia oversaw the fundraising, research and early writing stages until his retirement in 1997. William Nelson and Gregory McKee, his successors, continued to oversee the completion of the writing and the publication of the manuscript. They offered continuity and institutional support for all stages of the project and secured the services of the North Dakota Institute for Regional Studies at NDSU to publish and market the book.

The combined efforts of Senator Conrad and his staff and the Center for Cooperatives obtained initial funding from four donors. They are the North Dakota Farmers Union, the North Dakota Association of Rural Electric Cooperatives, CENEX Inc. and the North Dakota Water Association. The Farmers Union, however, the first donor to provide financial support for the project, became the real catalyst for securing the other funds. Mark Watne, cooperative development specialist, was central in this effort. It is not an exaggeration to state that Burdick would have not succeeded as a politician and his biography would not have been written without the encouragement and steadfast support of the North Dakota Farmers Union.

Dennis Hill, general manager of the North Dakota Association of Rural Electric Cooperatives, spearheaded the second fundraising project. Hill, as chairman of the Quentin Burdick Center for Cooperatives Advisory Board, put together a loan program from additional sponsors to complete the funding. Seven new sponsors agreed to loan money to the project with repayment from the proceeds of the book sales proportional to their share in the pool. The seven loan sponsors are: Minnkota Power Cooperative, United Power Association, North Dakota AFL-CIO, Upper Missouri G & T Electric Cooperative, Cass County Electric, North Dakota Coordination Council of Cooperatives and the Cooperative Power Association.

The Burdick family endorses the project and participated in interviews. Jocelyn Birch Burdick, Quentin's widow, made countless contacts and answered endless questions. The Burdick children, Jan Mary, Jennifer, Jessica, Leslie and Birch, gave key interviews and shared valuable insights. Several days of interviews with Judge Eugene and May Burdick recreated the milieu of Quentin's youth and the importance of the Williston and Minnesota years on his later life.

Every person who took the time and effort to be interviewed contributed to the project. All of their names appear in this book. Additional research requests were answered by many, but especially by Richard Baker, Kevin Carvell, Kevin Duchschere, Amy Hoffarth, Judge Herb Meschke, Garry Pearson, and most of all, by Sandy Slater and other librarians everywhere. Robbie McGurran transcribed most of the interviews and redid each a second time after careful editing. Her professional expertise produced cogent and readable interviews, which facilitated my repeated use of them.

Interviews took me many places. I borrowed automobiles from Doug Rand, and Harriet and Playford Thorson. Jennifer Burdick provided me with free board and room for my Washington interviews. Austin and Mary Engel gave me their basement room on several Bismarck trips. Others, too many to mention and probably impossible to list comprehensively, bought me a meal here or there. For all of these kindnesses, I remain grateful.

I would like to thank Suzzanne Kelley, editor, for breathing new life into this manuscript. Her editing added strength and sharpness to this biography.

Last but never least, Billie Jo, my wife, and Mecca, my daughter, always offered encouragement and support. They made the good days better and the not so good ones tolerable. They guarded the Burdick stuff as their own.

The author, however, not the contributors, is responsible for any final errors that survive the research, writing, editing and publication stages of this work.

Introduction

The title, *Quentin Burdick: The Gentle Warrior*, was selected from nominations made by those participants I interviewed for the book. At the end of each interview, I offered everyone the opportunity to partake in the final product by selecting a title for the book. It was one way for me to express my appreciation for the time and effort they expended in the interview process. Selecting a title seemed an appropriate exercise, as well as a fun one, and most enjoyed the opportunity to contribute to the contest. I promised the winner a free copy of the book and credit for the selection.

There were two caveats. The title must clearly distinguish Quentin Burdick from his father, Congressman Usher Burdick, and his younger sibling, Judge Eugene Burdick. A simple title, *Burdick of North Dakota*, might have worked well under normal circumstances and sent a simple message about a man named Burdick who worked hard and long for the people of North Dakota. It would not work, however, in this case. The Burdick family produced three individuals who held public office and garnered national recognition. The title also must not be vague or cute. I urged simplicity: a title that must include the name Quentin Burdick modified by a short descriptor, which ideally would capture his essence or historical contributions.

The two most repeated title nominations failed the above criteria. Several people who knew Quentin during his early career suggested the old Nonpartisan League slogan, "We'll Stick. We'll Win," as either the whole title or part of the title. Many others who knew him primarily during his senior years proposed the nickname, "The Q," followed by various descriptors, such as Burdick or Quentin Burdick.

I considered both suggestions. They were creative and captured in part a significant portion of Burdick's career. The Nonpartisan League connection stood at the base of Burdick's rise to political power in North Dakota. Baptized a Progressive Republican, he found more in common with the Nonpartisan League creed than mainstream Republicanism. He fought in the struggle to switch the League from Republican to Democrat affiliation. He ran as a League Republican for public office before he ran as a Democrat. However, history since 1958 remembers Quentin Burdick primarily as the state's first successful congressional Democrat, not as a pillar of the League. The other suggestion, *The Q*, was simply too vague and too much of an insider choice for popular consumption. It was a cute and warm nickname used primarily by members of his Washington staff during Burdick's final years.

Two other titles surfaced from the nomination pool. Former Democrat Senate Majority leader from Montana, Mike Mansfield, proposed the first: *The Quiet* Senator. The suggestion came at the beginning of our interview and before I even asked him to make a title suggestion. When I asked him to make an opening statement about who was Quentin Burdick, he quipped, "The Quiet Senator." Mansfield went on to explain his analysis. He said that he never knew a fellow senator who spoke less than Burdick, but quickly added it was not necessarily a negative trait. Lucy Calautti proposed the second nomination, *The Gentle Warrior*. Calautti is an astute analyst of North Dakota political history and was a longtime director of Senator Byron Dorgan's office, and also the spouse of Kent Conrad, North Dakota's other senator.

Both titles appealed to me. I played with them and inserted Quentin Burdick's name followed by a colon in front of each. The result was two short, but descriptive, titles, which were concise and clear and did not confuse Quentin with either Usher or Eugene Burdick. I had two good titles for the book and labored over which one to choose. In the end, I selected *Quentin Burdick: The Gentle Warrior*. There were several reasons. Calautti's title encompasses Burdick's lifetime and Mansfield's title works perfectly as a chapter title for Burdick's Senate years. There were many episodes in Burdick's life that support the label of a gentle warrior. He was a fistfighter, a football player, a trial lawyer, a Farmers Union organizer and a tireless candidate for public office. In all of these endeavors, Burdick was a fierce competitor — a warrior of sorts. Yet, for all his combativeness — and he demonstrated a tendency to reduce almost every confrontation to a sort of physical contest — Burdick was never bullish. There was a courtly, almost self-effacing, quality to his actions. Thus the adjective *gentle* to modify warrior stuck. The more I researched and wrote about Quentin Burdick, the more the title, *The Gentle Warrior*, appealed to me.

When I asked Calautti to explain her title choice, she paused briefly, but then responded rather forcibly. "I would call it *Quentin Burdick: The Gentle Warrior* because he wanted to be a warrior, and he liked to think of himself as a warrior, but he mostly played by the rules and when he went into these fights, he purred. He didn't roar!"

Wow! How Burdick would have roared after reading that interpretation! He would have turned his head slightly and pushed his jaw out even more. He knew full well the charges leveled against him by Byron Dorgan and other members of the North Dakota Democrat-NPL Party that he was, at least in his last years, a pussycat. It was time for him to step down in 1988 and turn over the keys of his Senate office to then Congressman Dorgan. The Dorgan challenge was never consummated. When the showdown came, the only competitor who showed up for the fight was Burdick, and he was roaring, not purring. The Dorgan challenge awakened the old man and reinvigorated his thirst for one more contest. In the fall, when Representative Earl Strinden, his Republican opponent, offered his hand at the conclusion of their debate at the North Dakota Heritage Center, Burdick grabbed it hard and pulled Strinden temporarily off balance. The gesture got enormous press and conveyed the image of Burdick's physical strength over a much younger opponent. It would be the final act of aggression by the Gentle Warrior.

On a personal level, I did not know Quentin Burdick. I met him on just a few occasions. Three stick out. The first occurred in June of 1972, when I was working for Senator Milton R. Young. The work allowed me some free time to solicit additional manuscript material for the Department of Special Collections in the Chester Fritz Library at the University of North Dakota (UND). My primary aim was to secure the papers of Senator Burdick. So one morning, I strolled over to the old Senate office building, where the state's junior senator was located, to see him. It was quite early, before the Washington heat and humidity hit the blacktop. He was not in. So I waited, and several minutes later, in he came. I quickly introduced myself, which seemed not to impress him at all, but before I could say anything more, he proceeded to go into an adjacent bathroom and started to shave. He just kept talking, so I just listened until he finished his morning shave.

When he finally sat down at his desk, we got down to business. Before I could say much, he asked me straight up, "What do you want those papers for?" I do not remember my exact answer because I was nervous. "For the university and history," I think was my reply. "Take 'em," he replied without hesitation. I was unprepared for his response or the immediacy of the transfer. I spent the next week in a wire cage labeled "Burdick" in the attic of what had to be the hottest building in Washington, packing hundreds of boxes of his material, as well as the many old records of his father, Congressman Usher L. Burdick.

I met Senator Burdick a second time, five months later. It was in October, and I was running for the office of North Dakota secretary of state on the Democratic-NPL ticket. I had sacrificed my annual vacation to spend most of the last month before the general election to campaign around the state. I was only 30 years old, had never run for public office before, and was running against the incumbent, Ben Meier, who had served in that position for most of my entire life. I was in Mandan on that particular day and was scheduled to go door to door with some local legislative candidates when Senator Burdick arrived at party headquarters. He took me aside and gave me some advice that I should not be too optimistic (I lost by more than 80,000 votes), but that I should learn from the experience and try again. I spent part of the day with him as we went door to door in a trailer court and some low-income housing for the elderly. He worked one side and I went down another side. He matched me stride for stride and his presence gave me confidence. He was then 64 years old.

The third meeting occurred in December of 1991. I knocked on his door in Fargo and Jocelyn Burdick invited me in. Burdick appeared a few minutes later in an old bathrobe and well-worn slippers. We sipped homemade hot chocolate in the living room, and I asked him whether he would consent to a series of interviews on his life. (I then was employed by the *Grand Forks Herald* as the editorial page editor.) He gave me the same straight answer he did almost 20 years earlier, and the interviews were scheduled for early January.

The interviews proved uneven. I struggled with many of the questions and he struggled with many of his answers. I tried to establish a rhythm to help him and to create an atmosphere to harvest history. I felt a deep sense of urgency that what I was doing would be the last opportunity for anyone to conduct an in-depth interview with Burdick. He was then 84 years old and not in good health. The interviews, titled "Conversations with 'The Q'," ran in the *Grand Forks Herald* in April of 1992, and they were as I had surmised — the last in-depth interviews with Senator Burdick to be published. He died five months later on September 8, 1992.

The 1992 interviews form the first cell of this biography. Several themes emerging ever so slightly in those interviews became major building blocks in the book. The first theme is family. Burdick experienced a difficult youth; at age 13, he was thrust into stressful circumstances in the Burdick household. His parents divorced in the fall of 1921, and Emma, his mother, and three children were left to make it on their own on an ill-conceived farming and ranching operation near Williston in the northwestern corner of North Dakota. The family earned little money and Quentin, as the oldest child, assumed the most responsibility. He became, by default, the titular head of the Burdick family.

The second theme evolves from the first. It centers on the relationship between father and son. The son tried in so many ways to be like his famous father, Usher. He played football at the University of Minnesota and the two became the first father-son lettermen in Gopher football history. He became a lawyer and then a member of Congress as well. Usher had accomplished all of these things with distinction and notoriety, and so did his son, Quentin. Still, there remained an incomplete bond between them. Football seemed to mend family hurts the most, but Quentin, unlike his father, spent a great deal of time on the Minnesota team's injured list. Quentin did not win an election to public office until 1958, the year Usher stepped down. Father's three additional marriages did not endear father to son, either. Usher's fourth marriage especially proved an embarrassment to his family and to Quentin. Usher died on Aug. 19, 1960, 11 days after his son began his Senate career.

The third great theme is football. At dusk, Quentin Burdick wanted more than anything to be remembered for being "a damn good football player." It seemed as important — maybe more important — to him as his long career in the U.S. Senate. Unfortunately, many of his football exploits are lost to history. If there had been an all-state high school team in North Dakota in 1924 and 1925, Williston's Quentin Burdick would have been on the team twice. He was the best rushing fullback on offense and the best tackler as linebacker in defense in the state during his junior and senior years. He was a tough, hard-nosed competitor and a natural blocker and tackler. However, his career at Minnesota was plagued by nagging injuries. In his senior year, Burdick inked more press for not playing than most players earned for playing.

The fourth theme is Burdick's contribution as the builder of the modern North Dakota Democratic-NPL Party. He was the standard-bearer of the successful party that made North Dakota a solid two-party state. He was also its first significant winner in 1958, a record he maintained without blemish, for the remainder of his life. Every public officeholder of the party since then owes at least one bow to the senator. This includes Governors William Guy, Art Link and George Sinner; Representative Earl Pomeroy and Senators Byron Dorgan and Kent Conrad. For them and others, Burdick toiled through the back roads of North Dakota politics for 26 years, without money and suffering six defeats before he hit political pay dirt. Since 1958, his hard work and political success have been shared by many others. He, more than any other single individual, worked to build the present-day North Dakota Democratic-NPL Party. There will be detractors to that thesis. This book devotes an entire chapter to Governor Guy and his relationship to Burdick, which was testy, to say the least. In the final analysis, however, Burdick, although lacking the organizational skills of a Guy or a Dorgan, remained the heart and soul of the party. When he ran, his party ran better. When he spent a considerable portion of his campaign funds on voter surveys, the party enjoyed higher turnouts.

Finally, this biography is about Burdick's Senate career. It spanned 32 years of his life, almost a third of his entire life. Yet, only one chapter is devoted to those 32 years. It is not an unreasonable question to ask why only one chapter, nor should my answer be considered unreasonable, either. Burdick, the man, was more important in the first 52 years of his life than he was in his last 32 years, an observation made perfectly clear in this biography. The fact that he served in the U.S. Senate did not alter his history lifeline. Although Burdick's Senate career was important, it was not historically significant to national history. He did not run for president or vice president, nor did he ever become a visible spokesman for liberal causes on the Senate floor. He remained like his predecessors, Senators William Langer and Milton Young, a sort of water boy for his constituents. For Burdick, riding in a July 4 parade in a small North Dakota town was deemed more important than speaking out about an important piece of national legislation. The strategy kept him in office longer and it made his life easier. He was a gentle warrior. Burdick was also a pretelevision senator and his career must be viewed in that context. Burdick performed best behind closed doors and without the intrusion of television cameras. He was a workhorse, not a show horse. The fact that he considered Garrison Diversion his most important contribution attests to the narrow nature of his Senate career. Burdick served more as a North Dakota senator than a United States senator. At the same time, Burdick was a consistent and strong supporter of national Democratic issues ranging from choice to civil rights to clean air. Ironically, his support for these liberal issues without personal fanfare kept him in office longer. He voted a liberal agenda and got away with it politically. But in the final assessment, his career must be placed more in his relationship to North Dakota than to Washington's world.

This is a good time to publish a biography of Quentin Burdick. His death more than a decade ago is recent but not too recent. It is close enough for those who knew him to remember his contributions and celebrate his accomplishments. At the same time, it is far enough removed from the present day to allow those who asked more of him to forgive and forget. Representative Byron Dorgan is now Senator Byron Dorgan. Although Burdick greatly angered him for putting his journey to the Senate on hold in 1988, he is now in the Senate. His career seems secure, barring some horrendous personal or political misstep. So telling Burdick's story now ensures that it will not be lost forever for those who knew him best.

Burdick should also be remembered for closing a chapter in North Dakota political history. He was the last of his generation to serve in public office. The last of a Depression generation that fought constantly for a vertical realignment of economic forces, which included the establishment of farm cooperatives, rural electric associations, telephone cooperatives and unions. Today all of these stand as a permanent part of North Dakota's economic and political landscape.

They did not for much of Burdick's life. He spent an enormous amount of personal energy and political capital to raise their level of power and acceptance. Burdick's serious side was a natural result of the era he came from. He was not just tight; he was obsessed with personal frugality. He wore the tattoo of the Depression clearly on his person. He was also suspicious of foreign military aid and a firm supporter of personal freedoms. These attitudes derived from the North Dakota of his father's era and the ideology of the Nonpartisan League.

There are other important legacies that Burdick represented, which are now gone permanently from our culture. He was the last of the pretelevision social capital politicians. He was the last great North Dakota political handshaker. The last North Dakota consumate parade participant. The last great North Dakota doorbell ringer. The last North Dakota political stump speaker. Finally, he was the last home-state politician to serve his state in the halls of Congress. Fargo was, since he graduated from the University of Minnesota, always his home. He worked in Washington, but he never left Fargo.

Senator Kent Conrad contrasted the Burdick era with the one he works in today: "I think [Quentin Burdick] represented a generation and a day that is slipping away," said Conrad in a March 27, 1995, interview. "It's a different era, a different set of challenges, and a different set of opportunities. I think he was one of the last of the senators from a different era — a time when the United States was in many ways defined by its conflict with the Soviet Union, with the two worlds, Communism and non-Communist, engaging in an intense competition militarily, economically, politically and socially. He was an old-time liberal, and I use those words with respect. It is a different time now with a different set of circumstances, and I think it calls for a different response. ... Yes, Quentin was of a different era, and we're unlikely to see someone coming from that same background emerge in the foreseeable future."

Age deserves respect. I hope readers of this biography share my respect for this unusual North Dakota political figure. I learned so much in researching and writing about his life, and I apologize to all for taking so long to complete it.

Dan Rylance
Oshkosh, Wisconsin
Summer 2006

- one -

Political Traditions

The coincidental deaths of Arthur C. Townley and Senator William Langer on November 7, 1959, and former Representative Usher L. Burdick on August 19, 1960, brought to closure more than a half-century of North Dakota political leadership. During their long political careers, all three men were at different times identified with the Nonpartisan League (NPL), the farmers of North Dakota and the Republican Party.

Townley founded the agrarian-based Nonpartisan League in 1915. Built on the philosophy of the American Society of Equity, the failure of Populism and the misdirection of Progressivism, the League roared across the wind-swept North Dakota prairie during the elections of 1916 and 1918. With total control of state government secured by the 1918 elections, it moved quickly during the 1919 legislative session to enact a program of state socialism. Its plank was ambitious and radical. The League sought to enact state ownership of terminal elevators and flour mills, guarantee fair inspection of the grain trade, exempt farm improvements from taxation, create a comprehensive state hail insurance program and establish state-owned banks.[1]

Although the NPL never officially became a political party in North Dakota, it acted like one for 40 years, and in 1956, became part of one. The League collected dues and published its own newspaper. It conducted precinct and district caucuses, held state conventions, and endorsed candidates for local and state offices. It created a unique logo – a rebellious goat – and its political battle cry, "We'll Stick. We'll Win," resonated from Crosby, in the northwest corner of North Dakota, to Rutland in the southeast corner, from farmstead to farmstead, and across section lines. From 1916 to 1956, it filed its candidates on a separate slate in the Republican primary. Since 1956, the league joined with the Democratic Party to form the North Dakota Democratic-NPL Party, but it no longer conducts separate league conventions or files a separate slate of candidates in the Democratic primary.

Townley never gained elective political office for himself. Encouraged by the success of the Nonpartisan League in North Dakota, he tried to take the League into the national arena. He opened a national office in St. Paul early in 1917, but his strong, unrelenting opposition to the United States entry into World War I weakened its progress and cost him a 90-day jail sentence in Minnesota for an alleged anti-American speech. The 1921, recall of North Dakota's League governor, attorney general and commissioner of agriculture and labor forced Townley's hand. He lost political control of the League to a committee and resigned his presidency in 1922.

Townley spent the remainder of his life searching in vain for the power he once enjoyed in North Dakota. He organized a National Producers Alliance and the American Temperance League. He tried many times unsuccessfully to win political office in North Dakota. He attacked William Langer's leadership of the second Nonpartisan League and became the state's loudest red-baiter, especially attacking the programs and policies of the North Dakota Farmers Union.

He died later in the same day, November 7, 1959, as his longtime nemesis, William Langer. Ironically perhaps, Townley died in a car accident doing what he always liked and did best, driving, searching, planning to raise money for still one more political enterprise. His estate, although never probated, was valued at less than $2,000. The fire that consumed his vehicle after the car accident destroyed his entire accumulation of personal possessions and historical records.[2]

William Langer, unlike Townley, was never a bona fide farmer, which was technically a prerequisite for membership in the Nonpartisan League. Townley and William Lemke, a friend and fellow lawyer, recruited Langer to be the League's first candidate for attorney general in 1916. Langer brought impressive credentials to the ticket as the son of a well-known Cass County farmer and banker, an aggressive and successful prosecuting attorney in Morton County (1914-1916) and a candidate with unbridled political ambition. Langer, however, was never a socialist. He remained a Progressive Republican. Nevertheless, Langer was astute enough to see the emerging strength of Townley's popular farmers' movement; he quickly jumped aboard and got elected as the League's first attorney general.[3]

Soon after the successful 1918 elections, Langer came in conflict with Townley's politics and policies. Langer charged NPL banks with fraud, and he successfully defended Minnie J. Nielson when Neil MacDonald, defeated by

Nielson, refused to give up his office for superintendent of public instruction. In the June 1920 Republican primary, Langer challenged Governor Lynn Frazier, the incumbent League governor, and lost a close election by 5,414 votes.[4] As penance, Langer spent most of the '20s in political exile for having betrayed boss Townley and the NPL membership.

Tough times in the '20s and '30s provided Langer with a second political opportunity. After 1928, he began to rebuild the Nonpartisan League, and in 1932, he stepped into office as governor. Langer's political machine replaced Townley's political machine. Although Langer was removed from office in 1934 for misuse of federal relief funds, he was re-elected governor in 1936 and defeated incumbent Senator Lynn Frazier for the U.S. Senate in 1940. By the 1950s, however, the second Nonpartisan League re-established by Langer was now a part of the emerging Democrat Party. In 1958, as a final gesture of hegemony in the then conservative-controlled Republican Party, they denied Langer his endorsement as a Republican for a fourth term as U.S. senator. The slight did not matter. Although Langer was nearly blind from diabetes and grief-stricken by the death of his beloved wife, Lydia, from cancer months earlier, his personal appeal to North Dakota voters carried him to one final victory.[5] He easily defeated the Republican nominee, Clyde Duffy of Devils Lake, and died in office a year later.

Usher Burdick never identified with Townley's Nonpartisan League. In fact, Burdick became one of its first political victims. He was bowled over by the League candidate for governor, Lynn Frazier, who defeated him by more than 15,000 votes in the 1916 June Republican primary.[6] But Burdick, like Langer, was a Progressive Republican. He launched a successful legislative career as a legislator from Munich in Cavalier County in 1908, garnering peer acclaim as speaker of the House in 1909 and state recognition as lieutenant governor from 1911-1912. Burdick's political fortunes seemed bright until he ran directly into Townley's political prairie fire. Burdick's 1916 defeat for governor put him on the sidelines of North Dakota politics for many years.

The Depression of the '30s also gave Burdick a second political opportunity. Burdick became president of the Iowa-based Farm Holiday Association. He spoke at farmers' meetings throughout the state, and his name became synonymous with protests against farm foreclosures — the core issue of the Farm Holiday movement.[7]

In the '30s, Burdick and Langer also became political allies. Langer, as governor, issued executive proclamations in support of Burdick's efforts against farm foreclosures. Burdick, as president of the North Dakota Farm Holiday Association, supported Langer in his unsuccessful attempt to remain governor.

Burdick began a second political career in 1934 with League endorsement to the U.S. House of Representatives, serving five terms. In 1944, he tried unsuccessfully to defeat incumbent U.S. Senator Gerald P. Nye in the June Republican primary, but he was re-elected to the U.S. House of Representatives in 1946 and served five consecutive terms until his retirement in 1958.

In 1958, North Dakota Republicans did the same thing to Burdick that they did to Langer — only worse. Mark Andrews, then a young delegate from Cass County, recalled what happened at the 1958 Republican state convention:

> They didn't refuse to endorse him. He didn't want to be [endorsed]. Usher said he was going to step down and announced his decision a few months before the convention. The thing they refused to do was when Usher showed up at the convention was to allow him to speak. The decent and courteous thing would have been to say, "Usher, old friend, you have served us so well for so many years, we would love to hear from you and present you to the podium." Then he would get a standing ovation and would talk to them as only he could talk, with some of his witticisms about North Dakota, about people in general and about them damn fools down in Washington. That would have been the graceful thing to do.[8]

However, the Republican leaders at the convention refused Burdick his one last public opportunity to say goodbye to the Republican Party that he had served all his life. Later Andrews walked with a sulking Burdick back to his room at the Patterson Hotel in Bismarck. "I was sitting in the hotel room," Andrews recalled, when Usher went to the telephone to call his son Quentin: "Quent, you've gotta to run for my House seat," Usher bellowed. "You have no idea what these blankety-blanks did."[9]

What happened made history. Quentin Burdick, a Democrat, ran for the U.S. House seat vacated by his father, Usher Burdick, a Republican, and won. In so doing, he became the first Democrat in North Dakota history to be elected to the U.S. House of Representatives. Less than two years later in June 1960, Representative Quentin Burdick ran for and won the unexpired term left vacant by the death of Senator William Langer, a Republican, and never turned back, serving as North Dakota's Democratic-NPL senator until his death on September 8, 1992.

Quentin Burdick nourished his political career from the same political soil cultivated by his father and Langer. He, too, was born and raised a Progressive Republican, growing up in the Burdick household weaned on the speeches of Theodore Roosevelt, Robert La Follette and his father. He stayed with the

Grand Old Party until after World War II, but then threw his Progressive support behind Henry Wallace's Progressive Party in 1948 and went to work for the North Dakota Farmers Union, helping to merge the Nonpartisan League with the Democrats. His constituents were the same, too — the farmers of North Dakota. The young Burdick began his practice of law as legal counsel for foreclosed-upon farmers sent to him by his father. He soon added other clients — a growing number of North Dakota Farmers Union members and Teamster Union truck drivers in Fargo. His symbol was still that old NPL goat, and he knew better than anyone the true meaning of the slogan, "We'll Stick. We'll Win," after losing his first six elections.

However, there were many changes, too, between the years of Usher Burdick, William Langer and Quentin Burdick. The experiment in state socialism was long over. Its two surviving socialist symbols — the State Mill and Elevator in Grand Forks and the Bank of North Dakota in Bismarck — stood proudly as monuments to North Dakota's socialistic past, but not as models for future expansion. North Dakota's shot at state socialism was radical and mildly successful in the beginning, but eventually the experiment ended. There would never be more state mills or state banks in North Dakota.

Most North Dakotans, however, felt comfortable passing their political support from Langer and the elder Burdick to Quentin Burdick. There was continuity in the name. There was strength of commitment and character. There was the fight for the same principles and for new ones, such as the growing cooperative movement, Garrison Diversion, more funding for the Rural Electrification Association, and continued support for new and better farm programs. The Burdick name made the voters' transition from Republican to Democrat smoother to follow and easier to understand. If Quentin was pinned with a liberal label, he sure did not act — or dress — like one. He usually wore rumpled suits and always donned a black homburg hat. Over time, this attire became his political symbols. He was Quentin Burdick, attorney at large, and the North Dakota people were his constituents — all of them.

To understand how Quentin Burdick became a Democrat and how North Dakota emerged as a viable Democratic state, one must briefly review the older political traditions of Populism and Progressivism: Townley's first Nonpartisan League and its opposition, the Independent Voters Association; Langer's second Nonpartisan League and its counterpart, the Republican Organizing Convention; the final separation of the Nonpartisan League with Republicans; and the growth of the Democratic-NPL Party since 1956.

Populists and Progressives

Sandwiched between the eclipse of Dakota Territory and the division of North Dakota and South Dakota into states in 1889, Populism was the first real political movement in both states. Its origins rested on two themes — one political and one economic. In political terms, Populism was a protest against 28 years of territorial apprenticeship (1861-1889). This was a period of increasing tension between a federal government that held most of the power in the territory and a growing local population anxious to exercise home rule as new states in the federal system. In economic terms, it was a protest against how the territory was being settled and controlled. The litany of complaints ran long. People saw themselves being exploited by railroads, grain trusts and bankers. Their specific grievances included excessive freight rates, unfair grain grading and weighing, high interest rates and monopolistic prices.[10]

Who were the Populists? Matching the South Dakota Farmers Alliance membership and ledger records with census and tax records in Marshall County in northeast South Dakota allows construction of a small but meaningful profile. Like most settlers, the members were farmers — more than 96 percent, 50 percent of whom owned land. They were immigrants who came primarily from Scandinavia and Germany. Only the "most foreign of immigrants joined the alliance."[11] They held debt. In fact, they held more debt than farmers who did not belong to the alliance. But they were more wealthy farmers, too. They were commercial farmers as opposed to marginal ones, which logically was a prime factor for their increased debt. If Marshall County was a barometer of membership for the region, "Fathers, foreign men, landed farmers and indebted farmers were the most likely to become Populists ... not poor, but propertied."[12]

Populism in North Dakota was less potent than in South Dakota. Although the states shared a common territorial heritage, Populism went different directions after statehood. South Dakota Populists formed a third party, while members in North Dakota flirted between fusion with the Democrats and being independent. Populists in South Dakota concentrated on economic issues while those in North Dakota were sidetracked with Prohibition. Henry Loucks was a stronger leader in South Dakota than Walter Muir, his counterpart in North Dakota. Governor Andrew Lee of South Dakota worked hard to implement Populist programs, while Governor Eli Shortridge of North Dakota never demonstrated Populist principles.[13]

According to historian D. Jerome Tweton, "Populism in North Dakota never developed as a vital force. Wed to fusion, at first with Prohibitionists and later with the Democrats, it downplayed the subtreasury system and other Populist proposals that would have altered the nature of government and society. Shortridge, the only independent to hold the state's highest office, never fully accepted the philosophy of Populism and indeed, worked against it."[14]

The victory of Eli Shortridge in 1892 under a Populist, Democratic, Independent or fusion label revealed a momentary victory of dissatisfied voters over regular Republicans on some local issues and individual personalities. Two years later, the stalwart Republicans — supported by a favorable press, fear of a third party, more money and the Depression of 1893 — ended third-party activity in North Dakota.

North Dakota Populists simply acted as though they did not know who they were or what they represented. A prime example was the results of the 1892 presidential race. James Weaver, the Populist candidate, narrowly defeated Benjamin Harrison, the Republican candidate, by less than 200 votes. But when the Electoral College met, one of the Weaver electors in North Dakota suddenly switched his vote to Grover Cleveland, the Democratic candidate.[15]

Despite initial failure, Populists in North Dakota set the stage for later political movements. The first generation of reformers reacted against exploitation and big business. North Dakota remained a colony of the Twin Cities' interests, whether those interests were in railroads, banks or the grain trust. Reformers recognized that farmers needed to be represented because they still exercised no political power. The Republican Party was too strong and popular to beat. It was the party of the North, of Lincoln, of the Union, of immigrants and homesteaders. A long-term successful political movement must be identified with rather than against the Republicans. Affiliation with an Independent party or the Democrat Party might work in the short term, but over time Republican loyalties were simply too strong to overcome. Prohibition was a side issue; the real issues were economic. This recognition was the key to farmer support.

North Dakota Populists also failed because of a strong political machine controlled by Alexander McKenzie, the chief lobbyist of the railroads. He stole the territorial capital from Yankton to Bismarck, hand-picked North Dakota's first eight governors, and ran state politics from his St. Paul and Bismarck hotel suites. McKenzie was the state's first political genius, but he stood on the other side of political reform. McKenzie was against change, not for it. "I never lead people," he once said. "I outguess them."[16]

Progressivism appeared much stronger in North Dakota than Populism. In fact, most treatments praise it in glowing terms. Historian Elwyn Robinson in *History of North Dakota* used one of the most powerful words in the historical lexicon by labeling the movement "the revolution of 1906."[17] Led by the election of "Honest" John Burke, a Democrat and lawyer, as governor, Progressives shaped the election in terms of McKenzieism and offered voters a straightforward alternative — purity in politics. George Winship, a leading Progressive and founder of the *Grand Forks Herald,* put the issue simply:

> There is just one issue before the people of North Dakota this year and that is whether the people are ready to take charge of their government or will permit three or four bosses to manage in their own interests and according to their own caprice. … The people know that the political government of this state has been an atrocious scandal, and they are earnest in their desire for better things.[18]

Who were the Progressives? They were much different than their Populist elders. They were lawyers and journalists, academics and small-business men. They were likely to be Protestant, although both Langer and Burke were Roman Catholics. They were college-educated, often the first generation of settlers or first-generation transients who came into North Dakota to make a better life. In defining who they were, it is obvious who they were not. Farmers were not a major part of the Progressive revolution in North Dakota.[19]

Obeying the law was central to the Progressives. "No matter whether we think it is unjust, no matter whether we believe in the principles of the law," Burke said, "it is our duty so long as it is the law to respect it and use our influence to enforce it."[20] Usher Burdick preached that philosophy as a legislator. William Langer practiced it as state's attorney and attorney general. Dozens of other lawyers scattered in county seats and cities around the state preached and practiced the same sermon. Fairness, openness and square deals flowed from the fountain of Progressivism; one of the best guarantees to ensure that it kept flowing was to enforce all good laws and eventually repeal the bad ones.

Many Progressives believed that representing the people was more important than representing a political party. Burke, for example, served as a Democrat, but he also appealed to traditional Republican voters because of his Progressive principles. Winship, as founder and publisher of the *Grand Forks Herald,* also put people ahead of party. Although he was a practicing Republican, his newspaper became a leading critic of the McKenzie ring, a supporter of Burke's administration and a promoter of fairness. His political philosophy, so succinct and relevant, remains the cornerstone of the *Herald* editorial page today and aptly personifies the mood of the Progressive era in North Dakota between 1906 and 1912. "It will be the people's paper, run strictly in their interests, guarding jealously their rights and maintaining boldly their cause."[21]

Professor Edwin Ladd, a promoter of good laws and the head chemist at the Agricultural Experiment Station at the North Dakota Agricultural College

(NDAC, later North Dakota State University) was a consumer products activist. Ladd spent a long and distinguished career crusading against adulterated foods, poisonous paints and fake fertilizers. From his Fargo laboratory, Ladd published bulletin after bulletin condemning consumer products that were unsafe for human consumption. Because of his activism, Ladd became nationally known and locally recognized. In 1916, he became president of NDAC, and in 1920, he was elected to the U.S. Senate, where he served North Dakota until his death in 1925.[22]

During the three legislative sessions of the Burke administration (1907, 1909, 1911) lawmaking reached a new, creative high in Bismarck. Under Burke's leadership and a supportive press, North Dakota Progressives wove two major themes into the state political tapestries. The first effort modernized state government. Lawmakers established a new system of state agencies and updated existing ones. For example, North Dakota established a juvenile court system, workmen's compensation, a public health laboratory and a library commission.[23]

The second theme was broader but equally significant. North Dakota established a model Progressive program to rid the state of bossism and return political power to the people. It followed national lines of Progressivism and included the direct primary, the initiative, referendum and recall, presidential and senate preference primaries, a commission form of government and corrupt practices measures.[24]

These were impressive legal gains for a young state more used to political control than active participation. By modernizing state government, Progressives sought to protect society with better management and accurate information. They hoped to achieve what Professor Ladd accomplished with pure food across a much broader spectrum of health, libraries, courts and regulatory agencies. Modernization, however, was not just about gathering the information; it required implementing expertise to put the data to work and to create public policy. As states modernized, they became equal partners, serving to instill governance over private enterprises more concerned with profit than the welfare of the people.

Removing state government control from the hands of McKenzie also required changes in the rules of politics. Direct primaries brought openness to state and local elections. It weakened McKenzie's power to hand-pick political candidates. Direct democracy by initiative and referendum gave ordinary citizens the opportunity to pass or refer laws. If the Legislature would not pass a good bill, the people could initiate their own law by petition. If the Legislature passed a bad bill, the people could refer it by petition. If politicians misbehaved, the people could recall them and force a special election by petition.

Two key questions linger about the significance of North Dakota's Progressive experiment. Did it succeed in its primary goal to curb the power of boss McKenzie? And, if it was so successful, what accounts for the roaring success of the Nonpartisan League five years later in 1916?

History does not offer a clear-cut answer to the first question. North Dakota Progressives asserted repeatedly that their movement buried the McKenzie ring. Burke left the state in 1913 to become U.S. treasurer under the administration of President Woodrow Wilson. Winship was forced to sell his *Grand Forks Herald* to local business interests who were not cut from the Progressive mold. Louis B. Hanna, a Fargo businessman and a conservative Republican, became governor in 1912. As for McKenzie, the historical record remains incomplete because of the paucity of material. "Men close to him assert that he still ruled but at long range," noted one source. "It is even said that McKenzie had a hand in organizing and directing the first activities of the League despite the popular impression that their political courses were as diametrically opposed as the poles."[25] McKenzie advised, "Never write a letter — walk across the state if necessary, but never write a letter. Sure, what you say goes up in smoke, but what you write is before you always," assured that few documents would detail his actions.[26]

Since McKenzie's power ultimately rode with the railroads, North Dakota Progressivism accomplished little. The ratification of the anti-pass bill in 1911 eliminated the political power of the free railroad pass, but the adoption of the direct primary made this form of political patronage, long a symbol of railroad power, less relevant anyway. In truth, new regulations did not lower railroad rates and licensing did not curb the abuses of the elevators. North Dakota Progressivism concentrated on bossism but ignored economic issues. It enacted elements of Wisconsin Progressivism political reform, but the Twin Cities' interests still controlled the state. It attempted reform under a Democratic administration in a state covered by a one-party blanket. It superimposed legislative reform but accomplished little for a farmer-producing class. It received much of its support from moralistic-minded Scandinavians but ignored the state's largest ethnic group, the Germans from Russia.

In time, North Dakota came to honor both the boss and the reformer. McKenzie died in St. Paul on June 22, 1922. Three days later, North Dakota officially accorded him a state funeral. The Northern Pacific Railroad transported his body from St. Paul to Bismarck, where it was met by three honor guards representing the North Dakota National Guard, the Masonic Lodge and the Roman Catholic Church. McKenzie's body lay in public view in the grand corridor of the old capitol; a memorial service in a standing-room-only crowd in the House of Representatives chambers followed.[27] McKenzie the boomer and McKenzie the boss came home to the city and state he controlled for many years. If his power had departed, his legacy remained.

In contrast, North Dakota waited until 1961, nearly 24 years after his death, to honor John Burke. A special appointed commission selected him as the state's single representative to be honored with a statue in the new Statuary Hall of the U.S. Capitol. Most states chose two, but Burke stood alone as a representative of North Dakota until the 21st century. Burke and the Progressive Era he represented came before the fray of Nonpartisan League and anti-League forces, which divided the state for the next four decades. Selecting Burke was not controversial. He was a safe, consensus symbol of North Dakota's Progressive Era. Selecting Arthur Townley or William Langer, or later choosing between Milton Young and Quentin Burdick, would prove much more difficult, ultimately creating deadlock, disagreement and hard feelings.

The answer to the second question is much easier to provide than the first since the Nonpartisan League shared little in common with Progressivism. The NPL was a sudden explosion of angry farmers, and its quick rise to power is a testimony to the organizational genius of Townley and the depth of the farmers' despair. "The abuses practiced by the grain trade were probably the principal stimulant for the development," wrote one agricultural historian, "but high railroad and interest rates added to the dissatisfaction with existing economic and political conditions."[28]

The First Nonpartisan League (1916-1921)

The first Nonpartisan League, established by Arthur Townley, was a return to the Populist Movement of the 1890s. Its overnight success grew out of the earlier political errors of Populism and the more immediate gains of Progressivism. The League learned from Walter Muir and the Populists the sheer political futility of running as an Independent or third party in a strong, one-party state. Astutely, it hid its socialistic ideology under the popular banner of the North Dakota Republican Party. The League stayed within the Republican family, believing that a June primary in a state with no voter registration was the best strategy to gain political power. For North Dakota voters, the primary became the main event. The Republican primary winner more often than not went on to defeat most Democratic opponents in the fall. When League candidates did lose in the primary, they immediately refiled their candidates in the November general election under the Independent Republican column, thereby splitting the vote three ways and employing a second opportunity to win. Such action was political genius and it worked to provide North Dakota with two-party representation under a one-party label.

Who were the Leaguers? The simple answer was farmers, but recent studies suggest that in 1915 and 1916, many of the Leaguers already had opted for membership in either the American Society of Equity or the North Dakota Farmers Union (or both) before they joined the League. Townley and his socialism salesmen were able to organize the farmers quickly because others had already organized them in the past.[29]

The League also continued the rationale of McKenzieism, but focused its party on the needs of a farmer-producing class. In doing so, it injected a class warfare theme into North Dakota politics. "Go home and slop the hogs," became the famous League slogan. It was a statement supposedly attributed to Treadwell Twitchell, a powerful Cass County Republican legislator, who reportedly told some farmers at the 1915 legislative session that running state government was none of their business. Instead, he said, they ought to "go home and slop the hogs."[30] The insult stuck. It soon became the rallying cry of League organizers and the best-remembered quote in the annals of League history.

The League inflicted harm upon itself as well. Its rhetoric, more than Twitchell's slight, ignited heated class warfare. The League pitted farmers against small-town businessmen, the farmers' wives and children against the nonfarmers' wives and children; the farmers against the elevator men; the farmers against the bankers; the farmers against the railroad depot agents; and the League newspaper editors against the non-League newspaper editors. These were tough, hard, bitter times, which politically divided small North Dakota communities between League and non-League factions and small towns against larger ones. People knew their place in this stressful environment, and they based their preferences for which stores they traded in on political affiliation rather than quality or discounted rates.

Public speech added to the stress. League rhetoric, especially during election rallies, raised furor. Townley's speechmaking, for example, bordered on demagoguery. He relished poking malicious fun at businessmen and lawyers: "I don't know what business you are in," Townley said, shaking his finger at the mayor of a small town, "but I will bet you belong to some association and that you pay more a year than these farmers do." When the mayor quietly explained he was a doctor and proud of paying $8 a year to the medical associations, Townley cut him off. "There you are," he shouted to the crowd.[31]

The League stressed loyalty. Its motto, "We'll Stick. We'll Win," was much more than just a slogan; it was a political catechism for behavior. Do not go your own way. Always follow League orders. The pain in penalties for those who did not stick was as strong as accolades for those who did. Townley's League demanded total obedience from all League members. During the legislative sessions, for example, the League caucused nightly at secret meetings held at the McKenzie Hotel to inform its members of the next day's voting agenda and to keep them in check. The caucus tolerated discussion and disagreements, but once on the floor of either chamber, unity prevailed. Townley and his lieutenants, such as William Lemke, ran the League as tightly as McKenzie had done earlier. It was just as secretive and equally as successful. The fact that the League conducted its closed meetings in a hotel named for Alexander McKenzie combined political irony with political continuity. New players played the same old game. "We have arrived at the place and the time to either accomplish the League program," Townley told League legislators at the opening of the 1919 legislative session, "or quit coming to Bismarck."[32] They chose to stay and went on to change the course of North Dakota political history in less than 75 days. During a regular session of 54 days and a special session of 17 more, the League put its stamp on North Dakota political traditions. It established two state industries — the Bank of North Dakota and the North Dakota Mill and Elevator Association. It established a new Home Building Association and strengthened the state hail insurance program. To ensure proper management and permanence, it amended the constitution, creating an industrial commission to manage all state industries. Three elected officers formed the commission: the governor, the attorney general, and the commissioner of agriculture and labor.[33]

The constitutional creation of the industrial commission was particularly insightful. It offered stronger protection for the public management of the newly created state industries. It prevented future legislative sessions from meddling in the operation of the state industries and their boards of directors. It also placed the ultimate control of the direction of these programs in the hands of the voters. When the people cast votes at each election for these three state offices, they were exercising the same rights as stockholders in selecting the chief executive officers (CEOs) of their company. That the twin pillars of the League's program — the Bank of North Dakota and the State Mill and Elevator — still exist today and are still managed by the same three elective positions is strong testimony both to the commission's creative wisdom and constitutional safeguards. The League plan worked.

Independent Voters Association

Substantive revolutions in government often cause counter-revolutions of equal force. The Independent Voters Association, or IVA as it was commonly called, was the counter-revolution to the first Nonpartisan League. Negative responses rolled in before the ink was dry on the League's blueprint for state industries. Initial criticism came internally from William Langer and other disgruntled League elected officials soon after the League's sweeping elective victory of 1918. Criticism broadened simultaneously with the establishment of a new faction in the Republican Party — IVA — a three-letter acronym designed to match the three-letter NPL. The IVA began to follow the NPL strategy of endorsing its slate of candidates and placing them in the June Republican primary. In the elections of 1920 and 1922 and the surprise recall election of 1921, the IVA broke League hegemony and seized political power in North Dakota.

Disgruntled leaguers and the IVA shared common goals; both factions hated Townley with a passion. "You and your hirelings have lied to and are deceiving the farmers of North Dakota," charged Langer, while the IVA made up lyrics to the tune of *Tramp, Tramp, the Boys are Sticking Us:*

> In our state oppression ruled, where the
> Townleyites hold sway,
> As they fake the farmers friend,
> They are drawing near the end
> It will be jolly fun to get their goats.[34]

Langer's monthly magazine, *The Red Flame,* distributed free, compared the League to Russian Bolshevism and called Townley "Comrade."[35] IVA cartoons charged the League with promoting "Free Love" in the public schools, and another depicted a mother praying on her knees, "Oh God! Save our homes, our churches, our schools and our state."[36]

This repeated anti-League rhetoric hurt League members as painfully as their rhetoric had hurt those opposed to their programs. The League membership was not an organization of Communists and free lovers. The bulk of the membership came from farmers eager for a chance to exercise political power and establish state-owned economic enterprises that freed them from the control of outside interests. The IVA attacks widened the social divisions and put NPL members on the defensive.

One point of contention between the groups occurred over the future of state industries. Langer charged League banking efforts with fraud, corruption and mismanagement. When he ran for governor in 1920 as the IVA candidate,

Langer sought to replace the managers but not to repeal the new programs. Although the IVA was astute enough to support the building of a state mill and elevator, it was unalterably opposed to the state engaging in any banking operation. So in a series of referral and initiated measures, the IVA sought to eliminate the newly created Industrial Commission and to repeal the charter for the Bank of North Dakota. They wanted to get rid of the managers as well as most of the programs.[37]

Who were the members of the IVA? As the IVA movement expanded, it became a harbinger for several factions, including disgruntled Leaguers from both the state and local level; conservative newspaper publishers such as Jerry Bacon, who bought out George Winship's *Grand Forks Herald*; Independents and a handful of Democrats such as J.F.T. O'Connor, a Grand Forks attorney; and Progressives still stunned by the League victories of 1916 and 1918. Usher Burdick, however, was never a member of the IVA.

Three election decisions ended the NPL's socialist revolution. In the 1920 election, the two factions split control of state government. The League retained control of executive offices, but the Legislature then was divided between the Senate (controlled by the NPL) and the House (controlled by the IVA).

In 1921, the IVA, sensing the tide was turning in its favor, experimented with the recall petition. It successfully recalled the three CEOs of the League's Industrial Commission — the governor, attorney general, and commissioner of agriculture and labor — and elected their own candidates, all by small margins. It was the first recall of state officials in the history of the United States. However, seven IVA initiated measures to limit or terminate the state industries failed.[38] Voters, unsure about the experiment in state socialism, fired the managers but kept the programs. In the 1922 election, the IVA gained total control of state government. It had completed its mission of ridding the state of Townleyism, but it remained stuck with key elements of the socialist programs.

Politically, the rest of the '20s became a stalemate of sorts. The NPL did not disappear. The IVA did not rule supreme. Both sides won elections and lost elections under a Republican tent and neither faction gained enough power to either eliminate or expand the League industries created in 1919. Democrats remained few and far between. When the price of wheat began its downward spiral in 1921, the state began to shift from prosperity to depression. Mortgaged farmers sitting with a second mortgage on a new quarter of land or a gas tractor or truck could not make payments on loans secured on the World War I price of wheat. Banks failed. Farmers lost their farms. Twenty years of depression, drought and despair followed six years of social and political revolution. Local political tensions exacerbated by class soon would give way to broader international and national economic tensions of unparalleled proportions. North Dakota's date with the Depression began in the '20s, not the '30s.

The Second Nonpartisan League

Two major political changes occurred in North Dakota in the '30s. At the presidential level, voters turned their backs on the Republican Party and picked Franklin D. Roosevelt to be their president. In both 1932 and 1936, Roosevelt carried every one of the state's 53 counties. This was unprecedented for a Democrat in a Republican state. Woodrow Wilson carried the state by narrow margins in 1912 and 1916, and Lyndon B. Johnson became the last Democrat to win the state in 1964 by a wider margin. For Roosevelt, especially a Democratic Roosevelt, to carry the state twice with such huge majorities amounted to shrieks for political change in a second decade of economic pain.

At the state level, voters gave William Langer a second chance. They elected him governor, the only Republican elected in 1932. At his shirttails marched almost an entire cast of Nonpartisan League cohorts also elected to save the state from bankruptcy and farm foreclosure. This second Nonpartisan League — Langer's League — became a driving force in North Dakota politics again. It lasted until 1956, when remnants of it merged with a growing Democrat Party to form the Democratic-NPL Party.

The second NPL shared many themes with its older cousin. Politically, it worked in much the same manner. It was still not a political party. Instead, it continued to endorse an entire slate of candidates for both local and state elections at NPL district and state conventions. Following the success of Townley's League, it, too, proceeded to file them all in the Republican column at the June primary. As before, June primary winners usually became November general winners. The second NPL also published a newspaper called *The Leader.* It collected dues. It maintained the famous caucus. It kept the goat as its symbol and repeated the ever-familiar motto: "We'll Stick. We'll Win."

For all the similarities in organization, however, there were vast differences in leadership. Langer was so unlike Townley. He possessed great personal charm, humor and physical presence. He genuinely liked being around people, joking, playing cards and telling stories. Although always controversial, he remains as one of the state's most beloved public servants, having spent his entire adult life representing voters as their state's attorney, attorney general, governor and U.S. senator.

Langer, like Townley, ruled with tight reins. He demanded as much loyalty from his organization as Townley had from his. Again, the nature of the demands was quite different. Langer was the master of "let's make a deal." If he offered someone a job, he expected a vote in return. If he supported your bill, he expected you would support his. This personal appeal to loyalty was different than obedience to ideology practiced by Townley. Loyalty to Langer was the key to his political power and longevity.

The policies of the second NPL, therefore, were also different – first because loyalty to Langer was the key to the whole operation, and second because the nature of the state's economy was so different. The second NPL never promoted an appeal for an extension of state industries. It was not a time for ideology. This was a decade of survival. Expectations were fundamental. Save our farm, get my husband a job, keep the children in school. But the NPL did rely on the Bank of North Dakota and the State Mill and Elevator to combat a second decade of economic disaster. Weather produced drought; grasshoppers and scant crops compounded the debt of the '20s. The NPL also participated in the start of a new federal-state relationship. Early New Deal programs probably kept North Dakota alive, but the growing tensions between Langer and Roosevelt's administrations created a new political atmosphere.[39]

Langer's NPL fought the Depression with bold and militant actions. He matched Roosevelt's call for a national bank holiday with a call for a state bank holiday. Langer used the office of governor as a "bully pulpit" to ease the burden of economic pain on the people of North Dakota. As farm foreclosures accelerated, Langer called out the National Guard to stop sheriffs' sales of farms. When farm prices continued to drop, Langer issued embargoes by executive proclamations to halt the state's shipment of wheat or beef. He openly criticized the direction of federal farm programs and called on other Midwestern governors to join him in his embargo policies.[40]

Langer was a more dominant, political player than Townley. Between the start of his administration in 1933 and his election to the U.S. Senate in 1940, Langer dealt all the major political cards during those eight years. Some hands he won. Some hands he lost. Some ended in a draw. But the dealer was always Langer. Everyone who wanted to play politics was forced to play at his table because he ran the game.

A few hands of political poker illustrate his influence. He played several hands with Roosevelt. He kept early federal relief money close to the vest. Roosevelt drew a stronger hand and prosecuted him for misusing federal money. Langer lost his governorship in the summer of 1934 because of his conviction in a federal court. Ole Olson, the lieutenant governor, replaced him. Lydia Langer replaced her husband on the fall NPL ticket but lost to Thomas Moodie, a Democrat. Moodie served less than 30 days as governor because Langer produced evidence that he was constitutionally ineligible because he had voted in the Twin Cities in 1930. Walter Welford, the NPL lieutenant governor, re-placed Moodie. Langer replaced Welford in 1936 after his federal court convic-tion was overturned.

There were more games. Langer challenged incumbent U.S. Senator Ger-ald P. Nye in 1938 and lost. He challenged incumbent U.S. Senator Lynn J. Frazier in 1940 and won. With Langer out of the governor's office, new factions fought for control. John Moses, a Democrat, replaced Langer as governor in 1938, served three terms and then defeated Nye for the U.S. Senate in 1944. However, Moses died of cancer a few weeks after being sworn in during March of 1945. With Langer off to Washington, the second Nonpartisan League be-gan to unravel. Political power was up for grabs.

The Republican Organizing Committee

A second Nonpartisan League produced a second anti-League counter-revolution. The Republican Organizing Committee (ROC) was another faction in the Republican Party with another innocuous name, such as the Indepen-dent Voters Association, and another shortened three-letter acronym designed once again to match the three-letter NPL. The ROC operated successfully in North Dakota between 1943 and 1956. It split the state even more between urban conservatives and rural liberals. It ceased when major realignments it precipitated in both the Republican and Democratic parties removed the need for it to continue.

The ROC made important contributions to North Dakota's political tra-ditions. It elected the only two North Dakota Republican governors ever to serve three terms, Fred Aandahl (1945-1951) and Norman Brunsdale (1951-1957). The ROC first appointed and then re-elected to the U.S. Senate Milton R. Young (1945-1981), who served longer in that body than any North Dakotan, Republican or Democrat. It gave the state 12 years of honest, efficient and uncontroversial management of government. It ended Langer's personal style of the Jacksonian spoils system. As the nation and state together moved from depression to prosperity, it ameliorated the mind-set of North Dakotans away from the Depression, drought and demagoguery to needed measures, such as a dependable water supply, rural electricity and paved roads.[42]

The ROC, like the IVA, sought to rid North Dakota politics of what it perceived as one-man control of state government. Its primary purpose was to take control of state government away from the second NPL and put its boss, William Langer, permanently on the sidelines. It succeeded with greater success than the IVA in accomplishment of its first goal. It all but destroyed the political existence of the second NPL at the state level by controlling both the executive and legislative branches of government. But unlike the IVA, which took Townley from power, the ROC failed to accomplish its second objective. Langer remained in Washington, the obvious political survivor of the state purge of his second Nonpartisan League.

In 1952, the ROC launched its most vigorous campaign to finally rid North Dakota politics of William Langer. ROC officials convinced Fred Aandahl, popular as the first ROC governor and now completing his first term as one of the state's two U.S. House members, to challenge Langer. "The man we have groomed for the job is Fred Aandahl," said Joseph Bridston, a leading ROC member of the state Senate. "He can easily defeat that boss of machine politics in North Dakota — William Langer."[43] Bridston knew the terrain. He had run a strong race against Langer in the 1946 Republican primary, losing by less than 14,000 votes. Six years later, the ROC was stronger. Aandahl was a better-known opponent and Langer's League was weaker. Aandahl was the candidate.[44]

In a shocking turn of events, at least to the ROC, Langer whipped Aandahl badly in the June Republican primary (107,905 votes to 78,359). The ROC campaign painted Langer as being soft on Communists and strong on creeping socialism. No response. The ROC charged Langer with being an errand boy for introducing too many private bills and doing too many personal favors for people in Washington. No response. Three weeks before the June primary, Langer opened his campaign for re-election. He attacked Aandahl's six House votes on federal support for the Rural Electrification Administration. Only two for six, said Langer, which he graded to a poor political score of "33 percent Aandahl." Langer's audacity caught Aandahl by surprise and in the heat of the race, he came up with a weak explanation five days later.[45] It did not matter. Most North Dakotans still approved of Langer's personal style of politics. Besides, doing favors for them in Washington was one reason they elected him in the first place. As for the trumped-up charges of being pink or red, they were old red herrings. North Dakotans had heard them all before.

The Democrats

Where were North Dakota Democrats all those years? The answer is quite simple. Before 1960, old Democrats won as individuals. After 1960, new Democrats won both as individuals and as a party. Old Democrats, such as Governors Eli Shortridge and John Burke, won as individuals when Populist and

Progressive reform traditions eclipsed traditional Republican voting patterns. Both men won on the strength of these reform issues, not on Democratic platforms. In the '30s, Governors Thomas Moodie and John Moses won as compromise candidates against the excess of Langer's second Nonpartisan League. Both were elected by conservative Republicans because they preferred them to Langerites, not because they were Democrats.

External factors determined their longevity. Populism was so weak and Shortridge so fickle that he served only one term. Progressivism was stronger and so was Burke. He completed three terms, but then left the state. Populist and Progressive reforms sought economic and political change, but neither established or built a Democratic Party. Roosevelt's personal popularity and North Dakota's dependence on New Deal programs offered Democrats a better opportunity to build a party in the '30s. But Langer's mastery of personal politics, Moodie's constitutional ineligibility and Moses' death prevented it. When voters tired of the second Nonpartisan League, they turned conservative and supported the ROC, in part, because there was no Democrat alternative and, in part, because North Dakota Democrats blew a golden opportunity.

New Democrats in the '60s were more successful. Two standard-bearers, Quentin Burdick and William Guy, won as individuals, but both contributed to building a Democratic Party as well. Burdick, the liberal, inherited Langer's Senate seat in 1960 and kept it until his death in 1992. Guy, the conservative, ended 22 years of Republican control of the governor's office, occupied it for 12 years, and saw Art Link and George Sinner each occupy it for eight more years.

Burdick appealed to those on the left — old Leagers, organized labor and members of the North Dakota Farmers Union. Guy appealed to those on the right — the business community, independents and members of the North Dakota Farm Bureau. Burdick met the broader challenges of the times by supporting civil rights, federal aid for education, pro-choice and anti-Vietnam. When Burdick's name led the ticket, more North Dakotans voted and more Democrats won.

Guy modernized state government. It was almost a fossil and hopelessly out of step with changes, which had occurred since statehood. In doing so, Guy demonstrated to a skeptical electorate that a Democrat could manage state government with efficiency. He worked hard to establish a party headquarters in Bismarck and brought younger men, such as Byron Dorgan, into state government. With Guy as governor, more North Dakotans came to appreciate his contributions and to identify them with the Democratic Party.

New Democrats failed to destroy the North Dakota Republican Party.

Milton Young and Mark Andrews consistently sent Democratic hopefuls to the sidelines in races against them. With minor exceptions, the Republicans continued their control of the citizen's Legislature. Earl Strinden, as House majority leader, however, more than matched the Democrats' executive power in the Legislature by becoming the first full-time legislative leader in state history. Most North Dakotans seemed satisfied with a division of power between two traditional political parties. Republicans lost their last congressional office in 1986 when Mark Andrews was upset by Kent Conrad. A schism within the Democratic Party in 1992 gave Ed Schafer the governor's chair. At the time of this writing, Republicans hold huge majorities in both houses of the state Legislature, while three Democrats — Byron Dorgan, Kent Conrad and Earl Pomeroy seem untouchable in Congress.

Endnotes

1. Larry Remele, "Power to the People: The Nonpartisan League," in *North Dakota Political Traditions*, 74.
2. Ibid., 92.
3. Rylance, "William Langer and the Themes of North Dakota History," *South Dakota History* 3 (Winter 1972): 47.
4. Ibid., 49.
5. Glenn Smith, "William Langer and the Art of Personal Politics," in *North Dakota Political Traditions*, 150.
6. Robinson, *History of North Dakota*, 336-37.
7. Mark Andrews, interview by author, April 19, 1995.
8. Ibid.
9. Ibid.
10. Schell, History of South Dakota, xi.
11. Dibbern, "Who were the Populists? A study of Grass-Roots Alliancemen in Dakota," *Agricultural History* 56 (October 1982): 681.
12. Ibid., 690.
13. Tweton, "Considering Why Populists Succeeded in South Dakota and Failed in North Dakota," *South Dakota History* 23 (Winter 1992): 331.
14. Ibid., 338.
15. Robinson, *History of North Dakota*, 224.
16. Wilkins, "Alexander McKenzie and the Politics of Bossism," in *North Dakota Political Traditions*, 26.
17. Robinson, *History of North Dakota*, 364.
18. Glaab, "John Burke and the Progressive Revolt," in *North Dakota Political Traditions*, 57.
19. Ibid., 43.
20. Ibid., 48.
21. *Grand Forks (ND) Herald*, May 1, 1997, 4.
22. Robinson, *History of North Dakota*, 261-62.
23. Glaab, "John Burke," 61.
24. Ibid.
25. Wilkins, "Alexander McKenzie," 3.
26. Ibid., 38.
27. Ibid., 36.
28. Fite, "Peter Norbeck and the Defeat of the Nonpartisan League in South Dakota," *Mississippi Valley Historical Review* 33 (September 1946): 217.

29. Remele, introduction to *Political Prairie Fire* by Robert L. Morlan, xii-xiv.
30. Morlan, *Political Prairie Fire*, 21.
31. Ibid., 29.
32. Tweton, "The Anti-League Movement: The IVA," in *North Dakota Political Traditions*, 98.
33. Robinson, *History of North Dakota*, 342.
34. Tweton, "The Anti League Movement," 103, 109.
35. Robinson, *History of North Dakota*, 345.
36. Tweton, "The Anti-League Movement," 11, 113.
37. Ibid., 114.
38. Robinson, *History of North Dakota*, 350.
39. Rylance, "William Langer," 51-51.
40. Ibid., 52.
41. Robinson, *History of North Dakota*, 410-11.
42. Rylance, "Fred G. Aandahl and the ROC Movement," in *North Dakota Political Traditions*, 151
43. Ibid., 180.
44. Ibid., 181.
45. Ibid.

- two -

The House of Usher

When Usher L. Burdick passed away quietly in a Washington, D.C., hospital on Friday evening, August 19, 1960, national and state newspapers rushed to judge and distill his 81½ years. It was a daunting task for so long a life in so short a time. His life was full; his achievements were many. His North Dakota legacy was assured. Burdick was a colorful and unique figure, whether he was found chatting with people on the street of a small town in his home state or sharing an anecdote with his colleagues in the U.S. House of Representatives.

Growing up adjacent to the Ft. Totten Sioux Indian Reservation near Devils Lake, North Dakota, his Indian boyhood friends called him Mato Sapa. Translated into English, the name meant either "Bear Black" or "Black Bear." Years later, when Drew Pearson, the longtime correspondent for the *Washington Post*, began to quote the congressman's home-brewed House homilies in his regular column, he referred to the aging Burdick as "a big shaggy bear of a man."[1]

Both descriptions proved apt. Burdick, both as a young man and an aging congressman, was a bear of a man. His huge physical presence always appeared larger than his actual 6-foot-1-inch frame. As a young man who played defensive end on two University of Minnesota Big Ten championship football teams in 1903 and 1904, he was sinewy and quick. He was thinner then and weighed around 220 pounds. As he grew older and less active, his stomach sagged and his weight steadily increased. His weight bounced between 260 pounds to more than 300.

There was another physical trait. Burdick walked with an athletic gait and pushed a long stride. He was a natural runner growing up on the reservation – a skill that later added to his many other football talents as a Minnesota Gopher.

As he grew older and walked slower, there remained a determined if not halting push to his stride. One Capitol Hill reporter described it as "a massive man who slogged along the Capitol corridors like a man pulling a sledge through melting snow."[2] Slogging along was a perceptive Burdick descriptor.

Burdick ate like a bear, too. People who observed him and friends who knew him understood his insatiable appetite. George Munyer, for example, who grew up in Williston, remembered Burdick gulping down huge amounts of food in a local cafe. "He ate two enormous platters heaped with pork chops, potatoes and a vegetable," said Munyer. "Then he quickly devoured two desserts which came along with the dinners."[3] Jack Traynor, a Devils Lake attorney and an old Burdick acquaintance, especially recalled his liking for Indian food. After running into him at the annual Ft. Totten Powwow not long before he died, Traynor quizzed Burdick about the food: "How's the stew?" asked Traynor. "Not so good," replied Burdick. "How come?" asked Traynor. "No dog meat," replied Burdick.[4]

Burdick was a stingy bear as well. John and Tish Kelly of Fargo, North Dakota, who were dating and working on Capitol Hill in the '50s observed him regularly. Although he loved to eat, he never wanted to spend too much money for it. "People in Washington used to tell me," said John, "how every day Usher would buy a hot dog for lunch and every day have an argument with the poor women selling the hot dog. He wanted a discount on the price of the hot dog because he bought them so often." Tish often witnessed the scene at noon. "I used to stand behind him in that line where I worked. That's exactly what he did. There was a cafeteria, but there was also a little stand where you could do some take-out. Usher argued about the price of that 15- or 20-cent hot dog every day!"[5]

Burdick also dressed like a shaggy bear. The clothes he wore never mattered to him. What he did wear often became the target of jokes and criticism. "Usher never used a belt for his pants," noted Terry Leonhardy, who grew up next door to the Burdicks in Williston. "He used twine to hold up his pants. One day when he was coming out of the Williston post office and he started walking down the street when a couple of the town matrons came up behind him. Well, the twine gave way! One of the women was heard saying to the other woman: 'Have you ever seen such dirty drawers in all your life?'"[6]

Representative Burdick often received the nomination for the worst dresser in Congress. Usually he paid little attention to the jokes. In 1954, however, when Burdick spoke against a huge congressional pay increase recommendation (a raise in pay from $12,500 to $27,500 per year), the *Atlantic Constitution* took after him. Burdick needed the pay raise. He "goes around with patched trousers held together with safety pins." "I do not," replied an angry Burdick on the House floor. "Everyone with whom I associate with knows it. I am not what you call a dandy in dress, but on the salary I now receive, I can and do wear good clothes. I may not wear them well, but they serve the purpose."[7]

Stained ties were a Burdick trademark. "I am just in receipt of six ties — very nice — ties neatly packed in a box and addressed to me," wrote Burdick to the O.J. deLendrecie Company, one of Fargo's premier clothing stores, "I do not understand the gift." Perplexed about something he would never buy and concerned about the propriety of any gift he received, he continued, "I am not aware of anything I have done for you or against you, [n]or am I aware of anything you ever asked me to do. There is so much bad rumor here in Washington in regard to gifts, that I felt bound to ask why the present was sent." There is no record whether Burdick returned the ties, the company responded, or that he ever wore them. Burdick's letter was dated the day after Christmas 1951.[8]

Beyond images of Burdick the bear, however, stood the carved figure of a Renaissance man. Obituaries from the East Coast to the Missouri River chiseled some of its shavings into print, but without ever understanding either the breadth or complexity of the model. Burdick was a man for all seasons. He was during his lifetime a pioneer, an athlete, a college graduate, a lawyer, a rancher, a politician, an oral historian and author of 27 works, a book collector (more than 25,000 volumes) and a book printer, a humorist, a man of many women and a father to three children.

The national press, which seldom understood the background of North Dakota politics, buried Burdick with the "m" word in American politics — maverick. It was much easier copy to use to describe him than attempt to explain the differences between a Progressive Republican, a Nonpartisan League Republican or a conservative Republican in North Dakota politics. Instead, Burdick's reputation was explained away as maverick for his abnormal political behavior in Washington. Although he was listed as a Republican, he voted against the party as much as he voted for it. He did not like many of the policies of the Eisenhower administration, so he regularly denounced them. He hated the soil bank program for farmers, so he repeatedly demanded the removal of Ezra Taft Benson, the secretary of agriculture. In Washington circles, that sort of performance earned him the maverick epitaph.[9] North Dakotans might use the term to identify a stray calf now and then, but never a politician. Where Burdick grew up, it was just normal behavior.

The Twin Cities press knew more about Burdick. They remembered him as a big but fast lineman who ran 100 yards in 10.5 seconds while wearing football gear. They knew him as a person who did not like the United Nations. They knew him as a defender of First Amendment rights and a possessor of rare, political courage in the days of McCarthyism to vote against bills that took away the rights of American Communists to maintain a political party. They knew about his political efforts during his last summer, especially when he spoke sometimes in Sioux, sometimes in German — sometimes on the same day — to get his son, Quentin, elected to the United States Senate.[10]

The North Dakota press treated Burdick's passing with deeper sympathy and more understanding. The *Fargo Forum* began by recounting his long public service, but then reflected on what was an important theme throughout his life. "He always clung to the romance of the Old West where he had played a part and much of his literary work dealt with that phase of the state's affairs."[11] Alden McLachlan, the *Forum's* political reporter for many years, wrote a personal column two days after Burdick's death. He told some great Burdick stories. Usher was the only member of the House of Representatives who was recognized by every cab driver in Washington. He was one of the few men all of the members stayed to hear when he spoke in the House. "These stories," McLachlan concluded, however, "don't add up to the total figure of Burdick, erudite and an athlete; whose careless appearance camouflaged a fine mind and rapier wit. ... Usher L. Burdick was never boring."[12]

The *Bismarck Tribune* gave insights into the complexity of North Dakota politics. Although Burdick was identified with the Nonpartisan League in his later years, he was never really a member of the organization. He was always a Progressive Republican. His appeal was to people and issues, not to political parties or factions within it. "Once he was asked if he intended to run for re-election. He replied he would if he sensed a draft. What constitutes a draft? he was asked. Answered Burdick: 'A couple of postcards.'"[13]

The *Tribune* touched a bit on family genealogy as well. Burdick was from old American stock. His family members were British colonists who came to the Massachusetts Bay Colony long before the American Revolution and the ratification of the Federal Constitution. They later became separatists, left the Puritan Bay Colony and followed Roger Williams to Rhode Island. Usher Burdick was from an old Yankee tree, living in a new, immigrant state filled with saplings. His memberships in Sons of the American Revolution, the Freemasons (32nd degree), and the Benevolent and Protective Order of Elks mirrored old Protestant institutions in the most free Protestant nation in the world. Although his father was a Baptist and his mother a Methodist, Usher belonged to no church.[14]

The *Minot Daily News* was closer to Burdick and Williston. It ranked him among the giants of North Dakota politicians. "He belonged in that group of the mighty — all highly skilled politicians of a generation now past — which included William Langer and William Lemke and others."[15] But for all their similarities, there were distinct differences. Burdick always placed more emphasis on accomplishing other things in life. He was never like Langer, for example, consumed with politics day and night. Burdick played the game of politics because he loved the game, but he strived to escape its trap of total absorption as often as possible. He was a Renaissance character more in the likeness of Thomas Jefferson than a consummate prairie Populist. Burdick's pursuit of happiness followed the traditions of John Locke and the disciples of the Enlightenment.

The *Daily News* failed to make the Jefferson connection. It did, however, scratch the surface of Burdick's Renaissance stature. It identified something clearly unique in its observation that Burdick "was in many ways the most versatile" of his contemporaries. Versatile because he wrote books on North Dakota history. Versatile because he raised purebred livestock, judged horses and organized farmers' associations. Versatile because he read and collected books on Western Americana and printed them, too.[16]

There was another facet to Burdick: He relished playing the character of the country bumpkin. He wrote the script and he literally played the part from the Missouri River to Capitol Hill. But beneath the colorful image, the nonconformist behavior and the untidy appearance lurked a true American homespun philosopher. Many of his views "were those of a practical man, often more conservative in temper than his history as a North Dakota Leaguer might justify. Often he sounded off with shrewd comments that had the cracker-barrel quality of a rural sage."[17] Burdick belonged among the cadre of rural humorists such as Mark Twain. "I was like the old farmer who said, 'I know the bee with his buzz, buzz, buzz,'" quipped Burdick, "'but I'm not the damn fool I useta was.'"[18]

On Monday and Tuesday, August 21 and August 22, 1960, friends and colleagues in Washington paid their last respects to one of its longtime residents. In a funeral service held on Monday, the Rev. Bernard Braskamp (the House chaplain) eulogized Burdick "as a man with a keen sense of humor and deep religious convictions."[19] Members of the House gathered on the floor Tuesday to talk about an old friend and to say goodbye to a fellow colleague. Representative Don Short, then North Dakota's only congressman, gave the traditional biographical sketch in keeping with the traditions of the House. "He was known far and wide for his stories of the West," Short said, "and he became nationally recognized as an authority on Indian history."[20]

Rep. John McCormack of Massachusetts and speaker of the House, spoke next. He and Usher were close personal friends; the tall speaker's remarks were filled with emotion. "In the passing of Usher Burdick," McCormack paused,

"I have lost one of my closest and most valued friends." McCormack eulogized his friend as "a people's congressman" and "an independent and constructive figure." Burdick, in McCormack's view, served as a connector between the modern days of America and those earlier ones that saw the development of the western part of the country.[21]

Rep. Sam Rayburn of Texas spoke next. "He was a rugged and fearless man," began the short, stout and balding Texan. "He served well his day and generation and promoted his country's welfare. He was bold; he was intelligent; he had characteristics of the highest type." Rayburn recalled how he also enjoyed sitting and listening to Burdick when he spoke on the House floor. "He was a big man in physical stature and a big man in brain, a pair. He knew how to be a friend and he was my friend, and I was his."[22]

Rep. Robert Levering of Ohio (married to Eileen Burdick, Usher's only daughter) brought the House to tears with personal recollections about his father-in-law. "I never knew a man like Usher Burdick," he began. "I knew him best for his love of the land, good cattle and horses. Only hours before his death, he was making plans to return permanently to the land where he learned as a boy to speak the Sioux language. I will always cherish the hours spent with him riding over his Missouri River ranch on a summer day when the sky is as blue as a baby's eyes and the clouds are as white as the first snow of winter."[23]

A young South Dakota congressman with a doctorate in history from Northwestern University inched closest to Burdick, the Renaissance man. George McGovern, who probably knew more in 1960 about American history then anyone in the House, placed Burdick in the broader context. "Usher Burdick," Professor McGovern began, "was endowed with the wit of Lincoln and the agrarian faith of a Jefferson. His philosophy of government cut across party lines and was limited only by his faith in America and particularly the rural people of America."[24]

Burdick's body was cremated and transported back home to Williston. On a fall day in early October, he was interred on a high bluff overlooking the Burdick ranch southeast of the city. Mato Sapa was home at last. The long winter would make this year's hibernation eternal. Here in the land of Lewis and Clark, Ft. Union, the Missouri River and his beloved ranch, Usher Burdick would finally find sleep forever. He had earned the rest.

To understand Quentin Burdick better is to know his father, Usher, a little more. What follows is not an attempt to craft a biography of Usher Burdick. Like the task thrown earlier to his obituary writers, there is too much to tell about him even in one chapter of this monograph about his oldest son, Quentin. But there remain Burdick bricks in the House of Usher that provide important building blocks to better understanding his oldest son. There are, at least, four themes, which include family, women, Golden Gophers and congressman at large, that bridge both generations of the House of Usher.

A Yankee Family

The Burdicks were a Yankee family in the New World. "I am the eighth generation of Robert Burdick, who settled at Salem, Massachusetts Bay Colony in 1635," Usher proudly wrote in 1955. "My ancestors came to England with the Norman Conquest, remained in England for a time and then went to North Ireland, where they remained 400 years. They came back to England, and could not find a peaceful life there, so they came to America."[25]

The first five generations of Burdicks remained in New England. But starting with William, Usher's grandfather, they started to migrate to the West. In Usher's lifetime, his family never stopped moving west. William died in Owatonna, Minnesota, where Usher was born. Azias, Usher's father, died in Port Angeles, Washington, about as far west as one could live and still put your foot down in the continental United States.

Going west in the mid-19th century was as common for Yankees as it was for newly arrived immigrants from Europe. It was an adventuresome time for the young nation and a difficult experience for those who made the journey. Settlers going west became transients and upstarts. They were transients in a continent as wide as the ocean. Mobility, not habitat, explained who they were and what they became. When they stopped being transients, they settled down and became upstarts or boomers. During the course of their journey, they experienced community before government. They learned to exercise America's law of majority rule and to practice one of its most common features: frontier justice. In their rush to get there first, they left many things behind.[26]

Usher was born on February 21, 1879, the youngest of six children, on a rented farm near Owatonna, Minnesota, located in the central part of the state. His father was Azias Perry Warren Burdick, born in Vermont. His mother was Lucy Farnum, born in New York state. Eugene Burdick, Usher's second son and the historical records keeper of the House of Usher, recalled a couple of family stories. His Grandmother Lucy was alleged to be a quarter Indian and a cousin of John Parson Weston, the ultimate transient who set the record in his time for walking across the United States. His grandfather, Azias, was a carpenter by trade and stubborn. "My mother used to say about him that when he would start to build something with a saw and hammer that she didn't think looked quite right, he would say in an old New England Yankee accent, 'When

I build stairs, I build stairs.'"[27]

As young adults, his parents moved west from New England in 1850 and married in Wisconsin. Usher wrote about their next two moves across the continent:

> In 1857, after the Sioux Indian Treaty of 1857, they moved to Minnesota. The Civil War soon came along, and my father enlisted in the Twenty-First Minnesota Light Artillery and served during the war in Sherman's army. Coming out of the war, a depression was on and there in Minnesota my father tried to pay for a farm, but in 1882 found he could not do so. Free homesteads in Dakota were advertised by the railroad companies, so in that year he gathered up what personal property he had and shipped by rail to Jamestown, North Dakota. From there we went by ox cart to Graham's Island, an island in Devils Lake, North Dakota. There I was raised in a farm life that was a continuous struggle. Dry years, early frosts, and prairie fires kept us very poor, but we were not worse off than our neighbors.[28]

Settlement in Dakota brought some continuity to the Burdick family. They were pioneers again, breaking virgin land in yet another new settlement surrounded by the newly created Sioux Indian Reservation. They quickly preempted 160 acres of prairie grassland sprinkled with scattered trees and began the transition from transient to upstarts. His parents found opportunities to earn cash income, which they immediately plowed back into an expanding ranch operation. Azias secured steady carpentry work in the summer at nearby Ft. Totten and then in Seattle during the winter. Lucy, assisted by daughters Ida and Carrie, took in washing and soon was called on regularly by a growing number of newly arrived settlers for her nursing services.[29]

Usher grew up in these pioneer circumstances. While his older brothers, George and Orlin, learned the carpentry trade from their father, the two younger boys, Lenny and Usher, took up ranching duties on the new homestead. They observed neighbors breaking oxen to the yoke and how to break the Plains sod. As more money was invested into the home place, they acquired new jobs and increased responsibilities —raising shorthorn cattle, Percheron horses and sheep, and planting wheat. Their days were filled with hard physical work and intermittent time to hunt and raise a little hell. Dreams of another lifestyle never entered their maturing young minds.[30] Usher later put into prose what he remembered from his youth:

> The month was June, the latter part of June. The whole prairie was a mass of colored flowers. It was like traveling through fairy land. The days

were hot, but the nights were cool and the sunsets were beautiful to behold. Streaks of gold, crimson, and purple followed the sun in its downward journey and, just at sunset, the western skies were richer in colors than any hand could ever paint. I have seen painting resembling it, but no coloring to equal it. I have since seen the paintings of the greatest artists who ever lived and none of them ever approached the coloring seen in the sunsets of the Great West. No hand can ever imitate the coloring which Nature so lavishly and so carelessly spreads across the skies in a western sunset.[31]

Life on Graham's Island also gave Usher a deep understanding of Sioux Indian culture. Custer's defeat, just a few years before, still stuck vividly in most Dakota memories, white and Indian. Soldiers, Indians and settlers alike recounted their recollections with the young boy eager to learn all he could about this important episode in American history. The deaths of Sitting Bull, Bull Head, Shave Head and 11 other Indians on the Grand River south of Ft. Yates on the Standing Rock Indian Reservation and the tragedy of Wounded Knee occurred when Usher was 11 years of age.

Young Burdick approached Sioux Indians with an open and inquisitive mind. He treated them as fellow human beings, not as conquered savages now removed from the expansion of the white man's frontier. He liked them and developed a lifelong interest in their ways and in their tenuous relationship with the federal government. He sought to learn their ways, to speak their language and to ride their ponies. He saw the transition from a horse culture to ranching and the mix of woodlands and Plains ways of life. He observed the pain of reservation life and the waning of the last days of the great Sioux nation. So close to what was once theirs, he began to collect artifacts, record oral traditions and write their history.

"The soup with chunks of dog meat swimming in it was in a large kettle and each individual dipped out his soup with a buffalo horn spoon," wrote Burdick many years later. He was recalling one of his very first invitations to eat with the Sioux in their dwellings. The occasion was a ceremonial one, and the soup served with dog meat was special in honor of the occasion. "I remember," Usher continued, "I had some difficulty in getting my soup out of the kettle as the top layer was covered with hair."[32]

Torger Sennes changed Usher Burdick's life. He taught him during the day in the country school and more at night as a boarder at the Burdick farm home. Sennes was tall — more than 6 feet 4 inches — and young, 21 years old. He was a recent immigrant from Norway and spoke with a thick Norwegian accent. Sennes knew the value of education and its potential to give young people living on the Dakota frontier an alternative to the hard, physical life of their parents. He was hired to teach at Graham's Island because the school was in chaos and he offered a strong match for its students. Some were big, teenage boys, even bigger than Usher, who enjoyed raising hell in school and forcing one teacher after another to quit.

On the first days of class, Sennes came prepared with a clever behavior management plan for misconduct. He simply sat at his desk in the front of the room and said nothing. He would announce recess and afterwards resume sitting at his desk for the remainder of the day. He repeated this same routine for a couple of days. Finally the students began to ask him questions: "Aren't you going to teach us something?"

"No," replied Sennes. "Well, why not?" "Well," he said. "You can't learn anything. You're just a bunch of savages." Sennes's answer of "just a bunch of savages" rankled Usher. It really upset him. So the next day at recess, he decided to say something to the other students. "Listen, you guys. We gotta do something about this." "Why?" asked one of the students. Usher responded, "We're not getting any schooling done. That's why."[33]

In time, the young teacher's efforts both at school and at home took hold. He took a big, strapping boy raised to be nothing but a rancher for life, and challenged him to learn something about the world of ideas. He modified Usher's hobby to hunt rabbits to read books. He urged him to attend Mayville State College and to further his education at the University of Minnesota. "To his efforts entirely," Burdick wrote many years later, "I owe the ambition I formed to acquire some education."[34]

Mayville solidified the changes in Burdick's life. He was the first of eight generations of Burdicks to attend an institution of higher education. The spark of learning ignited by Sennes in the country school burst into a life of learning. Searching for more knowledge, Burdick enrolled at Mayville State College in the fall of 1896 and graduated in 1900. Burdick loved Mayville so much that in 1955, he published *Reminiscences of Mayville: The State Normal School, North Dakota*. The Mayville years honed Burdick's study skills, expanded his social contacts and offered him new opportunities to participate in organized sports. "The teachers I met there and the people of Mayville," Burdick wrote, "had a great influence on my life in after years and there can be no doubt that these were the formative years."[35]

The small but excellent teachers college exposed Burdick to more ideas and a broader academic experience. It was really an optimum academic experience for the young man from Graham's Island. He took expanded classes in American history and sharpened his math skills. But he soon found new subjects, such as philosophy and psychology, more to his taste. He balked at first at the suggestion that he take Latin, but soon recanted. Later he acknowledged its great value for him as a lawyer. Some subjects naturally came easier than others, but his invitation to give the commencement address attested to his high standing among the faculty and his fellow students.

The town and gown atmosphere of Mayville matured Burdick's social development as an adult. He was born with a natural charm and a likable personality, but his manners were rough, even crude. Surrounded by cosmopolitan faculty and bright students, Burdick grew up socially. He attended classes with young men such as Ragnvold Nestos, who served as governor of North Dakota from 1921-1924. More importantly, he became attracted to Emma Robertson from Park River, North Dakota. Robertson was the brightest student in the 20-member class of 1900, and she seemed to like him, too. They began to court and were seen quite often with each other. They later became engaged and married. In the community, Burdick gained social acceptance. He was probably the best known student from the campus and was initiated into the Freemasons, the most popular fraternal organization of the time.

Burdick the academic student also became Burdick the Mayville athlete. Big, strong and fast, he took up boxing and football. In highly publicized boxing matches, he was the college candidate always willing and usually victorious in taking on any and all town contenders. He was introduced to football. He learned the key elements for the first time in a team sport, especially blocking skills, which he learned so well "that when I got on the Minnesota team I could take several men out of the interference in one play."[36]

Between school terms Burdick went back home. He taught summer school and worked on harvest gangs. After graduation, his father drove a two-horse spring wagon to carry him home from the train station. Curious about the value of learning and what Usher planned to do with his life, father began to ask son philosophical questions. "Now that you have graduated, I presume you know quite a lot," began Azias. "I was considered a good student," replied Usher. "I have learned a lot in a long life," said Azias, "and some of things I have learned are not found in books." His son urged him on, "Go ahead and tell me what some of them are." "Always remember that an empty wagon makes the most noise," said his father. "Anything else?" "Yes, also remember that if you play with a skunk long enough, you will smell just like him."[37]

Women in the House of Usher

"Many things attributed to Sitting Bull may be untrue," observed Evan S. Connell in *Son of the Morning Star*, "but one thing is beyond dispute: he liked women. He liked women enormously. He was married at least three times, possibly eight or nine times."[38]

The same observation can be written about Usher Burdick. He too, liked women enormously. He was married four times and may have been involved with other women besides. He liked to play men's games, especially politics and sports, but like Sitting Bull, his favorite American Indian hero, he too paid special attention to the ladies.

The historical record about how many women Usher Burdick actually married remains confused. All of his obituaries identify three: Emma Robertson, Mrs. Edna Sierson and Jean Rodgers Jackman. None wrote about a fourth woman, Helen Clark, who was Burdick's second wife in North Dakota during the '20s. Family interviews cloud her presence, but ultimately confirm that she was indeed Usher's second wife following his divorce to Emma in 1921.

In a 1992 interview with Senator Quentin Burdick and his wife, Jocelyn (Jocie) Birch Burdick, the first question about the women in Usher's life precipitated a heated but good-spirited exchange between the two of them over whether Usher was married three or four times. When asked, "Did your father remarry?" the senator replied, "Yes, he did." When asked if the second marriage lasted quite a long time, the senator answered, "No, I don't think so. His second wife was killed in an accident on a horse." Jocie interjected, "No, I thought it was his third wife. His second wife was the secretary. Right?" "Fifty years dims my memory, I guess," replied the senator. "I'm quite sure it was the secretary," continued Jocie, "because when you went to the University of Minnesota you weren't very pleased about that. The third one was killed on the horse, and the fourth one was the young woman who died." Burdick's response was immediate: "There wasn't a fourth!" shouted the senator. "I call her the third!" But Jocie was insistent, "Didn't he marry the secretary?" The senator ended the discussion by saying, "I have to fight this out with my wife."[39]

When Quentin's brother and sister-in-law, Eugene and May Burdick, were interviewed in 1995, there were more queries about the circumstances of Emma's divorce and the second marriage that Quentin could not remember. When asked for details about his parents' divorce, Eugene answered: "I'm not sure what the technical grounds were. I'm not sure if I ever read the complaint. I wasn't that interested to find out, you see. ... We knew that all this was traceable to the gal who worked in his office as secretary by the name of Helen Clark. She was a redhead, apparently sort of a siren-type secretary, and I would say that she simply seduced him! ... He married her in probably 1922 or 1923, but he divorced her, also, before the end of the decade." The line of questioning then led to a discussion about Usher's marital status when he was elected to Congress in 1934. "I'd say they were divorced in 1927 or 1928. They would go down to Minneapolis to see Quentin play football." Eugene continued by describing the incident that caused the marriage to break up. "When it came time to go to another game, she said to my father: 'Do we have to go again to watch that boob play?' Well, when she called Quentin a 'boob,' that destroyed the marriage. My father wasn't going to have her calling his son a 'boob' when he was star on the team as a blocking back. This really rankled him. I think that was the trigger of the divorce, don't you, May?" asked Eugene. "That's what Eileen, your sister always said," answered May. "Makes sense," said Eugene. "He wouldn't put up with that, so he got rid of her."[40]

Helen Clark was never an important figure in the House of Usher, especially for the children. She did, however, exist. The fact that the aging senator could not recall her or his father's marriage to her might be attributed to a blank spot in his memory. Yet, his anger and repeated assertions that she never existed might also hide denial. Eugene's defense of his father in the affair is also understandable, but one-sided. It may very well be that Clark did seduce Usher and forced the divorce. Seduction and divorce are seldom initiated solely by one party. It takes two to consummate an affair and two to terminate a marriage contract.

Emma Robertson Burdick was always the most important woman in Usher Burdick's life. They were married for more than 20 years and had three children: Quentin, Eugene and Eileen. Emma was born in Northwood, Iowa, in 1877. She had one older brother, William, and one younger sister, Evelina. Her parents were Scandinavians; her mother, Eva Maria Anderson, was Swedish, and her father, Hans Rasmussen, was Danish. Emma's family first moved from Iowa to a farm three miles east of Mayville, North Dakota. There her father changed the family name to Robertson because there was another Hans Rasmussen living in the same township and their mail was always getting mixed up. Her father, like Usher's father, was a carpenter by trade; later he became a banker in Park River, North Dakota. Emma married Usher in Devils Lake, North Dakota, on September 2, 1901.[41]

Quentin, Eugene and May spoke about their relationships with Emma. "I was very close to my mother," was Quentin's first and most important response. He described her physically as being of "medium height" and blessed with a "very joyous personality." He touted her as being "very well educated" because she graduated in three years from the University of Minnesota. He admired her independence and credited her with "doing lots of things by herself, including the farming operation" after the divorce.[42]

Eugene expressed the same fondness for Emma that his older brother,

Quentin, did. He described Emma as "bright, pert and pretty." He remembered her playing the piano and teaching piano lessons off and on. She was active in the Williston Women's Civic League, supported the public library and attended the Congregational Church. "She could talk about things intellectually," Eugene noted, "but she wasn't a polished housekeeper."[43]

"I think she was very liberal," said May Burdick. "She was a suffragette. She strongly believed that it was a woman's right to vote. She once confided to me that 'I'm so glad we never spanked our children.' She was a gifted drawer and did excellent figure drawings both in pencil and charcoal. She was an accomplished seamstress, an avid stamp collector, and reserved the radio every Sunday afternoon so that she could listen to the symphony broadcasted over the Canadian Broadcasting Company. Her hands and feet were so tiny that she could never find gloves or shoes to fit her."[44]

May, as daughter-in-law, observed other characteristics not noticed by either son. "She was highly opinionated. I remember once listening to her say that she didn't have any use for people who were not of her intellectual ability." Another time "she mentioned that everybody should know about money, every woman, every girl. ... I didn't know what she was talking about, so I didn't say anything."[45]

After the divorce, Emma never left Williston. She always maintained a cordial relationship with Usher and he with her. Rearing their children and seeing them marry and have children of their own kept them in touch, although not regularly. At some point, they discussed the possibility of remarrying. Emma was willing, but Usher "kind of stuttered and stumbled on that one," said Eugene, "and they didn't get remarried. She was willing to forgive him. While he still remained friendly, he didn't seem to be interested in marriage."[46] Emma died in a Fargo hospital on March 11, 1955, and was buried in the Williston Riverview Cemetery.

Burdick married two younger woman late in life. On July 31, 1955, he married Edna Sierson, a widow. On February 28, 1958, he married Jean Rodgers Jackman, a divorcée. Both women were considerably younger than the aging congressman. Although Sierson approached middle age, Rodgers was only 30. Death ended both marriages rather quickly. Sierson died on their honeymoon, less than one month after leaving the altar. Burdick died a few days short of six months after marrying Jackman

Burdick first met Sierson, a congressional secretary, in a parking lot on Capitol Hill. He came to her rescue when he overheard a rude parking lot attendant cursing her for parking her car crookedly.[47] Burdick and Sierson immediately struck up a conversation, started a relationship and soon married. For a honeymoon present, Burdick took his younger bride west to show her North Dakota and his Williston ranch. The honeymoon soon ended in tragedy. Eager to please Edna, Usher presented her with a horse named Cap. Eager to please Usher, Edna mounted the horse. The horse spooked and threw Edna off. She suffered a broken neck, a fractured skull and a massive brain hemorrhage. She died in three minutes.[48]

Burdick's fourth marriage to Jackman was contentious, fractious and embarrassing. She, too, was a congressional secretary, but where Usher first met her is not documented. The odd couple, however, fought like cats and dogs from day one in private and very often in public. He sued for an annulment in Fargo, North Dakota. She sued for temporary and permanent maintenance in Washington, D.C. Usher then withdrew the suit, saying she "can come back anytime she wants. She ran out on me figuring I didn't want her, but she was mistaken about that."[49]

In April 1959, Usher walked out on her while she was attending Sunday services. She immediately contacted the local police and reported that Usher was missing; she expressed concern that because he was diabetic and may have left without sufficient medicine, his life could possibly be in danger. The Washington, D.C., police immediately called Quentin, then a North Dakota congressman, and asked, "Where is your father, Usher?" Quentin did not have a clue where he was, but after some checking, he issued a brief statement from his office. "He isn't lost. He's en route to North Dakota."[50]

North Dakota Republican women scoffed at the fourth marriage. Usher, hearing of their gossip, made an unscheduled appearance before 150 of them gathered together in Bismarck. He minced no words and literally told them off: "I married the woman of my choice, and she made her choice," he told them. "I figured that was my own business, but in politics, I guess that isn't so." Usher refused to let the matter drop. "To show you how penitent I am if I had to do it all over again, I'd do the same thing. I've been without a home for 38 years and it's time I get one, and if they'll let me alone, I'll have one."[51]

Leslie Burgum, North Dakota's Republican attorney general (1955-1963) and a close personal friend of Usher, told his son, Tom (who later became one of Quentin's key senatorial aids), what happened at Burdick's next stop. According to Tom, "One of the great Usher stories occurred in Linton, North Dakota, which was one of his great political territories. My dad, Leslie, was there and Usher suddenly stopped halfway through his speech. 'You folks aren't with me tonight?' Burdick asked. Heads nodded. He could see a line of restless women standing at the back of the hall. "I think I know why. There is a little question about why I should marry a young woman?" Heads nodded again, especially from the women standing in the back. Usher could tell these women did not approve of him marrying the young woman. 'I'll tell you why!' he exclaimed. The crowd suddenly became quiet and the whole hall silent. 'Because I could not find anyone younger than that!' There was a long second of silence and then even the women broke out laughing. That was it. After that, the whole crowd was with him. Usher was a great speaker."[52]

During the Washington years, soon after his election to Congress in 1934, Usher bought a small tobacco farm near Cheltonham, Maryland, about 35 miles from the Capitol. The farm consisted of about 160 acres of rolling hills on soil exhausted from generations of growing tobacco, a few tobacco sheds, slave quarters and a two-story frame house surrounded by big trees. Eugene described it as being "in a state of bad repair," which his father was able to buy "not too expensively" because "he never liked to pay rent."[53] Usher corresponded with his daughter, Eileen, who was then (in 1940) a senior law student at the University of Colorado. He wrote in glowing terms about the plantationlike operation at Cheltonham and the bumper-crop harvest of tobacco, adequate corn and 25 bushels of potatoes. There were also two well-fed pigs and one big, fat tom turkey on hold for November slaughter. "I can see a year['] living already in sight," he told his unemployed youngest, even "if you don't have one law suit."[54]

The Golden Gophers

Usher and Emma Burdick never imagined going to the University of Minnesota. They planned to take their Mayville State College credits and enroll at the University of North Dakota in Grand Forks. Emma was admitted, but Usher was not because he lacked credits in chemistry. Disappointed, the young couple went east. Their first choice was the University of Michigan, but passing through the Twin Cities, they stopped at the University of Minnesota campus. They never left.[55]

All the members of the House of Usher knew what happened next. Usher was recruited almost immediately when he arrived on the Minnesota campus by Dr. H.L. Williams, the Gopher football coach. Williams saw a big, strong young man with a quick stride and a powerful frame. The story told in Usher's later writings and repeated without notes by his children assured that all of them would in time also be Golden Gophers:

> "Young fella, are you enrolled at the university?" asked Coach Williams.
> "No," replied Usher.
> "Why not?"
> "I could not get in because I wasn't smart enough. I didn't have any chemistry."

"Have you ever played football?"

"No. I sometimes played rugby but I never played football."

"Well, can you run?" asked Williams.

"Run," exclaimed Usher. "That's my profession."

"Well, come with me then," replied the coach.

Williams put Usher in a suit of football gear and timed him in the 100 yard dash. Usher ran it in 10.5 seconds.

"Well, young man," said the now happy coach, "I think you're smart enough."[56]

Usher became an outstanding football player at the University of Minnesota. He played right end for the 1903 and 1904 Gopher teams, which produced winning seasons and Big Ten football championship trophies. As the years went by and collegiate football increased in popularity, Usher became one of the early legends of Gopher football. He enjoyed the recognition and went back often to the campus for alumni events.

The greatest story about Usher's football days was told by himself in a letter to Dick Gordon, sports editor of the Minneapolis Tribune. He wrote the letter three years before he died. Usher wanted to clarify what happened in the fourth quarter of the 1904 game with Nebraska. The game was played in Minneapolis with fog getting thicker as the afternoon got later. Minnesota held a slight lead, but with only minutes to go, Nebraska pounded the ball down to the Gophers's 3-yard line, had a first down and were poised to score the winning touchdown. On their first down, Burdick somehow broke through the Nebraska line and sacked the quarterback for a 12-yard loss. Nebraska never recovered and Minnesota went on to win the game. In the years that followed, Coach Williams never understood — in fact, probably could not see — how Burdick got to the Nebraska quarterback so quickly.

With Williams dying in a hospital, Burdick called on his old coach two days before he died. Burdick told Gordon about their last conversation:

> I have always wanted to know how you broke thru the Nebraska line in 1904 and saved the game," asked Williams. "It was one of the greatest plays I ever saw any end make. How did you do it?"
>
> "Well Doc," replied Burdick. I didn't break thru the line. I just lined up with Nebraska. There was so much excitement," Burdick continued, "that I just figured I could make it, and if I didn't nothing would happen except we would be penalized for being 'offside,' half the distance to the goal line, which would have been one yard and a half. I knew Nebraska would not try an end run on first down. The result was that having got along side of the Nebraska quarterback, when the center snapped the ball, I guzzled the

quarterback up in my arms and ran 12 yards with him. No one noticed it, not even the Nebraska quarterback who was giving his line plenty of hell for letting me through."[57]

Usher and Emma graduated from the University of Minnesota in 1904. Over time, the House of Usher filled with more Golden Gophers. Quentin, Eugene and Eileen all attended the University of Minnesota and received undergraduate degrees. All three children followed in their father's legal footsteps, too, and went on to earn their law degrees. The boys stayed at Minnesota while Eileen went to the University of Colorado. Eugene inherited his mother's love of classical music and her artistic talent. He was an excellent sketcher and later did cartoons for several of Usher's publications. Quentin excelled in football. Usher and he became the first father-son letter winners in Gopher football history. Eileen, like her father, later raised livestock on her farm in Ohio.

Convinced that he had done a good job sending all three of his children to college and law school during the Depression, Usher took time to reflect. He was very proud of his efforts and his children's accomplishments. In 1935, with both boys now practicing law in North Dakota, he wrote a personal letter to John Burke, chief justice of the North Dakota Supreme Court, and his old Progressive political friend and former law partner. "I have had, as you know, a struggle to get these two boys through the University with two degrees each," wrote the father of the House of Usher, "and I don't know how I can be any better paid than the way they are living up to expectations, which I conceived a great many years ago." Quentin and Eugene were different, however, and Usher offered his comparison. "Eugene will never be the bull-dog that Quentin is but he may accomplish just as much by his peculiar way as Quentin will from his over-supply of fight. At least, I can say this, that they are both educated just as far as it is possible to give them an education and from now on they will have to remember the signals and play the best game they can."[58]

Congress

Usher Burdick went to Washington in 1935 as Congressman Burdick. He was 56 years old. Although he was too old to change basic patterns in his life, the new title, congressman, stuck and it became inseparable from his surname for the remainder of his life. He was always Congressman Burdick to most North Dakotans because they could not remember him as being anything else but their congressman. When Quentin Burdick replaced his father in 1958 and William Langer in 1960, continuity — not change — had occurred in North Dakota's congressional delegation.

Congressman Usher Burdick split the last 25 years of his life between Washington and North Dakota. His penchant for variety fit being a part-time legislator, a part-time Maryland farmer and a part-time Williston rancher. His congressional salary provided him with a steady income, but never earned him a congressional pension. He pursued his lifelong interests in books, finding more time and better resources to write, trade and print them.

What kind of congressman was he? This is not an easy question to answer, but by today's standards, one would have to say he was quite different. The United States House of Representatives of Usher is not the same House of Representatives, for example, of Earl Pomeroy, North Dakota's only representative today. Usher's House was an environment without television, press conferences or campaign financing. He came home when Congress adjourned every six months, not on weekends. He campaigned during the few weeks that preceded the election, not every day of the year. He was independent, not partisan. His elocution was courteous, not strident. He was charming and could even laugh at himself. He always carried himself as a gentleman. He developed many close personal friendships and probably, if one counted them, had more friends on the Democratic side than he did on the Republican side.

Constituents and siblings alike understood him in less scientific terms. They did not quantify his votes or check his attendance. They knew him as a domestic liberal, someone who supported more federal spending for agriculture, as they did. They understood his hesitancy to enlarge the country's involvement in the foreign arena. The fact that he was opposed to most foreign aid, hated the British Empire and was opposed to the United Nations did not bother most of them. When they thought about Burdick, they saw a wise and colorful rural philosopher who could speak on any subject and often did. They knew him as a common sort of person who could talk to any of them in their terms and always did. They knew him as personable and approachable, without airs. Finally, if he had a political profile, it was more about the freedom to speak than anything else. Usher Burdick was a great civil libertarian.

The poet, Ezra Pound, made a personal call to Burdick in April 1958. "This is a historic occasion," quipped the aging Idaho native in front of clicking cameras. Indeed it was. Pound came to thank the North Dakota congressman for helping to secure his release from Saint Elizabeths Hospital for the Insane in the District of Columbia. He had spent the last 13 years of his life locked up in that joint, and Burdick, among others, had worked to secure his release.[59]

Why would Burdick come to the aid of Pound? Pound was the voice of Radio Rome, the mouthpiece for Italian Fascism during World War II. He was the Tokyo Rose of the European front. He lashed out against the Allies,

President Franklin Roosevelt and the Jews. He was viewed by many Americans as a traitor. Yet, for all his sins, the government of the United States was unsure what to do with him. After he surrendered to the Allies in Italy in May 1945, the Army locked him up in a jail in Pisa. Seven months later, they shipped him to the United States. He was judged incompetent to stand trial for his alleged treasonous activities and was committed to a life sentence in a District of Columbia mental hospital.

There is no evidence that Burdick knew Pound, cared for his writings or supported his political views. But in 1957, Burdick introduced House Resolution 403, calling for a complete study to determine whether Pound was insane and whether there was justification for the government to continue his incarceration. The Burdick Resolution was stalled immediately, but he continued to raise the issue. Burdick's efforts, and those of many others, ultimately succeeded, and Pound paid him a visit to thank him for his efforts to secure his release.

Burdick's personal efforts on Pound's behalf capture the core of his civil liberties philosophy. There was political risk in joining the fight and no personal gain in continuing the effort. Still, he persisted without a lot of fanfare. When asked by a Pound biographer why he did this, Burdick answered: "I'm against people being railroaded into insane asylums."[60]

Tom Burgum recalled another Burdick effort he came across in 1974. Burgum was assigned the job of reviewing a general federal criminal reform bill that was introduced in the Senate. He pored over Senate background documents and a recently submitted ACLU report that was critical of many changes in the proposed bill. The handiwork of Usher kept reappearing in citation after citation in several of the documents. Curious and surprised, Burgum called a senior staff person. "What is all this Usher Burdick stuff?" he asked. "Oh, my God," came the response. "Didn't you know that Usher Burdick was a great constitutional civil libertarian in the House during his time?"[61] Burgum was speechless. He, along with many other people, did not know that.

Burdick cultivated a Jeffersonian image among Washington Hamiltonians. Since he preferred a country life to city life, he became identified as a sort of rural sage. He liked playing the part. "Living like this," he told a Washington reporter in 1936, "I can do a better job in Congress."[62] Burdick was referring to life on his Maryland homestead. He described his morning routine of cooking breakfast, doing dishes, milking a herd of goats, and then driving 34 miles on country roads to get from his farm to the U.S. Capitol every morning to be a congressman.

His congressional peers seemed awed by his wide range of interests. Terry

Leonhardy, who was a career officer in the U.S. Foreign Service, was reassigned to Washington periodically. He remembered participating in a foreign service officer escort program held regularly between the State Department and members of Congress. It was a day with a foreign officer type of affair and Leonhardy enjoyed getting out of the office and mingling with members of Congress. "Do you know Representative Burdick from North Dakota?" Leonhardy would ask each time he escorted a designated congressmen. "Smartest man in the House," they would respond invariably. "Smartest man in the House."[63]

Burdick was not only smart. He was loyal to his friends and their descendants. Mark Andrews, longtime North Dakota member of Congress, spoke firsthand of Burdick's loyalty to his family.

> My father was Usher's campaign manager for his first two Congressional campaigns in 1932 and 1934. Dad died when I was twelve and we lived in a little apartment in Fargo. I slept on a Murphy bed and really didn't have much to go on and the war was beginning to get pretty active. Dad had some kind of an idea back in the thirties that West Point would be a great place for me to attend. All of a sudden out of the blue came this letter from Usher. "Your Dad was a great friend and he always said he would like his son to go to West Point. Would you be interested? If you are, I have a principal appointment for you." Now Dad had been gone five years. There was nothing the Andrews family could do for Usher but he remembered through all that period of time. Yes, I took the appointment to West Point in 1944. I was all of seventeen years of age.[64]

Usher Burdick retired from the U.S. House of Representatives in 1958. He was an old man then, 79 years, and would not live much longer. He had served his state for 10 terms in the House. It was a long tenure, longer, in fact, than any North Dakotan before or after him. He quit in the sunset of his life rather than die in office. This was somewhat atypical behavior for many veteran politicians who often went the other road. Certainly it was unlike his North Dakota congressional colleagues, Representative William Lemke and Senator William Langer, and later, unlike his son, Senator Quentin Burdick.

Usher's retirement, however, came begrudgingly. The conservative-controlled North Dakota Republican Party literally closed the door on him to win their nomination for another term. The flap about his fourth marriage dimmed his chances to win as an independent in the primary. Family and friends urged him to call it quits. Besides, he was old, tired and forgetful. But none of these negative factors forced his decision to hang up the jersey in the final analysis.

Usher Burdick retired because of one positive factor. He had a son, Quentin, standing on the sidelines. Quentin was 50 years old, prepared and primed to take over the fight and to continue serving North Dakota for another 30 years. Usher removed his worn-out political jersey because he, unlike any other North Dakotan politician, had a formidable substitute to wear the Burdick jersey — another Burdick — the young Burdick. This was retirement in a personal sense, but not a family sense.

The fact that the name of the jersey read Democrat, not Republican, caused some concern in Usher's master plan. But he had planned his final act well. The negative circumstances surrounding his departure from the Republicans made his political endorsement less difficult. It made him a free agent. He could campaign for a Democrat, and the Democrat he was campaigning for was his son. Family loyalty would supersede any charge of party disloyalty, and it did.

The political plan of the House of Usher worked to perfection. Quentin, running as a Democrat, won his father's seat in the 1958 election. Less than two years later, in June 1960, the young Burdick defeated Governor John Davis for Langer's unexpired term in the U.S. Senate. This play was not in Usher's political game plan. He opposed the idea and urged his son to stay in the House. But with an open Senate seat caused by Langer's death, his son wrote his own game plan and won one of the closest Senate races in North Dakota political history.

Usher Burdick died only 11 days after Quentin was sworn in as North Dakota's junior senator. The last two years of his life had been exciting even beyond his own wildest dreams. He had lived to see two members of the House of Usher elected to the House, Quentin and Robert Levering, his son-in-law. He died knowing there was also a member of the House of Usher in the U.S. Senate. Well done, Usher, well done.

Endnotes

1. *Washington (D.C.) Post*, Jan. 8, 1950.
2. *New York Times*, Aug. 20, 1960, 19.
3. George Munyer, interview by author, Sept. 24, 1993.
4. Jack Traynor, interview by author, April 1995.
5. John and Tish Kelly, interview by author, Jan. 22, 1995.
6. Terry Leonhardy, interview by author, Sept. 19, 1996.
7. *Congressional Record*, 83rd Congress, 2nd Session., 1954, vol. 100, pt. 1, p. 765.
8. Usher L. Burdick, letter to the O.J. deLendrecie Company, Dec. 26, 1951, folder 14, box 16, Usher L. Burdick Manuscript Collection [hereafter BMC], University of North Dakota.
9. *New York Times*, Aug. 20, 1960, 19.
10. *Minneapolis (Minn.) Morning Tribune*, Aug. 20, 1960, 1.

11. *Fargo (N.D.) Forum*, Aug. 20, 1960, 1.
12. Alden McLachlan, "Usher Burdick will be Remembered for His Fine Mind, Rapier-like Wit," *Fargo Forum*, Aug. 21, 1960.
13. *Bismarck (N.D.) Tribune*, Aug. 20, 1960, 1,2.
14. Ibid.
15. *Minot (N.D.) Daily News*, Aug. 20, 1960, 1.
16. Ibid.
17. Ibid.
18. Dick Dobson, "Rep. Usher Burdick: Salty Wit His Trademark," *Fargo Forum*, June 30, 1964.
19. *New York Times*, Aug. 23, 1960, 29.
20. *Congressional Record*, 86th Congress, 2nd Session, 1960, vol. 106, pt. 13, p. 17030.
21. Ibid.
22. Ibid., p. 17031.
23. Ibid., p. 17033.
24. Ibid., p. 17032.
25. Usher L. Burdick, letter to L.C. Connell, Jan. 27, 1955, folder 7, box 33, BMC.
26. Boorstin, *The Americans: The National Experience*, 52-97.
27. Eugene Burdick, interview with author, Feb. 28, 1995.
28. Burdick letter to Connell.
29. Usher L. Burdick, Autobiographical Notes, 1951, folders 2 and 12, box 36, BMC.
30. Ibid., 13.
31. Ibid., 10-11.
32. Ibid., 4.
33. Eugene Burdick interview; Burdick, Autobiographical Notes, 15.
34. Burdick, *Reminiscences of Mayville*, i.
35. Ibid.
36. Ibid., 4.
37. Burdick, Autobiographical Notes, 16.
38. Connell, *Son of the Morning Star*, 231.
39. Quentin and Jocelyn Burdick, interview with author, Jan. 6, 1992.
40. Eugene and May Burdick, interview with author, Feb. 28, 1995.
41. Eugene Burdick interview.
42. Quentin Burdick interview.
43. Eugene Burdick interview.
44. May Burdick interview.
45. Ibid.
46. Eugene Burdick interview.
47. *Fargo Forum*, Aug. 3, 1955.
48. Ibid., Aug. 3, 1955.
49. Ibid., June 26, 1958.
50. Ibid., April 7, 1959.
51. Ibid., March 27, 1958.
52. Tom Burgum, interview with author, March 25, 1995.
53. Eugene Burdick interview.
54. Usher L. Burdick, letter to Eileen Burdick, Sept. 25, 1940, folder 14, box 16, BMC.
55. Eugene Burdick interview.
56. Burdick, *Reminiscences of Mayville*, 11-12; Eugene Burdick interview.
57. Usher L. Burdick, letter to Dick Gordon, Feb. 18, 1957, in possession of Jennifer Burdick, Baltimore, Md.
58. Usher L. Burdick, letter to John Burke, July 18, 1935, folder 7, box 5, BMC.
59. Wilhelm, *Ezra Pound*, 313.
60. Meachum, *The Closed Panther*, 94.
61. Burgum interview.
62. "Here's a Congressman with a Busy Routine," 1936 newspaper clipping, folder 8, box 33, BMC.
63. Terry Leonhardy interview.
64. Mark Andrews, interview with author, April 19, 1995.

- three -

Place

A s a place, Munich, North Dakota, is unprepossessing. Its drift prairie landscape is slightly more rolling than the Red River Valley, which absorbs its eastern flank. Yet, still less than the more pronounced rolling landscape that begins to ascend slowly in height and appearance as one heads west toward the Missouri River and Montana. Its modest elevation of 1,601 feet positions it in the midsection of the state. The drift prairie is a transition zone, which corrals 40 percent of North Dakota, conveniently curtained between two geological faults – the Pembina Escarpment to the east and the Missouri Escarpment to west.

As a place, Munich symbolizes in a broader context the American region of the Great Plains. It sits on the eastern rim of this huge region, which runs 2,500 miles north and south and up to 600 miles east to west between the 98th meridian and the Rocky Mountains. Somewhere near Munich, the prairie environment begins to give way slowly to the plains. The flat valley starts to roll into soft plains, the Great Plains. Somewhere around Munich, adequate rainfall stops, and less than adequate rainfall begins. Skinny, vertical sights, such as telephone polls, replace the more familiar river-bordered trees. Finally and perhaps most dramatic, is the constant presence of wind, more wind, every day, any day. Wind is the permanent Plains resident that chills in fall, freezes in winter, warms in spring and bakes in summer.

Historians and travelers alike repeat these same natural images in different words and at different times. The Texas historian, Walter Prescott Webb, who first immortalized the region in his classic work, *The Great Plains* (1931), painted in broad strokes the region's three key elements: treeless, rolling terrain and insufficient rainfall. Webb described the shear immensity of the region – containing 20 percent of the land area of the continental United States and portions of

10 states — sparse population and a lack of any large metropolitan areas.[1]

William Least Heat Moon in his van, Ghost Dancing, traveled west to east near Munich in the early 1980s. His travel narrative, *Blue Highways: A Journey through America* (1982), describes what place here seemed to be after one hurried visit. "North Dakota up here," he noted "was a curveless place, not just roads, but land, people too and the flight of birds."[2] Everything appears angular, he writes: "Fence posts against the sky, the line of the jaw, the ways of the mind, lay of the crops."[3] Locals seemed concerned but reconciled to the presence of ICBMs with their multiple, destructive nuclear warheads. "We live on top of them here," one resident exclaimed. "We grow the bread you and the Russians eat right over the missiles."[4]

Ian Frazier, in his national bestseller, *Great Plains* (1989), chronicled his interpretation of the region in still more wonderful prose. He describes it as the "air shaft of the continent" where the "wind blows all the time."[5] Plains storms fascinate him. "Up ahead, in North Dakota," he writes, "storm clouds come all the way down to the ground like an overhead garage door."[6] Frazier, like Least Heat Moon, also notes the presence of the nukes, observing, "a nuclear-missile silo is one of the quintessential Great Plains, objects."[7] Frazier adds two more themes to the region: since 1930, two-thirds of all the counties of the Great Plains have lost population, and more than 50 percent of the nation's coal reserves rest under its soil.[8]

On the sparse Great Plains region, space always costs more money. "The further people live from the city," the law of economics dictates, "the costlier and less available modern services are likely to be."[9] Public and private costs of services are greatly increased by distance. Roads cost more per capita. Education costs more per student. Health services cost more per patient. Electricity and telephone cost more per customer, and air transportation costs more per mile. Adaptations to reduce this social cost of space provide few alternatives for those who live there. For families, it could be to maintain two homes — one in the country and one in town. For government, the choices are quite simple: Either consolidate basic services such as county government, education and law enforcement, or just continue to pay the higher costs by duplicating services. For private enterprise, the choice is to consolidate basic services such as health care, businesses and transportation, or simply discontinue them altogether. Over time, however, more duplication of government services remains than private enterprise.

The future of the Great Plains was addressed comprehensively by the federal government in the wake of the Depression, drought, and despair of the years between World War I and World War II. In a letter of transmittal to the

United States Congress in February of 1937, President Franklin D. Roosevelt submitted "The Future of the Great Plains" study. He urged Congress to take a long-term approach to the prospects for the region. "Depression and drought," Roosevelt wrote, "have only accentuated a situation which has long been developing."[10] In this broader context, the agricultural practices developed in the more humid east simply fell short in the semiarid region of the Great Plains.

The report called for a new federal-state partnership to save the Great Plains. It suggested a variety of adjustments, which included investigations and surveys, development of water resources, preaching and practicing conservation, controlling insects and pests, and mobilizing capital resources and credit.[11] The report also identified the region's greatest economic problem, which was the squeeze of a flexible price system for agriculture and an inflexible price structure for industry. The report cited mobilization of capital resources as both a responsibility and an opportunity for the federal government to become a prime player. It identified the Farm Credit Administration as a federal agency "through which part of the existing difficulties may be resolved."[12]

Lack of water and abundance of lignite coal drew special attention. The report cited the absence of water in the Red River of the North during the worst years of the drought with a staggering, almost unbelievable statistic — no water flowed at Fargo, N.D., for 584 days between July 25, 1932, and June 14, 1936.[13] Clearly, the Great Plains must discover new means to utilize water because the single, greatest natural handicap of the Great Plains would always be the lack of sufficient rainfall. If water was deficient, vast undeveloped lignite deposits should be mined, with the first stage being to generate electricity. An ironic proposition perhaps, since development would demand more water to produce the electrical power.

The political realities of the region remain quite simple. The first generation of Plains politicians worked for change to create regulations that ensured regional fairness in economic dealings with the rest of the nation. A second generation also worked for change and jumped aboard New Deal and Fair Deal trains to establish and fund myriad federal programs for agriculture, rural electrification and water diversion. Since the Eisenhower years, the Plains politicians work primarily for continuity. Their agenda is to protect the regulations and government programs established by their Plains forefathers. The issue for them and their constituents is not the creation of new federal programs, but to protect those that already exist. In other words, change the formula, but do not eliminate the program.[14]

Political styles differed between promoting change or protecting continuity. The first and second generations of Plains politicians were protesters and screamers. They drew attention to the unfairness of railroad rates, low farm prices or large numbers of farm foreclosures by giving speeches, drafting legislation and raising hell. They were Chautauqualike actors playing the roles of the depressed and the deprived under the tents of their constituents and among their colleagues in Washington. The louder their protests, the more attention they drew to the region's problems and the longer they stayed in office.

The protesters are no more. Managers act in their place. Their style of drawing attention is gone, too, replaced by a style of trying *not* to draw attention. Today's representatives work quietly to maintain the existing programs. They protect the existing federal programs, and serve as liaisons between federal agencies and interest groups in their own states. Few aspire to create new programs. Instead, they barter between administrations and members of Congress to ensure that vital programs for their region survive. They make less noise, probably give fewer speeches, but conduct more meetings. The harder they work, the more their states receive in federal dollars, and the longer they stay in office.

North Dakota's two longest serving congressional representatives, Senators Milton R. Young (1945-1981; Republican) and Quentin N. Burdick (1958-1992; Democrat) illustrate the change from protester to manager. Both served their congressional apprenticeships during the Great Depression — Young as a North Dakota state senator representing farmers of LaMoure County; Burdick as a practicing attorney in Fargo representing urban indigents, labor strikers and foreclosed farmers. Neither, however, were political screamers — Young, in part, because of a speech impediment; Burdick, in part, because of a personal reserve.

When voters sent them to Washington, their behind-the-scene style fit easily into the new style of the Plains politician. They became federal managers for North Dakota programs. Both acquired nicknames, which personified their Senate work. Young became "Mr. Wheat" and Burdick became "Mr. Pork." Young used his position on the Senate Appropriations Committee to protect the farm subsidies established in the 1930s. He accomplished this feat not by giving speeches, but by marking up bills and forging alliances with Southerners who sought the same protection for their farmers. Burdick used his chairmanship of the Senate Appropriations Subcommittee on Agriculture to add many North Dakota projects to final appropriation bills.

Both North Dakota senators bridged the era of change and continuity. Their politics were in marked contrast to those of their predecessors. Young, who was appointed to the Senate in 1945, stayed away from foreign affairs, which had led to the defeat of Senator Gerald P. Nye (1925-1944) in 1944.

Burdick, who won a special election in June of 1960 to fill the unexpired term caused by the death of Senator William Langer (1941-1959), never participated in the antics of filibuster or debate that characterized the career of "Wild Bill." Yet, both Young and Burdick learned lots from Langer. They continued the service to state theme, which Langer raised to a new political art form for their North Dakota constituents. Their offices served like foreign consuls in the federal capital. They answered their mail, talked endlessly by telephone and came home regularly. They were quiet businessmen working in a complex world where federal spending fed the hungry appetite of state needs.

Beginnings

The historical significance of Munich stands not in its uniqueness but in its similarity. There were many towns just like Munich scattered throughout the Great Plains in general and North Dakota in particular. Each created with a different settlement name, but all exhibited similar settlement patterns. Some bore Norwegian names such as Viking and Voss, or Russian names such as Balta and Volga, French names such as Des Lacs and Souris, Indian names of Minnewaukan and Makoti, German names such as Fulda and New Leipzig, and English ones such as Victoria and Wimbledon.[15] All looked and felt the same. Each community conformed to uniform railroad townsite designs. Each town mapped out carbon copy main streets filled with eager and enthusiastic residents. Munich, like most of its small town cousins, mirrored a prairie mosaic of ethnicity, railroad expansion and boom in the first years of the 20th century on the Great Plains and in North Dakota. Munich was not different as a place. It was the same as most anywhere else in the state.

The Munichs of North Dakota never reached the large numbers anticipated by their founders. Their importance always rested in their beginnings, not their growth. In a repeated cycle, these frontier communities marketed wheat for needed cash in exchange for manufactured goods. The railroads that created them in the first place never lost money on their economic existence, and the Twin Cities emerged as the alpha and omega of trade and their dominant economic overseer for decades.

Their sons and daughters left like carloads of durum wheat when parents pulled stakes or opportunities simply ceased. All shared in a common, simple, small-town beginning. Some residents achieved more success than others, but history measures the success of North Dakota's decision makers by their achievements — not their place of birth. We admire Lawrence Welk for his music, not his Strasburg, North Dakota, birthplace. We know Angie Dickinson for her television and movie roles, maybe her shapely legs, but never her Kulm, North Dakota, birthplace. Many remember Eric Sevareid's long and distinguished career in journalism, but few pay scant attention to his Velva, North Dakota, birthplace. We can recall Senator Milton R. Young's long tenure in the United States Senate, but we seldom refer to his Berlin, North Dakota, birthplace. Similarly, when we think of Senator Quentin Burdick's long stewardship to the people of North Dakota, his uncommon birthplace in Munich does not seem to matter. It need not. What was important about the Munich communities of North Dakota was not their town sites but their citizens. Quentin Burdick was born in Munich, but he could have been born in similar communities anywhere in the state. It would have made no difference. His town of birth remains less important than his place in the region or the state as a whole.

The community of Munich paid scant attention to Burdick for most of his public career. The town celebrated its Diamond Jubilee in July of 1979. The three-day event centered on an all-school reunion and dance, the showing of a Walt Disney movie, the production of a canned stage show, and a Saturday morning parade. Locals hawked the sale of a Diamond Jubilee history book and cookbook while seniors sold homemade quilts. Burdick did not attend the celebration.[16]

In the summer of 1984, the Munich community invited Burdick home for a special occasion. Town boosters decided to promote their community by touting it as the birthplace of the state's senior senator. The town fathers unveiled a new sign near the southwest entrance of the community, which proudly read: "The birthplace of U.S. Sen. Quentin Burdick." The sign cost $350, was 10 feet by 5 feet, and made of weather resistant redwood, "So it could last forever," as one of the builders explained it.[17]

As part of the ceremony, Burdick was invited to speak. It was a hot summer day in mid-July. Burdick appeared almost overdressed touting a new, pale blue blazer sport coat and unfamiliar footwear — a shiny new pair of shoes. He left his famous homburg hat in the car because it was just too hot. A modest crowd, estimated to be about 60 in number, gathered in the city park, a drained cattail slough. There was no podium or platform. Instead, someone backed up a pickup truck, flipped down the tailgate and rearranged some bales of hay. Burdick hopped into the back of the pickup and rested one leg on a bale of hay. He spoke without notes.

"I arrived here June 17, 1908," he told the crowd, adding quickly with a half smile, "of course I hadn't been anywhere else before." Burdick went on to speak informally about his birthplace and to extol the values of rural America. He warmed the crowd by reminding each of them of their place and importance as a sort of symbol of what rural life was all about. At one point, he seemed almost lost with a personal, philosophical abstraction of where he had been: "How different it all is from the city of Washington."[18]

Quentin Ames, one of the organizers of the celebration, was especially pleased with Burdick's appearance. "My dad and Senator Burdick played together in Munich," Ames explained. More proudly, he went on to exclaim: "I'm named after Senator Burdick!"[19]

Suezette Bieri said it was one of those rare occurrences in life that you remember all the time because what transpired was so powerful. "I mean, here you are in a small town in northeastern North Dakota filled with ordinary people honoring a man who by chance was born there and became a United States Senator," Bieri said. The speech by Burdick that afternoon made her proud to be a North Dakotan and an American: "I suddenly understood why this very old man ... must have been [powerful] as a public speaker when he was younger because even at this age, he could just take this crowd and sweep them up and make them part of this great democratic experience."[20]

It was never made clear whether Burdick incorrectly stated the date of his birthday or whether the *Grand Forks Herald* simply erred in reporting it. Burdick was born on June 19, 1908, not June 17 as reported in the newspaper.[21] It really did not matter. Burdick was never known for correctness in every detail anyway, and for this occasion, nobody cared. The fact that he was actually born in Munich, not the date, was the only thing that really mattered. Political buffs allotted more significance to the fact that he had purchased a new pair of shoes for the occasion than whether he recalled the correct date of his birth. The new shoes sent only one message: Burdick was getting ready to run for re-election in 1988.

In December of 1995, the *Grand Forks Herald* wrote the final chapter in the Burdick-Munich saga. The Burdick home in Munich stood empty. A big for sale sign sits in the front yard; interested buyers seem nonexistent. Repeated attempts by local civic groups to restore the house as a local Burdick museum met with continued failure. The weatherworn house with peeling paint and a couple of broken windows attests to a town without a past and a senator without a birthplace.[22]

Burdick Beginnings

Usher Burdick came to Munich in December of 1904 primarily to settle down and to make money. Of the latter goal, after several years of college life at the University of Minnesota, he had little. Therefore, when a business proposition came his way from David H. Beecher, president of the Union National Bank in Grand Forks and avid admirer of Usher's football success, to establish the First National Bank at Munich, Burdick took the offer under advisement. With the purchase of $5,000 in bank stock obtained from his father-in-law, Hans Robertson of Park River, Burdick accepted the title of cashier and the job of credit officer for a salary of $125 a month. In addition, Burdick was encouraged to supplement his salary by practicing law, a trade as important to the new bank as it was to Burdick himself.

In the beginning, there was neither a town of Munich nor a First National Bank. In early December, Burdick took an overnight train with William Budge of Grand Forks to inspect where the townsite was located. Budge was a land speculator and close, personal friend of James J. Hill, whose Great Northern Railroad was grading a branch line from Lakota, North Dakota, to the Canadian line. Burdick and Budge spent the night wrapped in a bundle of buffalo robes to stay warm as the temperature dropped to 30 below zero in Munich's only building, an unheated sod house. In the ensuing weeks, Burdick erected a small house on the lot where the bank was to be and transported his wife, Emma, by sled to the site. In the beginning, the house served as both a residence and a bank.[23]

Burdick the football player quickly became the town's leading upstart and boomer. During the next six or seven years, he always appeared busy with some new business venture. At public events, he gave the speeches. When the town needed a site for the church, he donated the land. When the town organized its first public school, he served on the school board. When the town residents looked for a candidate to represent them in the state Legislature, he ran. Although we know little about his family life, the pages of the local newspaper swell with Burdick activities and accolades. "Mr. Burdick is a young man, barely turned 30 and is full of vim," touted the *Munich Herald & Tribune*. "As a business man, he stands at the top of his class and is conscientious and upright in all his dealings."[24]

The bank operation encompassed more than making loans. The bank was also in the business of selling city lots and establishing other businesses to fill the main street. As bank officer, Burdick signed off on all loans, but his hands were busy making Munich into a prosperous and progressive community. He established a sale barn for horses and organized the Munich Machine Company, which sold wagons, buggies, plows and a full line of farm machinery. He soon invested in a herd of Percheron mares, a fine stallion named Gasolite and registered Hereford cattle. And his calling card, "Usher L. Burdick, Attorney at Law," ran noticeably on the front page of the weekly newspaper.[25]

Burdick the business booster soon became Burdick the civic leader. He and William Budge donated land for the Presbyterian Church and Burdick helped construct the first school in Munich in 1905. Fourth of July events always found Burdick as the main speaker or master of ceremonies. When a speech was over, he quickly donned the hat of a Wild West show character or gunned his Buick around the dirt racetrack. In 1909, Burdick and his Buick won the automobile race at Hampden. Either by speech or by race, Burdick symbolized the freedom of new beginnings and the model of citizen involvement.[26]

The ultimate synthesis of booster and civic leader came in 1907. When the long winter of 1906-1907 reduced coal supplies in Munich, Burdick held up the branch line train heading north with four cars of coal slated for Sarles but none for Munich. "The crowd became angry and it looked like trouble," Burdick recalled about the incident many years later. "I volunteered to take possession of one car and weigh out the coal to the citizens in and around Munich." Although the railroad crew bluffed resistance, Burdick distributed the coal. He collected the money and gave it all to the railroad agent.[27] Munich homes were warm again. Burdick, the football player, had made another great play.

Whether by design, reward or a combination of both, Usher Burdick launched his political career at Munich. In the factional split caused between stalwart and insurgent North Dakota Republicans, Burdick joined the Progressive wing. He ran and won a legislative seat in the North Dakota House of Representatives from Cavalier County in 1906 and 1908. Once he tasted the political pulse of state politics, his political career seemed to grow as quickly as Munich's main street. He was elected speaker of the House in 1909 and a year later became a successful candidate for the office of lieutenant governor.

A new player in state politics, Burdick's speech echoed the words of his political mentor, President Theodore Roosevelt. He sought office to represent the people, "with special privileges to none and a square deal for all."[28] When asked how he would preside over the state Senate if elected lieutenant governor, Burdick replied he was in favor of recorded roll calls. "I want to see every bill have a fair hearing and if any be killed that there be a record of the killing."[29] By the end of the 1911 legislative session, Burdick began to sound like a future candidate for governor. "I am not trying to play Cincinnatus and arrange to be suddenly surprised by a nominating committee while driving oxen in the field." Burdick said in one breath. Then he quickly continued, "I stand squarely for those principles so ably advocated by Senator LaFollette and Theodore Roosevelt and I will not compromise my belief in those policies for any public office."[30]

Sometime during his heady rush for a career in politics, Usher Burdick made the decision to move his family west to Williston. The move was not out of character, however, even with his new-found love of politics. The Burdicks were transients. As Eugene Burdick described it, "He was kind of a, not a wanderlust exactly, but going to the pastures where things were going to develop, going to the end of the line."[31] Their whole history was one of continual movement somewhere else but always west. Emma Burdick did not support the move. She wanted very much to stay in Munich close to family and friends. She could not understand why Usher suddenly and abruptly decided to move to Williston. Sometime during 1910, Emma and their 2-year-old son Quentin moved to Williston. Because of business dealings and running for a state office that same year, Usher withdrew from Munich in stages. It was not until the fall of 1911 that his name disappeared from the published list of bank officers of the First National Bank. In early November, Burdick sold 36 of his 46 purebred horses at a well-attended auction in Munich.[32] The sale was his last official act.

In the dusk of his life, Burdick wrote about those Munich years in some detail. The words written by the old man still flowed with the excitement of new town beginnings. Older European names such as Berge, Deitschman, DeVries, Grimson, Kleinschmidt, Neussendorfer, Schmiddlekofer, Skjervheim, Thorfinnson and Wiems assimilated quickly to become accepted American names. He remembered the fast pace of erecting new homes and the numerical order of each new store, as well as the personal satisfaction of his civic participation and political success. "While the days were rough, I was young and full of energy," Burdick wrote. "Now at a distance of 48 years, I look back to my days there as the happiest of my life."[33]

Quentin

In the Burdick home on June 19, 1908, Emma gave birth to her first child, a boy. The boy received the name Quentin Northrop Burdick. Although there are some family doubts about the circumstances of the naming, it is quite certain that he was named Quentin in honor of Quentin Roosevelt, the youngest son of Theodore Roosevelt, and Northrop for Cyrus Northrop, the president of the University of Minnesota — Quentin for the seed of Progressive Republicanism explicit in his father's brand of politics; Northrop for excellence in education shared by both parents with college degrees.[34]

The biggest story on June 19 was the Republican nomination of William Howard Taft of Ohio for president. Nominated the day before in Chicago on the first ballot, Taft's story swept front-page news across both national and state newspapers. The North Dakota Republican delegation joined the Taft parade, proudly casting all eight of its votes for Taft. "Mr. Taft stands against all privilege," exclaimed President Theodore Roosevelt, his most enthusiastic supporter, in the *New York Times,* while an exuberant Mrs. Taft found only two words: "Oh Will!" to express her joy.[35] The *Bismarck Daily Tribune* ran Taft's photograph on the front page, predicting a sure victory in November with the headline, "Our Next President."[36]

Upbeat best describes the economic climate as well. Although there were less than 100 stocks listed on the New York Stock Exchange, stock prices remained strong on Wall Street. ATT, the nation's only telecommunications company, closed at 118, while the two major Midwest regional railroad stocks, the Great Northern Railway (131) and the Northern Pacific Railroad (136) also closed strong. Realtors were touting new homes in Hayworth, New Jersey, only 14 miles from New York, for under $10,000.[37] Fancy dairy butter in 5- or 10-pound jars was listed in the *Fargo Forum* for 22 cents a pound.[38]

Crime was neither a national preoccupation nor a local priority. Cy Seymour, outfielder for the New York Giants, probably made the catch of the day in New York by dashing across the field and, with his bare hand, catching a ball surely "sailing toward the Harlem River." The catch brought 12,000 cheering fans to their feet and produced a big headline, which read, "Seymour's Catch Checks the Cubs."[39] In Fargo, George Schas, Hector Barnes' chauffeur, also got caught. He was arrested for speeding on Broadway "at a time when that street was crowded" and for doing it "a number of times."[40] Peter Matthews, who was running from creditors, apparently committed suicide in a Wahpeton, North Dakota, hotel, where he was found "hanging by his neck to a bedpost."[41]

June of 1908 was a busy month for Usher Burdick, too. He was a candidate for re-election in the June Republican primary for the Legislature. Usher later wrote that he and Emma could not agree on a name for the baby and his absence probably delayed their decision. He wanted to name the boy Quentin, while she wanted another name, presumably Northrop. When the children in the neighborhood kept pestering him for a name, Usher gave his choice. "I told them one day that Quentin was the name of the baby. That settled it; the kids started calling him Quentin, and that name stuck."[42]

Quentin Burdick could not explain his middle name. "I can't answer that question," he said in response to a query in 1992. "It isn't a family name."[43] His younger brother, Eugene, had not the slightest hesitation when asked the same question three years later. The name Northrop was given to Quentin in honor of Cyrus Northrop, the president of the University of Minnesota when Usher and Emma were students there. As for Quentin's inability to recall the story behind his middle name, Eugene at first seemed flabbergasted. "Isn't it funny that he could not remember that?" However, quickly recovering almost in the same breath, he answered his own question: "Well, when you interviewed him, he was slipping."[44]

Namesakes add flavor to biography. Quentin Roosevelt was the fifth and youngest child of Theodore and Edith Kermit Roosevelt. He lived a short but active life. He was born in New York City on November 19, 1897, and died behind German lines on July 17, 1919, when his plane crashed after shooting down a German plane near Chateau-Thierry. He was only 21 years old. Herman Hagedorn, Theodore's close friend, wrote that Quentin's death hit his father particularly hard. "The old side of him was gone," recalled Hagedorn. "The boy in him was dead."[45] Less than six months later, the father was dead, too.

Roosevelt biographers paint a prankster image of Quentin growing up in Washington during the years of the Roosevelt presidency. He and his older brothers Teddy and Archie were referred to as the "White House Gang." They flattened the south lawn for a baseball field, and Quentin once took his Shetland pony, Algonquin, upstairs in the elevator to visit Archie, who was sick in bed.[46]

Special occasions such as the New Year's Day open house at the White House always put Washington police on alert, especially for Quentin. "As the crowd approaches the portico, nine-year-old Quentin Roosevelt waves an affable greeting from his upstairs window. The policemen eye him sternly: he has been known to drop projectiles, including a snowball so gigantic it completely flattened one officer, to the uncontrollable hilarity of the President."[47]

Cyrus Northrop served as the second president of the University of Minnesota (1884-1911). During his tenure, the school emerged from a small state university to the beginning of a great American university. Enrollments increased, new schools were organized and new buildings constructed. Most importantly, however, was the hiring of quality faculty who would distinguish themselves and the institution in the decades to come. "He endeared himself to the people, won support from every group," praised Minnesota historian Theodore Blegen years later. President Northrop, "as the years went by became the most beloved of all Minnesotans."[48]

Few records exist about Quentin Burdick's first two years of life. His early years were uneventful and ordinary. His loving mother reared him in a small town in northeastern North Dakota. His father was always busy with some new business activity or preoccupied with some new political challenge. Quentin grew to know and love his mother, but he never experienced the same emotional attachment to his father. This father-son relationship, however, was usual for the time. Mothers reared their children in every small town, while fathers worked to support them and to acquire property. What was unique about this father-son relationship was the disconnect of Usher's wild ambition with Quentin's child rearing. Usher's world was so much bigger than most fathers of his generation. Quentin often learned about his father through public action, not personal contact. He seldom experienced having a father who worked regularly during the day in town or on the farm and stayed home at night. Their relationship was often different than the norm. He was the son of a football and political legend. He was not Quentin Burdick; he was the son of Usher Burdick.

This father-son relationship, which began in the first two years of Quentin's life, did not change much over the next 52 years. Quentin filled his father's shoes as a University of Minnesota graduate, a Golden Gopher football player, a North Dakota attorney and a seasoned politician. On the surface, they served North Dakota through opposing political parties: Usher served as a Progressive Republican and Quentin served as a liberal Democrat. Political labels, however, do not mean much to North Dakota voters most of the time. In political terms, there were more similarities between Theodore Roosevelt's Progressivism and Franklin Roosevelt's New Deal liberalism than differences. In personal terms, there were more similarities between Usher and Quentin Burdick than differences, too. Important to voters was that they spelled their last names the same, but perhaps most important was that North Dakotans became familiar with both the name and the person who reappeared regularly for almost nine decades between 1908 and 1992.

Endnotes

1. Webb, *The Great Plains*, 3.
2. Least Heat Moon, *Blue Highways*, 283.
3. Ibid., 284.
4. Ibid., 286.
5. Frazier, *Great Plains*, 3.
6. Ibid., 138.
7. Ibid., 200.
8. Ibid., 9.
9. Anderson, "Space as Social Cost," *Journal of Farm Economics* 32 (August 1950): 411.
10. "The Future of the Great Plains," Report to U.S. House of Representatives, 75th Cong., 1st Session., 1937 (Washington: GPO, 1937), 5.
11. Ibid., 66.
12. Ibid., 95.
13. Ibid., 141.
14. Danbom, "A Part of the Nation and Apart from the Nation" in *Politics in the Postwar American West*, 175.
15. Wick, *North Dakota Place Names.*
16. *Grand Forks Herald*, June 27, 1979.
17. Mike Jacobs, "A senator comes home," *Grand Forks Herald*, July 15, 1984.
18. Ibid.
19. Ibid.
20. Suezette Bieri, interview by author, Jan. 17, 1995.
21. Jacobs, "A senator comes home."
22. Kevin Bonham, "Decline of the house of Usher," *Grand Forks Herald*, Dec. 10, 1995.
23. Burdick, *A Short History of Munich*, 3.
24. *Munich Herald & Tribune*, Aug. 20, 1908.
25. Ibid., June 18, 1908.
26. Ibid., July 8, 1908.
27. Burdick, *A Short Story of Munich*, 4.
28. *Munich Herald*, May 5, 1910.
29. Ibid., Dec. 29, 1910.
30. Ibid., Aug. 31, 1911.
31. Eugene Burdick, interview by author, Feb. 28, 1995.
32. *Munich Herald*, Oct. 12, 1911.
33. Burdick, *A Short Story of Munich*, 19.
34. Eugene Burdick interview.
35. *New York Times*, June 19, 1908, 1.
36. *Bismarck Daily Tribune*, June 19, 1908.
37. *New York Times*, June 19, 1908, 10.
38. *Fargo Forum & Daily Republican*, June 19, 1908.
39. *New York Times*, June 20, 1908, 7.
40. *Fargo Forum & Daily Republican*, June 19, 1908.
41. Ibid.
42. Burdick, *A Short History of Munich*, 5.
43. Quentin Burdick, interview by author, Jan. 6, 1992.
44. Eugene Burdick interview.
45. Pringle, *Theodore Roosevelt: A Biography*, 601.
46. Miller, *Theodore Roosevelt: A Life*, 16.
47. Morris, *The Rise of Theodore Roosevelt*, 16.
48. Blegen, *Minnesota: A History of the State*, 423.

- four -

The Williston Years

Quentin Northrup Burdick was a Williston boy. Here, on the banks of the Missouri River, his life really began. His parents moved to Williston in 1910 when he was only 2 years old. There he remained until graduation from Williston High School in 1926 at age 18. There he also returned during the next few summers to work while a student at the University of Minnesota. There, too, are buried both his parents — Usher, the congressman, on the ranch, and Emma, his mother, in the city cemetery. Although Quentin never returned to practice law like his younger brother, Eugene, he always considered Williston his home and a major influence on his life. Quentin understood the west in North Dakota — the importance of the Missouri River and the hardships of ranching — because he was part of the place.

There were many positive aspects for a young boy to grow up in Williston in the early two decades of the 20th century. The community was booming with more residents; 3,124 in 1910; 4,178 in 1920; and 5,106 in 1930. The public schools were bursting with fresh faces, better-trained teachers and optimum student participation. Football was increasing in popularity as a high school sport. College was an alternative for some of the brighter students. The Missouri Valley provided opportunities to hunt and fish. The ranch provided an outlet from town life and the opportunity to raise cattle and horses. Town residency gave access to a larger community and a real neighborhood.[4]

Quentin experienced a normal childhood in many ways. He attended Williston Public Schools for 12 years. He proved to be a good student. He made friends among the boys, but demonstrated little interest in the other sex. He liked to hunt, tinker with cars and pull off a few school pranks. Most of all, he loved football. He trained all year for a half-dozen games each fall. He was by all accounts a tough, hard-nosed player who played linebacker on defense and fullback on offense. He excelled in crisp blocks, punishing tackles and bull-you-over runs. He usually carried the ball straight up the middle. Once through the line, he looked to run over rather than around the remaining defenders. He was neither mean nor dirty, but he played hard. If you came in contact with him, you seldom forgot the impact. He never ran from a fight, but he never provoked one, either. His gentle but warriorlike qualities, fundamental skills, work ethic and his father's legacy made him a strong candidate for the University of Minnesota football team in the fall of 1926.

Quentin experienced an abnormal childhood in other ways. His father was an aspiring politician, a colorful personality and often the talk of the town. Quentin could never escape the label of being Usher's son, although there were many incidents during his lifetime when he would have preferred the disassociation. The divorce of his parents in 1921 caused public embarrassment and personal hurt. It also placed additional work on Quentin's shoulders. Although he was only 12 years old, he took those duties seriously. He grew closer to Emma, but remained in awe of Usher. Drought, poor farm prices and inexperience in ranch management added to family stress and poverty. Quentin became the surrogate head of the Burdick family. Emma depended on him while his younger siblings, Eugene and Eileen, began to view Quentin more as a provider than an older brother.

The Williston years produced fundamental characteristics in Quentin. He was quiet like his mother. He preferred doing to his father's talking. He liked physical contact and aspired to be a better football player than his father. He often reduced some of his future political opponents to physical opponents, challenging them to a match rather than a public debate. He was habitually serious and always a worrywart. He took life more gravely than most boys of his age and never let go of it. He found relaxation difficult, and rather than do nothing, he always kept himself busy with newfound projects. He was astute, but never took to bragging. He played every contest to win and hated to lose. But for all his competitiveness, there was a courteous demeanor about him. Quentin Burdick appeared always the gentleman, but once thrown into the fray or pushed into a corner, he became the gentle warrior.

Place

Physical differences dot the North Dakota landscape between Munich and Williston. The 300-mile journey west is split almost equally between the expansion of the Drift Prairie and the emergence of the Missouri Plateau. Elevation hikes ever so gradually from 1,601 to 1,877 feet above sea level. Annual rainfall drops precipitously, however, from 20 inches to 12 inches. The soil gets lighter. The grasses grow thinner. The music of the cottonwoods replaces the silence of the elms. New creatures, such as rattlesnakes, fight field mice and prairie gophers for survival. The sky seems closer and the wind blows stronger. As one approaches Minot, the "Magic City," with two-thirds of the journey completed, the broader canvas changes from soft rolling hills to bigger ones with more definition and texture.

It is hard to determine exactly where western North Dakota begins along this old Great Northern Railroad-Highway 2 journey. Certainly, it happens a few miles northwest of Minot, as one turns right and climbs the big hill and heads west toward Stanley and Williston. However, what makes the western test here so evasive is that the Missouri River, the real dividing line between eastern and western North Dakota, is so far west at Williston that it almost touches Montana.

The southern journey across the state makes the east-west test much easier. Author John Steinbeck captured the difference when he traveled with his dog Charlie on old Highway 10 in the early '60s:

> Someone must have told me about the Missouri River at Bismarck, North Dakota, or I have read about it. In either case, I hadn't paid attention. I came on it in amazement. Here is where the map should fold. Here is the boundary between east and west. On the Bismarck side it is eastern land-scape, eastern grass, with the look and smell of eastern America. Across the Missouri on the Mandan side, it is pure west, with brown grass and water scorings and small outcrops. The two sides of the river might well be a thousand miles apart.[1]

Although the east-west division is not as graphic as along the southern route, it does occur. Residents think of themselves as westerners with as many suspicions about those who reside in Fargo and Grand Forks as those who live in the Twin Cities. One can debate endlessly with good arguments either way as to whether Minot or even Devils Lake is the line of division on the northern route. What one cannot debate is that at journey's end, the Williston Basin, remains as the most important link North Dakota enjoys with the broader themes of western American history. Williston is both western North Dakota and western United States.

If Munich existed without a historical past, the Williston area was born with one. "Make no mistake about it," notes Ben Innis, Williston historian, "The Missouri is the reason for our founding and our being" because "for more than forty years the great river served as the main highway of the north western American fur trade."[2] Indeed, Williston's location on the Missouri River, and its proximity to the Little Missouri and to Missouri's confluence with the Yellowstone River, position it in a unique geographical location for important historical events that took place before there was a North Dakota.

The Missouri, however, is more than just a river. It is the nation's longest flowing river – 2,465 miles from Three Forks, Montana, to its mouth above St. Louis, Missouri. In addition, 10 states share in the broader landscape of the Missouri Basin. For writers of prose, the Missouri is neither a river nor a river basin. "I have come to look upon the Missouri as more than a river," wrote John G. Neihardt, who swam it as a boy and canoed it as a man. "To me it is an epic."[3] For writers of American places, its influence is mitigated only by patterns of settlement and discovery. "If the historic direction of settlement had been west to east instead of east to west," observed Wallace and Page Stegner, "we would probably be calling the great concave of the continent the Missouri Valley, not the Mississippi Valley, and [we] would recognize both the Mississippi and the Ohio as tributaries of the Missouri, which is the longest river on the continent and one of the longest in the world, and which below the junction completely converts the placid Mississippi to its own wild ways."[4]

The Missouri is also the river of many nations. Indian nations who observed its unique ways gave descriptive names to label its behavior. For example, "Minni-So-Say" or "Muddy Water" to the Sioux; "Mati" or "Navigable-Stream-Full-Of-Dirt" to the Hidatsas, and "Mata" or "Meridian Boundary Between Two-Pieces-Of-Land" to the Mandans. American observers added to the river's lexicon with epithets such as the "Big Muddy," "Misery River" and "Graveyard for Steamboats," and popular sayings such as "too thick to drink and too thin to plow."[5]

The Williston area is also synonymous with two 19th-century American forts – Ft. Union and Ft. Buford. Ft. Union, the largest and most important trading post on the Missouri, was constructed in 1829 by John Jacob Astor at the confluence of the Missouri and Yellowstone rivers. Abandoned in 1864, the National Park Service acquired it in 1966. Through the efforts of North Dakota historical, park and tourist officials and federal funding initially secured by Senator Quentin Burdick, Ft. Union stands as one of the most striking historical reconstructions in the nation. Ft. Buford, east of Ft. Union, was an American military fort from 1866 to 1895. It is now a North Dakota historical site administered by the State Historical Society of North Dakota.

Ft. Union, of all the Missouri River trading posts, was the largest and certainly the most significant. For years, it was the final destination for the steamboats that plied the Missouri. It was the great rendezvous center for North

American traders with Sioux, Hidatsas, Mandans, Arikaras, Crow, Crees, As-
siniboines and Blackfeet Indians who came together each spring to trade beaver
furs and buffalo hides for enormous profits back East. It was a departure point
for trapper Jim Bridger, river man Mike Fink and CEO fur trader Kenneth
McKenzie. It was a respite for European noblemen such as Prince Paul of Wur-
temberg and Maximilian, Prince of Wied. It served as an art colony for the
Swiss artist Karl Bodmer, the American naturalist John James Audubon and
the American painter John Mix Stanley. It was a reprieve for the missionary
Catholic priest, Father Pierre Jean DeSmet; the surveyor, Isaac Ingalls Stevens;
and for one of President Lincoln's Civil War generals, George B. McClellan,
who would not fight. It was also a site of cultural genocide against the Indians
— a source of small pox and alcohol.

Ft. Buford served a narrow but no less important mission. It was there in
1877 that Chief Joseph and his band of Nez Perce were held briefly. And it was
at Ft. Buford in 1881 that the Sioux, led by Chief Gall and Sitting Bull, surrendered to American military forces after being forced to leave Canada.[6]

Family

The opening of the Missouri Plateau consummated the second and last
great Dakota Boom, beginning in 1898 and ending at the eve of World War I.
In the space of almost two decades, one-quarter of a million settlers poured into
North Dakota. Most settled in the western portion, arriving rapidly via a greatly
expanded network of competing railroads. The availability of free land by homestead entry or cheap by railroad sales enticed the majority to come. Almost all
of the settlers pictured themselves as small farmers committed to the same crops
grown by their ancestors. Few thought themselves in the class of foreign or rich
American ranchers with big spreads.

Williston became a center for part of this expansion in the northwest
corner of the state. It was a mere campground of worn tents and crudely constructed log cabins when the Great Northern Railroad blew its whistle in 1887.
Williston grew rapidly from village (1884) to city (1904) and cemented its hold
as the seat of Williams County, one of the largest of the state's eventual 53
counties. Its population increases matched its growing importance, jumping
from 763 residents in 1900 to 3,124 by 1910.[7]

The young Burdick family joined this boom milieu in 1910 in a move
based on sound planning. Usher saw great financial opportunity in relocation
to the Williston Basin area. He never entertained for one moment the idea to
be a farmer on a quarter or two of land in this semiarid region. His background

was not that of a newly arrived immigrant. He knew better. What he planned was a real opportunity to expand his cattle and horse operation. He envisaged a big market for quality livestock and sturdy, dependable farm workhorses in this growing region. He wanted to make a better living by selling his proven stock to these newly settled small farmers, to breed their cows and mares with his blue-ribbon bulls and stallions.

Usher put the pieces of his operation into place quickly. He toured the country on more than one occasion before moving his family out there. His first purchase was two quarters of land in Stony Creek Township minus about 35 acres of railroad right of way. The site was a mile south and a mile east of Williston proper. He then added an additional 320 acres of quality river bottomland. In subsequent purchases, he bought more land east of town (Todd Place) and later another parcel some 20 miles east of Williston (Half-breed Point). The Burdick ranch grew into a three-segment operation with a home base near town, excellent river bottomland for growing hay and plenty of room for cattle.[8]

Variety and research always characterized Burdick's approach to his ranching business. He spent countless hours reading up on new breeds of cattle and horses; he gauged their quality at local county fairs, and when he found a good line, he would buy some and introduce them to his customers. At first, he concentrated on raising primarily purebred cattle and never really got out of the cattle business entirely. But his first choice was always raising quality breeds of horses, which was probably a return to his boyhood experiences in Ft. Totten near Devils Lake, North Dakota. He invested in a herd of Percheron horses and Belgian mares. Some time around 1916 or 1917, he got intensely interested in Shetland ponies. He took the train to Wisconsin to look at some and ended up buying a whole railroad car full of them and promptly shipped them back to Williston. Usher Burdick was the first person to introduce the pony in North Dakota and "he sold them all over."[9]

So far, things went well. Usher's ranch operation produced almost to perfection. He was pleased with his decision and the early success of his business. If a local farmer wanted to purchase quality cattle or farm workhorses, he contacted Usher Burdick. If a farmer wanted stud services for his cows and mares, he also contacted Usher Burdick. The Burdick name became synonymous with quality animals. He sold a lot of them, especially horses.

Then came the bad news. Burdick did not receive much money for all the horses he sold. When he made a sale, the buyer got the horse and Burdick received a promissory note. He got just a piece of paper in exchange for the sale or stud services. No conditional sales contracts in those days forced on-time payments, and often the notes went completely unpaid. According to Eugene, the situation got worse:

> In 1920 or 1921 the Federal Reserve Board called in those notes that the local banks had discounted, sold to the Minneapolis banks. When they called those in for payment, the local banks had to go back on the people who sold the notes, namely, my father, since he was the endorser on the notes that were paid to him. When my father went to collect the note from the fellow he'd sold the horse to, the man didn't have any money. The price of cattle had dropped tremendously, and the price of horses had dropped. This big Percheron stallion that he had, which was a very, very valuable horse in the teens was sold in 1921 for $700. These people couldn't pay these notes.[10]

Usher also packed a promising political career west. He was literally the biggest Progressive Republican in the entire state. His career was on fast track. In 1909, his Progressive colleagues recognized his leadership qualities by selecting him as speaker of the House. In 1910, voters all across the state preferred him, too, electing him lieutenant governor alongside incumbent Democratic Governor John Burke. Not to be outdone, Williams County voters put him on their ticket in 1912 by electing him as their state's attorney. During these first years in Williston, Usher Burdick was as busy being a successful politician as he was being a successful rancher.

Unfortunately, political losses came to match economic losses. What had risen so fast came down proportionately at the same speed. Two losses in Republican primaries for governor in 1914 and 1916 abruptly ended Burdick's first political career. He lost a close race to incumbent Governor Louis B. Hanna in 1914. However, the fury of the socialist Nonpartisan League, headed by Lynn J. Frazier (a farmer from Hoople, North Dakota), smothered the hopes of North Dakota Progressives and the political future of its tallest player, Usher Burdick.

Family shared in both the difficulties of the ranching venture and the political verdicts. It is hard to imagine, however, that the family's routine intersected on a daily basis with Usher's. In truth, Emma Burdick raised the family. Her husband was always busy and much of his work took him away from her and the family. For example, 1911 was only their second year in Williston, and Usher spent almost the entire first six months living in Bismarck. As lieutenant governor, he presided over the state Senate (January 3 to March 3), which was his only official duty. He earned no annual salary for the executive post, only a legislative salary of $5 per day during the session. After the session adjourned, he stayed on at the capitol (with no salary) to preside over the impeachment trial of District Judge John Cowan.

Two major events, however, soon happened to the Burdick family. The marriage produced two more offspring. Eugene was born at the ranch in October 1912. Emma delivered Eileen in the downstairs bedroom of the town home in March 1917. Before Eileen's birth, Usher and Emma decided to move the family from the ranch to Williston. It would be the first and only real home for the entire Burdick family and Emma's residence for life.

The Burdick house at 811 Second Avenue West was a single-story, wooden structure, small but adequate for a family of four. It offered a parlor, dining room, kitchen, master bedroom, a coal-burning furnace and indoor plumbing with hot water. After Eileen's birth and the arrival of Emma's mother, the Burdicks lifted the roof and added a second story with three bedrooms — one for the boys, one for Eileen and one for grandmother.

The house was never filled with stuff; it was rather bare, even Spartan, in furnishings. The parlor or family room contained Emma's piano, Usher's bookcases and an old Victrola phonograph record player. The children played their favorite record, *The Japanese Sandman,* hundreds of times. Perhaps the most striking feature of the room was a huge portrait of Usher as lieutenant governor, which hung prominently alone on one wall.

The residence was located in the good part of town, which in those days simply meant it was located on the *right* side of town — in this instance, it meant the east side of town among the elite homes of the community. Locals soon dubbed it "pious hill," in recognition perhaps that the occupants were all successful, practicing Protestants who owned their own businesses.[11]

The Burdick family, like the majority of American families, was matriarchal. Mother Emma was the primary parent in charge of raising the children. Usher's symbol, the portrait hanging in the parlor, suggested his domain lay elsewhere than in the home. Quentin recalled, "my father didn't give my mother too much money to live on."[12] He was family, but his interests primarily lay elsewhere. It is hard to know what kind of relationship he had with his family. He did tell all of the children that if they did not take up smoking, he would send them all to college, which he did. College education was very important for his children. Terry Leonhardy, a neighbor boy the same age as Eugene, observed that for all the years he lived next to them, he never understood the Burdick marriage.[13]

Usher's relationship to his oldest son remains obscure. "I don't remember much except him asking about school," said Quentin. "I said, I'm fine."[14] There was one public event that bonded father and son — Boy Scout Week in

February of 1917. Quentin was 16 years old; Usher was so proud of him because during the week Quentin's fellow Scouts elected him president of the Williston City Council for a mock session. The front-page headline read, "Mayor Burdick Gives City Safe Administration." The article author went on to editorialize under a headline, "Good Citizenship in the Making," that the event was "an outward reminder of the fact that the modern boy is acquiring the sense of citizenship."[15] The week concluded with a father-and-son banquet in the basement of the Congregational Church with an attendance of 350.[16]

Age ameliorated the sibling relationships. Quentin was four years older than his brother and almost nine years older than his sister. He got alone with both of his siblings, but was closer to Eugene because of age and gender. The two youngest, however, were another story all together. "Eugene and Eileen were never friendly disposed toward each other," recalled Leonhardy. "They fought like cats and dogs." Leonhardy recalled one incident when Eileen came over to play with his sister. Eileen was spitting mad and told Leonhardy's family that her brother "wanted salad at all his meals."[17] Quentin stood aloof from most of their disagreements.

The relationship between Quentin and Eugene remained important to both brothers. Leonhardy, who was the same age as Eugene, said Quentin was worshipped by his younger brother; he could do no wrong in his younger brother's eyes. One summer, Adler Beitsch, who lived back door to the Burdicks, came home from college. He was a couple of years older than Quentin, who was still in high school. They got into a terrific scrap and Beitsch beat the hell out of Quentin. Eugene was distraught and very upset. He never got over it. Adler had beaten up his hero![18]

Eugene, in a moment of serious thought, expressed the following about his brother, Quentin: "He lacked the capacity to express admiration. I don't know about love, but certainly admiration or any compliments for success." As example, Eugene recalled a conversation with his brother: "Look at the picture I drew," asked Eugene. "Well, so what," responded Quentin. Quentin sort of questioned lightly, secretly admiring the drawing, but he never passed a compliment on it. Eugene further described Quentin's outlook by saying, "The same thing was true about crying or something like that. You're not a man if you cry. If he was hurt, he'd try to stifle his crying emotions. Only sissies cry."

The children did enjoy shared activities. They liked to play cards, especially hearts. Their favorite radio show was "Amos and Andy," a program their mother ignored. They attended Sunday school regularly at the big Congregational Church. May Burdick, Eugene's wife, who was raised a Roman Catholic, called it a congregation consisting of as "tight right-wing Republicans you can find and always will."[20] The boys both had .22 gauge rifles and liked to hunt. Eileen, who carried the big bones of her father, was the best storyteller of the bunch and a tomboy. May relates this story as evidence of Eileen's tomboy antics: "I remember one time Eileen told me that she and the neighbor girl, who lived next door, were in the backyard and got into a real scrapping fight. Quentin was sitting on the porch behind the kitchen. 'Scratch her eyes out, Mary,' yelled the girl's mother. 'Kick her in the stomach, Eileen,' countered Quentin."[21]

School Days and Friends

Quentin attended all 12 grades at Central School in Williston. When asked about his school experience, he replied with a nonacademic answer: "I was a pretty busy boy. I was president of my class two or three years. I played football and I debated."[22] Eugene seems to know more about his grades than Quentin did. "I think he was a good student," recalls Eugene. "I don't think he was straight A's, but above average."[23]

Aside from football, Quentin was involved in a variety of school activities. He was chosen associate editor of the Coyote yearbook as a junior. He played the part of author Paul Green in the senior class play, *Fifty-Fifty.* He graduated with a class of 37 and offered the class prophecy. He said he hated snobs, loved to sing, wanted to be a farmer, and that all of his best pals were on the football and basketball teams. The Williston newspaper published a taste of school humor under the heading "Jokes":

> Miss Griffin: What does the prefix "mag" mean?
> Burdick: Big.
> Miss Griffin: Well, give me a word that contains this prefix and use it in a sentence.
> Burdick: I like magpie.[24]

Like most normal teenagers in the last years of high school, Quentin enjoyed a prank or two. "Did you ever try to pull a cow up steps?" Quentin asked during an interview. "I put a cow in the superintendent's office. That was nice surroundings and I didn't get caught. This was on the second floor of the school," Quentin continued with a half smile. "They tried to find out who did it, and it was my father who told them. Nothing happened though. It was tied."[25]

Eugene told one better on his brother.

> I can tell you an episode about Quentin and the school house. This was one he was really ashamed of afterwards. It wasn't hard to get into the building, and once in the building it was easy to get to the belfry and get

up and ring the bell. ... I never did it, but I knew that Quentin and some of his friends did get up there. They had to climb outside a bit to get into the belfry area to ring the bell. On this particular night there were two or three of them up there ringing the bell when they had a confrontation with Chappie Ricard , the chief janitor. He wrestled with them and in the process either slipped or fell. Well, here is Chappie falling off the roof and the building is a two or three story building with an edge and a rather steep slope. ... As luck would have it, there happened to be a chimney right there and he slid off the roof right into the chimney. What a terrible thing that would have been if he'd fallen off. It would have killed him sure as the world. It was about a thirty-five-foot fall to the ground.[26]

Corey Wegley was to Quentin what Huckleberry Finn was to Tom Sawyer. He was older by four or five years and experienced in the ways of the world. He was a rough-hewn sort of character and not too well educated. He was physically imposing and possessed street smarts while engaging in lots of male activities, which appealed to the younger Quentin. In a way, Wegley became Quentin's father figure and certainly his closest friend. Corey liked to hunt. Quentin liked to hunt. Corey was an adept boxer. Quentin desired to be a good boxer. Corey was deep into learning to wrestle and bought wrestling lessons from Farmer Burns of Iowa. Quentin read every lesson and then forced little Eugene to be his practice dummy. Corey knew about sex. Quentin did not. Their relationship revolved around all of these activities and more. However, even stingier with praise than Quentin's father, Corey never handed out one single compliment to Quentin for any progress he made in any of their activities. The lesson stuck. "I don't recall Quentin passing out any compliments to anybody on anything," said sad Eugene.

Although Corey knew about women, Quentin in those years was not interested.

When asked directly in an interview, "Who was your first love?" Quentin replied, "Oh hell, I didn't have any loves. Hell, I wasn't a sissy playing around with girls. I was a football player!"[28]

Emma tried with poor success to encourage her son to date. She even picked out a girl for him. She liked Muzette Wills, one of the girls in his class at school, but Quentin demurred. Finally, out of frustration and to get his mother off the issue, he consented. He asked Muzette to go out with him and drive around in his car. Emma was delighted and the rest of the family saw an opportunity too good to ignore. Eugene and some of his friends enticed Eileen to be the spy on her brother's first date. She did not require much coaxing. The kids arranged to hide her on the floor in the back of Quentin's car long before he went to pick up his date. They covered her with an old blanket and instructed her to remain silent at all costs. They wanted her to listen carefully and report back the entire conversation she heard between the two. Everything went according to plan until the dust seeping up under the floorboard raised such a cloud that Eileen let out aloud sneeze. End of date. Quentin drove home furious with the whole incident.[29]

Divorce

There were some early signs that Usher and Emma's marriage was troubled. It is impossible to document an exact beginning, but the discord probably began the very day Usher made the unilateral decision to move Emma and baby Quentin west to Williston. Usher, of course, was an incurable romantic and remained so his entire life. Change accelerated his being. It made him more of what he was and what he intended to be. He thrived on the excitement of new places and the thrill of new beginnings. The Missouri Plateau gave him yet another opportunity to be reborn, to be something different again. It provided him with the opportunity to expand his cattle and horse operations and to live under a bigger tent – the big sky. He was tired of Munich and bored with his bank job. He wanted out and Williston seemed the perfect setting to make a move. It was the west; a place so full of the past and so filled with promises for a better future. Instead of simply collecting Americana, Usher would now have the chance to become a living part of it as well.

Emma viewed the move differently. She thrived on continuity and abhorred change. In Munich, she felt security for herself and her young son, close to her parents and friends. The Williston move upset her. It made her nervous and apprehensive. She quite honestly did not want to live there, but like most women of her time, she went west with little public protest, only private trepidation. Emma was a small-town female who was used to safe, small-town living. She did not know anything about being a rancher's wife and she had no real desire to learn, either. She possessed a college degree, enjoyed the fine arts and reading. Change simply frightened her existence. Unlike her adventuresome husband, there was not a romantic bone in Emma's Scandinavian body. She wanted the security of community, the support of an extended family and some intellectual stimulus. Williston, to her way of thinking, offered none of those things. Under big sky and no shelter, Emma would become less of what she was and what she intended to be.

Wallace Stegner, the great American writer, captured the essence of this region in the early years of the 20th century. In *Wolf Willow: A History, a Story, and a Memory of the Last Plains Frontier*, he described his boyhood years, growing up west and north of Williston on the Montana-Saskatchewan border. Stegner described the place and what a romantic such as Usher saw as potentially wonderful and what Emma feared as potentially devastating. "It is a country to breed mystical people, egocentric people, perhaps poetic people," observed Stegner, "But not humble ones. At noon the total sun pours on your single head; at sunrise or sunset you throw a shadow a hundred yards long. It was not prairie dwellers who invented the indifferent universe or impotent man. Puny you may feel there, and, vulnerable, but not unnoticed. This is a land to mark the sparrow's fall."[30]

The Williston move proved Stegner correct. Usher adjusted easily to his new environment, while Emma struggled with hers. Stodgy, but never egocentric, she felt vulnerable and less noticed. Other factors soon tugged and pulled on their weakened state of matrimony. The ranching operation hit hard times. Bankruptcy became a familiar family word. Usher's aspiring political career fell as quickly as it had risen. Helen Clark fancied Usher. Usher fancied her. The divorce was final in 1921 and Usher married Helen soon after. Usher left for Fargo to practice law with an old friend, John Burke, and to explore another new adventure — owning a bookstore. Emma remained in Williston where she never wanted to be in the first place. Now, however, she was without a spouse and stuck on an ill-fated ranching operation with three young children: 12-year old Quentin, 8-year old Eugene and 4-year old Eileen.

Both spouses sought to keep their divorce a private affair. There were many compelling reasons — some public and some private. Divorce in the 1920s was not as socially acceptable as it is today. Community custom preached a higher standard. Peers viewed divorce as a sign of failure for both spouses, so society dictated a different course. No matter how painful the marriage or how difficult the circumstances, parents must stick it out, especially when young children were involved. Christian traditions also preached a different sermon — divorce was morally wrong; it was a sin to be divorced. Convention aside, Usher sought to dissolve the bonds because he was having an affair with another woman. Adultery cut even deeper, hurting the wife while damaging the offspring. Emma never wanted the divorce no matter how great her personal hurt or embarrassment. However, when Usher insisted he wanted out, she gave in to his wishes. She sought silence as her wisest course.

For a while, their strategy worked quite well. Neighbors noted no changes in either parent or among the children. Usher was still absent as often as he had been since moving to Williston 11 years ago. Everyone in the community knew him as a man with a thousand and one interests. He was always busy going here or there. His time away from home about equaled his time at home. At first, politics took him away to Bismarck. Then it was his ranching business, which included the buying and selling of horses and Shetland ponies. Emma, on the other hand, was stoic. She was a private person before and after the divorce. She did not have close, female friends or many social contacts. She liked to chat with neighbors but never to gossip. The fact that she still loved her husband sealed her silence. Finally, she was still the mother to their children and she wanted them to respect their father, divorce not withstanding.

Unfortunately, loyalty to each other obfuscated a primary responsibility to inform their children. Neither Quentin nor Eugene was told by either parent. Quentin learned about it through his friends, but could not remember any details. Eugene, on the other hand, remembered exactly how painful the news was to him.

"As a matter of fact, I learned about it on the street. One of the school kids said something like, 'Your parents are divorced,' and I said, 'I don't understand it fully.' I thought they'd been misinformed, to put it mildly. Then, I'm not sure that I confronted my mother about it. I don't think I really confronted her, but something happened one day that I was possibly a little bit out of control. I don't remember what the episode was, but it precipitated in Quentin telling me that our father didn't live there anymore. I was broken up. He was the one that confirmed it to me – Quentin. Quentin knew about it, but I had to have the kids on the street tell me. I didn't believe it!"[31]

Time healed the pain but not the disappointment of the divorce. "I missed a lot of things a father could give a son if the marital relations had been normal," lamented Quentin.[32] Yet, in some ways the family tried to maintain a normal relationship with Usher, primarily at Emma's insistence. "We still had regard for our father," continued Quentin. "He would show up once a week or something. I suppose the family was out of joint, and it wasn't as pleasant or harmonious, but we took it quite well."[33]

"He shouldn't have done it," exclaimed Eugene about his father's actions. "He really fancied himself as a lady's man" and "he could be buttered up by a woman so fast."[34] In time, Eugene forgave his father for his transgressions. In the '30s, he became quite close to him, shared his interest in collecting Indian artifacts and doing photography for him. When Usher aged, Eugene wrote his will and handled his legal affairs for him as well. But he still remained critical of him for being "a little bit too fickle" and that "people could flatter him to no end."[35]

Quentin, on the other hand, never went into the motives behind his father's actions. He saw the divorce as primarily a major change in his youth rather than a character flaw in his father. "In that time when I was growing up and he was having marital problems with my mother, I was about in the eighth or ninth grade. I was helping my mother oversee the farm. She didn't know much about it. I took on the responsibility a lot of kids that age would not have."[36]

How often and where Usher stayed after the divorce is debatable. Although he went to Fargo to practice law, he kept an eye on the ranch and took in as many of Quentin's football games as possible. (Emma never went to the games because of the divorce.) Both boys said their mother kept an empty bed for their father and that he slept there in the home whenever he came back. "When he came to Williston," said Eugene, "he'd reach over and grab the cribbage board and just automatically start dealing the cards. He also liked to play hearts; we played a lot of hearts and cribbage."[37]

Terry Leonhardy disagreed. "He was never in that house" after the divorce. ... He always stayed in the Great Northern Hotel and would take the kids next door and feed them."[38] He also claimed Usher usually only came to Williston about once a year to see the children after the divorce. "He would take them to a local clothing store to buy them some clothes or buy them a car and then he would take off again. Sometimes he would take them to Seattle."[39]

Emma, like Usher, probably never lived a day of luxury in her entire life. They were both frugal people living in a self-sufficient age before the dawn of consumer madness. Their marriage was parsimonious from the very beginning. The move to Williston created additional fiscal hardships, forcing them to get by on still less long before their divorce. Emma's mother came to live with her daughter and became a permanent member of the Burdick family. The divorce caused more economic difficulties and forced still more economic adjustments. Emma took in boarders and raised chickens out back. Neighbors were curious and unsure exactly how the family supported itself after the divorce. "I always had the feeling that they were just barely eking it out," recalled Leonhardy.[40]

Eugene gave a more detailed and accurate account of the family finances during those years. His mother rented out the farm to George Halverson, but eventually lost the hay meadow on foreclosure. She contracted an annual 50-50 split on 40 acres of wheat and rented out the river bottomland (blue joint grass) to dairy farmers such as J.R. Cherry. She sold 100 shares of AT&T stock inherited from her father. Evelina, her younger sister, regularly mailed her small stipends to help defray the cost of their mother's care. Most importantly, Usher never abandoned his financial obligations to the family. He bought the children clothes and the family cars, and sent all three of his children to college and law school during the Depression. "I suppose we didn't have enough," Eugene said.

"We weren't as poor as some people. We weren't on a strict outright dole, but it was tough to make ends meet."[41]

Football

It is difficult to contrast North Dakota high school football in the '20s with the present. They were entirely different eras, and during Burdick's youth, football was just emerging as a school sport. Aside from the layout of the field and the scoring, there were clearly more differences than similarities with today's game: no conferences, division playoffs or all-state players, and few state championships. Money was tight. Teams scheduled games close to home and rarely, if ever, took overnight trips. Seasons were short and bad weather often forced cancellations for games, which were never made up. Facilities were sparse. The game took place on pasturelike fields or on dirt fields without grass. Outdoor lights did not exist, so games usually began on Saturday afternoons. High school football games were never scheduled during a week of school. Even the basic shape of the ball was odd. It was rounder, like a homegrown citron melon. It was something to wrap your arms around to protect and only in desperation to launch into the air for a teammate to drop, or worse, for an opponent to intercept.

If the basic apparatus was embryonic, so was the major cast and the script. The coaching staff usually consisted of one man, often a former college player who worked somewhere in the community but seldom taught in the school. Coaching high school football was his hobby and his life. It gave him a chance to stay involved in the game he loved so much, and to take charge of it with younger players. No pay for his services was offered and none was expected. There were minimal school rules of eligibility, no parent interference, and no player complaints because none would have been tolerated. The coach under this system ruled supreme. He ran his own little program away from school and after school. The more games he won, the longer he coached, and the more absolute his power became.

Game strategy was simple. The coach fielded his best 11 boys. He played them both ways for the entire season and for each entire game. If his team lacked 11 good players, which it usually did, the coach tried to hide their weaknesses as long as possible. If his team possessed an exceptional player or two, which it usually did, he would exploit them as often as possible. Substitutions were rare. A starter was only pulled if he made a dumb mistake or received a crippling injury. Games were won or lost by how a team executed the basics. No fancy stuff. A team scored points by running the ball at the other team, not passing. A team avoided points scored against them by playing basic, tough defense.

The players understood the system. They knew the coach was God and that the season was short. If you wanted to play, you played by his rules. The rules were quite simple. A player worked like hell to make the starting 11, avoided mistakes at all costs, and hid injuries. There were no tomorrows, physical trainers or after-game whirlpools. Personal honor and satisfaction came after the heat of competition and the thrill of victory. After-season recognition was important, but playing was everything. If not this season, then hopefully the next one.

For all the apparent differences between then and now, there were also striking similarities. Football was already beginning to symbolize something more than just a contest between 22 young men on a Saturday autumn afternoon. It was rapidly becoming the major contest for community competition. It pitted one town's knights against the knights of another realm in a contest of physical strength, rather than smarts. The fact that the teams played outside in an open battlefield with medieval- looking equipment made the event more real, more exciting and certainly more masculine. A community that consistently won contests earned the image of a stronger town than one that continually lost.

The local press soon realized the importance of the sport for the community. Home games received ample coverage, while serious attempts were made to cover road games, too. Good players and good plays were praised with growing regularity and readers became more aware of who they were and what they had accomplished. Victories were celebrated in bolder and larger type. Defeats were minimized with a wait-until-next-year verse. The ultimate accomplishment was an upset victory against a larger and more powerful adversary.

Most high school players then as now never expected to play college football. In fact, many were not even college-bound. Those who did matriculate went unrecruited and unannounced. There were, however, a few exceptions. An outstanding player with size, strength, speed and a desire or means to attend college could play college football. However, the opportunity was the exception, not the rule. A family football legacy was even more rare. Few boys had fathers who went to college, let alone lettered in the sport.

The Williston community took enormous pride in the success of its football team. The Williston Coyotes played a regular schedule of five to seven games. They generally whipped weaker Montana opponents, such as Culbertson and Wolf Point due west on the Missouri River, and experienced tougher games with Sidney and Miles City southwest on the Yellowstone. The proximity of Sidney often resulted in an annual two-game affair. The rest of the games were set against North Dakota opponents. Smaller teams, such as Bowbells and Minot Normal, proved easy wins, and then all attention turned to the pivotal game of the season — the annual tussle with Minot High School. In 1919, after completing an undefeated season, Usher Burdick was asked to submit his all-time North Dakota mythical high school football team. He did. All the players he selected were Williston Coyotes.[42]

The success of the team reflected the personality of its coach. Joe Cutting was a University of Minnesota graduate and an outstanding player. "The smallest guy who ever played in the line for the University of Minnesota," recalled one proud Williston fan. "He was only 165 pounds, but tough as nails."[43] Cutting worked full time as a pharmacist at the Williston Drug Store. Come fall, however, he became Coach Cutting. He coached for free. He produced a long string of winning teams who mauled their smaller opponents by huge scores while whipping arch rival Minot High School by much closer margins.

Cutting coached his teams like General George Patton ran the U.S. Third Army during World War II. He taught fundamentals, fundamentals and still more fundamentals. He adhered to the philosophy that a winning coach should only use his best 11 players for the entire game. He hated to put in subs. He churned the sidelines during the games at a furious pace, coined new words and did a whole lot of swearing.

"I remember one time he sent in a play to pass," said Terry Leonhardy, "and after the play, the intended receiver came back to the sidelines." Leonhardy recalled Cutting's response:

> "Moses," yelled an angry and loud coach. "Did you crap in your pants?"
>
> "No," came a quiet reply.
>
> "Well, you sure run like it."[44]

Eugene Burdick closely followed Quentin's performance in games and on the practice field. He even survived a brief stint as a backup quarterback. He described Cutting as "extremely demanding" with zero tolerance ever for fumbles. "If you fumbled a ball on the football field, you practically lost your job."[45] Not surprising, perhaps, the Williston teams seldom fumbled because the coach drilled them day in and day out not to lose the football.

Cutting ran a tight command. He did not take criticism lightly and showed absolutely no toleration for anyone who attempted to encroach on his job. For example, he chased an eager but naïve Williston superintendent of schools off the practice field one day because the man came to offer his services as an assistant coach. "I'm the coach here," yelled Cutting in front of all the players. "If you want to take over, fine."[46] No takers. The school superintendent was already walking off the practice field by then.

Quentin Burdick proved to be an outstanding football player under Cutting. He played five years for him between 1921 and 1925. Burdick was primarily used as a practice dummy as an eighth-grader, showed promise as a ninth-grader and played half time on the varsity as a sophomore. Burdick lettered in both his junior and senior years and was chosen captain in his last year. By his senior year, he had grown to 5 feet 11 inches and 175 pounds. He loved the game, especially the physical contact. He worked endlessly to improve his skills and to strengthen his body. He became a sure tackler, a vicious blocker and a strong, straight-ahead runner. Off the field, he was a gentle sort, not tolerating small talk or bragging. On the field, he played like a warrior, never speaking to opponents — just playing hard to win. If there had been an all-state North Dakota high school football team selected in 1925, Quentin's name would have appeared twice as a middle linebacker on defense and a running back on offense.

It is a safe assumption to make that Cutting saw tremendous football potential in Quentin from the start. He knew Usher as a great football player earlier at his alma mater, and Quentin was a chip off the same block. Cutting taught him the basic skills of blocking and tackling, especially to drop a would-be tackler just above the knee and then in the next instance to drive your shoulder into his waist. Quentin excelled at blocking; he learned how to tackle with both hands, to match speed with speed, and to block shoulder to shoulder. He liked hitting on defense as much as blocking on offense.

Quentin responded silently to the constant negative reinforcement of Cutting's teaching methods. He never looked for or expected a compliment because he knew that Cutting was incapable of ever offering one. Instead, he took the hard knocks and just hung in there. "If Quentin didn't do exactly as he wanted him to do it," recalled Eugene, "he'd physically kick him in the butt. I mean literally. I've seen him do it."[47]

As a sophomore during the 1923 season, Quentin alternated one running back spot with Charlie Carpenter. At the annual awards banquet, Cutting handed out only 10 varsity letters that year. Since he believed in awarding letters only to those players who played full time, he decided not to give them to Carpenter and Burdick since they had only played half time. But to compensate for his decision and their half-time efforts, he gave each of them a consolation prize, a reserve letter — a small patch with a little "w" circled by a funny stitch. Disgusted, Quentin went home that evening and sewed it on his jock strap.[48]

Burdick was a starter the next year. The 1924 season began well. Williston humbled the Sidney team by a score of 77-0. Rain canceled its second game against Minot Normal High School. Burdick's junior year of football ended in the first quarter of the next game with Wolf Point when he broke his left elbow. Brother Eugene recalled all the details: "Quentin was carrying the ball around the right end. It made a substantial gain towards the goal line. There was one player that still had a chance to catch him. In trying to dodge that player, Quentin hurdled where he thought he was going to be tackled. The fellow tripped his foot and spun him in such a way that Quentin landed on his left elbow. That's when he broke it, and that was the end of the season."[49]

The 1925 season proved better. "Before the largest gathering of rooters that has assembled on the local grounds this season," reported the *Williston Herald*, "the football teams representing the Williston and Minot high schools battled to a scoreless tie Saturday afternoon in the annual clash of these rivals for championship honors."[50]

Although the tie was a bitter pill for the undefeated Coyotes to swallow on their home field, Burdick excelled. It was his last and best game ever as a Williston High School football player. The local press touted his superior play in a bold, heavy black headline, which read: "Burdick is Star Player."[51] The game statistics supported the hometown booster accolade. Burdick lugged the ball for 128 yards from scrimmage. This was more than the total yards gained by the opponents passing and running. Equally impressive was his defensive prowess, especially his interception of a Minot pass in Williston territory in the fourth quarter.

Williston tried furiously to score in the last quarter. They ran Burdick up the middle on every other play. He carried the ball 11 times in the quarter. The game ended, however, without a Williston score — Burdick with a run and then a badly thrown incomplete forward pass; game over; no score. Williston ended the season with five wins and the disappointing tie. Burdick ended his high school football career with a truly outstanding performance before the hometown fans, but he failed in his final attempt to defeat Minot.

In the middle of an interview with Senator Burdick in 1992, an abrupt switch in a line of questions from politics to football seemed to irritate him at first. When asked, "Do you remember October 24, 1925," he sort of glared and jutted his chin up a little as he said, "Oh, my God! Do you?" But when he was provided with a second clue, "The game ended in a zero to zero tie," he plowed right in and vividly remembered the game he played 67 years past. "Oh, yes. That was the game with Minot. I was captain." The newspaper account of that game noted that Burdick carried the ball for more than 120 yards and made some big plays on defense. Burdick added, "I was middle linebacker. On offensive, in those days, the fullback was in close and the halfbacks on the side."

Williston retained its undefeated season, but Burdick felt his team should have scored a win with this last game. "We had a fellow on the team that didn't want to take any chances. I won't mention his name, but I thought we could have won the game. But we didn't. That is all I can say."[52]

The 16 years and a few additional summers Quentin spent in Williston shaped his adult life. They were his most important years. They shaped his personality and formed his character; neither trait would change a great deal in the succeeding years of his life. When he boarded the train for the University of Minnesota in the late summer of 1926, he was physically prepared to don the same uniform worn by Usher many years earlier. Football, football, football was the most important single interest of his being. He wanted to play it so bad and succeed that it occupied much of his thinking. Quentin went to Minnesota to get a college education, but his prime reason for attending was to play football on Saturday afternoons in Minneapolis, just as he had in Williston for the past three falls.

Emotionally, Quentin was less prepared for the journey. He was naïve in many ways and had no idea what to wear or how to act in many social situations. The success of football and the hero worship accorded him hid some basic insecurities. He hated to lose, yet he knew what defeat meant. It was just that he preferred to win — always. His love for his mother was secure — perhaps the most secure experience in his family upbringing. He loved her very much and remained devoted to her for the rest of her life. His relationship with his father was more unsettled. He was still searching for some common bond that would unite father and son. In the back of his mind, that bond was playing football at the University of Minnesota and playing it better than Usher did. There was a lot of emotional pain about the divorce that Burdick kept inside. As for Eugene and Eileen, they both would follow his Minnesota footsteps. But for the most part, the train track that took Quentin to Minneapolis was in many ways the same track that ended many of his relationships.

Endnotes

1. Steinbeck, *Travels with Charlie*, 138.
2. Innis, "A Brief History of Williams County, North Dakota: 1805-1910," in *The Wonder of Williams: A History of Williams County North Dakota* Vol. 1, p. 5.
3. Neihardt, *The River and I*, 2.
4. Stegner, *American Places*, 25-26.
5. Innis, "A Brief History of Williams County," 6.
6. Ibid., 36.
7. Robinson, *History of North Dakota*, 173; Wick, *North Dakota Place Names*, 209.
8. Eugene Burdick, interview by author, Jan. 28, 1995.
9. Ibid.
10. Ibid.
11. Ibid.
12. Quentin Burdick, interview by author, Jan. 6, 1992.
13. Terry Leonhardy, interview by author, Sept. 19, 1996.
14. Quentin Burdick interview.
15. *Williston Herald*, Feb. 14, 1924, 1.
16. Ibid., 6.
17. Leonhardy interview.
18. Ibid.
19. Eugene Burdick interview.
20. May Burdick, interview by author, Jan. 28, 1995.
21. Ibid.
22. Quentin Burdick interview.
23. Eugene Burdick interview.
24. *Williston Herald*, Dec. 17, 1925, 5.
25. Quentin Burdick interview.
26. Eugene Burdick interview.
27. Ibid.
28. Quentin Burdick interview.
29. May Burdick interview.
30. Stegner, *Wolf Willow*, 8.
31. Eugene Burdick interview.
32. Quentin Burdick interview.
33. Ibid.
34. Eugene Burdick interview.
35. Ibid.
36. Quentin Burdick interview.
37. Eugene Burdick interview.
38. Leonhardy interview.
39. Ibid.
40. Ibid.
41. Eugene Burdick interview.
42. Ibid.
43. Leonhardy interview.
44. Ibid.
45. Eugene Burdick interview.
46. Leonhardy interview.
47. Eugene Burdick interview.
48. Ibid.
49. Ibid.
50. *Williston Herald*, Oct. 29, 1925, 1.
51. Ibid.
52. Quentin Burdick interview.

- five -

The Minnesota Years
(1926-1932)

When young Quentin Burdick boarded the Great Northern for Minneapolis in the autumn of 1926, he left western North Dakota for urban Minnesota. There on the banks of the mighty Mississippi, he would spend the next six years of his life at the University of Minnesota. They were significant years for him, transition years spent between his Williston boyhood and Fargo law practice. He came as an 18-year-old freshman in the fall of 1926 during the hegemony of feel-good Republicanism. He left in June of 1932 as a 23-year-old law graduate near New Deal's dawn. He participated in intercollegiate sports, where he earned a varsity letter in football and a short stint on the wrestling team. He pledged Sigma Nu fraternity and served as eminent commander (president). Two fraternity brothers, Morteer Skewes and Ken Byerly, both Minnesotans, became his best friends. In the absence of athletic scholarships, he paid his college expenses by working a couple of summers in Williston and later in his father's uptown Minneapolis bookstore. Finally and perhaps most significantly, he met Marietta Janecky, a Carleton College coed and a New Prague, Minnesota, native, on a blind date. She became his first and only serious girl friend. They married in March of 1933.

"I majored in football and minored in law," said Burdick proudly in a 1980 interview.[1] The statement was probably an apt analysis of his state of mind between his late teen and early adult years. He enrolled at the University of Minnesota because both his parents were proud graduates of that fine institution. He and his siblings never thought of applying anywhere else, let alone being allowed to even consider it. They were sons and daughters of the Maroon and Gold growing up on the plains of western North Dakota. Quentin was even christened with Cyrus Northrop's name, one of the school's most respected presidents.

Although young Burdick came to Minnesota to play football and earn a law degree, there was more in retrospect to his journey. For the son of a Midwestern Progressive, on the eve of the Great Depression, to be arriving in Minneapolis would be the equivalent of a young Russian moving to Moscow or a young American moving to Washington, D.C., today. Anyone who truly understood how North Dakota operated during the colonial period of its history certainly came to understand the power and influence of its economic master, Minneapolis, as well. One urban historian described Minneapolis as "an imperial city at the headwaters of the Mississippi" and "strategic to the plains of Minnesota, the Dakotas, parts of Montana and Wisconsin."[2]

Imperial and strategic were positive words to disguise a more painful relationship between colony and lord. Minneapolis controlled this upper region of the country; it served as the nation's midsection Wall Street, the scion of the grain trade and the residence of the Ninth Federal Reserve District. Here each year farmers sold their wheat below the cost of production and then borrowed money above the cost of production. Here stood the headquarters of the chief flour-producing centers of the nation — the mighty General Mills and the popular Pillsbury, whose tattoo identified every other elevator across the northern Great Plains. Minneapolis was also home to the railroad carriers, the Great Northern and the Northern Pacific, who made tons of money shipping anything in or everything out. There were other corporate cousins as well who controlled trade, dry goods, manufacturing and insurance interests. Here, too, cultural and religious power concentrated, especially among Lutherans and Roman Catholics who genuflected toward Minneapolis. As a symbol of political change, it also became briefly the hopeful headquarters for Arthur C. Townley's ill-fated National Nonpartisan League — a farmer's political organization created to rearrange the vertical landscape between consumer and producer with a radical plan scorched by American loyalties of the First World War. Although Quentin probably did not arrive in Minneapolis with these thoughts in mind, it is hard to imagine that Usher's son failed to understand some of their historical significance.

The University of Minnesota complemented the strength and character of Minneapolis, a city within a city standing stately on the east bank of the Mississippi. The university's academic programs ranked among the very best the nation provided and bore the stamp of President Cyrus Northrop (1884-1911), its imprimatur. The institution was described as "a federation of schools," a collage of colleges, which included "schools of law, medicine, agriculture, engineering, mines, pharmacy, dentistry and education."[3]

Growth in enrollment and physical plant best describes the campus in the '20s. Enrollment surged to 10,718 full-time students in the winter quarter of 1927. The figure caused celebration and pushed Minnesota to the fourth largest university in the country, while the *Minnesota Daily* billed itself as "the world's largest college newspaper."[4] Appropriations for buildings soared to $3.5 million the following year, allowing for the addition of six new structures and "the greatest program in the schools growth."[5]

The performing arts and athletics received equal support from state, alumni and campus leaders. Pushed for bigger and better facilities for campus and community events, the institution constructed the Northrop Auditorium and Williams Stadium to take care of the increased demand for both. Behind the Grecian form to balance arts and athletics, however, was a growing American tendency that began to spell football with bigger letters. "Across the nation, the great company of spectator sportsmen had come into existence," noted University of Minnesota historian James Gray, " ready to fill the stands for any show of prowess[,] but ready in particular to become the ardent fans of any excellent football team."[6]

Fellow North Dakotan Eric Sevareid, whose family moved to Minneapolis in the '20s and attended the university in the '30s, put football in a more cynical vein. He labeled football jocks "the behemoths of the gridiron," yet acknowledged that it "was an honor to sit beside one of them in class." By the mid-'30s, however, Sevareid editorialized that Minnesota football was "out of hand" and that "downtown sports writers seemed to have acquired as much authority over the university's policies as the regents."[7]

Burdick arrived in this powerful urban center and leading institution of higher education sometime in September of 1926. The campus numbers were twice the size of his hometown and larger than most North Dakota cities (bigger than Bismarck and the same size as Minot). The freshman class of 1930 was the largest in the school's history. More than 3,000 young men and women joined in a week filled with fun, excitement and adventure. School officials were defensive in announcing the return of the famous freshman green beanie (first since 1920), stating only that it was required as a means of freshman identification and not as vehicle for hazing.[8]

The school pushed the eager, young frosh through a host of institutional hoops. They first lined up for a medical exam, where they were tested for incipient dementia, praecox, small pox and tuberculosis. Their heads were photographed next for the required institutional mug shots. Then their brains were tested for I.Q. scores — the results were immediately locked in the administrative archives. Senator William Borah, the Progressive Republican from Idaho, gave a thundering convocation speech, reaching high C with everyone in the auditorium: "I find the Constitution so important I would go through fire and sword and blood if necessary to uphold the Constitution held so dear by Washington, Lincoln and Roosevelt."[9]

Campus politics provided few instances to challenge the Constitution. Students voted in minuscule numbers on straw votes for president and the repeal of Prohibition. The biggest campus issue centered on the suspension of Harrison Salisbury, the managing editor of the *Minnesota Daily*, and John Moorhead, the business manager of the Gopher yearbook annual. Both young men received one-year suspensions for violation of the no-smoking rule in the university library.[10]

Burdick never rubbed shoulders with Sevareid. He lived a college student life much different than Burdick's. After graduating from Minneapolis Central High School in 1930, he and his companions canoed down the Minnesota and Red River to Hudson Bay. The trip, which almost cost the young adventurer his life, also landed him an office boy job with the *Minneapolis Journal* upon his return. He quickly moved up the ladder, first as copy runner and then reporter. He worked days on the newspaper and attended night school at the University of Minnesota. His fellow evening students — much different than those who lived on campus and attended traditional daytime classes —were identified as "housewives who had married too young and wanted to catch up," "middle aged workers from the flour mills," and "scores of young clerks."[11]

Sevareid, whose Velva, North Dakota, banker father went broke on unpaid loans and drought-spoiled wheat crops, viewed the regular campus and especially the fraternity crowd with disdain. "We had no campus life," wrote Sevareid. "In the dusk, when we arrived for classes, we passed the fraternity boys in their slacks and sweat shirts lolling on the verandas of their stuccoed houses ... . It was a distant impenetrable world of the specially chosen which I never expected to enter."[12]

The Sigma Nus

Morteer Skewes and Ken Byerly became Quentin Burdick's two closest friends at the University of Minnesota. Skewes was a skinny, 16-year-old farm kid from Laverne, Minnesota. His small community was located in the southwestern corner of the state, just a skip and a hop from Sioux Falls, South Dakota. Byerly was a willowy, hockey player from the Iron Range in northern Minnesota, where he graduated from Virginia High School. He was a year older than Skewes and a year younger than Burdick. He also proved to be a lot more street smart than his two fraternity brothers. Byerly was not a new kid of the block. He was born in Chicago and spent part of his youth there before moving to the Range.

They all met in the fall of 1926 as pledges at the Sigma Nu fraternity. Skewes, like Burdick, enrolled as a pre-law student and, like Burdick, earned a bachelor of science, literature and the arts degree before earning his law degree. He was one of Burdick's constant companions in the fraternity and his room-mate during their last year of law school (1931-1932) when they moved out of the house and rented two rooms off campus. Byerly's tenure was shorter. He stayed only four years and graduated in 1930 with a degree in business admin-istration.

At first glance, they seemed like an odd threesome. Skewes was clearly the runt of the litter. He was small and slight of build, compared with the muscular Burdick and the slender but taller Byerly. He probably earned the best grades of the lot, not because he was any brighter, although he possessed a trenchant mind, but simply because he studied more. He was a soother, a confidant who was always willing to just sit and listen. He was hard to dislike. Byerly was bois-terous, cocky, outgoing, self-confident and easier to dislike. He was worldlier than the other two and probably relished telling them a tale or two about his manly experiences. He was also loyal to his friends and steadfast against his enemies. Before the end of the freshman year, the three pledges bonded. They spent time together on weekends and took in a party or two at nearby soror-ity houses. They followed Burdick's football career. Skewes became Burdick's personal trainer. Skewes learned how to put back Burdick's trick knee and thus escape hospital time. Byerly became his personal adviser, especially in matters dealing with dress, social behavior and women.

In-depth interviews with Skewes and Byerly provide a rare glimpse of their friend, Quentin Burdick, during the Minnesota years. After graduation, Skewes returned to his hometown, were he practiced law for more than 60 years. Byerly moved around often, later becoming a professor of community journalism at the University of North Carolina. He retired to Lewistown, Montana, as emeri-tus publisher of the local newspaper run by one of his sons. Both men speak candidly and freely about their insights into the personality and character of "Quent," as he was nicknamed in those university days.

First impressions stick. Skewes recalled a hungry Burdick who bird-dogged a freshly baked angel food cake sent to Skewes one weekend by his mother. Al-though they knew each other as first semester pledges, they were not close until Quent discovered the cake early during the second semester. "He became my pal for the rest of the day," recalled Skewes with a chuckle, "and toward evening, he asked what we were going to do that night. When I replied I had no plans, he suggested that we go to a show. Afterward, he brought a whole quart of ice cream."[13] Skewes soon discovered the real motive behind the movie, the ice cream and the appetite of his Williston fraternity brother:

> We went back to the house and Quent offered to bring some tableware and plates up to my room. When we were both there, he suggested that we have cake with the ice cream, so I got out the cake my mother had sent and handed it to him as he expected me to do. I figured he would slice off a piece, but he asked if I could eat half of it. When I answered that I preferred to have just one piece, he asked if I could eat a third. When I replied, "Maybe," he gave me about a third and took the rest for himself. That's when I realized that I had found a new friend![14]

Byerly got to know Burdick in the compulsory Reserve Officers' Training Corps (ROTC) class they took together. ROTC was a required class in those days for all male undergraduate students. It was not a very demanding class, however, and most of the one-hour class periods, which met three times a week, were spent marching around campus. "Everybody hated it, except a few," recalled Byerly. "But we didn't hate the Army and we didn't hate the United States or anyone else." One day in the fall of 1926, the two were marching side by side and Burdick turned to Byerly with a rye comment that sounded like a challenge. "I'm going to get out of this," boasted Burdick. "The hell you are," replied Byerly. "There's not a chance." Burdick, much to Byerly's surprise, soon got out of the class. "He was a football player, and a very good one," noted Byerly, "and because of it he did get out of ROTC."[15]

The "big fight" that took place behind the Curtis Hotel in the fall of 1928 stands out in Skewes and Byerly's recollections as perhaps the most telling incident of the Quent they knew. As eyewitnesses to all or part of the event, they relish in repeating it with laughs and physical gestures. They enjoy replaying its youthful spirit in the sunset of their lives. It was one of those unforgettable memories of college days and Quent was center stage.

Saturday night in the fall of 1928, the Curtis Hotel dining room was full of St. Paul Democrats touting Al Smith, the governor of New York and the first Roman Catholic nominee in American history, as their presidential candidate against Herbert Hoover. Their candidate, Smith, was not among the guests, but when Dick Long's orchestra belted out Sidewalks of New York, everybody in the dining room joined in the singing.

The Curtis was also a popular stomping ground for college students — an excellent place to eat and the prices were right. Saturday nights offered one of the best deals in the Twin Cities. For $1, each person received a steak dinner, the sounds of music and the opportunity to dance. This particular night, a group of Sigma Nus was enjoying its own fun amidst the fanfare of the Smith for president celebration. When the band played the New York City theme song, they joined in the singing, but to demonstrate their free spirit and independence, they let go with a chorus of boos at the conclusion of the song.

Their rudeness was too much for one partisan sitting at an adjoining table. He jumped out of his seat and headed for the fraternity table. He was of good size, possibly Irish, and in fine spirits. Skewes provided the play by play:

> "Did you boo?" said the man looking directly at Burdick who happened to be the biggest one at the table.
> "Sure," said Burdick, who had not said anything, but who would rather fight than not.
> "Come outside and I'll show you," came the challenge.
> "Sure," responded Burdick.

Byerly remained at the table with the others while Skewes graciously agreed to serve as Burdick's second. He witnessed the whole fight. "They got to the side of the hotel, out by the alley, and Quent went to remove his coat. While he was doing it, this fellow took a sock at him and knocked Quent down. Quent got up and pummeled that guy. We had to pull him off. Quent hadn't even booed, but he could not resist the temptation."[16]

Meanwhile, back inside, the other Sigma Nus sat nervously on the edge of their chairs waiting for the outcome of the fight. They did not have to wait very long before Burdick and Skewes soon returned. When Burdick simply began to eat the rest of his dinner, without a word about the fight, Byerly demanded to know what the hell happened. Skewes began to provide the details, but everyone wanted to hear it from Burdick, the fighter. "He just sat down as if nothing happened," said Byerly, "and went on eating. No bragging. Nothing." Byerly was flabbergasted and noticeably disappointed. "Burdick never picked a fight and he never crowed. Never."[17]

Skewes, the second, probably spent the rest of that evening replaying the fight to all the Sigma Nus. Burdick, the participant, never talked about it. A year or so later, Byerly and Burdick got involved in another incident. A Minneapolis cab driver tried to overcharge them for a cab ride back to the fraternity house. He claimed that the fare was for three zones. Burdick argued it was only for two. When Burdick got out of the cab, he only paid the cabby for the two zones. Before they got to the sidewalk, the driver came after Burdick with the crank of the coin box raised over his head in one hand. Burdick swiftly disarmed him. He took the crank out of his hand and forced him to the ground on his hands and knees. No trash. No violence. Burdick and Byerly quietly continued walking up to the fraternity house and Burdick never brought up the incident.[18]

Aside from being the Gentle Warrior of the Sigma Nus, Burdick endeared himself to his fellow fraternity brothers for other reasons. Although physically imposing, he was neither cocky nor pushy. He was a rock of security, not a threat, to all and each of them. His gentleness and quiet demeanor, unless challenged, imbued a mysterious strength of character. He was dependable, compassionate and sincere.

Quent was "a fellow that you could go around the world with," said Skewes. "He was well-liked, well-known and well-thought of." He was active in a lot of things. He was "always frugal, never a dresser," and "hated hospitals."[19] Byerly was more critical and perhaps more discerning. Quent was "very stubborn" and "very naive." He had a sense of humor, but for most of the time was "pretty tense" and "kind of a patsy."[20] When Byerly recalled the coat incident, he broke into bits of laughter as he tried to explain just how green and gullible his Williston friend could be:

> At that time the campus style was overcoats — quite long, below the knees, and in black or dark blue. The hat was black or dark blue, but preferably black. Burdick was always looking for bargains and one day he went down to Washington Avenue and bought an overcoat. He came back to the fraternity house and started to show it off. "How do you like it?" [Quent asked.] "Quent, that coat stinks!" I had told him the style on campus. This coat was ugly. It was white with big, black balls. "That's completely out of style. It's awful!" [Quent's immediate response was:] "That son of a bitch told me that's what the boys are wearing on campus." He got madder than hell. The next morning he cut his early class and went down and got his money back. From then on I bought his clothes.[21]

Schoolwork did not appear to tax any of them. All three were better than average students, but not top students. They studied when tests required that they study, but all were busy — Burdick and Byerly with sports and Skewes with working at a café. The academic environment differed in those days, too, especially in law school. Many students held full- or part-time jobs while attending law school, except for a few weeks before exams. Library research and extensive papers for each class were rare. School consisted primarily of memorization and practicum exercises in class.

Skewes described Quent as "a good student" who earned primarily "B grades in college." He could have been "an A student if he had wanted to be, but there was little pressure to do so." In their senior year of law school, both men hit the books, and as a result, their grades reached new highs. In law school, Burdick was "always considerate of the other fellow" and on "close terms with Jewish classmates," as was Skewes. Both worked on several class projects with the only African-American student in their class.[22]

School expenses ran about $750 a year. Tuition was $20 a quarter for undergraduates, slightly higher for nonresidents and for law school. Each student also paid an incidental fee of $7.50, which covered health services, including two free nights in the hospital and a copy of the daily student newspaper. The fraternity charged $1 a day for board and $15 a month for room.[23]

Social life, like money, was meager. Byerly enjoyed more dates than his two shyer friends combined. "We never went out much," explained Skewes. "We didn't have that kind of money."[24] The truth was that neither Quent nor Skewes showed much interest in going out. The fraternity hosted two parties (one formal and one informal) every quarter, and for most of their college years, provided them with their only dates.

Quent used to pull pranks on some of the sorority houses just for fun. He would dial their number and in an exaggerated voice would say:

"Is Boo there?"
"Boo who?"
"There, there, don't cry, little girl!"[25]

With no meals served at the fraternity house on Saturday night, the three would go searching for a place to eat. Quent introduced his friends to Chinese food. He would insist on going to one restaurant about four blocks away. They would order a big plate of chow mein for 35 cents.

The last year of law school (1931-1932), Skewes and Burdick decided to move out of the Sigma Nu house. They were tired of being elected to this or that office and doing much of the work. They also wanted to be on their own and away from the younger members of the fraternity and to concentrate on their studies. The first move proved unsatisfactory. They did not like the landlords. By the end of the fall quarter, which was right before Christmas, Skewes came out of the residence to find Burdick waiting for him in the car.

"Jump in the car, Mort," ordered Quent. "We're moving."
"Good," replied Skewes. "I'll go and get my things."
"You don't have to," said Burdick. "I got 'em all in the car."[26]

They drove around the rest of the afternoon looking for another place. They discovered a nice looking house at 1704 Brooke Avenue Southeast. They stopped the car and both went up to the door. The owner of the house told them in no uncertain terms that they were not interested in renting to any university students. They simply did not like them. The two law students continued to plead their case, and during the conversation, the subject of football came up. As Skews recalled:

> "Are you Burdick, the football player?" asked the man.
>
> "Yes."
>
> "Just a minute, then. I will go and ask my wife."
>
> In a few minutes, he returned and told us they would rent to us.[27]

In the spring quarter of 1930, Byerly tried to persuade Burdick to go on a blind date. It was a hard sale.

> "Gosh, I know a beauty, Quent," said Byerly. "You should see her!"
>
> "Oh, hell," replied a doubting Burdick.
>
> "No, you should. "I'll make the date over the telephone."
>
> "OK."
>
> I made the date and Quent went down and met her at Sanford Hall. I went to bed and about 11:30 p.m. Burdick comes into my room and wakes me up. "You sure played a dirty trick on me," said Burdick.
>
> Quent carried on like this for about five minutes while I just listened. Finally I said: "Oh, bull suit!"
>
> "That's the loveliest girl," replied Burdick with a smile. "She's beautiful!"
>
> That's when it started. This was the spring of 1930.[28]

Skewes confirmed the obvious. "He fell pretty hard for her. She was the love of his life."[29] "I think," added Eugene, that "Marietta was his first and only love."[30]

Marietta

Exquisite physical beauty and genuine personal charm epitomize Marietta Janecky. Family and friends described her as "very beautiful" and "very charming." Males sometimes paused as they search for a more descriptive word than beautiful to paint her portrait. Finding none, most opted for the modifier "very," and repeated it a second time as if to make it clear. Females strongly second the physical characterization of her beauty, but in a surprisingly nonthreatened tone. They liked her. When Marietta entered a room, everyone noticed her — the dark complexion; the dark hair pulled straight back; the long, gold earrings; and those marvelous hats. Whatever Marietta wore, she wore well. Yet, she possessed an inner beauty as well. She conversed with a natural charm devoid of ostentatious mannerisms. She awed most men and was still admired by most women, strong testimony both to her physical and spiritual attributes.

Comments in her senior yearbook at Carleton College in 1932 touch the same chords as those who knew her later as Marietta Burdick:

> She should be awarded a palm, a gold medal, or something — for she is of a rare feminine species — the non-catty kind. Her sweetness is coupled with a quiet intelligence, her looks have smitten many a West-Sider, and she dresses right smartly. She's smart — we've never yet seen an East-Sider that majored in chemistry who wasn't.

Eugene, her brother-in-law, remembered her as a "Grace Kelly type" while Jan Mary Hill, her oldest daughter, characterized her as a "kind of Gloria Steinem of the 1950s."[31]

Marietta Janecky was born on May 7, 1912, in New Prague, Minnesota, a Czech community 45 miles southwest of Minneapolis. She was the oldest child and only daughter of Dr. Joseph and Mary Jelowski Janecky. Her parents were second-generation Czech-Americans who found ethnic continuity in the communities of New Prague, Hutchinson and Spring Lake, Minnesota. Her father was the town's only dentist. Her mother, a homemaker, was the real source of family strength. The Janeckys lived comfortably and were socially active. Joseph played golf regularly and the family spent summers at their cottage on Spring Lake.

The children of Quentin and Marietta Burdick knew lots about their maternal grandparents. "My grandfather, Joseph," recalled Jan Mary proudly, was a "very forward-thinking person. He was a thinker and an atheist who married a Catholic girl."[32] Jennifer Burdick recalled his contributions in the field of dentistry. He was a fine dentist who "experimented with orthodontics before orthodontics became very popular."[33] Joseph and Mary spoke their native language fluently and subscribed to the New Prague Czech newspaper in their home.

The Janeckys lived together almost like a clan. They did nearly everything together. Family came first and the parents were described as "the centrifugal force of a very, strong, close family."[34] Marietta had five younger brothers: Woody, Franklin, Clayton, Joseph and Burton, the baby. Woody, next to Marietta in age, was her favorite. He followed his father's example and became a dentist, establishing a practice in Barnesville, Minnesota, in the lower Red River Valley, 20-some miles southeast of Fargo, North Dakota. Franklin opted for another profession; he became an optometrist and settled in Crookston, Minnesota, in the upper Red River Valley, 20 miles east of Grand Forks, North Dakota. Clayton and Joseph became career officers in the U.S. Navy following their service during World War II, and Joseph, like his older brother Franklin, became an optometrist. Burton was "mentally handicapped at a young age as a result of encephalitis or meningitis, not properly diagnosed."[35] A large child, he was soon institutionalized because his mother simply could not handle him. His departure from the close family caused much unhappiness, but his visits home each summer ameliorated some of their grief.

The influence of this strong and close-knit family stood in stark contrast to the childhood of Quentin growing up in Williston. Marietta enjoyed a secure and warm childhood surrounded by doting parents and a basketball team of adoring but teasing male siblings. The goal of self-fulfillment, independence and the pursuit of professional goals acquired through higher education stood out in her upbringing. "She was not supposed to stay home and just bear children," recalled Jan Mary. "There were bigger and brighter things for her."[36] The pursuit of a college education in those days — especially a degree in chemistry, spoke loudly to her independence and idealism.

Two other matters weighed heavily on her childhood — the first related to religion and the second to health. Marietta never experienced a traditional religious upbringing. Joseph, her father, affluent by profession, espoused atheism and socially got away with it in the community. He rejected all types of established religions. He preferred to think freely and rationally about ideas of the mind and spirit without the practice of a religion. He was never unkind or boastful about his philosophy, nor did he carry guilt as a result of his positions He simply rejected all religion. Mary, her mother, lived with the religious guilt of a fallen-away Catholic for the remainder of her life. "It was a sad part of her life," observed one of her grandchildren. "She always went to church, but she left the Catholic Church."[37] Marietta grew up in a home of love, but without the curse of personal, religious guilt. She did not belong to any church growing up in New Prague and seldom attended one later as an adult in Fargo. The second matter was of a physical nature: Marietta was never strong. She was always a sickly child and prone to respiratory illnesses because of contracting scarlet fever as a young child.

After graduating from the New Prague High School in 1928, Marietta enrolled at Carleton College in Northfield, Minnesota. It was then (as it is now) a small but excellent liberal arts college located a short distance due east of her hometown. Because of family wishes, academic needs or both, Marietta transferred to the University of Minnesota. "Her father had been a University of Minnesota man and he wanted her to go to the university very badly," recalled Quentin, "and so her junior year, she switched. During that year is when I met her. She stayed there that one year and went back to Carleton. I had a long drive then!"[38] Both Eugene and Byerly disputed Quentin's memory of why and how long Marietta actually spent at Minnesota. Both insisted that she enrolled for only one quarter and did so because she needed to take certain chemistry courses that were either not available or offered when she needed them at Carleton.[39]

Regardless of the actual time Marietta spent at the University of Minnesota, it was when she met her future husband. Whether Marietta fell head over heels in love with Quentin, as he did with her, is not known. He was, however, a good catch. His curly hair, athletic stature and quiet demeanor made him attractive to women even though his clothes suggested someone out of tune with style and taste. He was handsome, the strong, silent type, naïve or innocent or both. His sexual experiences were nonexistent; house money at the fraternity placed high odds that he was a virgin the day he got married. Moreover, he opined a future. He wanted to be a lawyer and seemed proud of the fact that Usher was already planning for him to take over his Fargo law practice following his graduation.

There is only scant knowledge on their courtship. Quentin did not elaborate in interviews. Jan Mary, Jennifer and Jessica Burdick knew virtually nothing about their parents' dating and courtship. Jessica, the youngest, who was only 10 when her mother died, asked the question that all of Marietta's daughters wanted to know the answer to: "Why did [Marietta] major in chemistry?"[40]

What was clear about their relationship was that Quentin became an accepted member of the Janecky clan and loved it. It was a family, full of caring, teasing and excitement. Marietta's parents took to Quentin immediately and welcomed him into their home, while her brothers played one trick after another on their future brother-in-law to see if he was worth of their sister's commitment. It was also clear that Quentin failed to introduce Marietta to his family. He seldom mentioned her to his brother and never took her home to Williston before they were married.

The wedding was a quiet affair. They were married in a short service in the New Prague Community Baptist church on Saturday night, March 18, 1933, at 7 p.m. The ceremony was described as a "simple service in the presence of immediate relatives of the families."[41] It appeared, however, that only the Janecky family was present. Eugene, for whatever reason, was not there, nor was Eileen. If either Usher or Emma Burdick were present, there is no record or recollections to substantiate it. Ken Byerly and Morteer Skewes were absent as well. Byerly had left Minnesota, but Skewes, who returned to Laverne, said he could not afford the trip.[42] Thomas Kelly, who was listed as Burdick's groomsman, was an unknown.

The *New Prague Times* covered both a hometown shower for the bride and the wedding ceremony. The groom was described as a Fargo attorney and a "former University of Minnesota football star," while the bride was characterized as a "charming and accomplished young lady" who had "attained various scholastic honors in her college work."[43] The groom was three months short of being 25 years old; the bride two months short of 21. They were to make their home after April 18 at 1614 Eighth Avenue South, Fargo, North Dakota.

During World War II, when Woody Janecky was serving in the armed services, Dr. Joseph and Mary Janecky moved to Barnesville, Minnesota. It was suppose to be a short stint. Woody asked his father to take over his dental practice until the end of the war, but with other dentists in New Prague, Joseph decided to stay in Barnesville. Mary wanted to return to the Czech community, but the presence of Marietta and two sons in the Red River Valley compensated for the move. They later purchased a lake home on Pelican Lake, east of Barnesville. Joseph died in 1977 and Mary in the early 1980s. Both were in their 90s.[44]

Skewes and Byerly lost track of Marietta through the years. Skewes recalled that he and his wife once dropped in on the Burdicks in Fargo and got a fine tour of their Red River residence. In 1947 or 1948, Byerly stopped in Jamestown, where they lived for two years. Although Quentin was away, Marietta commented, "he was off again saving the world." It was not a statement made in anger or disgust," noted Byerly, but "a shrug of acceptance or resignation."[45]

The Pummeler

The University of Minnesota Golden Gophers football team and Quentin Burdick, one of its star players, shared a common legacy of disappointment between the years 1926 and 1931. The team compiled a respectable record of 33 wins, 14 losses and three ties during those six years. Alumni, fans, students, coaches and players expected more, but neither Big Ten nor national championships came their way. The Gophers beat arch rival Michigan only once (1927) and tied Notre Dame the same year. They piled up huge scores against weaker opponents such as North Dakota (1926 and 1927) and South Dakota schools (1930). Big Ten opponents proved much more difficult. The 1927 team went undefeated in eight games, but two ties against Indiana and Notre Dame blemished their season's record and prevented national ranking and conference honors. The 1930 season was a major disappointment. The team won only three games while suffering four losses against Vanderbilt, Northwestern, Michigan and Wisconsin and a tie with Stanford.

Quentin Burdick gave his heart and sacrificed his body for Gopher football. There was nothing more important to him than football, football, football during those years. He aspired to be the very best and trained endlessly to build strength and add weight to his body. In the spring and fall quarters, he practiced on the football field, on the track and in the weight room. In the winter quarter, he wrestled and boxed to stay in shape. His total commitment, nonetheless, earned no reward when it came to his personal goals. He played varsity on both offense and defense. He lettered, and by doing so, became the first son of a former Minnesota player to do so. His football career, however, was dogged by nagging injuries that ultimately prevented him from becoming the great football player he always wanted to be. The physical pain he inflicted so surgically on opponents extracted a toll from him, the inflictor, as well. With an extra year of eligibility, he labored for almost two years to rebuild a knee permanently weakened by the removal of cartilage and ligaments.

What kind of football player was this young man from Williston? In the autumn of his life, Burdick confided that he was "a damn good football player."[46] At age 81, that epitaph was more important to him than his long service in the Congress of the United States. It was not a boast, just a matter of fact. No crowing. He wanted history to know that he was a damn good football player. Unfortunately, sources to back up his claim are incomplete — coaches and players are deceased. Clips from the student newspaper and the recollections of Eugene and his two college friends, Skewes and Byerly, offer the best documentation.

Both of Burdick's friends described him as a pummeler. Skewes used the word repeatedly to characterize the way Burdick played football. "He was a pummeler. Instead of ducking somebody, he'd rather hit 'em and knock 'em down."[47] Skewes explained this word further by recalling a specific play with some detail: "We were playing Northwestern at Evanston. Quent had the ball and a clear shot for a touchdown. There was one fellow between him and the goal line. Quent went out of his way to knock that fellow down and, of course, he didn't make the touchdown."[48]

Byerly knew exactly what Skewes meant by the word pummeler. "That's Quent," chuckled Byerly, "that's Quent."[49] In other words, if given the choice between hitting an opponent and running away from him to score a touchdown, Burdick preferred to run at the opponent and try to knock him down. If he scored in the process that was fine, but the main object was to knock over the opponent. Byerly explained the same strategy when Burdick played defense:

> I was out for football one spring practice. Burdick and I were practicing punt returns together with another fellow. He was supposed to fetch the ball and we're supposed to tackle him.

"Just steer him my way." said Burdick with a grin, "and I'll get him."
"Wham! It would be the deadliest crash."
So I'd steer gladly. He loved to hit![50]

A closer examination of Burdick's football career reveals elements of brilliant play and besetting injuries. During his six years at Minnesota, Burdick played only two complete seasons. The first full season was in his freshman year (1926), a year in those days when freshmen were not eligible for varsity participation. The second occurred in his junior year (1928), when he played on both sides of the ball as a blocking back on offense and a linebacker on defense. His outstanding play earned him the coveted "M" varsity letter. A nagging knee injury sidelined him for two full seasons. The first injury occurred during his sophomore year (1927), the year he was touted to be a starter on the varsity team. The second came in 1930 as a red-shirted senior. Burdick played partial seasons in 1929 and again in 1931. After the surgical removal of torn cartilage and ligaments from his knee, however, Burdick's lateral movement was gone. Physical injuries from football were not the only problems; Burdick was plagued with other medical problems, too, including operations to remove his tonsils and appendix. By 1931, Burdick hated hospitals as much as he loved football.

Freshman candidates for Minnesota football in 1926 competed against each other for future varsity consideration. With 200 students expected to try out, Sherman Fingers, the freshman coach, explained how the process would eventually produce good varsity players. "The men will be divided into squads of from 17 to 20, with one coach over each section," said Fingers. "These teams will play a series of contests between themselves and whenever a man shows enough of him to warrant promotion, he will be transferred to what will be known as the 'freshman varsity.'"[51]

The primary award for freshmen prowess was varsity punishment. The main contribution of the newly established freshman varsity was to get the hell kicked out of them by the varsity team. Monday practice was particularly brutal, especially after losing a game the previous Saturday. The older jocks got in their licks by an extra hit here and there to make up for Saturday's dumb mistakes. The rest of the week's practice for the freshmen was not much better. On Tuesday, they donned the uniforms of the next opposing team for the upcoming game. They ran the opponent's plays until after dark, usually viewing the crisp fall sky from their backsides. Freshman participation was basic training and only those who liked the contact survived the pain.

Of the 135 men who actually showed up for freshman football, two got press. Burdick with a misspelled first name, "Clentin," was listed as a promising 170-pound back.[52] The other was Bronco Nagurski, a 210-pound lineman from

International Falls, Minnesota. Burdick excelled in blocking for those who carried the ball in the old single-wing offense. Nagurski, with a body of a bear and the legs of deer, excelled in creating big holes in the offensive line and making quick tackles on defense. Both were among the 40 outstanding freshman honored at the "M" banquet in late fall and both were expected to show varsity colors come spring practice in March.[53]

Physical conditioning for spring football began in February, but Burdick never quit staying in shape. Between the end of football in November and the first official day of spring practice on March 28, 1927, Burdick pumped iron and ran sprints. He added a dozen pounds to his frame and dreamed of making the starting team for Doc Clarence Spears' varsity team in the fall.

"Spring practice will be serious business at Minnesota this year," opined the *Minnesota Daily*.[54] Outstanding freshmen such as Burdick and Nagurski certainly concurred. Both made strong impressions on the coaches as they made significant progress during spring practice. Coaches remained unsure, however, where to best play Nagurski. They moved him to end to capitalize more on his speed, but still showed no intent to make him the All-American running back he later became. Coaches used Burdick as both a blocking back and running back. What he lacked in speed he overcame with strength. His punishing blocks and killing tackles made him a spring star. He got more press than Nagurski for "ripping off quite a bit of yardage" and for being "fast for his weight."[55] His first name was then spelled correctly and he was identified as the son of Usher Burdick who played for the Gophers in the early 1900s. At the annual spring game, the Maroons, with an all-freshman backfield and Nagurski controlling the line of scrimmage, defeated the Gold team by a score of 6-0. Burdick "counted 12 yards in six tries."[56]

What exactly happened next in Burdick's football career is not entirely certain. What is certain was the growing popularity of Gopher football. Tickets were hiked 50 percent in price and buyers came from 37 states and Canada. "Football hangs in the air," forecasted the student newspaper; "the cold, crispy autumn winds have brought out overcoats, coal men and football players. Out of the field padded men dash hither and thither, falling on the ground with ambitious grunts."[57]

Burdick reported in an interview that he earned a varsity letter as a sophomore. He was mistaken. Burdick did not play on the 1927 Minnesota football team. There is no record of what happened to him either following spring practice or the start of fall practice. He was not one of the five sophomore letter winners.[58] One can only surmise that he suffered the first of several knee injuries, although the student newspaper makes no mention of a gimpy knee during this season.

In the spring of 1928, Burdick was up and running again. His name appears regularly on the varsity roster with potential as a varsity player, just as in the spring practice of 1927. "Burdick was the fourth man in the backfield," reported the newspaper, although "his efforts were confined to blocking."[59] While Burdick appeared healthy once again, the real star of spring practice was Fred Hovde, another North Dakotan from Devils Lake, who took over the quarterback slot.[60] He also represented the Sigma Nus in the annual spring all-Minnesota intramural track meet and placed fifth in the hammer throw.[61]

Burdick played his best football as a junior in 1928. The Golden Gophers compiled a respectable 6-2 record. They defeated Creighton, Purdue, Chicago, Indiana, Haskell and Wisconsin, but two one-point losses to arch rival Iowa (6-7) and Northwestern (9-10) darkened an otherwise successful season. Burdick played regularly in the backfield and stayed healthy most of the season. He started in the first home game against Creighton before 26,000 screaming fans, almost the population of Fargo — North Dakota's largest city in 1930. He played every game and scored the only touchdown of his entire collegiate career. In December, he and 23 other players walked up to receive the coveted "M" sweater at the annual football awards ceremony.[62]

Coach Spears rotated Burdick and Nagurski in different positions throughout the entire season. Burdick played some games as a running back and others as a blocking back. Nagurski nagged to carry the ball, winning that right late in the season. They stood tall together on the defensive side with Nagurski at end and Burdick at outside linebacker. As the season progressed, the two men — both short on words but long on results — learned to respect each other's abilities. According to Byerly, the two developed an unusual routine during the season. "Burdick and Nagurski would square off before practice. Burdick, who weighed much less, would throw Nagurski. Just throw Nagurski! Nagurski would get up kind of embarrassed and look at Burdick and say: 'I don't know how you do it!'"[63]

In the last home game of the season, Burdick had the opportunity to score a touchdown. The outcome of the contest against a weaker opponent, the Haskell Indians, was determined early in the game. The Gophers eventually won by a score of 52 to zip. As the game got out of control, the Gopher players began to enjoy the game even more. Burdick vividly recalled what transpired:

> Most of the time I was a blocking halfback, but I liked to carry the ball, too. So I talked to our center in the huddle.
> "Damn it, I would like to carry the ball once in awhile."
> "We can fix that."
> When we got within 5 yards of the goal line, he gave me a wink and said:

"Instead of hiking the ball to the fullback, I'll hike it to you."
He did and I made the touchdown.[64]

Although Emma Burdick never came to watch her son play any games, Usher sat with Eugene at many home games. The diminutive son and big bear father made an odd couple in the Minnesota stands. Usher would get so excited that he would move an entire row of spectators left or right, depending on which direction the Gophers were advancing the pigskin. "When Minnesota players got the ball," recalled Eugene, "the empathic response of my father was tremendous. He just pushed it. Pushed it! He just pushed me about a foot or two trying to get that score. That is empathy! I attended several games with him like that."[65]

During the 1929 winter quarter, Blaine McKusick, the Minnesota wrestling coach, recruited Burdick. Alvin Teeter, the regular heavyweight, was sidelined with illness, and McKusick was desperate to find a respectable competitor before the upcoming match against the University of Chicago. Burdick was a regular in the gym during the football off-season and McKusick knew who he was, so one day he approached him about joining the wrestling team. Burdick listened to the proposal and gave his word to the coach that he would give it a try for the good of the alma mater. Less than two weeks later, Burdick took to the mat. "The football blocking back, Quentin Burdick, entered his first match," reported the student newspaper, and "gave his experienced Chicago opponent a hard battle and nearly succeeded in winning before he himself was downed."[66]

The newspaper clip told only part of the story; Byerly recalled the rest. McKusick set Burdick up. He never told him that his opponent was the heavyweight champion or that he outweighed him by more than 40 pounds. The gullible Burdick never gave his opponent a minute of thought until he saw him the day of the match. Then in a panic, he started to worry. According to Byerly:

> Here is Burdick sitting on the bench watching the first wrestling match of his life with great interest but he doesn't know what the hell is going on. Finally it came his turn.
> "Sure, he is the champ, but he's kind of a sissy," encouraged the coach in Burdick's ear. "If you hit him hard, he'll crumble!"
> Burdick rushed out of his corner and with his open hand closed the guy's eye. He just clobbered him! The next few minutes were the damnedest wrestling match I ever saw in my life. The guy got mad. Burdick had him in a position two or three times and if he'd known anything about wrestling, he could of got him, but he didn't know it. Eventually the guy beat him on technique. Burdick came home to the fraternity house and for two

days said nothing. Just sat around sort of dazed. Finally on Monday night, he came up to my room.

"You know, Ken, McKusick lied to me."

"How's that?"

"He told me that this guy wasn't really tough and when I came out that he would fold. McKusick lied to me!"[67]

Although Burdick did not wrestle against Iowa and Illinois the next two matches, he did post a 17-9 victory against Northwestern on the last match of the year.[68] Burdick did not wrestle again for the Gophers, but occasionally he did some sparring with the boxing gloves. McKusick found other replacements. The incident, however, demonstrated something basic about Burdick's character. He was unbelievably strong and equally naïve.

Burdick carried his fall success into spring practice. He sought to improve the quality of his game and ensure a starting slot on the 1929 team. Coach Spears used the spring practice to move Burdick around from position to position. He tried him at left tackle for a couple of days and then switched him to quarterback. When the annual spring championship rolled around, however, Burdick resumed his normal position as a blocking back. "It was his ability to block out tacklers," praised the *Minnesota Daily*, "that made [it] possible for other backs to get good gains."[69] The Maroons lost to the Gold team 7-6 and "Burdick's try for a point after touchdown was blocked."[70]

The 1929 season produced another 6-2 season for the Golden Gophers. They defeated Coe, Vanderbilt, Northwestern, Ripon, Indiana and Wisconsin, while losing two heartbreakers to Iowa (7-9) and Michigan (6-7). The season ended with All-American honors piled on Nagurski, who was by then becoming one of the premier running backs in the country. Burdick played a superb game against Vanderbilt but re-injured his knee in the Iowa game. The injury sidelined him for the remainder of the year, preventing him from earning a second varsity letter.

The severity of the knee injury ultimately proved fatal to Burdick's football career. "The doctors took the ligament out," said Eugene. "They didn't try to sew it or reattach it like they would today. They removed it, so he never had that lateral support for his knee."[71] Burdick spent days in the university hospital with a weight hanging over the bed to pull the knee back into shape. Frustrated by his confinement and concerned about school, he called Skewes for assistance to escape from the hospital. Skewes recalled the conversation:

One morning he called me up and told me to bring his books and meet him at the school.

"Where are you?" I asked. "Are you out of the hospital?"

"Yah, but ..." Burdick replied.

"Where are you?"

"I won't tell you!"

"Do they know you're gone from the hospital?"

"No. I sneaked out"

"How did you get out?"

"I broke off a broom handle and used it for a cane."[72]

After the knee surgery, both Minnesota football and Burdick's career took a transition course. Coach Doc Spears resigned at the close of the 1929 season to accept the head coaching position at the University of Oregon — a much higher paying position. The Gophers faced a major rebuilding program the next year. Minnesota quickly hired Fritz Crisler, the assistant football coach at the University of Chicago, to replace Spears. His 1930 team suffered a losing season, winning only three games, losing four and tying one. Burdick was red-shirted for the knee injury he suffered in 1929, but he was unable to play any football in 1930.

At the start of fall practice in 1931, Crisler called on Burdick to assume a leadership role on the team. He extended Burdick's eligibility for a second year, and Burdick was a seasoned player on two of the Nagurski-led teams of 1928 and 1929. "There is no tackler so vicious as the Williston power boy," Crisler told the Twin Cities media. "He seems to have just what we need and what nobody else on the team has been able to give us."[73]

After a couple of days of fall workouts, however, Burdick collapsed one afternoon from a sharp pain in his right side. Doctors diagnosed the pain as acute appendicitis and recommend surgery immediately. Burdick, who knew that surgery meant the end of his football career, stalled for time. He requested that his mother be present before surgery and the doctors agreed to wait for her arrival unless the pain got worse. Emma never came and the next day Burdick disappeared from the hospital. He just disappeared and spent the next couple of days quietly sleeping in a friend's dormitory room.

Undaunted, Burdick suddenly showed up the next week for football practice. The pain was gone and he was eager to play: "And don't let anybody tell you that I won't be ready — because I'll be there," snapped a feisty Burdick to an eager news reporter.[74] Still weak from the past week, however, Burdick was forced to sit out the first two games against North Dakota State and Ripon. By the end of September, Burdick was stronger and demonstrating considerable improvement in the backfield.

On the first Saturday in October, Burdick got the call to start against the Oklahoma Aggies at Memorial Stadium. He was primed and excited about playing again in front of the home fans after a long absence. Minnesota easily defeated the Aggies by a score of 20 to zero. Burdick played well in the first quarter but was hurt soon into the second quarter. Attendants carried him off the field on a stretcher in a drizzling rain. The knee he worked so hard to rebuild lasted less than half a game in the first real test of its strength.

The next week, the Gophers boarded the Great Northern Empire Builder for the long trek west to play Stanford. The *Minnesota Daily* said that Burdick would be "a stimulating factor which could not be overlooked," although his position "will be on the player's bench in civilian clothes."[75] Injury or no injury, his hometown of Williston had planned a special stop for the train to honor their hero, and Burdick had called home to tell Emma to "Get out the band."[76] When the train stopped at the depot early in the morning, the Williston High School Band stood waiting on the platform. A Twin Cities reporter traveling with the team filed the following story for his Minnesota readers:

> The finest demonstration was at Williston, North Dakota, the hometown of Quentin Burdick, where several hundred friends of the injured halfback (he of the punch-inviting jaw and pugilistic nose), headed by a band and mayor, turned out to pay tribute to one of the finest boys that ever wore a Minnesota uniform.[77]

Burdick missed both the Stanford game and the following game against rival Iowa. Only barely, according to Dave Woodward (the team trainer), who acknowledged that Burdick's return to practice surprised him and his fellow teammates. "He had a pretty bad knee," said Woodward, "but it must have been his spunk that brings him out for practice."[78] The next week, Burdick played his last game against Michigan. Again, he was carried off the field with an injury to the same knee. Burdick's football career was officially over. A couple of weeks later, with no further reason to hide, Burdick had his appendix removed.

The Gophers compiled a respectable 7-3 season. They defeated North Dakota State, Ripon, the Oklahoma Aggies, Iowa, Wisconsin, Cornell of Iowa and Ohio State while losing to Stanford, Northwestern and Michigan. Coach Crisler resigned shortly thereafter to take the head coaching position at Princeton. His replacement, Bernie Bierman, soon ushered in a new of year of Minnesota football, capturing four national titles in 1934, 1935, 1936, 1940 and 1941.

Burdick's final comeback proved to be a disappointment. Red-shirted for almost two years and now a senior in law school, he worked unsuccessfully to play one more season. His weakened knee, however, never responded satisfactorily to even his most rigorous exercise program. At age 23, Burdick could still hit any opponent hard and run forward and backward with good speed, but his lateral movement was gone. He could not play football with one good knee. His football eulogy, written by sports editor Ed Shave in the *Minneapolis Journal*, captured painfully in print what Burdick certainly felt inside:

> Quentin Burdick is the pathetic figure on the Gopher team. Quentin with his hopes, ambition and longing to play for Minnesota is hobbling around with the aid of a cane and being barely able to navigate. I doubt that if you thumb back the gridiron pages and delve into history, a lad can be uncovered who has tried higher, suffered more and yet been unable to attain his desire.[79]

Family and Politics

Skewes and Byerly shed some light on the Burdick family. Both recalled Usher, whom they said came to the campus often to watch Quentin play football. They liked to listen to him and his engaging personality captivated them. "Usher was a stubborn old bastard," said Byerly, "but a decent, lovable, old bear."[80] Skewes knew Usher well "because he was visiting Quentin and later Gene." Emma seldom visited the campus. In fact, Skewes said he could not recall ever meeting her during his entire time at the university.[81] Byerly did. She "seemed shy" and "didn't say much" on the one or two occasions he met her.[82] Both men knew and liked Eugene (Gene to them) who demonstrated a pleasing sense of humor and an admiration for Quentin best described as awe.

Quentin seldom shared any personal information about his parents' troubled relationship. Skewes knew of the divorce but said Quentin never once discussed the matter with him. Byerly was unsure about whether the Burdicks were divorced or not, but observed on more than one occasion that family matters weighed heavily on his friend's mind. "You don't know,' Quentin would say to Byerly. "You just don't know what went on in my family." When Byerly heard those words, he just kept his mouth shut. He never asked what happened and Quentin never explained what happened. "But I want to say again," said Byerly, "Quentin and his father were good friends at the time. Very good friends. They respected each other. He never talked about his mother much, but I could tell he loved her."[83]

Quentin Burdick did not turn into a liberal during the years he attended the University of Minnesota. He, like his best friends, lived those years apart from the divisions that were beginning to change American politics. They talked more about personal matters than national politics — what they were going to do on Friday night, the upcoming game on Saturday, and whether any of them had the courage to ask the cute coed to a movie. They were simply not involved in campus political rallies or Minnesota politics. They did not discuss the virtues of being a conservative or being a liberal, let alone belong to either the Republican or Democratic Party. They were nonparticipants, nonvoters, in the American political process during those years. None of them cast a vote until the 1932 election and it is possible that all of them voted for the incumbent, Herbert Hoover. Certainly Byerly and Skewes did, though they were concerned about their future after graduation, not the country's. Their world then was much smaller than the world they would enter after graduation. "At that time," said Byerly, "Quentin's aspirations were not political, just to be a lawyer in North Dakota."[84]

This is not to imply, however, that these two friends who knew Quentin better than anyone did not observe any political characteristics. They did. "He was extremely honest," said Byerly. "His principles were high. He wanted to do what was right."

His fraternity brothers elected him again and again for offices he never sought. "They respected him even though they did not know him."[85]

As their president, Burdick strictly enforced all house rules. He was particularly insistent about enforcing prohibition. No liquor was allowed in the house and no liquor was to be available at any house parties. Unlike most other fraternities, Burdick tried to keep Sigma Nu dry, a difficult undertaking no doubt. He led by example. He never took a drink in college. For those with more thirst, he established rules of enforcement. He appointed Byerly house manager and called him "Sniff," an appropriate nickname for an obvious task.[86]

The Depression in North Dakota changed Burdick from a nominal conservative to a liberal. "Here was Burdick in college, who was very conservative, and here comes the Depression," noted Byerly. "Quentin becomes very radical, very radical — and he even backed Communist principles!"[87]

The last time Burdick and Byerly met was in the late '60s. They were both stuck in the Minneapolis airport awaiting late-night flights to Fargo and Billings. They had several hours to chat and shoot the bull about a ton of topics. Byerly recalled asking Burdick, "Are you still a wobbly, you dumb bastard?" "No," replied a suddenly excited and defensive Burdick. "No. I am the most conservative guy in the world. The way I get elected is I give service to the people of North Dakota."[88]

The Minneapolis Bookstore

As the Depression deepened, Usher Burdick searched for new ways to support his children's education. He still owned property and livestock in Williston and his Fargo law practice. Nevertheless, as the '20s' clock clicked closer to the '30s, neither endeavor produced much income. The Burdicks, like many of their contemporaries, found themselves strapped for money by the mid-'20s. They were cash poor, and with all three children expected to attend the University of Minnesota, income became an even more pressing issue. Usher explored other ventures to raise funds. He became co-owner of Bunny's Bookstore in Fargo. Books were one of his favorite pursuits and Bunny Smith was an old acquaintance. Leaving Smith to run the bookstore, Usher took to the road. He sold fire insurance and mortgages throughout the upper Midwest. "A bank would take a mortgage," explained Eugene, and "he would peddle them among his friends in Minneapolis, selling their mortgages at a discount."[89]

Sometime in 1929, Usher purchased the Adair Bookstore in downtown Minneapolis. It was a novel idea to support the three children while they attended the University of Minnesota. By then, Quentin was completing his junior year, Eugene was enrolled for the fall and Eileen was set to follow in 1933.

Usher came upon the venture by regular haunts of bookstores and mortgages. In 1929, the Adair Bookstore was in bankruptcy under a receivership. Usher learned of this, contacted the receiver and chatted with him about the progress of the bankruptcy. The receiver told him that his work on the store was nearly complete since he had liquidated most, if not all, of the marketable books. After some haggling, the receiver quoted a price of $1,500 for the remainder of the store's contents and the equipment. Usher accepted the terms. He was then the owner of two bookstores, one in Fargo and one in Minneapolis.

The bookstore stood next door to the Nicolette Hotel on Hennepin Avenue. It was not an impressive structure — a tall, skinny, three-store affair, not in particularly good physical condition, and only about 25 feet wide. The excellent location — in the heart of downtown Minneapolis before the days of malls and adjacent to the city's premier hotel — overshadowed its poor appearance. Usher rented the premises for $75 per month.

Along with the books, Usher acquired a lot of junk. The first floor contained the only remaining marketable commodities: the books unsold by the receiver, some old coins and a few used stamps. The second floor housed piles of bound magazines and lots of unsorted material. The third floor swam in piles of pure junk, single copies of everything with no organization to any of it. It was a mess. "We had all kinds of stuff," recalled Eugene, "about 125,000 copies of books and volumes."[90] Fussy and better organized than either his father or older brother, Eugene probably possessed a more accurate count of inventory. He was also the only Burdick to live in the bookstore. He spent his first summer, 1929, in the Twin Cities, sleeping on a cot on one of the upper floors. "I got city broke there," Eugene reminisced with a smile.[91] He was a mere lad of 17 that summer, his first extended absence from Williston.

Why did Usher put down $1,500 of real money to buy a rundown second-hand bookstore in the middle of the Depression? Considering his penchant for quick deals and poor proceeds, the store turned out to be a profitable business. It paid the rent, the salaries of two employees, and the college expenses of Quentin and Eugene. The bookstore made a killing each fall in buying and selling used trade books, especially in the Twin Cities market for used high school textbooks. "It was the school books that made money," said Quentin. "It wasn't the best of times, so they didn't want to buy a new book. The economy wasn't too good, even then, and they wanted cheaper books."[92] Both Quentin and Eugene recalled vividly the brisk demand to buy and sell used textbooks and the money it brought into the bookstore. "The first week of school each fall, those kids would be lined up along the whole block on Hennepin Avenue," remembered Quentin.[93] Eugene described the book traffic scene inside, seeming to know the exact profit margins. "We'd have the students come in on one side of the table, where we would buy [the books], and on the other side we'd sell them. We might buy them for 50 cents and sell them back for a dollar." Quentin agreed but said overall, "we made it on volume not price." Eugene said he could only remember one new book, "The Specialist" written by Chick Sale, which ever made money for the bookstore. "It sold for $1, like hot cakes."[94]

There was much more to the Burdick bookstore business than just books. Quentin and Eugene relished Usher's attention and inclusion in a real business operation, man to man. Both sons bonded with their father during the bookstore operation, especially Quentin. "Come with me," Usher instructed Quentin. "It's yours. Go to it."[95] Usher also provided the boys with cars for pleasure and work. He purchased a two-door Nash coupe with a rumble seat. The Nash was "a very, very nice car that wasn't terribly expensive," said Eugene, and it allowed them to get around the Twin Cities without relying on trolley cars. Usher also delivered them an old Reno (an early Oldsmobile). This was a touring car, much bigger, and one they used for hauling books.

The bookstore provided Quentin with a rare opportunity as a young man to share a real experience with his father. Quentin already followed in his father's football steps and later his political career, but those endeavors were more stressful and not shared. The bookstore relationship was unique. It remained through all the years in Quentin's memory as something father trusted to son, and son responded in kind.

Eugene shared many more personal experiences with his father than Quentin did. In 1931 and 1932, Eugene spent the summers with Usher on North Dakota Indian reservations. They drove all over. They visited with elders, attended powwows and even did some archeology. Eugene learned how to speak Sioux and took notes and photographs for his father. In later years, he drew cartoons for various Usher publications, took care of his properties in Williston and carried out all his personal legal work. Quentin never shared in those experiences, in part, because of age and location, and in part because of temperament. He was not as organized as Eugene, and Usher understood their differences.

As the years went by, the small Minneapolis bookstore operation blossomed into a wonderful, living memory of a father-son relationship, as well as a profitable business venture during the Depression. "I made enough money to put myself and my brother through school," exclaimed a proud Quentin. "I ran the bookstore for three or four years ... then Eugene helped, well, he helped a bit!"[96] Eugene, who was in Minneapolis the entire length of the bookstore operation, would undoubtedly dispute the accuracy of his brother's recollection. Eugene indicated that both of them worked at the bookstore on weekends, but two salaried employees ran the store on a day-to-day basis.[97]

Morteer Skewes and Ken Byerly shared their recollections about the bookstore. The used textbook trade made a lot of money for the bookstore and paid for Quentin and Eugene's college education. But the actual time the Burdick boys spent working there was negligible. Skewes went to the bookstore many times, but "never saw them do any work there. They didn't have time for that. They just went there to get some money."[98] On one occasion, Skewes recalled, he and Quentin got into a discussion about the ownership of the store:

> "The owners were a Massachusetts Trust," said Quentin.
> "What the hell is that?" asked Skewes.
> "I don't know." replied Quentin.[99]

Byerly shared the same thoughts as Skewes. "I used to go with him once in awhile. We'd go down there and sit around. Right around the corner was a bum's hangout on Washington Avenue."[100] Quentin never went near the bookstore during the football season. When he did go down there, he would just spend an hour or two looking around. The bookstore was a social place to be around, not a place to actually work.

The amount of time Quentin and Eugene actually spent working in the bookstore was not of great historical importance. They probably worked there more than what their peers observed but less than what they recalled 60 years later. The significance of this chapter during the Minnesota years was a real, living memory of a successful bookstore operation between father and sons. No more. No less.

Usher owned the bookstore until March of 1933, "when we could no on longer pay the rent" and after "we had milked it for four years."[101] The building was eventually torn down and made into a parking lot. In 1934, with his election to the U.S. House of Representatives, Usher and the children shared his first regular salary in a long time.

Quentin Burdick's Minnesota years are significant. They provided a bridge between his boyhood and his adulthood. Those six years sharpened his character and deepened the personality traits already apparent to those who knew him. "Quent was a very unusual man," mused his college friend, Byerly, some 65 years later. "He was very bright — not a top student — but a very bright student. He was naïve. He was tough. He was a great football player. The boy rocked them!"[102]

Byerly's characterization points to some of Burdick's strong personal traits. There were others as well. Burdick's personality evolved from family hurts and football experiences. There was a clear core of set values discernible by the time he graduated from law school in June of 1932. He never altered them for the remainder of his adult life. There were detours, perhaps, but Burdick always stayed on the same road. His standards included desire for physical contact, high tolerance for pain, a dogged persistence, a self-effacing modesty, chastity, loyalty and a nonintellectual bent toward society.

Burdick embraced physical contact in any form. He simply desired it and never ran from a chance to engage in it. It might take the form of a Saturday night fight in the alley, a simple boxing workout in the gym or a conference wrestling match. It was always and forever any football practice or game regardless of the weather or his physical condition. Burdick just physically loved to hit and to be hit. He relished in the sheer contact, win or lose. He was never the instigator or the bully, however, except in a legal role of player or wrestler when he was allowed to throw the block, make the tackle or hit his opponent with an open hand. He never fought dirty nor did he seek revenge. He was always a gentle, willing warrior of sorts, who, once drawn into the fray, never looked back nor took prisoners. He was a formidable, imposing and silent combatant who challenged his opponent by physical strength rather than verbal trash. When the match was over, he shook hands and went on with his business. There were no bragging rights or replays. What was done was done. Period.

Burdick demonstrated a high tolerance for pain. He was continually prone to injuries but learned to keep going in spite of them. He escaped from the university hospital on at least two occasions just to remain competitive. He played football hurt more than most members of the Gopher team played football well, and he did so without rants of unfairness or bouts of complaining. He accepted the pain and refused to give up because of it. His dogged persistence complemented his high tolerance for pain. These were distinct parts of his personality although not separate. One facet seemed to take strength from the other. The greater the pain, the stronger the effort he applied to overcome.

There was also a self-effacing modesty to Burdick. His fraternity brothers observed it early in his Minnesota years. They respected him for it. Here was a football star and the strongest Sigma Nu living among them, yet, Burdick never bragged or crowed to any of them. Some found it odd, to be sure, but none found it displeasing. The flip side of the modesty, of course, was an almost innate inability to give anyone a compliment. Burdick could not heap praise on anyone anymore than he could heap praise on himself.

Burdick was always a sucker for a good cause. Friends concluded it was simply a trait of being naïve. This Williston boy had led a sheltered life and because of it was an easy target to be hustled, but the circumstance was probably more complex than that. Burdick was naïve, but the pain felt by others deeply affected him. His big heart and strong body were always available to lend a helping hand. If this characteristic was naïve, it was also humanitarian.

Burdick experienced life in terms of contests — the issue of fairness was paramount in his world. He witnessed a vertical landscape, a who's on top and who's on the bottom sort of equation. He sought to rearrange the pile but never the playing field. He was conservative in the sense that change should be orderly and based on fairness, not theory or change for change's sake.

Burdick learned to love a woman — only one woman. He was a tease in an innocent, adolescent manner, but he was also courtly and chaste. He was sexually innocent with other coeds, and once drawn to Marietta, remained chaste and loyal to her until her premature death in 1958. Burdick loved the physical presence of Marietta. He worshipped her and seemed perfectly content just to be around her, to see her, to talk to her and to hold her. With Marietta in his arms, the gentle warrior experienced security and peace in her love.

The Fargo years took the core values of Burdick's Minnesota years and pushed them into a different context. Burdick, the blocking back, became Burdick, the people's attorney. He defended the small farmer against the banker who sought to foreclose his farm. He represented the Teamster truck driver who longed for a decent wage and the right to strike to get it. These were different contests, but they existed in Burdick's mind as physical contests of sorts. He approached political problems with the same persistence and physical strength as he did football. Although he no longer wore the Maroon and Gold, his rumpled black attire symbolized those he represented. The establishment, those on top of the economic pile, soon learned that Burdick the lawyer was as formidable and persistent as Burdick the football player. The gentle warrior was still in the game.

Endnotes

1. Binford, "The Senator and His Lady," *Howard Binford's Guide* 13 (July 1980): 30.
2. Gray, *The University of Minnesota: 1851-1951*, 1.
3. Blegen, *Minnesota: A History of the State*, 423.
4. *Minnesota (Minn.) Daily*, Sept. 28, 1926, 1.
5. Ibid., Sept. 27, 1927, 1.
6. Gray, *The University of Minnesota*, 547.
7. Sevareid, *Not So Wild A Dream*, 48-49.
8. *Minnesota Daily*, Sept. 28, 1926, 6.
9. Ibid., Oct. 1, 1926, 1.
10. Ibid., Jan. 4, 1930; Jan. 24, 1930, 1.
11. Sevareid, *Not So Wild a Dream*, 33.
12. Ibid., 34.
13. Binford, "The Senator and His Lady," 31.
14. Ibid.
15. Ken Byerly, interview by author, April 21, 1995.
16. Morteer Skewes, interview by author, April 15, 1995.
17. Byerly interview.
18. Ibid.
19. Skewes interview.
20. Byerly interview.
21. Ibid.
22. Skewes interview.
23. Ibid.
24. Ibid.
25. Byerly interview.
26. Skewes interview.
27. Ibid.
28. Byerly interview.
29. Skewes interview.
30. Eugene Burdick, interview by author, Feb. 28, 1995.
31. Jan Mary Hill, interview by author, May 2, 1995.
32. Ibid.
33. Jennifer Burdick, interview by author, March 26, 1995.
34. Hill interview.
35. Ibid.
36. Ibid.
37. Ibid.
38. Quentin Burdick, interview by author, Jan. 6, 1992.
39. Eugene Burdick and Byerly interviews.
40. Jessica Burdick, interview by author, Jan. 28, 1996.
41. *New Prague (Minn.) Times*, March 23, 1993, 1.
42. Skewes interview.
43. *New Prague Times*
44. Hill interview.
45. Ken Byerly, letter to author, April 27, 1995.
46. Quentin Burdick interview.
47. Skewes interview.
48. Ibid.

49. Byerly interview.
50. Ibid.
51. *Minnesota Daily*, Sept. 28, 1926, 9.
52. Ibid., Sept. 29, 1926, 5.
53. Ibid., Oct. 10, 1926, 6; Dec. 3, 1926, 4.
54. Ibid., March 29, 1927, 1.
55. Ibid., April 26,1927, 4.
56. Ibid., May 14, 1927, 4.
57. Ibid., Sept. 27, 1927, 4.
58. Ibid., Nov. 26, 1927, 1.
59. Ibid., March 31, 1928, 6.
60. Ibid., April 4, 1028, 6.
61. Ibid., May 24, 1928, 6.
62. Ibid., Dec. 4, 1928, 1.
63. Byerly interview.
64. Quentin Burdick interview.
65. Eugene Burdick interview.
66. *Minnesota Daily*, Feb. 15, 1929, 4.
67. Byerly interview.
68. *Minnesota Daily*, March 9, 1929, 4.
69. Ibid., April 30, 1929, 4.
70. Ibid., May 4, 1929, 4.
71. Eugene Burdick interview.
72. Skewes interview.
73. Dan Rylance, "Quentin Burdick's 1931 hospital escape is hard to beat," *Grand Forks (N.D.) Herald*, July 30, 1992, 4.
74. Ibid.
75. *Minnesota Daily*, Oct. 20, 1931, 4.
76. Rylance, "Quentin Burdick's 1931 hospital escape."
77. Ibid.
78. *Minnesota Daily*, Oct. 20, 1930, 4.
79. Rylance, "Quentin Burdick's 1931 hospital escape."
80. Byerly interview.
81. Skewes interview.
82. Byerly interview.
83. Ibid.
84. Ibid.
85. Ibid.
86. Ibid.
87. Ibid.
88. Ibid.
89. Eugene Burdick interview.
90. Ibid.
91. Ibid.
92. Quentin Burdick interview.
93. Ibid.
94. Eugene Burdick and Quentin Burdick interviews.
95. Quentin Burdick interview.
96. Ibid.
97. Eugene Burdick interview.
98. Skewes interview.
99. Ibid.
100. Byerly interview.
101. Eugene Burdick interview.
102. Byerly interview.

- six -

Fargo

Fargo ranks as North Dakota's most powerful city. It has been that way for most of the city's 130-year history and all of the state's. Fargo sprang up overnight, first as a transportation link for Red River steamboats on the Winnipeg to St. Paul trading route in the 1870s, and then as an important railroad terminus for three railroads crossing open spaces to settle newly established territories. The Great Northern and the Northern Pacific depots at the north and south points of Broadway stood as ports of entry for settlers and freight heading west across the Great Plains. When highways and airlines eventually replaced tracks, Fargo was where federal highways intersected and where the leading air terminal sent North Dakotans to and from the state.

Population and politics powered Fargo as much as transportation. The city ranks first in state population for all of the 20th century. Combined with the cities of Dilworth and Moorhead on the Minnesota side of the Red River and West Fargo on the west, the greater Fargo-Moorhead community today is the largest population center between the Twin Cities and Spokane. Although never blessed as the state capitol site, Fargo, or "Imperial Cass" as it was soon nicknamed by jealous state competitors, emerged as the center of economic and political power in North Dakota. Fargo was for most of its history a staunch Republican stronghold where victorious state candidates compiled insurmountable margins to sustain their journey to less hospitable western precincts. The opulent homes on Fargo's South Eighth Street between Fifth and Tenth avenues stood as symbols of banking, newspaper and Republican power.

Population changes over time made Fargo a home for Democrats, too. Since the emergence of the North Dakota Democrat-NPL Party in the '60s, successful Democrat state candidates have cached large majorities in Imperial Cass to sustain their victories over some western counties. There were many factors that contributed to Fargo changing from the state's leading Republican city to one of the state's most dependable Democratic ones. The Great Depression forced many North Dakotans to abandon their farms and small towns. Great numbers left the state never to return, while others moved to larger communities within the state. Many who stayed moved to Fargo. They came for jobs, to raise families and to start a new life. They were New Deal orphans in a Republican city. Nowhere was this more evident than in the growing numbers of truck drivers who joined unions to seek higher wages and better working conditions. The *Fargo Forum* remained safely in Republican hands, but Democrats delivered milk and coal.

These new arrivals forced the Fargo community to rethink its long held attitudes about relief. The first change came in 1930, when Cass County officials struggled with their 1931 budget. They had no choice but to cut back on relief payments for the upcoming year. Revenues were shrinking and welfare roles were skyrocketing. Welfare costs had tripled between 1928 and 1929. The next year was worse. Local officials sounded warnings about what choices must be made for work and relief eligibility between new and older residents. "There is not sufficient work here for those who live here," exclaimed Fargo Mayor A.T. Lynner, "and Fargo and Cass County doesn't intend to support any poor who do not legally reside here."[1]

As the Depression widened, the city turned to volunteerism. Fargo declared war on the Depression on March 29, 1932. At 9:00 a.m., for a full two minutes, the Fargo fire whistle blew to signal the start of the engagement. City veterans, local members of the American Legion, led the war effort. The weapon of choice was money. The Legionnaires pledged $117,550 to employ as many unemployed Fargo men as possible. When the city fathers suggested the money be used to repave part of Broadway, the veterans unanimously endorsed their proposal. The war was on![2]

More fronts on the war against the Depression occurred during the summer of 1932. Elected officials matched private efforts with public ones. Fargo city commissioners took a cut in salary. They reduced their monthly salary by 5 percent, from $100 to $95. Streetlights were dimmed to save money on electricity. The school board passed new initiatives for the upcoming school year: there would be no kindergarten programs for school children. The board cut programs rather than reduce teacher salaries.[3]

As North Dakota's farm economy continued its downward plunge, many residents turned their attention to the November 8, 1932, presidential election. The issue was whether the federal government shared a responsibility for the welfare of its citizens. The result was a Democratic rout in a Republican stronghold. New York Governor Franklin D. Roosevelt humbled Herbert Hoover, the Republican incumbent, by a wide margin of 178,350 votes to 71,772. The majority of Fargo voters stuck with Hoover economics, but the margin was narrow; Hoover received 6,052 votes to Roosevelt's 5,239 votes.[4]

New Deal programs appeared in Fargo before the close of 1933. Money became a stronger and longer-term front in the war against the Depression. In August, city fathers called for a community parade to show their support for President Roosevelt's National Recovery Administration (NRA) program. Mayor Fred Olson encouraged everyone to take part. Business owners closed their stores to allow employees to attend the parade. The event culminated in a program of speeches at the city auditorium, and the *Fargo Forum* reported the event was extremely successful with thousands of people marching.[5] Before Christmas, more relief arrived. On the morning of December 1, 200 men were put to work on various city projects — cleaning the banks of the Red River, cutting tree stumps or working at city hall.[6] Political rhetoric was becoming an economic reality.

As 1932 passed, Usher Burdick slowly ascended the narrow steps to his small Fargo law office above Wimmer's Jewelry at 2½ Broadway. It seemed a good moment to seek solitude and to reflect upon the many changes that had occurred so quickly to the American people and his life during the past few years. He wanted to put pen to paper, but finding something to write it in his messy office proved time consuming. Finally, Usher grabbed a piece of blank stationary titled "J.K. Rishel Furniture Company of Williamsport, Pa[.]," and started to write:

> The year 1931 was a bad year. In many respects 1932 was still worse. Prices of farm products dropped to the lowest in our history. Farmers couldn't pay and finally gave up all hope of paying. The situation in September was headed straight for bloodshed, but Roosevelt came forward as the one hope. The Revolutionary spirit entered in a grim determination to oust Hoover and the disciples of moneyed interest. The result was amazing and the people thru Roosevelt won a smashing victory and allayed for the time any further thoughts of an open revolution. It probably ended it for a century for the people feel they can rescue their government anytime they earnestly put forth united action.[7]

For all the pain of the '20s, the coming of the New Deal revived Burdick's spirits. The deepening of the Depression made him more determined and rekindled his old Progressivism. He took on new public issues, stumping for the repeal of Prohibition and the creation of an allotment plan to save busted wheat farmers. In 1932, he sought public office again, running in the Republican primary for Congress as an Independent. He did not win, but his run paved the way for his election in 1934 and showed his determination to be part of the solution, not the problem. This was Burdick's first election contest since losing the Republican primary for governor against Lynn J. Frazier and the Nonpartisan League in 1916. Times were so different now. The roar of state Socialism was muted by human cries for jobs and crops. Ideology was shoved aside for economic survival. In losing, Burdick also discovered old League enemies: the likes of William Langer and William Lemke stood beside him as Depression-fighting allies. They were now all in this together. The Depression provided all of them with a new agenda and each a second political career, which ended only in death or retirement. All would serve through the Age of Eisenhower.

Burdick family fortunes went forward as well. The '20s were filled with memories of the divorce and separations from the children. The '30s, though difficult, inspired resolve. "All the family are in good health," wrote Usher, "and the shortage of our cash has not subdued our spirit. We are all willing to take our stand with the people, and if all are hard-up it doesn't matter." Most important to Usher, however, in 1932 was the progress of his oldest son. "Quentin graduated from Minnesota, regained his health and has made a signal start in law," observed a proud father. Quentin, after six years in Minnesota, was coming home to North Dakota.[8]

Quentin Burdick arrived in Fargo during that eventful summer of 1932. He came to practice law as a member of the law firm of Burdick, Burk and Burdick. He was the second Burdick of the firm. He was fresh out of law school and eager to make a career for himself and to follow in the footsteps of his more famous father. The Burdicks, like most North Dakotans, existed on a shaky economic foundation during these years. The firm attracted a steady stream of callers, but few paid for services rendered. The firm's portfolio, by Fargo legal standards, was paltry, on the fringe, maybe even off the edge of acceptable legal standards, even for those days. Burdick clients were railroad bums, downtrodden indigents, renters who could not pay, foreclosed farmers and police-busted Teamsters. The firm was not in the practice of protecting property and represented few clients who wore white shirts and collars. They spent most of their time listening to the problems of the poor and often went to court on their behalf. Burdick, Burk and Burdick was as much in the business of depression healers as it was in the profession of practicing law. It was a tough time to practice law and even harder to make a living at it.

Quentin Burdick embarked on a long and distinguished legal career during the summer of 1932. He was lucky to be offered the opportunity to enter an honorable profession in one the most revolutionary years in all of American history. He was admitted to the North Dakota bar on July 15, 1932, and worked briefly at home in Williston before moving to Fargo in the fall. There he practiced law until he was hired by the North Dakota Farmers Union in the late 1940s. He maintained an active law license through 1963 and kept an inactive status thereafter, according to records in the North Dakota Supreme Court.[9]

Little fanfare greeted Quentin Burdick's arrival in Fargo. The *Fargo Forum* published a brief business clip announcing the formation of a new law firm, "Burdick, Burk & Burdick," with offices in Fargo and Williston. Quentin was identified as the son of Usher Burdick and a former University of Minnesota football star. The latter received more attention than the former, and the clip recaptured in a nutshell the legacy of Burdick's athletic career. "A brilliant football player," began the piece, quickly adding, "Quentin's athletic career was continuously interrupted by one of the strangest successions of injuries ever to befall anyone."[10]

No one knew that sports obituary better than Quentin. He would repeat it the rest of his life without notes. The words had dogged him throughout his Minnesota years. Gifted potential that never reached full achievement. Now those words were pressed again as he began the practice of law in his new home of Fargo. It was a second start in a new field of dreams. The uniform of the maroon and gold was replaced by a black homburg — a hat that became a symbol of Burdick's 27-year legal career and an even longer political one.

There were a couple of reality checks up front. Quentin either knew these facts before his arrival in Fargo or learned of them soon after. The first was about his father's law firm and the second was about his Fargo office.

Although Usher Burdick established a law practice in Fargo shortly after the divorce in 1921, he made little use of it. There were so many things he wanted to do, and practicing law day in and day out simply bored him to death. Usher did, however, associate with a number of lawyers who did practice law while he engaged in his pursuit of happiness. The lawyers included John Burke, Harold Shaft, Roy Redetzke and Walter Burk. "Those were his partners," recalled Eugene. "Most of those partnerships were in name only. I'm not sure there was much of an exchange of money as a division. They probably each contributed their own clients. Maybe even trial lawyers. That was the arrangement they had before Quentin came along. Then it became Burdick and Burdick. It was Burdick and Burdick 'til I was admitted in 1935. Then it still operated under Burdick and Burdick, but the Burdick and Burdick was Quentin and Eugene. We were partners in name only. We helped each other on occasion when we needed it."[11]

John Burke and Usher Burdick shared a Progressive past. They held common political beliefs throughout the early years of the 20th century, but especially in 1911-1912, when they served together as North Dakota's governor and lieutenant governor. Their paths, however, diverged soon after. Burke's Progressivism and Democratic affiliation earned him a position in Woodrow Wilson's administration. Burke served eight years as treasurer of the United States (1913-1921). Burdick's Progressivism and Republican affiliation, on the other hand, bore little fruit. In 1916, the Nonpartisan League swept away the influence of the Progressive wing of the Republican Party. In 1921, however, the lawyers' paths crossed again and the two old friends agreed to practice law together in Fargo. It was a warm and amiable relationship, which lasted until 1925, when Burke was elected to the North Dakota Supreme Court, where he served with distinction until his death on May 14, 1937.[12]

As fathers, the two old friends shared common aspirations about their sons, too, yearning for them to be lawyers and to practice law in North Dakota. John Burke was very proud of his son, Tom, 12 years Quentin's senior, who went to Harvard as an undergraduate and then returned to North Dakota to study law. He never went to law school, which was not a requirement in those days. "The way I remember it, on a chair, a straight chair," recalled Eugene, "Tom Burke had the faculty to balance on the hind legs and just sit there hour after hour. He was supposedly studying law, which he did. He got through his reading law there in his father's and my father's office, and he passed the law."[13] Tom later followed his father, serving on the North Dakota Supreme Court for 17 years (1939-1966).

Usher shared similar visions for his two sons. Burke followed their progress almost as much as that of his own son. He had little choice in the matter. Usher kept him informed on a regular basis of where both Quentin and Eugene were in school. On one occasion, the elder Burke took young Eugene aside and told him a wonderful story about the joy of practicing law with his father. The act was complimentary in an odd sort of way and the young boy never forgot it. "Your father made the best use of the little law he knew of anyone I've ever known," noted Burke.[14]

Usher's other associates, Shaft, Redetzke and Burk, were all young lawyers fresh out of law school. Each was deeply appreciative of the opportunity to practice law anywhere and to be associated with a state figure. Shaft, who later moved to Grand Forks and became one of that city's most prominent lawyers, remembered those early days of law practice in Fargo with much nostalgia. He and Usher exchanged letters soon after Quentin's election to the U.S. Senate in 1960. "I was thinking about those lean years in the twenties," Shaft began, "when your meager practice was stretched to feed my growing brood. Politically, you were about three floors below the basement —and financially you were some distance below that."[15] It took the ailing Usher several weeks to reply. "It's a long time since you used to sit up in that hot office," recalled Usher, "and hunt around for business enough to pay your grocery bill."[16] One month later Usher was dead.

Wimmer's Jewelry, at 2 Broadway, was described in the '30s as "an ancient building."[17] It stood vertically at the intersection of the Northern Pacific railroad tracks (east and west) and Fargo's most important downtown street, Broadway (north and south). The single-digit address documented the southern start of Broadway as it went straight northward to the city's center. Near the Northern Pacific Depot and Front Street, which parallel the tracks, residents in this part of Fargo were more aware of railroad bums and transients who arrived and departed regularly than their affluent business cousins up the street.

The Burdick law office located above Wimmer's bore the address 2½ Broadway. The entry was a rather steep incline up narrow steps, followed by a quick right turn through the office door. The inside was modest — actually, much worse than modest. Quentin could not recall any specifics about the layout, but Eugene kindly described it as "skimpy," with "a single typewriter" and "a couple of chairs."[18] Chester Serkland, a longtime Fargo attorney who spent the summer of 1934 there studying for the North Dakota bar, knew the environs better than the Burdick brothers. The office had "beaten-up desks, old chairs and no rugs," Serkland recalled with a slow, Scandinavian smile that implied irony. Only "a drop cord from the ceiling" and "a small light from the table" lit the room. There were a couple of old, dusty bookshelves that contained copies of the *Northwestern Reports* and statutes of North Dakota, as well as a handful of miscellaneous volumes. That was it. The room barely qualified as a law library by most standards of the day, but it was sufficient for basic research to practice law.[19]

Taylor Crumb, another attorney, shared the second floor. He was an aggressive lawyer with a severe physical handicap. He was "a little hunchbacked fellow," recalled Eugene. "He wheezed because of the restriction caused by the curvature of his spine. He was a little banty rooster lawyer, very tough. He was friendly to his cohorts on the other side of the hallway. They did a lot of interchanging, discussing things and what not. He was not only hunchback, but one leg was shorter than the other. He walked like the Hunchback of Norte Dame."[20]

The law office and its cast of characters would fill a Damon Runyon sketchbook with a Fargo twist. Here in the middle of nowhere, though the nerve center of North Dakota, the likes of Basil Valentine, Waldo Winchester, Dave the Dude, Madam La Gimp and Lame Louise could be observed daily just like on the sidewalks of New York.[21] The rehearsal for the popular musical *Guys and Dolls* could have been conducted in the Burdick law office. Central to the Fargo scene, however, resided young Quentin with rumpled attire, a big heart and a black homburg — symbolic of his trade and ambition.

Although Usher seldom appeared in person, his handiwork remained synonymous with the office and almost everything Quentin touched in his first years of practice. In 1932, the small office became a campaign center for Usher's first bid for Congress. In 1933, the office switched to a place of last resort for mortgaged farmers sent there by Usher, who became the president of the newly organized North Dakota Farmers' Holiday Association. In 1934, the office again became a focal point for Usher's second and successful bid for Congress. "Well, when I was studying there in 1934," recalled Serkland, "we were in a deep depression and there was unemployment. There was an older fellow who was in there steadily — every day by himself. I think he was an old client of Usher's. From the way he talked to me, I think he was a Communist, if not a card-carrying Communist, he believed in it because of all the tough times. He used to carry a newspaper *[The Daily Worker]* with him whenever a new issue came. It was published in New York. He was bothering Quentin with that stuff. Quentin would kick him out and sometimes he would then come over and want to read me a paragraph. Of course, I was new and young and a guest in the office, so I would just listen and hope he'd quit. Quentin, I know, wanted to get rid of him, but the guy just came and came. My recollection is that Quentin didn't want him hanging around any longer and kicked him out. I'm sure he was Usher's client who kind of felt he had a place in there."[22]

After Usher went to Washington in 1935, the office served even more as a quasi-congressional office for the newly elected congressman. "It became somewhat of a focal point of politics," said Eugene, "because Usher was in Congress and Quentin was manning the Fargo office." Eugene, who spent part of that summer there, said there were political allies and hacks always hanging around the small office. "People like Ole Gunvaldson, editor of *The Normanden*, the state's largest Norwegian newspaper, would be there talking politics. There would be quite a few that would come up. They'd be distracting of Quentin's time. Then he had to sift out those who could maybe spare a few dollars from those who couldn't. So he had a rough time practicing law at that time."[23]

Quentin recalled those first years in great detail and with some anger. "It was tough," he began. "There was no money. It was tough." A typical day began about 10:00 a.m., when someone would just drop in to talk about their problems. "We would talk, and talk and talk until maybe noon," recalled Quentin. "Nothing else took place in the office and when noon rolled around, they got up and said if anything comes of it, we will let you know. They would come with no cash, no nothing, just used my time. They stole my time back then right and left."[24]

If clients did pay, they seldom offered cash. "We were paid in chickens generally, or a slab of bacon." Then Quentin's voice raised a notch or two and his words began to summarize: "There were two things clients always told me. First, I voted for your father. Second, I would get a slap on the back and the same words; 'If anything comes of it, I'll call you later.' I heard that a hundred times! They used up the whole morning time, but it didn't make much difference because there wasn't anybody waiting anyway."[25]

In a rare letter written to his mother, Quentin presented a somewhat different interpretation. "I handle all the law work now and try all the cases," boasted a proud son. "In fact, I have tried them all since I came here and I have been most successful. Dad's reputation as a lawyer is based on a great deal of bluff, but if he can keep the public bluffed I guess that's all right too. If he could read the law, no one could ever beat him. Of course, now he is not interested in the law business."[26] Quentin also told Eugene he was the busiest lawyer in Fargo, but that he did not make a dime.[27]

Quentin's early practice centered on crumbs, not big clients. His first law case symbolized the meager work he was engaged in during his early years of practice. It involved a petty crime. Someone stole something because the individual possessed no money to purchase it. Unsure of himself, Quentin took the case only on the promise that his father would be present in the courtroom to provide encouragement and assistance if necessary. When Usher said, "Yeah, I'll be there." Quentin took the case. When the trial day arrived, naturally, Usher didn't show up."[28]

Quentin logged most of his trial time before the justice of the peace, the lowest ladder in the system and much akin to the current small claims court. Lawyers arrived with minimal preparation and little paperwork. The justice of the peace kept his own records. In court, surprises ruled the day. The hearing often became a test of quick on-the-spot thinking rather than expounding on legal precedence. "It would be most informal," recalled Serkland. "Your client or witness would tell a story just like in other courts and other defendants would say anything and then the judge would rule. Bingo!" Money judgments rendered for those who could not pay were never finalized. "Nothing would happen to anybody," recalled Serkland.[29]

Burdick and Serkland basically engaged in the same type of legal practice before the '30s. The two young lawyers often appeared in court together on a weekly basis representing opposing sides. Serkland recalled, "It usually amounted to representing individuals who either had a bill coming from somebody, or wanted to evict someone, or else I was on the other side, [with] the person who was trying to pay the bill or was being evicted and an occasional plaintiff who had been in an accident."[30] Serkland frequently appeared in court representing a particular Fargo landlord who demanded either his tenants pay up or get out. Burdick would be there, too, representing the same tenants who testified that without work, they could not pay the rent and they had no other place to live. The two men also represented thieves caught stealing sheep or a few chickens and a growing number of drunk driving cases tried in County or District Court.

In court, Burdick was a prowler ready to pounce. He was full of nervous energy, but sat otherwise stone serious. His imposing athletic frame, unkempt hair and ill-fitting clothes added to his courtroom image. "Physically, he looked rough," said Serkland. "I don't want to say he didn't dress well, but he didn't dress poorly. Probably somewhat rough outer coat, but much better than Usher. Usher would beat anyone."[31] More to the point, Serkland reported that the congenial and helpful characteristics he observed about Burdick in the office disappeared in trial. The courtroom setting was different. When a trial was in progress, suddenly the whole atmosphere changed. "When we were fighting each other in these petty little cases, he'd be quite aggressive," said Serkland, "not a bit friendly at that point."[32]

Out of court, Burdick approached people differently. Although never gregarious, he appeared more relaxed and outgoing. He was also very approachable, even kind, especially to members of the bar, who for their part demonstrated little time for his politics or his person. Two stories circulated among Fargo lawyers that reveal Burdick's kindness to others in time of need. The first one involved Serkland. Chester Serkland was a Minnesota native of the Red River Valley who came to Fargo in June of 1934, fresh out of law school from Colorado. He wanted to spend the summer studying for the North Dakota bar, to settle down and practice law in Fargo. Serkland made the rounds among several of the city's elite law firms seeking just a desk and access to books so he could soak up some North Dakota law. No one took him. "The two older lawyers I went to were discouraging," noted Serkland, "instead of helping me."[33]

Burdick, who probably had the least of any law firm to offer, gave Serkland free access to his office for the summer. It was a small gesture of professional courtesy to assist a young fellow lawyer who, like Burdick, was also trying hard to make a start in the dark days of the Depression. Serkland never forgot Burdick's kindness as the years passed by. "I've never thought of him in any other way but friendly. Sometimes a little reserved or something, but always friendly. He was never rude to me."[34]

Mart Vogel, a Fargo native, who began to practice law a few years after Burdick and Serkland, recalled another incident in more detail:

> An example of Senator Burdick's kindness was when he agreed to donate blood to a partner of mine in the early 1940s. My partner, George Thorpe, who was the head of the law firm I was employed by, was a very conservative, reactionary person. He was completely opposite from Quentin or his father, Usher, who had a very liberal outlook on life, as well as the practice of law. I don't suppose that my senior partner, who was in his early 60s, ever exchanged a word with Quentin, although he certainly did with Usher. I was asked if I couldn't get somebody to give blood to Thorpe[,] who was about to die. Mrs. Thorpe had called me to say she had been unable to get any of her husband's conservative friends to do the necessary, so would I see what I could do. I called Quentin, and he agreed immediately, even though he knew Mr. Thorpe was a member of the opposite pole of his own thinking. The two of us went over to the hospital and had our blood checked. Mine was not compatible with Thorpe's, but Quentin's was just right. I think, at that time, the job of transferring blood was done directly from donor to patient. Thorpe was well aware that he was getting blood from this wild-eyed radical, Quentin Burdick. Thorpe snapped out of it and lived for several years after that, but we kidded him from time to time about his carrying around the blood of Quentin Burdick. I even think, secretly, he was pleased. I'm sure he also thanked Quentin for this donation, which was somewhat unusual. I think Quentin may have given several pints of the necessary fluid to Thorpe. It certainly is an example of the kind of guy Burdick was, and he remained that way all of his life. He had a very deep feeling for people in trouble and particularly a deep feeling for handicapped persons, families and kids.[35]

Fargo's proximity to Minnesota allowed Burdick to ferry some of his law practice across the Red River, especially at Crookston and Moorhead, the county seats of Polk and Clay counties. Burdick soon found himself practicing law in Minnesota without a license. He never took the time to take the Minnesota bar examination, against the advice of his law classmates. Burdick, instead, found another way to keep his Minnesota practice legal. He called Morteer Skewes, his law school roommate, who was licensed in Minnesota and asked if he could use his name to practice law in Minnesota. "He used my name all the time on pleadings," recalled Skewes with a chuckle. "I was involved in a lot of litigation up there I didn't know anything about."[36] The practice was not uncommon, but one day Skewes inquired if one of these times he might be called to appear in court. Burdick immediately reassured him that it would never happen and, of course, it never did.[37]

Burdick continued to operate a solo law practice in Fargo until he was hired as general consul for the North Dakota Farmers Union in the late 1940s. The Fargo office changed little in appearance from Usher's day. The desk stayed piled with unsorted papers. There was no clerical help. The room was dark. The furnishings remained skimpy and unkempt. Friends recall watching Burdick type his own pleadings on an old, black typewriter. Burdick supplemented his legal practice by preparing tax returns for clients and anyone else who came through the door. He soon found himself extremely busy with tax work from January to April; the large volume of returns produced badly needed additional income for his family.[38]

Burdick made several appearances before the North Dakota Supreme Court in the ensuing years. The highest state court consisted of five justices, and although more formal than the Cass County justice of the peace setting, it operated without any supportive legal staff or much of the present modern court structure. The Burdick name was well known among the Supreme Court judges. Associate Justice John Burke, of course, was almost family. It never bothered Usher to give him advanced notice of Quentin's appearances.

One North Dakota Supreme Court case stands out in significance above the others. *Heuer v. Heuer* was heard before the Court on March 28, 1934. The case was heard on appeal from the Cass County District Court. Quentin Burdick represented William Heuer, the plaintiff. Sure & Murphy of Fargo represented Henry Heuer, the appellant, uncle of William. The lower court ruled for the plaintiff and the defendant appealed.

The facts in the case were clear. Carl Heuer (father of William and brother of Henry) purchased land in Cass County in 1910. When William married shortly thereafter, he and his wife moved onto the land with his father. It became their home for 30 years. They made many improvements, paid the annual property taxes and raised a family of 11 children. The land in question became their home. Although Carl told William the farm was his, he also explained to him that he would hold the deed so that his son would never lose or sell it. In 1919, Carl bought more land and borrowed the money from his brother Henry. He mortgaged the land he gave to William to secure the loan. Carl died intestate in 1930 and the deed was not filed until after his death.

On the surface, the case appeared a simple one. The oral transfer of land was insufficient to meet the legal requirements of the statute of frauds. The law required that any transfer of real property must be in writing in order to be effective. Carl did not meet that standard and the gift by parol — word of mouth — was void based on the law. Henry, as brother, was entitled to a portion of the property. The land did not belong to William because there was no written record to prove title to the land.

The case under normal circumstance should have been decided strictly on the statute of frauds. Courts in those days were very supportive of those with moneyed interests. Henry was the lender. There was no deed to support William's claim to ownership of the land. Nevertheless, Burdick won the case at the District Court level. He introduced other facts and circumstances that demonstrated that the law was intended to be a shield, not a sword. He presented all sorts of relevant testimony from neighbors and even Carl, who was deceased. Burdick got away with that by arguing that another law, the Dead Man's statute, which prohibited the use of statements of the deceased in court, did not apply in this case because the action was between a donee (recipient) and a lender, not between someone and the heirs of the deceased person. The evidence introduced by Burdick proved that many people knew that Carl gave the land to William. The District Court agreed with Burdick and William kept the land.

Appeals to the Supreme Court often are decided on technical points of law rather than human circumstances. Usher sensed this might occur in this instance, so he did a little pretrial lobbying on his son's behalf. He wrote Justice Burke in January 1934 about the case. "When you get a chance to see the case of *Heuer v. Heuer*, be sure to look into this carefully as it might not receive your careful inspection in the natural hurry in that court," wrote Usher. "This is a meritorious case and I believe the facts and the law are such that the court will grant relief. All I ask is that you be sure to consider it, no matter who is assigned to write the opinion."[39] Burke quickly responded in a short, handwritten note: "You can be sure that I will give the case studious attention."[40]

In a unanimous 4-0 decision, the North Dakota Supreme Court affirmed the lower court ruling. "The question here," wrote Justice William Nuessle, "is as to whether a valid title may be predicated upon the facts and circumstances established in the record."[41] Nuessle wrote and Justices Alexander Burr, Burke and Adolph Christianson concurred that title could be established. "We hold, as did the trial court, that the plaintiff has sustained the burden that was placed upon him and has established his case by that weight of the evidence which the law requires."[42]

"The court ruled yes, indeed, this fellow did own it," said Eugene. "Quentin tried the case and won it. He became well-recognized as a very competent lawyer as a result of the case." Eugene went on to explain that the significance of the case was that it established the principle of estoppel, "which is a stop to deny that he made the transfer. In other words he was estopping the donor or the people claiming under the donor from claiming that he had not made a transfer. When you make a representation that someone relies on to their detriment, that is known as estoppel, so it treats it as a fact even though it's not a fact."[43]

Garry Pearson, a University of North Dakota law professor and prominent Grand Forks estate lawyer, also commented on the case. "There is no new principle of law involved, nor is there anything particularly unique in the underlying story about how the uncle attempts to shaft his nephew," wrote Pearson. What impressed Pearson were the trial lawyer skills of Burdick. "This case could have gone the other way had it not been properly tried, and even then, given the prevailing mood of the courts, could easily have been lost even if Clarence Darrow had represented William."[44]

Burdick's early Fargo law practice, however, stood out more for his representation of two different groups during the Depression than for his appearances before the state Supreme Court. The first group was the growing number of North Dakota farmers who were being foreclosed on throughout the state. The second group consisted of Fargo truck drivers fighting for a collective bargaining agreement and the legal right to strike. Representing busted farmers was assigned to Quentin by his father. There was little, if any, discussion. As Usher traveled around as the first president of the North Dakota Farmers' Holiday Association in 1933, he simply would announce that any farmer seeking legal representation should contact Quentin in Fargo. Fargo Teamsters sought out Quentin because he was the one city attorney who most identified with their plight and political situation.

Usher Burdick reflected about 1933 as he had done previously in 1932. He wrote about the same themes again — country and family — and he clearly seemed upbeat about the progress made in one year with both. As the nation rose slowly from the depths of the Depression, Quentin and Eugene also were on the move. "Quentin has made good as a lawyer," Usher noted with pride, "and has now built up a reputation in criminal and equity cases that will assure him a promising and paying law practice." Eugene was hard at work completing his schooling at Minnesota and he would be headed back to North Dakota in 1935. Although Usher observed that Eugene was "still showing signs of a gifted artist" like his mother, Emma, "he refuses to study the subject."[45]

Usher, as father, harbored no doubts about his two sons' future personal and professional relationship. Such relationships proved difficult. The brothers were simply incompatible. "I am of the opinion," Usher observed, "that Quentin and Eugene will not mix well. Each is an intense individual and neither can understand why the other should know anything."[46] Usher's discerning observation then played out in full view years later among their fellow North Dakota lawyers. "I knew the judge and Quentin," observed Bob Vogel, an associate justice of the Supreme Court, "and there were never two brothers more unlike. One was rather formal and very dignified, and Quentin was relaxed and common."[47]

Holiday for Farmers

During the intense heat of McCarthyism in the '50s, Mrs. Helen Wood Birnie of Long Beach, California, testified before a subcommittee of the House Un-American Committee in Chicago. She pointed her finger directly at the North Dakota Farmers' Holiday Association and testified that it had served as a front for Communist Party agitation in North Dakota during the early '30s. The testimony of Wood Birnie, a former Communist, never made national headlines. There were much bigger fish to fry in the federal government and the entertainment industry. Her testimony did bring, however, an instant retort from Congressman Usher Burdick, who played a key role in the organization.[48]

"She is about as near the truth as the North Pole is to the South Pole," retorted an angry Burdick. He lambasted the charge on radio and wrote in more detail in his March 24, 1954, newsletter. "I had more to do with the organization of the North Dakota Holiday Association than anyone else, and was elected the first president of it. It was not organized by communists, but by good loyal American citizens." Burdick went on to explain how bad things were and what actually happened. "In North Dakota foreclosures and dispossessions were rampant. ... We didn't propose to repudiate our debts, but wanted time until conditions changed. Later some communists did get into it, as they try to do in all organizations, including this government. As president of the group I had more trouble with the communists than I did with the Union Central Life Insurance Company, which was carrying on a spree of wholesale foreclosures."[49]

Burdick also gave a brief historical sketch of the organization's beginnings and goals. The name holiday was patterned after a procedure used in a country bank in Iowa. When a large number of depositors began to withdraw all their money, bank officials declared a holiday and closed the doors. In a few days, enough cash was secured to reopen, but when most depositors learned that their deposits were secure, they agreed to keep the money in the bank. The bank holiday precipitated an unprecedented step with a happy ending. "Farmers and businessmen in Iowa got together and organized a 'Holiday Association' as they reasoned that if a holiday could save banks it could save farms," said Burdick.[50]

The North Dakota Farmers' Holiday Association began overnight during the summer of 1932. The first meeting, in late July, was promoted by the North Dakota Farmers Union. The call, however, attracted a wide range of farmers, Leaguers and politicians. The Farmers' Holiday tent was wide open, and except for a few members of the North Dakota Farm Bureau, included a broad range of farmer interests and county representation. A second meeting took place in early January 1933. Membership multiplied rapidly, 46,000 in six months, and peaking at 70,000 by the end of the year.[51] Usher Burdick was elected temporary president at the first meeting and permanent president at the second meeting. "I spent the entire year speaking for the Holiday Association," he wrote privately, "and at the close of the campaign December 23, 1933, we had succeeded in educating the people of North Dakota to stop foreclosures and dispossessions. Governor Langer worked well with us during the year and actually has done more for poor people than any governor in the history of the Territory and State."[52]

The North Dakota chapter, like its Iowa parent, started on a platform of market strikes. In other words, farmers called for a holiday on the sale of their produce until prices rose higher. When that did not work and prices fell lower, the farmers shifted to more basic concerns. The Farmers' Holiday soon became most identified with taking whatever steps were necessary to halt involuntary sales, foreclosures and evictions. Keeping the farmer and his family on the farm until the Depression was over became central to their organization and a key to their popularity. *Moratorium* became the buzz-word in North Dakota, and Burdick led the charge. "We held meetings and talked to people of the State until there was built up a powerful public opinion against foreclosures. William Langer was governor of the State at that time, and to make our effort to stop foreclosures more effective I prepared a moratorium, which the governor signed and supported with the State Militia whenever it was found necessary. The foreclosures stopped. The loan companies howled and wailed, but we explained to them that if they would be patient the day would come when they would all get their money, and that no farm families would be hustled out of their homes and carted to the cities to swell the unemployment ranks and put a further strain on public relief."[53]

As federal aid poured into North Dakota, the membership of the Farmers'

Holiday Association declined as rapidly as it began. But there were other factors for the decline, too. Farm conditions improved. It rained again. War threats in Europe bolstered the economy. The North Dakota Farmers Union grew in numbers, programs and services. Finally, new leaders lacked the firepower of men such as Usher Burdick. As a newly elected congressman, he took their concerns to Washington, but replacements lacked his energy and charisma.[54]

The Burdick family participation in the North Dakota Farmers' Holiday Association was significant in many ways. First and foremost, it gave Usher a platform. At age 53, he suddenly reappeared on the political stage. He loved the limelight and relished the passion of the crowds. Here was a Chautauqualike speaker with a flair for theatrics, standing alone in front of a captivated audience of foreclosed farmers. This was as good as it gets. There was no better setting for Usher before this time, nor would there be ever after. This was drama, his finest hour, and one that only he was perfectly dressed to play. No costume designer could have done better.

Usher began each rally with a few stories. Stories told in simple language that carried an unmistaken message. The messenger always offered hope, never despair. Times would get better if the farmers would just stick together. Eugene, who traveled with his father during the summer, recalled his favorite story that his father often told:

> There was a farmer that was taking a trip to town with his cream can. There had been a heavy rain the night before and the stream was full. As he rattled through the creek bed, the cover of the cream can fell off and in floated a couple of frogs. Both of the frogs tried to escape, but neither could find a way out. "Well, this is curtains for me," said one frog to the other. Then he bellied up, drowned and died. "No way," said the other frog. "I'm going to fight it out to the end." So he thrashed and kicked and thrashed and kicked all the way to town. When he got to town the farmer began to pour out the cream. The dead frog came out, but the other frog was sitting up on a ball of butter that he'd churned himself.[55]

The farmers understood the story. "The morale is not to give up. Keep fighting because there will be someway to get out of this. Keep thrashing," said Eugene. "Keep thrashing."[56] When the talk was over and questions were answered, Usher and his entourage would pass the hat. They asked for a 50-cent donation, which entitled each contributor to full membership in the Holiday Association. A sign-up sheet was also circulated to register those who made contributions. Some signed it while others did not. After a bit of food and more talk, they moved on slowly to another small town. The rallies never stopped and

Usher never quit telling stories.

The most volatile incident occurred at Wing, North Dakota. Located in Burleigh County, north of the state capital in Bismarck, Wing, with a population of about 200, was typical of the small villages where many of the Holiday rallies were held. Wing, however, was ripe with violence. It was a planned attempt by Communist organizers to get Czar Burdick and put down his message of hope before a large gathering of farmers. Mother Bloor, a member of the Communist Party who operated out of Plentywood, Montana (straight west of Williston), spearheaded the plot. "There were a lot of farmers there that were ready to go Communist," recalled Eugene. "In fact, a lot of them had declared that ... the only way they would succeed was to have forcible overthrow of the government. They were really violent, I mean violent, not vehement."[57]

Usher and Eugene drove into Wing without any knowledge of what was planned. The local Council for Defense, the county organization for the Holiday Association, which organized the event, did not have a clue, either. As Usher began to address the crowd, hecklers began to interrupt him. This was a hostile crowd. He soon found himself bombarded by questions about where this country was heading. The more he talked, the more questions he had to answer. The crowd became restless as the dialogue went back and forth. The hecklers wanted to know why it was better to work within the American system of government than to abandon it. Many did not buy the story of the frogs. Each of their questions brought longer answers. The crowd listened intensely as the Communists scored points and Burdick scored points. "It took him five hours of nonstop talking to the group before they came around," stated Eugene. "That was the longest speech that I've heard. He stayed with them. In the end, he had all of them with him. That's one of the most significant events I ever saw in North Dakota politics. It proved to one and all that Burdick was not a Communist, because he was dressed down as being the czar, something to be gotten rid of. They never attacked him physically with guns or anything, but it wouldn't have surprised me if they had now in retrospect," said Eugene.[58]

Usher recalled the Wing incident in his response to Wood Birnie's allegations. "There were communists in the Holiday Association because they could not be kept out," admitted Burdick. "I knew their plan and worked night and day to circumvent them. I clashed with them time and again at public meetings, for I was well aware of the criticism they had leveled against me. At one meeting they said, 'Burdick, you are trying to patch up this old machine of government, when you ought to spend your time developing a new government.' I answered by saying, 'How are you proposing to get rid of the present government?' The reply was 'By force.' I promptly remarked that they couldn't muster enough force to take the village of Wing [then with a population of less than 100]."[59]

There was Burdick family significance to Usher's leadership in the Farmers' Holiday as well. His appearances offered a unique opportunity for his sons to see their father perform. Sure, they could recall stories about his oratory growing up as young boys in Williston. But now father and sons were all older. The times were different, too, and this was high drama. No replays. Usher's sons witnessed firsthand the rare forensic skills of their father in person. The experience was very special. At no time in their entire lives were the Burdick boys more proud of Usher as when he stood in front of North Dakota's farmers in the heat and dust of the early '30s. Eugene spent more time traveling with Usher than Quentin. He took photographs and stored memories of summertime spent with him. Quentin attended the first Farmers' Holiday rally and a few others, but more importantly, he became his father's self-appointed legal counsel to the entire organization.

Quentin Burdick, through Usher's announcements at rally after rally, quickly became the official attorney for the North Dakota Farmers' Holiday Association. There was no formal vote of the organization, just Usher's instructions. When Usher was asked about an upcoming sheriff's sale or an eviction, he simply referred the party to his son, Quentin the lawyer, in Fargo. Since there are no preserved records of the Holiday Association or Burdick legal files, it is impossible to reconstruct the exact nature or amount of legal work Quentin performed for the Farmers' Holiday Association. How many farmers actually went to him for advice or legal action is unknown.

Interview questions about his legal work yielded only meager results.

"I was the attorney for the Farm Holiday boys," recalled Quentin, "with portfolio but without money." It was a general statement he repeated, but it was never punctuated with specifics. "There were some legal questions, of course, trespassing at times and all that stuff. I got a little smattering of law from them but no money," Quentin replied. In response to another question, regarding stopping foreclosures, evictions, etc., he said, "Oh, hell, yes, all of them. More than not they would come to court at some stage. Those were tough days."[60]

Eugene's version collaborated how the referrals began and expanded on the amount of work involved. "At these meetings, they'd say, 'What can I do? The sheriff is having a sale at our farm next week. What can I do?' And, my father would reply, 'Talk to Quentin in Fargo.'" Eugene said he heard this question again and again while traveling with his father. "Quentin handled hundreds of cases like this," he said, "maybe thousands."[61]

Whether Quentin stopped one farm foreclosure or hundreds, the legal relationship with the Holiday Association reaped long-term benefits, including a tremendous legal education. Here was a young attorney fresh out of law school thrown into one of the most controversial public debates of the Depression. Should debt be postponed until good economic times return? He learned firsthand the personal suffering of debt and the laws of bankruptcy that governed and failed to govern. He met a wide variety of clients, district judges and more county sheriffs than most of his bar brothers. He tasted grass-roots participatory democracy, although he never earned a dime from his legal work. In addition, there were political IOUs. Quentin Burdick, like his father, bore an institutional mark stamped with a Holiday Association tattoo. He was one of them. He was their attorney and they never forgot his efforts on their behalf. The negative side, of course, was the radical nature of the organization. It put him left of most of his contemporaries and even branded him with Communist activities. In North Dakota, Quentin, like Usher, was a radical.

Fargo Strikers

Fargoans snuggled safely in their homes as the evening of January 21, 1935, approached. It was Monday and a bitter, still cold hung heavily over the city. Bright northern lights could be seen dancing across the clear sky as one drove north on Highway 81. It would be a lot colder come Tuesday morning as the weatherman predicted an overnight low of minus 32 degrees. Under normal winter conditions, the city stoked approximately 1,500 tons of coal per day. But this was the end of January and winter weather in North Dakota was never normal. Never. Fargo furnaces would burn a lot more coal than normal this week in January 1935. A lot more, or would they?

Suddenly, although not totally unexpectedly, the security of Fargo's safe, warm residences was placed in jeopardy. Late Monday afternoon, 300 Fargo truck drivers, members of Drivers Union 173, walked off their jobs. They were on strike and served notice that starting Tuesday morning, no more coal or ice would be delivered until Fargo coal and ice companies met their demands. It was a propitious time for Fargo truck drivers to call a strike. They sought finally to achieve union representation now guaranteed by federal law. It was an awful time, however, for the city of Fargo to be without heat. The rights of union recognition would soon clash with the needs of public safety.

In the national arena, the Fargo strike was not an isolated occurrence in 1935. Times were changing. The Democratic administration of Franklin Roosevelt ushered in a new era for organized labor. Suddenly the federal government became a friend of labor. The NRA, established in 1933, gave American labor unions new political and legal power. According to North Dakota historian

D. Jerome Tweton, labor "gained the right to organize and bargain collectively through representatives of the workers' own choosing and a prohibition of the 'yellow dog' or anti-union contract."[62] National union membership soared from 3.2 million in 1933 to more than 9 million by 1940.[63] The Fargo Trades and Assembly suddenly came alive with new hopes and new members. Young union members, especially among truck drivers, warehousemen and chauffeurs, infused the older membership with new ideas and more than 400 new members. Labor was on the move even in North Dakota's winter cold.[64]

As the striking truck drivers abandoned their trucks, union leaders presented a list of four demands to the Fargo companies. If not met, the strike would continue indefinitely regardless of the cold. If the demands were met, the strikers would return immediately to work. The four demands were:

1. The recognition of Local 173 as the legal bargaining agent for the truck drivers.
2. The recognition of seniority rights for union members.
3. The rehiring of several drivers who were fired for union activities.
4. The establishment of a board of arbitration to settle wages and other unresolved matters.[65]

Fargoans awoke Tuesday to a coal crisis. The *Fargo Forum* reported that there were already 750 homes out of coal and that police protection to allow one truck per company to deliver coal on an emergency basis was being thwarted by large numbers of union members. Other scattered incidents caused some concern. An empty coal truck was found overturned in a company lot. Union members drove continually around city streets in two large trucks to prevent any coal deliveries.[66] All strike news became Page One material. The message came across clearly. The strike was causing hardships on the citizenry. Violence was commencing. Nowhere was the plight and hardships of the strikers reported. The safety of Fargo was in jeopardy and the union caused it.

Two individuals emerged as key players in the infant strike. A.R. Bergesen, a conservative Republican and Cass County state's attorney, became almost immediately the leading spokesman to end the Fargo strike. By day two of the strike, Bergesen threatened wholesale arrests for striking drivers if they continued their tactics of threatening scabs and ignoring police protection for emergency deliveries of coal. He took this action, in part, because he believed strongly that the strike was wrong, but also because he was concerned about keeping the peace. Fargo police convinced him that the matter would soon get out of control. They expressed concern that they were unable to cope with the situation. There were too many union members and too few policemen. He was the chief law enforcement officer for the county and he quickly took the initiative.[67]

Miles (Mickey) Dunne of Minneapolis emerged as the leading union strategist. His official title was business agent of Local 173. He was one of the infamous Irish Dunne brothers of Minneapolis, a dissident Trotskyite and a major participant in the 1934 Minneapolis truck drivers strike — a strike characterized by one historian as one that "lasted thirty-six days and had cost ... the city $50,000.00. Bank clearings during the strike were down $3,000.00 a day, approximately $5,000.00 was lost in wages, and the maintenance of the National Guard had cost the taxpayers over $300,000.00. The violence had left four dead and scores injured."[68]

Dunne left the Twin Cities to insure a union strike victory in Fargo. His labor experience made him a strong leader. He loved playing center stage. Although he studied to be an actor as a young boy, he spent most of his early years as a Twin Cities coal truck driver. His participation in strikes as an adult compensated his adolescent urge to act. He usually performed well under pressure. Dunne was short, with slick hair, and he wore fancy clothes. He was Irish to the core. One journalist described him as "convivial, fond of companionable drinking, prize fights, football, hunting and fishing." There was nothing more Irish than his quick wit and vitriolic tongue, which proved formidable against stubborn adversaries. He also opined a spirited editorial. Dunne's leadership was a key factor to Local Union 173's success.[69]

Tensions eased somewhat during the remainder of the week. Both sides waited for the other to make the first move. Union officials prepared a brief statement to explain the purpose of the strike. They reiterated that the strike was about gaining union representation, not about raising the current hourly wage of 45 cents. As a concession to public safety, the union also agreed to a 24-hour truce on Wednesday to allow coal to be delivered to those most in need.[70] At the same time, the union pressed forward with demands and demonstrations. Strikers took to the streets and marched peacefully through Fargo. Their numbers were estimated to be about 200, but when they passed the North Dakota Agricultural College campus on the city's northwest side, students and faculty joined the march. Together, as they turned south back toward downtown, they were heard singing: "We want union recognition!"[71] In other developments, the union rejected management's proposal to call off the strike if they would agree to an election monitored by the National Labor Relations Board.[72] It was too late for that.

The cold continued as the weekend neared. The strike remained in full force, but there were no more reported incidents of violence or harassment.

Both sides were talking. Union officials noted an increasing number of police vehicles stationed outside of their headquarters at 514½ First Avenue North, but no arrests had been made. According to plan, the first week of the strike would end on Sunday, a day of rest for all. Monday would take care of itself and maybe calm, compromise and normal coal deliveries would prevail. Fargo needed the black chunks to stay warm.

But a different sequence of events occurred. Sunday was ugly, very ugly. By day's end, there were almost 100 union members squeezed into the second floor of the Cass County jail. What began as a day of rest suddenly exploded into a day of violence. The basic facts of what happened were never in question. The reasons why it happened or who bore the responsibility for what happened were never agreed upon. The day pitted nonunion workers and the Fargo police against union members and their families. It was one of Fargo's darkest days. It was far worse than anyone could have imagined. Sunday, January 27, 1935, Fargo exploded.

The day began peacefully for Local Union 173 and their families. It always did on Sundays when union members and their families gathered at union headquarters above the Rusch Printing Company and across the street from the Donaldson Hotel for a social gathering. It was a day of rest, and considering the hardships of the past week, a special time for solidarity and renewal. The upstairs hall was packed from wall to wall as women worked in the kitchen to prepare a warm meal and youngsters ran about playing games. Most of the men seemed oblivious to both the women's work and the children's noise. More important matters weighed on their minds. Some chatted about the strike and swapped stories. In one corner, an elderly guest speaker tried to get the men's attention. He was a New Deal man, a fervent employee of the Federal Emergency Relief Administration (FERA) who was attempting to organize a class to study the history of American labor.[73]

The Fargo Labor Hall stood as a symbol of Depression life for working families in Fargo. "What comes to mind graphically about the Depression," recalled Burdick, "was the second floor building for working people, union people and otherwise." He was sometimes present at the Sunday gatherings and said it was a special place where "they would bring their families, wives and children. It was a community kitchen. I remember that just like it was yesterday."[74]

Six hours that Sunday changed the Union Hall and crowded Burdick's memory with a more painful one. After dinner, word reached the Union Hall that a crew hired by the Moorhead Ice Company was loading ice at the Red River. Many union members grabbed their hats, coats and some clubs and drove quickly to the river site. They were on strike. No ice was going to be loaded or delivered until the strike was settled, even on Sunday. In less than an hour, between 50 and 80 union members surrounded the ice laborers. They told them to stop working. Court testimony later documented that the strikers repeatedly yelled such things as: "This is your last load;" "Go home and don't come back;" "We mean business. No fooling;" "If you come back, it will be just too bad for you;" "You are nothing but a bunch of rats;" "You better quit or we will make you."[75]

Large numbers of the Fargo police force arrived within an hour of the fracas. They dispersed the crowd and separated the two sides. They made several arrests, charging the strikers with causing a riot. They also searched union members and confiscated a number of wooden sticks and lead pipes. Although most of the confrontation ceased before they arrived, a few strikers resisted arrest. According to union sources, a policeman clubbed Jack Eastman (one of the union strikers) over his head, splitting it open.[76] Eastman was one of the strikers arrested and hauled off to jail. The strike became a police versus union fight.

More police (regular and special), numbering more than 300, quickly drove to the Union Hall and surrounded the Rusch Building. The scene took on more of an atmosphere of war than civil unrest. It was unbelievable. As the police waited, a couple a regular Fargo police officers climbed the stairs to the Union Hall and knocked on the door. They demanded the immediate arrest of the union leaders. Those most responsible for inciting the riot, they believed, were now hiding among the women and children. When voices inside called out demanding to see a warrant, none was produced by the two officers. The scene shifted to a tense standoff between the police and the union members and their families. The police could not enter. The union could not leave.

At some point in the next hour, Fargo police decided to employ a second strategy. It was a radical decision. If the union leaders would not surrender, the police would raid Union Hall. It was reported by several that they heard Officer Andrew Quam give what amounted to "an added warning" to the union crowd and then he "lifted the tear gas gun" and "fired bombs through the upper parts of the windows."[77] Miles Dunne wrote the union account of what happened next:

> Before the women and children could be rushed to safety tear gas bombs began to crash through the windows and pandemonium reigned where all had been quiet and pleasant only a few minutes before. An eight year old boy was struck in the face by a bomb and badly injured. A tiny infant was seen in her mother's arms choking and gasping for breath. The FERA instructor, an aged gentleman struggled toward the doorway. As the gas forced the workers from the hall the police herded the men into the street,

together with a number of bystanders who happened to get in their way, and paraded them with much cursing and jeering to jail.[78]

Dunne's prose did not exaggerate the raid. A shaken reporter for the *Fargo Forum* waited in the cold for the first sign of activity in the aftermath of the tear gas volley. His words, like Dunne's, captured the exodus: "The officers formed a gauntlet from the hall entrance to the streets, cleared a space there to assemble the prisoners and soon they came staggering down the stairs eyes straining from the effects of the gas, many walking unsteadily — women not molested — but men were marshaled into a line almost a block long."[79]

Sunday night ended much differently than it had begun. It was still winter in January, of course, but for those concerned about the strike on both sides, things had changed dramatically. Many strikers of Local Union 173 were now under arrest. The numbers of detainees were unprecedented, almost 100 members. They were transported to the Cass County jail on Fargo's near south side. The second floor suddenly took on the appearance of a college dormitory rather than a North Dakota county jail. The second floor proved inadequate for the crowd. With only 20 bunks available, the majority simply sprawled out on the cold, concrete floor and tried to sleep.[80] In the meantime, the arresting officers pored over a cache of union records and weapons seized from the Union Hall in the state attorney's office in the courthouse building next door.[81] The Fargo coal strike was headed to court.

It is not clear when Quentin Burdick first learned of the events, but by Sunday evening, he became the union's attorney. During a 1992 interview, Burdick delivered a long and detailed narration about that Sunday of some 56 years before. His reply was instant, detailed and quite emotional. "We had an eager beaver as a police officer, Andy Quam," began Burdick.

> Have you heard of him? He was going to fix those people. Now remember, there is just families up there. Nothing was going on. He claimed there were some clubs up there. There may have been some clubs, but they weren't being used. He came down there with his squad and they shot tear gas bombs through the windows. There was nothing up there!

Burdick's speech quickened as he continued. "Quam came down the stairs and separated the women and children. A lot of the men were lined up just like POWs. Now Quam was supposed to be a hero or something for doing that of course. Now bear in mind, there was nothing going on up there. No speeches. No nothing. This was even Sunday that they made the arrests."[82]

Burdick arrived at the jail sometime late that afternoon or early evening. He came at the behest of union members and their families. "There were so many of them they didn't have room for them so they had to select the ones they wanted to put in jail," recalled Burdick. "Then the rest came to me. Women crying. Kids crying! 'Do something.' I scurried around. ... I'm trying to give you a picture of that day. This was raw dope. Every place you went there was crying. The wives, mothers and kids were crying. Things were not good at all."[83]

The state wasted little time in arraigning the 94 jailed strikers. The Monday hearing originally scheduled for the county courtroom was hurriedly moved to the larger District Court chambers because of the huge crowd of spectators. These were primarily the wives and relatives of the accused who wanted to see their loved ones and find out what charges were being made against them. Bergesen represented the state and the North Dakota National Guard sent an official observer. Keeping the peace in Fargo evidently was now becoming a state issue as well. "Quentin Burdick was counsel for all of the Union members," noted the *Fargo Forum*, "and any others who cared to accept his services."[84]

The proceedings took little time. Each of the defendants were charged with "rout," a lesser charge than "riot." Under North Dakota law, rout was a misdemeanor; if convicted, the guilty would be fined from $100 to $500, and would serve from one day to one year in jail. To save time, the court brought the accused in groups of 10 to 20 men before the judge. The common charges were read and each defendant pleaded not guilty. The crowd, to the objection of the court, cheered when certain names were read off or when they pled not guilty. O.L. Aasgaard, the elderly FERA employee, was released by the judge. He broke no North Dakota law on Sunday for his attempt to organize a labor history class. The records note, however, that another Norwegian-American, Jasper Haaland of Grandin, North Dakota, an avowed Communist, was among those not released. Trial date was set for Thursday, February 14, 1935, in Cass County Court with Judge P.M. Paulson to preside.[85]

Burdick worked overtime in the 16 days prior to the scheduled trial. There was much work to be accomplished. His first priority centered on the release of the dozens of union members in jail. The work involved raising bail money and attending bond hearings in court. His hard work paid off. On the eve of the trial, only four men of the original 94 were still incarcerated. They were Hugh Grieves (laborer), Hugh Hughes (butter maker), Chris Sorum (laborer) and Carl Pilcher (truck driver).[86]

Burdick's second task was more political. He did not want more strikers charged with additional crimes. Enough was enough. Tempers ran high, however, and more altercations took place. Strikers beat up Sven Erdahl, a driver for the Gate City Fuel Company; Charles Hail, a scab (strike-breaker), who was caught delivering coal to the First Baptist Church; and Martin Kisser at the

Newberry Store.[87] Although not every incident resulted in an arrest, some did, each requiring legal representation and the detailed process of trying to bail them out. Some arrested were repeaters. Ernest Goldschmidtz, for example, was among the original group arrested Sunday, but Burdick posted bail and he was released. On February 8, Goldschmidtz was arrested again for beating up a coal truck driver at the corner of Tenth Street and Thirteenth Avenue North. This time, the beating was more severe and the charges more serious. He was charged with aggravated assault and battery — a felony — and held under a $1,000 bail. Burdick requested a preliminary hearing at the arraignment, but posted no bail. Goldschmidtz stayed in jail this time. Burdick also kept Dunne out of Fargo. He housed him in the Comstock Hotel in Moorhead and told him to stay there.[88]

Burdick's third task was trial preparation for his biggest case since coming to Fargo. He did not want to lose. Never a stickler for detail, he secured the services of fellow attorney Lee Brooks. Brooks help put together the defense case, including the interviewing of key witnesses, and he would also assist Burdick in the trial proceedings. This was a huge case and Burdick realized the necessity of securing help. He could not do it all himself. Together Burdick and Brooks would represent the union against Bergesen and Assistant State's Attorney Roy Redetzke, Usher's former law partner.

The trial lasted six days. It was almost exclusively a prosecution show. The state called more than 40 witnesses and introduced mounds of physical evidence. The defense produced only two witnesses and took less than two hours to present its entire case. The prosecution succeeded in tying physical evidence seized at the Union Hall with those strikers who went to the river. The defense objected time and time again —sometimes even shouting at the court — to the introduction of seized records and alleged weapons. Judge Paulson, however, ruled consistently for the prosecution. Burdick won only one motion during the entire trial. It was a motion to dismiss charges against two of the defendants because there was no evidence to place them at the scene. When the prosecution made no objection, Paulson accepted the motion.

The trial produced a couple of humorous sidebars. On the first morning of the trial, Judge Paulson stopped the proceedings to deal with another strike-related issue. Bergesen wanted him to issue warrants against four members of the union for printing and distributing a special one-page strike bulletin in Fargo. The state's attorney wanted to slap them with contempt of court charges. Burdick objected and when he explained that Dunne was writing the sheet from his Minnesota hotel room, Paulson released them without penalty. The mysterious Dunne fellow, however, perked Paulson's interest, so he left the bench and went to his office and called him. He asked Dunne if he would voluntarily come across the river to testify. Dunne said, "No." Paulson then offered him immunity if he came over. Dunne still refused. Paulson then instructed the four Fargo men to make sure that no further articles were published. He was concerned that it might influence the jury. Dunne kept writing and the union continued to publish and distribute it.[89] On Saturday, Paulson again recessed the court. It was a matter of great importance. Henry Ferderer of Mandan and Matilda Meyer Wise of Fargo sat patiently waiting in his office to be married.[90]

Jury deliberations consumed 21 hours. At first, the jury peppered Paulson with questions primarily about the legal definitions of the charges. The verdict was never in doubt. The jury found all 16 defendants guilty as charged on the eighth ballot. There was only one juror who voted consistently for acquittal, and never more than three. Union leaders William Cruden, Austin Swalde and Hugh Hughes were sentenced to six months in jail. The other 13 were sentenced each to two months in jail.[91] The state easily won its case.

What happened?

The prosecution repeatedly told the jury that this case was not about the legal right of Local Union 173 to unionize. Redetzke reiterated the claim one more time in his closing remarks: "The right to work for the support of his family regardless of whether he belongs to a union or not had not been tread upon."[92] Redetzke was dead wrong. The whole case, indeed the whole episode, centered about the right of the union not to deliver coal in the cold of North Dakota winter. The jury, though, agreed with Redetzke, and so did the vast majority of the city's residences. The union strike was wrong and the weapons confiscated from their den were evidence enough to convict them of a crime against the citizens of Fargo. It was their own fault and they were punished for it.

The defense spared no words in condemning the verdict. "There was no riot on the river on January 27," said an angry Brooks, "until the police and special police arrived and started one." Burdick took another shot at the Fargo Police Department. "Why were special police, armed with clubs, stationed across from the union hall two days before the alleged riot?" he asked. Both men believed the police were out to get the union and to bust it. They precipitated the riot and the raid on union headquarters proved it. The weapons they confiscated had nothing to do with what happened at the river. The state's case was circumstantial, but the jury bought the prosecution's argument. As for the trial itself, Burdick minced no words: "I have seen the biggest circus I ever saw in this courtroom," he began. "The state has brought in everything but the elephants and a brass band in an attempt to impress the jury. I have never seen such a fragmentary case brought into court."[93]

The union joined their attorneys in condemning the whole affair. "Local

173 is making a fight that the whole labor movement can well be proud of," wrote Dunne from his Moorhead hideaway. "We are fighting against the greatest odds. All the combined power of the organized employers — the banks as well as their press, the *Fargo Forum* — have been turned against us."[94]

The strike aftermath lingered in Fargo. Speakers for both sides made the rounds at various public forums. In April, Eli Weston, who represented the employers during the strike, spoke before the Fargo Kiwanis Club. He posed a broader picture of a titanic struggle taking place between the forces of good and evil — good being represented by the American system of government and evil by the spread of European Communism. He made three bold accusations. First, the Fargo strike was "absolutely controlled and managed by Communists." Second, there were more Communists hard at work in seven North Dakota counties (Bottineau, Mountrail, Burke, McKenzie, Williams, Slope and Bowman), especially "among school children." Finally, he warned about the infiltration of Communists in institutions of higher education. "The activities of a group on the payroll of the Agricultural College," he stated, "have all the earmarks and resemblance of Communism."[95]

In October William Mahoney, former mayor of St. Paul, spoke at Fargo's Fall Festival. He was more supportive of the labor movement in general and the new opportunities presented by the New Deal. "The day is passed," he said, "when every demand for labor was met with legal contest. In this new attitude of government toward labor, their right to organization is recognized and the result will be a more softened human viewpoint. Labor needs the protection of laws."[96]

The Fargo trial verdict did not end the controversy. The Nonpartisan League, a friend of organized labor, controlled the North Dakota House of Representatives and launched a legislative investigation. Burdick appealed the convictions immediately to the North Dakota Supreme Court. What began in Fargo would be determined in Bismarck. The actions in Fargo were now on trial in North Dakota. Burdick was still in the game. He was still fighting.

On March 2, 1935, Representative William Godwin of Mandan, North Dakota, introduced House Resolution M. He was the House majority leader; the resolution passed immediately with the full backing of the Nonpartisan League caucus and the few Democrats led by Minority Leader Thomas Burke. The resolution language was decidedly pro-labor. It questioned the acts of the Fargo Police Department and especially those of Bergesen, the Cass County state's attorney. It called for a committee of five to investigate the facts "in order to insure that no injustice shall be done to any citizen of the State of North Dakota." It gave the committee broad investigative powers and passed an emergency appropriation measure of $810 to conduct the investigation.[97] The resolution was unusual. The expenses were considerable considering the topic and year.

The *Fargo Forum* blew a gasket at the House initiative. The strike was solely Fargo business, and state lawmakers should keep their noses out of it. How dare the North Dakota Legislature question a Fargo decision. "The real purpose of the resolution and the creation of the investigating committee," editorialized the newspaper on Page One, "is to come down to Fargo to put a few officials and others 'on the pan' as they used to say in the slang of another day."[98]

The special House committee wasted no time. It completed its investigation in one week and issued a written report. It contained five conclusions and made two recommendations. The conclusions probably appeased neither side, although much of the language was sympathetic to the plight of Local Union 173. The committee found no evidence that any constitutional rights were violated, but that the activities of the strikers extended beyond a peaceful picket. Other conclusions recognized the right of truck drivers to be recognized as a union and to strike. Unfortunately, their strike timing was lousy. It occurred in the worst weather of a state winter and "when there was an acute public necessity to have fuel" and that "it was the duty of the officers to protect coal deliveries." Having established that, the committee also included language that seemed to call for more tolerance toward the Fargo truck drivers. It said that "in fair sympathy with the men who are striking to better their working conditions ... that sometimes allowance must be made under such circumstances."[99] What allowances and under what circumstances was left unexplained. It was legislative words, not action. The committee made no mention of the convictions.

The two recommendations were directed squarely at the Fargo Police Department. The officers goofed. Both recommendations addressed what the police did at the Union Hall on Sunday afternoon, and the committee took exception to their behavior. If police officers are making an arrest under the authority of a warrant, they must inform the defendant and show it to him. That was not done at the Union Hall. Second, the use of tear gas must be tempered with the seriousness of the crime. It should be confined to more serious charges where the arrest was being made for a felony, not a minor infraction.

In October, Burdick appeared before the North Dakota Supreme Court. He was in Bismarck to appeal the conviction of the "Sixteen" involved in the January Fargo strike. "None of the defendants in this action," he argued, "was connected with any of the facts construed to be violence." Burdick further stated that none of the "Sixteen" were participants in the fight near the icehouse on the Red River and that the clubs later seized from the Union Hall "had no connection with this offense." He supported his testimony with dozens of items seized by the Fargo police from the Union Hall, which included wooden clubs, axes and lead-filled hoses. He said again, as he had in the trial court, that these items were in no way connected with the particular incident.

A.R. Bergesen, Cass County state's attorney, who brought the original charges against the union members, spoke again for the state. He conceded the state did not have to prove that these men were actually present at the riot. Moreover, he conceded that other facts presented in court were never denied by the defendants. Finally, Bergesen restated his claim: "The state contends they were the leaders and were responsible for the acts committed by the rioters." The court took no immediate action on the appeal.[100]

On December 7, 1935, seven years before the Japanese attack on Pearl Harbor, the North Dakota Supreme Court issued its decision on the Fargo coal strike case. In a unanimous decision written by then Chief Justice John Burke, the court made two major decisions. It affirmed the lower court conviction of 13 union leaders. It reversed the conviction of the three union leaders: Cruden, Swalde and Hughes. In overturning their convictions, Burke wrote "it is not illegal for members of a labor union to go on strike," and he added that there was "evidence insufficient to connect union leaders with the riot."[101]

In addition, Burdick appealed two motions he made and lost during the trial. The court listened carefully to his arguments, but ruled that the lower court made no error by not granting separate trials for each of the defendants or in considering evidence on union activities and weapons seized from their headquarters.[102] Undaunted, Burdick requested a rehearing. The court denied it on January 26, 1936. Case closed.

Labor learned hard lessons from the Fargo coal strike of 1935. Federal legislation, which guaranteed local unions could organize, did not guarantee implementation at the local level. Unions were still bad vehicles for many regardless of the federal legislation. The strike in the cold of winter killed the union. The action turned the public and the local government against the union. The violence that followed did not make the strike right. It made it worse. Keeping Fargo warm was more important than recognizing the right of Local Union 173 to organize and to strike. The excessive force used by the Fargo police was glossed over because the end in this case justified the means. Although both the state Legislature and the state's highest court later said unions had a right to organize, the fact was they really did not, at least not in Fargo during the cold winter of 1935. In late March, the International Teamsters Union revoked the charter of Local Union 173. That decision ended the strike as well as their union.[103]

A tired and frustrated young attorney learned some hard lessons. He had lost the legal battle, just as the union did. Public support was simply not there. Most Fargoans sided with the prosecution. Burdick became even less popular in legal circles, if that was possible. He was too radical for the Fargo bar establishment. He also bore personal rejection for his union representation. He was like John Adams, who represented the British troops in Boston, a traitor to his class. The rejection hurt him personally and his young spouse, Marietta. And like his legal work for the farmers, there was little money earned from representing the Fargo coal strikers. "That was the attitude in Fargo at that time," said Burdick. "You couldn't do that today, I don't think. You couldn't march those fellows down Main Street. Labor is more respected today than it was then. Does that answer your question? Can you see now how I got to be known as a radical?"[104]

Burdick's support for labor proved significant over time. The union members did not forget what happened in Fargo and what he did for them. "He was there to represent them and to help them keep out of jail," said David Kemnitz, president of the North Dakota AFL-CIO in 1995. "He was also instrumental after that in getting a resolution passed during the North Dakota legislative session."[105] Arvin Kvasager, longtime Teamster leader in Grand Forks, said he was told about the Fargo strike early on in his career. "Yeah, and Quentin Burdick was a young attorney," recalled Kvasager. "He didn't get any money for it, but he got a lot of publicity."[106]

Playing Politics

Quentin's politics were as clearly stamped as a birthmark. He was the son of Usher Burdick, a Bull Moose Republican and more recently a Nonpartisan League supporter. The Depression made for strange bedfellows; Usher, newly elected Governor William Langer and Congressman William Lemke found themselves with second political careers primarily as the friends of mortgaged farmers and enemies of bankers and the *Fargo Forum*. Their political solutions were radical and usually included a variety of legal and extralegal means to postpone debt until the nation recovered economically.

It was sometimes difficult for Quentin to chart an independent course from either the Progressive Republicanism of his father or Langer's Nonpartisan League political machine. They were all under the Republican tent, but young Burdick preferred not to be beholden to either man. "I don't think there was a particular time that I signed an application or anything like that," recalled Burdick about his relationship with the Nonpartisan League. "Sure, I was part of the League because my father was and I went to a lot of meetings with him. So there was no formal declaration like giving blood or anything like that."[107] Still, it was easier to say no to Langer than it was to his father. When cornered, Burdick said he sometimes tried to hide behind the fact that he was "a professional man" in order to avoid "having to take a stand between the two of them."[108]

Both men, however, kept the pressure on young Burdick to do things their way. Quentin still occupied Usher's Fargo law office, and he soon found himself as Usher's self-appointed legal counsel for the Holiday Association. He really had no choice in either matter because he seldom said no to his father. Besides, Usher never asked Quentin whether it was OK with him or not. He simple sent people to him without any advance notice. Langer, on the other hand, worked in more devious ways to capture Quentin's support. There were at least three documented cases of Governor Langer courting Quentin's favor in the '30s, which reveals much about Langer's cunning and Burdick's stubbornness.

The first incident involved a personal check written by Langer to Burdick in 1933. The amount was for $50. Burdick never cashed it. Family members later found it among many personal possessions after Burdick's death. No one offered any explanation for its origin or why a man as frugal as Burdick did not cash it.[109] He certainly needed the money considering his financial circumstances, and it probably would have paid the grocery bill for a month or two. The amount was considerable for the times. The check might have been a graduation gift, a wedding present to Quentin and Marietta, or Langer's way of saying. "Now you owe me one." In any case, Burdick declined to cash Langer's check. Many years later, Burdick told Tom Burgum about the check. "Smart," said Burgum. "He was hurting and he did not cash it."[110]

The second incident occurred shortly thereafter. Governor Langer contacted Burdick and asked if he would introduce him at a political rally. It was to be held in a southeastern North Dakota town not too far from Fargo. Burdick agreed to the governor's request and drove there well in advance of Langer's scheduled arrival from Bismarck at 2:00 p.m. Burdick was quite nervous; to make matters worse, Langer showed up two hours late — evidently on purpose. Burdick characterized Langer's political style and recalled the incident in great detail:

> Well, you've seen these barkers at carnivals and you've seen these slick salesman. Langer was an operator. I saw him one time the first year I was back from college. He was scheduled for a speech in Kindred or someplace at two o'clock. About four o'clock he came in just huffing and puffing. He was all lathered up. The people were still in their seats. The Townsend Plan [old age security pension] was in vogue in those times and

everyone read about it. Langer came in and they all whooped and yelled even though he was two hours late. I went up to the platform and introduced him. He had a hell of a voice you know. He said: "I want you to know I am one hundred percent for the Townsend Plan." Then he repeated it: "I want you to know I am one hundred percent for the Townsend Plan." Then there was a little more excitement and he repeated it for a third time: "I want you to know that I am one hundred percent for the Townsend Plan." And he left the stage. That was it. ... He sat outside the town for two hours so he could make a grand stage entrance. I had to handle a thing like that — warming up the audience. That's where I got my experience! Sure is [a hell of a deal]. After you talk about this and that, what the hell do you say next? But that's all Langer said — those three repeats.[111]

The third incident was more controversial. It involved a physical confrontation between John Holzworth and Burdick in the Cass County Courthouse during the 1938 election when Governor Langer was a candidate for the United States Senate against incumbent Senator Gerald P. Nye. Holzworth was a popular freelance writer and an old Langer friend. They both graduated from Columbia University in 1910. Langer commissioned Holzworth to write a book about him titled *The Fighting Governor: The Story of William Langer and the State of North Dakota*. The book was primarily political puff written to defend Langer's checkered past and to prove that his actions as governor during his first administration (1933-July 1934) were in the best interests of his constituents — even though Langer was removed from office in the summer of 1934 because of a federal felony conviction for using federal relief funds for political purposes. Somehow, shipments of the book were held up, so Langer sent Holzworth to Burdick to resolve the matter. When Burdick was asked to confirm the truth of the incident, he told his version:

Oh, yeah. I remember [knocking John Holzworth down the stairs in the Cass County Courthouse]. He was a buckswalter sort of a guy, a jolly good fellow, king of the walk and that kind of stuff. ... He was surely cocky and he wore outdoor clothes, not business clothes. Some sort of corduroy and he had two dogs with him. Here he is coming into Fargo with a damn shotgun, his corduroy outfit and the two dogs ready to take over everything. He came in just like a gentleman senator.

As Holzworth came up to the office, Burdick continued, "he said, 'God damn it.' Those were his words, Mrs. B. [Jocelyn was present]." Jocie reminded him, "I've heard those words before." Burdick went back to the story:

Holzworth said, "The election is next Tuesday. I have a bunch of books that I want released to be used in the campaign, but they tell me the trucking company won't release them.' Let's get replevin action and get them. So I got the forms all typed up and ready to be served and what do I find out. The outfit re-bonds and replevin [called claim and delivery] only works unless the other party secures you by putting up a bond themselves. We were back where we started. They re-bonded because politicians didn't want those books to be circulated. When Holzworth found that out, he let out a stream a mile long. "You're a hell of a lawyer!" Listen, I said. I can't do a thing about it. That's the law. That's the rules. Unless you can prove to me that the bond is no good or something, that's practice and that's the way it's done.

The longer he was there, the madder he got. I tried to calm him down and get him out into the breezeway before we hit the stairs. But he called me a bad name again: "You're a hell of a lawyer." ... When that came out, I smacked him. He wound up in the middle level of the stairs at the Cass County Courthouse about twenty feet below. I must have cold cocked him a good one. He was holding his jaw and was bleeding a little bit. He was going to have me arrested. Judge John Pollack was District Judge at the time and just by accident he saw the incident. The whole damn thing! He wouldn't give him a warrant [Burdick laughed]. Good Republican and he wouldn't give him a warrant. Holzworth tried to get me arrested![112]

Although Burdick never bragged about the incident at the time, his replay many years later suggested he relished the confrontation. How accurate was his memory? Mart Vogel, a close personal friend of Burdick and fellow attorney, heard about the altercation second hand. He also remembered hearing about it on a radio broadcast soon after it happened. More significant was the rounds it made among Fargo attorneys for several days after.[113] Serkland was late coming to court that morning and was an eyewitness. "I was there," he said. "I heard a rumpus. I was at the bottom of the steps of the second floor. The rumpus was on the third floor. They got into a wrangle about something just as they got out of the courtroom. I heard something, a noise, and pretty soon this fellow launched down on the landing between the second and third floors. I looked up and saw a surprised look on his face."[114]

The incident was significant. When confronted with a personal challenge to his honor, Burdick hit his accuser. It was an automatic response. He was 10 years removed from playing football and fraternity fun, but the incident brought the same physical response he demonstrated at the University of Minnesota. Burdick did not follow up the first punch by a second or in any way proceed to continue the attack at the bottom of the stairs. He said nothing to his accuser and did no crowing about it later. The Gentle Warrior simply hit Holzworth and walked away. That was the end of the matter, period.

The incident carried political as well as personal overtones. Burdick, by throwing a punch at Holzworth, indirectly hit Langer. It was a clear sign that Burdick was his own man and that any personal attacks on his character would be met swiftly and decisively. The incident never earned Burdick a seat among Fargo's top lawyers. He was still the son of Usher and too radical for their taste. Yet, the fact that young Burdick cold-cocked a Langer crony must have brought some chuckles from the legion of Langer haters. Maybe young Burdick was not all bad. The incident sent another message to the Fargo bar. Quentin Burdick, the lawyer, not only looked rough and physically intimidating in court; he was. Look out! It was unwise to mess with him. Do not cross his path, insult his integrity and avoid trying to humor him or one might end like Holzworth, tumbling down a flight of stairs in the Cass County Courthouse.

The Burdick family jumped into politics repeatedly during the Depression. For Usher, it was a new ball game. He won five consecutive terms to the U.S. House of Representatives starting in 1934. He and Lemke, who first won in 1932, consistently headed the Republican column, beating several Republican conservatives in the primary and humiliating weaker Democrat opponents in the general election. The two old warhorses were labeled Republicans in national counts, but in North Dakota, they always wore League uniforms. Eugene Burdick entered local politics in 1936. He ran for Williams County state's attorney and lost a close race. Two years later, with a stronger campaign, he won. He was re-elected in 1940 and 1942 before stepping down to devote full time to a growing private law practice. Quentin, in the meantime, joined the fray. "I ran for every damn thing I could find," he said.[115] He ran three times for elective office in Cass County and lost each time. In 1934, he ran against A.R. Bergesen for Cass County state's attorney, losing badly by almost 7,000 votes. Two years later, he ran for the North Dakota Senate in a much closer race. He lost in the Republican primary by less than 700 votes to veteran Republican incumbent Senator Arthur Fowler. In 1940, Burdick again sought the office of state's attorney, losing to Ralph Crowl by almost 2,000 votes.[116]

There were obvious reasons for Usher and Eugene's victories and Quentin's defeats. The Depression and the presidency of the North Dakota Farmers' Holiday Association lifted Usher to the forefront of North Dakota state politics in the '30s. He was a big, colorful and impassioned stump speaker who articulated the problems of the debtor class and who understood bankruptcy from personal experience. He spoke the farmer's language in a period of great doubt about the future of American agriculture. Eugene, fresh out of law school, ran with high voter identification in the Burdick home county. Virtually every Williams County resident knew the Burdick name, and although some may have parted with Usher on specific matters, Williams County proved good League and Farmers Union territory for his return to politics. Eugene stayed away from partisan politics, although he always identified himself with the Progressive Republicanism of his father. On the back of his calling card were printed the words: "I am not bound to win, but I am bound to be true. I am not bound to succeed, but I am bound to live up to what light I have. I must stand with anybody that stands right; stand with him while he is right and part company with him when he goes wrong." Abraham Lincoln[117] Eugene was short in stature like his mother and less outgoing than his father. He was also very bright and knocked on every door to win a local office at the same time his father was carrying the county for a seat in Congress. Voters elected a veteran fighter to save the family farm and a young lawyer to prosecute lawbreakers in Williams County. Both were Burdicks.

The first political road Quentin took was much more difficult. He was not playing on home turf like Eugene. The Burdick name gained little yardage in Cass County. In fact, the name was a negative factor among most Fargo lawyers and the majority of Republican voters. Williams County might have launched Quentin's political career much earlier, but it was not going to happen in Imperial Cass for a much longer time. Burdick always made two standard statements when asked to explain these early losing races. "Bear in mind, each time I ran I got more votes," he said. He repeated it in a much louder voice, "I was gaining votes!" His second statement announced that Cass County was always "the worst place in the state" for him to run.[118]

There is fiction and truth to Burdick's assessment. It was incorrect for him to state that each time he ran that he received a higher percentage of votes. He did not. He was soundly beaten in 1934 and 1940 for state's attorney, but ran a surprisingly strong race for the state Senate 1934. Many Cass County voters evidently wanted him representing them in Bismarck more than serving as the county's chief law enforcement officer, especially with his union connections. He was viewed as being on the wrong side of the law. In 1939, Burdick was elected chairman of the Cass County Republicans. He succeeded Lee Brooks for the post. Burdick promised two things for the organization: He would work to establish a sound constructive program for 1940 and to increase the membership of the young GOP in Fargo.[119]

Losing in politics was not anymore acceptable to Burdick than losing in football. Burdick never said he was disappointed in losing, only claimed that things were getting better — when in reality there were not. Nevertheless, he must have been terribly disappointed in the results. Overall, the House of Burdick was doing well. Father, Usher, was now serving in Congress and younger brother, Eugene, was in charge of legal affairs for Williams County. Only Quentin had failed to win playing the political game. In retrospect, there was more than just a bit of political irony to note that Quentin Burdick, who later became the leading vote getter for the North Dakota Democrat-NPL Party, only won one elective office after eight years of trying: the president of the Cass County Young Republicans!

Since the tremendous success of the movie by the same name, Fargo now stands for other things as well. Suddenly everyone who was born in or who lives in Fargo talks with a heavy Norwegian accent. If you meet someone and the conversation turns to *place* and you say you are from Fargo, the response often comes with a big smile and a comment like, "you betcha!" The movie also established Fargo as a city where deals can be struck. Clearly the Scandinavian accent fits North Dakota's ethnic patterns. Minot, however, lays more claim to Norwegian ancestry than Fargo and most who actually live there do not speak with a Norwegian tongue. On the other hand, consummating deals is old Fargo cuisine. Fargo has always existed as a place where important deals are made. Fargoans sought and secured a second state university in 1960 and built North Dakota's biggest dome in the 1990s. The genius of Fargo under either Republican or Democratic labels is to control power, and the city underneath the dome or outside of it remains the strongest city-state in North Dakota.

Quentin Burdick played on Fargo's turf, too. He worked hard to build a small law practice. His clients were primarily the city's downtrodden — those unknown souls who were most deeply affected by the Depression. His surname, like that of his father, was always identified with busted farmers and farm organizations that proposed extreme measures to keep farm families on North Dakota farms. Quentin Burdick alone, however, became the leading city attorney to represent striking truck drivers. In Fargo, he also attempted to launch a successful political career, which went nowhere. Finally, Fargo was a place to start a marriage, build a home and raise a family. Burdick came to Fargo in 1932 to forge new beginnings. He never left the city except for a brief sojourn to Jamestown, North Dakota. In 1992, he was honored in one of the biggest public memorials every held in Fargo. Fargo is always good at hosting big events, even for a senator named Burdick, who in the '30s was neither liked nor appreciated by most of the city's residents.

Endnotes

1. *Fargo (N.D.) Forum,* Dec. 30, 1930, 1.
2. Ibid., March 29, 1932, 18.
3. *Fargo (N.D.) Forum,* Nov. 11, 1932, 1.
4. *Fargo Forum,* Nov. 11, 1932, 1.
5. Ibid., Aug. 29, 1933, 1.
6. Ibid., Nov. 30, 1933, 1.
7. Usher L. Burdick, Autobiographical Notes, 1932, folder 12, box 36, Usher L. Burdick Manuscript Collection [hereafter BMC].
8. Ibid.
9. Penny Miller, Clerk, North Dakota Supreme Court, letter to author, June 6, 1944.
10. *Fargo Forum,* Oct. 16, 1932, 3-1.
11. Eugene Burdick, interview by author, Feb. 28, 1995.
12. North Dakota, *Centennial Blue Book,* 464.
13. Eugene Burdick interview.
14. Ibid.
15. Harold Shaft, letter to Usher L. Burdick, July 1, 1960, folder 14, box 16, BMC.
16. Usher L. Burdick, letter to Harold Shaft, July 1960, BMC.
17. Mart Vogel, interview by author, Jan. 19, 1995.
18. Eugene Burdick interview.
19. Chester Serkland, interview by author, Feb. 13, 1995.
20. Eugene Burdick interview.
21. *The Damon Runyon Omnibus,* 29, 129, 172.
22. Serkland interview.
23. Eugene Burdick interview.
24. Quentin Burdick, interview by author, Jan. 6, 1992.
25. Ibid.
26. Quentin Burdick, letter to Emma Burdick, Nov. 11, 1933, in possession of Jennifer Burdick, Baltimore, Md.
27. Eugene Burdick interview.
28. Ibid.
29. Serkland interview.
30. Ibid.
31. Ibid.
32. Ibid.
33. Ibid.
34. Ibid.
35. Mart Vogel interview.
36. Morteer Skewes, interview by author, April 15, 1995.
37. Ibid.
38. Mart Vogel interview.
39. Usher L. Burdick, letter to John Burke, Jan. 12, 1934, folder, 7, box 35, BMC.
40. John Burke, letter to Usher L. Burdick, Jan. 15, 1934, folder 7, Box 35, BMC.
41. *Heuer v. Heuer, North Western Reporter* 253 (North Dakota 1934): 858.
42. Ibid., 860.
43. Eugene Burdick interview.
44. Garry Pearson, letter to author, Feb. 15, 1998.
45. Burdick, Autobiographical Notes, BMC.
46. Ibid.
47. Bob Vogel, interview by author, Feb. 15, 1994. Holiday Association (master's thesis, University of North Dakota, 1969), 82.
49. Ibid. 50. Ibid., 84.
51. James W. Dodd, "Resolutions, Programs and Policies of the North Dakota Farmers' Holiday Association, 1932-1937," *North Dakota History* 28 (April-July 1961):108.
52. Burdick, Autobiographical Notes.
53. Remele, "The Public Reaction," 85.
54. Dodd. "Resolutions, Programs and Policies," 117.

55. Eugene Burdick interview.
56. Ibid.
57. Ibid.
58. Ibid.
59. Remele, "The Public Reaction," 85-86.
60. Quentin Burdick interview.
61. Eugene Burdick interview.
62. D. Jerome Tweton, *In Union There is Strength* (Grand Forks: The North Dakota Carpenter [Craftsman Heritage Society], 1982), 58.
63. Joseph R. Conlin, *The American Past: A Survey of American History*, 5th ed. (New York: Harcourt Brace, 1997), 761.
64. Tweton, *In Union There is Strength*, 58.
65. *Fargo Forum*, Jan. 22, 1935, 1.
66. Ibid, Jan. 23, 1935, 1.
67. Quentin Burdick Interview.
68. Thomas Blantz. "Father Haas and the Minneapolis Truckers Strike of 1934," *Minnesota History* 42 (Spring 1970):14.
69. Dale Kramer. "The Dunne Boys of Minneapolis," *Harpers* 184 (March 1942):389.
70. *Fargo Forum*, Jan. 24, 1935, 1.
71. Ibid., Jan. 25, 1935, 1, 7.
72. Ibid., Jan. 26, 1935, 7.
73. *Special Strikers Bulletin*, Feb. 2, 1935, No 1.
74. Quentin Burdick interview.
75. *State v. Russell et al.*, *North Western Reporter* 264 (North Dakota 1935):534.
76. *Special Strikers Bulletin*, Feb. 2, 1935, No 1.
77. *Fargo Forum*, Jan. 28, 1935, 6.
78. *Special Strikers Bulletin*, Feb. 2, 1935, No 1.
79. *Fargo Forum*, Jan. 28, 1935, 1.
80. Ibid., Jan. 28, 1935, 8.
81. *Special Strikers Bulletin*, Feb. 9, 1935, No 7.
82. Quentin Burdick interview.
83. Ibid.
84. *Fargo Forum*, Jan. 29, 1935, 7.
85. *Special Strikers Bulletin*, Feb. 2, 1935, No 1.
86. *Fargo Forum*, Feb. 13, 1935, 2.
87. Ibid., Jan. 30, 1935, 9; 1, 1935, 1.
88. Ibid., Feb. 9, 1935, 1.
89. Ibid., Feb. 16, 1935, 2.
90. Ibid., Feb. 17, 1935, 1, 4.
91. Ibid., Feb. 21, 1935, 9; Feb. 24, 1935, 1.
92. Ibid., Feb. 19, 1935, 10.
93. Ibid., Feb. 20, 1935, 9.
94. *Special Strikers Bulletin*, Feb. 15, 1935, No 11.
95. *Fargo Forum*, April 24, 1935, 10.
96. Ibid., Oct. 5, 1935, 1.
97. *Laws of North Dakota*, 24th session, 1935, 459-460.
98. *Fargo Forum*, Feb. 27, 1935, 1.
99. Ibid., March 3, 1935.
100. Ibid., Oct. 2, 1935, 1.
101. *State v. Russell et al.*, 536.
102. Ibid., 535, 538.
103. Henry Martinson, *History of North Dakota Labor* (Fargo: Labor Temple, 1970), 34.
104. Quentin Burdick interview.
105. David Kemnitz, interview by author, April 26, 1995.
106. Arvin Kvasager, interview by author, Jan. 29, 1995.
107. Quentin Burdick interview.
108. Ibid.

109. Jocelyn Burdick interview.
110. Tom Burgum, interview by author, March 24, 1995.
111. Quentin Burdick interview.
112. Quentin Burdick interview.
113. Mart Vogel interview.
114. Serkland interview.
115. Quentin Burdick interview.
116. *Fargo Forum*, n.d. (?)
117. Eugene Burdick interview.
118. Quentin Burdick interview.
119. *Fargo Forum*, June 16, 1939, 1.

- seven -

A North Dakota
Farmers Union Man

The stories of how Arthur C. Townley ignited the political consciousness of North Dakota farmers before the dawn of World War I appear often in North Dakota history. The stories relate how his Nonpartisan League (NPL) grew rapidly into a formidable farmers political organization; how in 1919, it took total control of state government and established a dossier of state-owned enterprises; how his disciples preached a simple, Socialistic message: Economic disadvantage suffered by farmers could only be overcome by state ownership of banks, and the milling and marketing of its own wheat.

North Dakota history is less conversant about the demise of Townley's NPL — how its radical message and almost instant success spawned a conservative countermovement. Less is known and appreciated about the Independent Voters Association (IVA), which successfully embarrassed NPL candidates in Republican primaries, recalled the NPL's top three constitutional officers in 1921 and thwarted the expansion of more government-owned businesses. The IVA, like its antithesis, the NPL, also preached a homily — a sermon that centered on the virtues of free enterprise, especially in the aftermath of Russia's successful Communist revolution. State Socialism as practiced by the NPL was simply un-American.

The titanic struggle between Socialism and Americanism ended in a political draw. Both the NPL and the IVA survived under the Republican flag throughout the remainder of the '20s, but neither faction ruled absolutely. Although William Langer took control of the NPL in his successful bid for the governorship in 1932, old tensions from the '20s suffocated in the dust of the Depression. The rhetoric of mistrust remained as the base of ideological differences, but sheer economic survival posed entirely different conclusions and solutions. The '30s proved to be much more difficult than the '20s.

No state ideologies or policies saved North Dakota during the Depression. Certainly the existence of one bank and one mill and elevator did little to save North Dakota agriculture from economic disaster. The problems were too big and ran too deep for just two small state institutions to handle. The disciples of free enterprise faired no better in providing remedies. The organization offered no solutions to unprecedented unemployment, bankruptcy and a legion of foreclosed farms. In the final analysis, only Roosevelt's New Deal and the tremendous economic explosion spawned by the Second World War saved North Dakota from economic ruin.

If Townley's Nonpartisan League proved to be the most successful political organization in North Dakota, the North Dakota Farmers Union (NDFU) became the most successful cooperative enterprise. Its complicated beginnings weave an intricate story of the complexity of North Dakota farmers between two world wars. And its decision in 1947 to get directly involved in the political process led to the switch of the NPL into the North Dakota Democratic Party nine years later.

The NDFU sprouted from the failure of other farm organizations in the 1920s. The first kernel of growth came from the demise of Townley's defunct National Nonpartisan League in 1923. It was a last-ditch effort under a new label and it was called the National Producers Alliance, but everyone connected with it simply referred to it as the Producers Alliance. It was Townley's last concerted attempt to organize the nation's farmers. When he quit and handed over the reins to others, they quickly became the organizers of the Farmers Union. The Producers Alliance was the transition between the end of Townley's NPL and the beginnings of Charles Talbott's NDFU. Townley's last message, "the cost of production should be the basis of the prices farmers receive," became the cornerstone of the NDFU.[1]

Other seeds contributed to the gestation of the Farmers Union. The failure of another farm organization, the Farm Bureau, for example, certainly was a contributing factor. The bureau began with much fanfare in North Dakota in 1920 and attracted the likes of Usher Burdick, who served as its first president. Its political conservatism, however, soon soured many farmers and Burdick resigned his position as a symbol of farmers' dissatisfaction with the organization. Another failed program was an attempt by the North Dakota Wheat Growers Association to improve wheat prices. It established a wheat pool and a cooperative marketing plan to push up the price, but by the end of the decade, it handled only a very small portion of the wheat grown in the state. More than anything, however, the NDFU became a home for North Dakota farmers who joined Townley's NPL in 1915 and 1916. A decade later, farmers were tired of the political rhetoric and the constant warfare with the IVA. They accepted the reality of the end of their Socialist experiment, but they also knew the dire consequences of not sticking together. By 1925, all North Dakota farmers were in deep financial straits and there was no viable farm organization capable of helping them out until the NDFU began to organize.[2]

The Talbott family was synonymous with the tremendous success of the Farmers Union from its establishment in 1927 through the 1970s. The Talbotts instituted a remarkable record of service and personal dedication, as well as tight control of the organization for three generations. The founder, Charles Talbott, served as the first president (1927-1937) until his premature death in an automobile accident. He was succeeded by his son Glenn, who served as the second president (1937-1961) and daughter, Gladys Talbott Edwards, who served as the first education and junior work director before assuming the position of director of the Department of Education for the National Farmers Union (1941-1953). Stanley Moore, Charles's grandson and Glenn's nephew, served as the fourth president (1975-1980) after many years of prior service with the organization.

The Talbotts' service mirrored various stages in the first 50 years of the Farmers Union. Charles gave it shape, size and ideology. He, like Townley, was a master stump speaker and crowd pleaser. According to his reputation, he "could organize almost any farmer by a personal contact" and "convert the most stubborn farmer at a public meeting."[3] In the first year (1927-1928), the NDFU grew from 369 to 767 local chapters and increased membership from 10,000 to 22,000.[4] Clearly, many North Dakota farmers had found a new church; they liked the messenger and the message.

Talbott's main message encouraged everyone who joined to work together for the betterment of all. He downplayed political differences and reminded his audiences that infighting did nothing to improve their economic conditions. At one local meeting after another, he promoted cooperation rather than competition. He sold a good product and spoke a great line. "This is not a political organization," began Talbott. "We are building an organization to save ourselves from bankruptcy and protect ourselves against those who prey upon us and exploit us. At the market place there is no such thing as Nonpartisan or IVA wheat, cattle, or hogs. They are neither Protestant [n]or Catholic commodities when they get to market. The Protestant buyer skins the Protestant and the Catholic the Catholic. In business all charity, politics, and religion are forgotten."[5]

Slowly under Talbott's leadership, the NDFU began to establish cooperative- owned businesses to provide lower costs and share higher profits. There would be no state banks and state mills with Farmers Union labels, but there would be a wide selection of services and programs. Farmer-owned cooperatives would replace state-run industries. Growth was slow but steady during the troubled '20s. The Farmers Union opened its first oil company in Jamestown in 1926 and sold its first insurance policy two years later. On the eve of the New Deal, the cooperative enterprise was the second largest distributor of gasoline in North Dakota, behind only the giant Standard Oil Company.[6] Talbott's hard work paid off. His NDFU was the strongest of any state Farmers Union organization in the country.

Charles also developed important contacts with the Roosevelt administration. He became a federal favorite among state Farmers Union directors and lobbied for stronger foreclosure laws, relief and soil conservation payments, and Farm Security Administration loans to farmers that allowed them to purchase stock in various Farmers Union operations. Equally important, he secured major appointments in North Dakota to administer the growing number of federal programs. The NDFU served in an advice and consent role for Democratic administrations on many matters dealing with federal agricultural policy.[7]

Glenn Talbott went even further. He became the real architect of the cooperative movement. According to Charles Conrad and Joyce Conrad, authors of 50 Years: The North Dakota Farmers Union, Glenn "looked on the cooperative movement as a departure from the capitalistic system that could become an alternative to it."[8] He possessed less personal charm than his father but exercised more political power. He ran the Farmers Union with an iron hand and often behaved a lot like Bill Langer, whose political organization ran North Dakota during those years. He was aggressive, dictatorial and very successful. He made enemies as well as allies. Gorman King, a Valley City Democrat, recalled a fight between his grandfather and local members of the Farmers Union over an elevator he owned in Drake, North Dakota, southeast of Minot. The farmers wanted to purchase it, but King's grandfather did not want to sell it to them. "They told my grandfather Henry either sell it to them or they would build their own," recalled King. "My grandfather said they were all Communists — that is the word or label they used because the Farmers Union came out of the cooperative movement, which is not Communist at all. But that is the way it was sold. They organized [on] main street in all the towns and it was an easy way to call them a Communist and then walk away from it."[9]

Under Glenn's presidency, the Farmers Union evolved into a more profitable and powerful organization. There were even Farmers Union locals operating at both the University of North Dakota (UND) and the North Dakota Agricultural College (NDAC), and the Co-Op House in Fargo housed 76 members and owned two buildings near the NDAC campus. In 1941, the organization generated $45 million in revenues and served 129,000 patrons, and "cooperatives had become an important factor in every community in North Dakota."[10] Success, however, bred contempt. In particular, the cooperative movement prompted a conservative Republican backlash during the 1947 legislative session. Ultimately this backlash forced the organization to fight political attacks by becoming a political player. The 21st-century two-party system in North Dakota would not exist without Glenn's leadership. He was a major force and the Farmers Union a key factor in the merger of the NPL and the Democratic Party in 1956. Glenn Talbott was the ultimate North Dakota insurgent in the 1950s.

Gladys, working with both her father and then her brother, shared her many abilities with the organization. She made it a special place for women and single teachers who were both accorded full membership. To her, the Farmers Union was a community of farm families working side by side. When things got tough, she became stronger. She was its inspiration, the voice of hope for many years. She took special interest in programs and camps for the children of Farmers Union families. She trained young people in four-minute speech contests providing valuable experience and confidence. Governor Arthur Link of Alexander, North Dakota, was a regular participant seen often with his fiddle, his long waving hair and a handsome smile at various Farmers Union youth events.[11]

Stanley Moore took over the reins of the NDFU in a much different era. Like Glenn and Gladys, he grew up in the organization, serving as secretary and administrative assistant to then-president Ed Smith before being selected as the fourth president. By the mid 1970s, it was a much different organization than the one started by his grandfather or the one enlarged by his uncle. Success, trust and compliance replaced the fervor for the cooperative idea. Continuity, not change, was his major goal and one that proved difficult with declining membership among third-generation families, tensions over eminent domain practices of Garrison Diversion, and the threatened impacts of coal development. The Farmers Union reached maturity and its members were seniors.

The Burdicks were very close to the Talbotts and the work of the Farmers Union. Usher and Charles were old friends, as well as longtime participants, in working for better farm policies. Usher spoke at the first Farmers Union convention in 1927 and gave a powerful address. More importantly, of course, was his presidency of the North Dakota Farmers' Holiday Association, which occurred with Talbott's blessing. "I brought a little baby back from Iowa," said Talbott, "and Burdick made it into the largest farm organization in North Dakota."[12] Throughout Burdick's congressional career, he always received strong support from the organization although never formal endorsement because they were nonpartisan. Usher, in turn, appeared as a regular at Farmers Union gatherings and served informally as Charles's "legal consultant."[13]

There was more to their relationship. They were close in age — Charles was born in 1876 and Usher in 1879. They shared the same farming experiences and loved to chat about those early days. Neither cared a damn for clothes or fancy cars. Charles wore an old sheepskin coat and often drove an old Ford without a top. This attire matched Usher's to a T. They probably could recognize each other on any section road in North Dakota without taking a second look. They were salty creatures, too, with a good eye for attention and a quick tongue for one-liners. One Sunday morning, for example, Charles was found sleeping on a bench during a Co-Op Institute. The man who found him asked, "Charley, why aren't you in church?" Talbott replied, "Well, I got all the religion I can stand right here in the Farmers Union."[14]

After the tragic death of Charles in 1937, Glenn took control of the NDFU. His presidency did not come without a tough contest, but it proved to be a wise choice for the organization. Glenn was 36 years old. He possessed only an eighth-grade education and a talent for playing the violin until a hunting accident at age 16 permanently injured his left hand.[15] Glenn's education was primarily in-house. He was really a Farmers Union offspring groomed in every aspect of the movement. He was a popular speaker, an excellent organizer (who also spoke German), and had worked in various grain marketing jobs prior to being elected president. His nephew, Stanley Moore, admired his uncle's speaking abilities. He was "very analytical" and "very dynamic," but not a "story teller" like his father. His speeches were dogmatic and demonstrated a good thought process, and "his logic was reasoned logic, and he would develop a whole theme of it. I think he was a good speaker," said Moore.[16] Some people detected a strain of inferiority about his lack of formal education. "Glenn Talbott didn't go to college," said Gorman King, "and one of the biggest things in his life was when he got the honorary degree at NDSU when he was quite old."[17]

Glenn Talbott and Quentin Burdick also shared a close working relationship. It was a much different one than that of their fathers — one that never centered on farming backgrounds, tall tales, or social and personal relationships. It is even conceivable that they were never really close, personal friends. They were certainly, however, close colleagues who respected and learned from each other. Their working relationship began in 1943 when Glenn hired Quentin to be legal counsel for the NDFU. It lasted for 15 years until Burdick resigned in late 1958 after becoming the first Democrat in North Dakota history to win a seat in the United States House of Representatives. Although they were close in age (Glenn was eight years older than Quentin), they shared little in common. It was strictly an employer-employee relationship. Glenn was the boss; Quentin was the worker. But differences in their relationship should not detract from its significance. Talbott exerted more influence on Quentin than any other male, except for Usher. Talbott's work assignments prepared Burdick for his political career in many aspects. Talbott provided Burdick with many opportunities to speak, provide legal counsel and plan political strategy. "Quentin would make appearances at Farmers Union conventions," recalled Link. "He would make speeches. He was their legal counsel because at that time co-ops were having a tough time being accepted. At best, cooperatives, and particularly the Farmers Union, were considered Socialists, and at worst Communists."[18]

It is not clear who or exactly what circumstances prompted the arrange- ment. Maybe it just occurred. It is always possible Usher played a hand in it, too. It was clearly in his character to do so as past events demonstrated. But it is also entirely possible that Glenn and Quentin simply worked it out by themselves. They knew each other through their fathers' association and both attended the first NDFU convention. Both were involved in Farmers' Holiday activities, and both were in need of each other's services. The Farmers Union required a full-time legal adviser and Burdick desperately needed more work. Whatever the circumstances, time proved it to be a satisfactory and mutually beneficial relationship. Burdick worked for the Farmers Union longer than any other employer except his constituency.

The immediate effect on Burdick was his pocketbook. The Farmers Union deal rescued him from his paltry Fargo law practice. Burdick's brother said "it stabilized [Quentin's] income at a time when things were a little rough."[19] It provided him and his family with a guaranteed monthly income, the first in his 11 years of law practice. "Nobody was making any money practicing law in Fargo in those days," said Jim Jungroth, who later became his legal assistant. "So they offered him like $300 a month to be the general counsel for the Farmers Union and do whatever chores the Farmers Union needed doing."[20] The work primarily centered on representing the Farmers Union Insurance Company in court. In other words, Burdick continued his practice of being a defense lawyer, with a concentration of settling accident cases. However, as general counsel, they had him doing everything. "He did political work. You name it. Where they needed a lawyer, he was there. When they needed a speaker, he was there. It was whatever needed doing," recalled Jungroth. "I don't think he did as much organizing as other folks, but I think he did a lot of speaking."[21]

In 1947, Talbott asked Burdick to be the NDFU chief political lobbyist. He represented them at the North Dakota legislative session that year, and soon after he was appointed executive director of the newly formed Farmers Union Progressive Alliance. The Progressive Alliance was a PAC (political action committee) established by Talbott to do political work for the Farmers Union while maintaining some independence from the parent organization. The Progressive Alliance lasted for a few of years and centered on educating Farmers Union members to become more politically involved. The position provided Quentin with a political forum and he traveled throughout the state in that capacity, attended Henry Wallace's 1948 Progressive Party convention and became deeply involved with the insurgent movement, which worked long and hard to bring the NPL into the Democratic column.

Talbott also cut some political rope for Burdick. Quentin ran for governor in 1946, U.S. senator in 1956 and the U.S. House in 1958 without Farmers Union political endorsement while remaining on the NDFU payroll. It was a big bonus for a poor candidate with no personal income. "He had a guaranteed economic base from the Farmers Union," observed Lloyd Omdahl, "and so he had a certain amount of security and could engage in this kind of thing. A lot of other people can't enjoy that kind of backing, like if they are lawyers, they have to practice law. They can't be running off for office like that all the time. Quentin Burdick enjoyed a certain amount of economic security in the process and political support. The Farmers Union was in sympathy with what he was doing all the time so he had a better situation than a lot of other people."[22] In other words, without Farmers Union support, Omdahl maintained, it is doubtful that Burdick would have been a candidate in all of those elections.

For all the rope extended by Talbott, he also held a tight rein on Burdick. "Glenn was a very strong, dominating individual and Quentin had to rely on that for his paycheck," said Gorman King. "You must recognize the character of Talbott. He was a very, very strict disciplinarian in his organization. There wasn't any arguments about it, whether it came from Quentin or his wife." King noted that whenever "you talked with Talbott, you had to back out of the room just like you were talking to the Pope. He had them cowed!" and Burdick "had to take that because that was the way he had to eat."[23] Others softened the harshness. "They were very, very close," observed Charles and Joyce Conrad. "Glenn was the boss. Glenn wrote the changes, but Quentin was his political adviser. They made the decisions together." At the same time, the Conrads acknowledged that sometimes "Talbott was not a man to be trusted."[24] Stanley Moore said his uncle never talked with him a great deal about his relationship with Quentin, but Moore thought "they had a high regard for each other" and that "it was a [mutually beneficial] relationship."[25]

When asked about his relationship with Talbott, Burdick answered slowly but bluntly in his typical delivery of one-liners: "I don't want to say anything to detract from his reputation." He continued, "Let's see what would be the best example [pause]; I remember one word that sticks right out that had to do with that bunch in St. Paul [Bill Thatcher and GTA]." Burdick imitated Talbott: "'By God,' he said, 'We'll mandamus them!'" putting the emphasis on the first syllable. "I could not help but break out laughing," continued Burdick. "That's man-da-mus, of course. He was 'mandamusing' everybody. He would pick up words he heard some lawyer use and he didn't know what the hell they were. He'd always 'mandamus' everybody, but we never had any difficulty [understanding him]." When asked if he had any other comments about his employ with Talbott, he remarked, "Glenn Talbott was the best on the stump." When encouraged to say more, Burdick added, "I often wondered if I made a mistake going there, but maybe I didn't. I don't know. I sure roped in a bunch of farmers in the state eventually."[26]

Many North Dakota Democrats knew Burdick's decision was the correct one. "My first recollection of Quentin was a young attorney working for the NDFU," recalled Governor Link. "I guess I sort of sprouted my public awareness involvement coming from a Farmers Union co-op background and finding that Burdick's fight for the farmers' cause was the same as the Farmers Union."[27] When Burdick spoke before Farmers Union conventions years later as senator, he reminisced about working for the organization. Burdick especially loved to talk about the '30s, recalled Karl Limvere, a longtime Farmers Union official. "He reminded Farmers Union audiences frequently that his dad was the president of the Farmers' Holiday Association and every time Usher met a farmer in trouble, he would say: 'I know a good lawyer for you!'"[28] Lynn Clancy, a second-generation Farmers Union member, said everyone of his generation knew that Burdick had been "a lawyer for the Farmers Union and the Farmers Union respected him because of his work."[29]

Farmers Union Progressive Alliance

In 1947, the Republican Organizing Committee (ROC), the powerful conservative wing of the Republican Party, launched a major attack against the NDFU. It began during the legislative session and was spearheaded by Grand Forks state Senator Carroll Day. Day was a powerful voice in the Senate, a skilled attorney as well as associate and friend of the private insurance industry.

The attack was twofold. First, it proposed to tax the cooperatives. Second, it wanted to put all of the Farmers Union insurance programs out of business. Three separate Senate bills were introduced to achieve both ends. One bill (SB 201) expanded the state's income tax to include all cooperative earnings not distributed in cash to its members, and cleverly excluded rural electrics and other cooperatives. A second bill (SB 51) gave the state commissioner of insurance absolute authority to terminate fraternal licenses annually. A third bill (SB 281) required all mutual insurance companies to maintain 100 percent premiums in reserve.[30] In taxing profits, Day sought to punish the very heart of the cooperative movement — profit sharing with its members. In putting unreasonable restrictions on the fraternal insurance companies, the net effect was to prevent the cooperative from doing any insurance business in the state.

Although the Farmers Union participated in important legislative initiatives in the '30s, its core organization had never been directly assaulted by the political process. In 1932, the Farmers Union initiated the anti-corporation farming act and in 1937, supported the passage of the anti-deficiency judgment law, which protected farm foreclosures from the absence of competitive bidding. At the same time, the Farmers Union failed to initiate a graduated land tax, repeal the state sales tax or initiate a four-mill levy for the school equalization fund.[31] Political defense, however, proved a much more difficult choice in the '40s than playing offense in the '30s.

The frontal attack of 1947 forced major changes in Talbott's organization. The ROC attack was so bitter against him personally and so vindictive against the pulse of the cooperative movement that the Farmers Union opted to fight political fire with political fire. The immediate first step was to defeat the three Senate bills and to keep Talbott out of trouble during the session. To those ends, Talbott wisely dispatched Burdick to Bismarck to lobby against the bills and serve as a blocking back in the many heated exchanges he got into with Day. All three bills easily passed the Senate, but in the House, Burdick helped to craft a coalition of NPL members, Democrats and a few ROC associates with large Farmers Union constituents to defeat all measures. When Day and Talbott got into a shouting match over Day's demand that Talbott turn over the entire membership of the Farmers Union to him, Burdick stepped in, successfully arguing that such a request went way beyond the rules.[32] Although the session ended on a positive note for Talbott, the whole experience had scared the hell out of him. As for Burdick, he relished in victory. "Yes, I got there in the heat of it" and "they didn't get one damn thing passed either."[33]

In June, Talbott announced the formation of the Farmers Union Progressive Alliance (FUPA) and named Burdick executive director to run it. Talbott did not want the Farmers Union to get directly involved in politics, so he opted for a separate organization, a PAC, to do the work. Its purpose was to "form an organization and carry on political action among farmers and the people of the state from a Progressive viewpoint and in the end to protect the interests of cooperation and cooperative services in the state."[34] In other words, the FUPA would work with any individual or group who believed essentially with the philosophy of the Farmers Union.[35]

In announcing its establishment, Talbott tried to mask a clear distinction between the FUPA and the NDFU. The alliance would operate under three guiding principles: It would not form a separate political party, give blanket endorsement to any political party or use the Farmers Union for political purposes.[36] No one who knew anything about North Dakota politics took Talbott seriously about the independence of the new organization. The alliance was controlled by the Farmers Union, who paid its expenses and determined its overall strategy.

Burdick, in response to Talbott's new assignment, moved to Jamestown later that year. He officially closed his Fargo law office, resigned as executive director of the North Dakota Democratic Party, and took a reluctant spouse and three children with him. He built a house and his presence demonstrated a total commitment from him and his family to be at the center of the operation, which, of course, was the headquarters of the Farmers Union in Jamestown. "The only reason Burdick decided to come to Jamestown," said Tom Burgum, a longtime Burdick Senate aide, "was because this was the most critical period of the Farmers Union for more progressive action in North Dakota."[37]

In the next couple of years, Talbott's new organization under Burdick became the biggest political motivator of change in North Dakota following the Second World War. It was a new grass-roots organization working with farmers, labor and political agendas for people who shared common interests but belonged to different organizations. Burdick schooled local alliance members to attend county NPL conventions, to obtain seats as delegates and then elect delegates to the state convention. It was an open process and alliance delegates were elected in large percentages. Once there, the alliance caucus cut deals with the NPL leadership in the endorsement process for each state primary candidate. The League would select one candidate. The alliance would pick the next candidate, and so forth down the entire ticket. After the convention, the alliance worked to get out the vote through local efforts, including the distribution of absentee ballots. Although the League and alliance often found themselves fighting over procedures and blaming each other for defeats or claiming credit for victories, the table was being set for major changes ahead.

Burdick took a lot of credit for the success of the alliance. "I organized it," boasted Burdick. "The Farmers Union for years had been beating their chests. They were nonpolitical. We wanted to solve the problems of the farmer through legal, economic and judicial means. Here comes the Legislature, which damn near upsets them the year before and almost took away their charters away and everything else."[38]

Burdick continued, "It was saved, but looked like it wasn't going to be saved a second time and that is why they came to me. They asked me if I wouldn't spend time fixing it up. I fixed it good! The Farmers Union went political. This was all born the first two years because we didn't know legally what we could do. After all, we were a business organization and so we decided to create this name and this organization. But I only lasted one year. We were too successful."[39]

Not always successful. Political solidarity, for example, between the much older NPL and the much younger FUPA never materialized. Although the FUPA endorsed the entire NPL ticket in 1948, tensions persisted. One meeting in particular that year turned into a shouting match between Frank Vogel, Coleharbor, North Dakota, and Burdick. Vogel, a staunch League legislator in the '20s and loyal member of Langer's administration in the '30s, held strong personal doubts about the two organizations working together from the start. Working "alongside the Farmers Union is darn poor politics," said Vogel.[40]

Vogel's assessment drew a bitter and instant response from Burdick. Showing noticeable anger, Burdick ripped off his suit coat as if he was preparing for battle. He told those at the meeting that the FUPA had helped the NPL win in 1948. "Yet you say here today that we are almost a handicap," Burdick told Vogel. "Some of you old timers resent new blood coming in and taking over."[41]

Political tensions occasionally spurned physical confrontations. A much publicized incident between state Senator Orris Nordhougen of Leeds, North Dakota, and Burdick occurred in the lobby of Bismarck's Patterson Hotel at the start of the 1951 legislative session. The Patterson was a favorite watering hole for politicians and lobbyists. According to newspaper accounts, the two men became involved in a personal argument, which "resulted in Burdick slapping Nordhougen," and then he "immediately apologized."[42]

The small slapping incident was symbolic of broader issues of ideology. Nordhougen, who operated an independent elevator and implement dealership in Benson County, saw the growth of Farmers Union Cooperatives as a threat to his own economic well-being. Burdick, on the other hand, believed that cooperatives were legitimate forms of much needed competition. He was testy about negative comments made to him about the illegality of cooperatives conducting business alongside private enterprise.

Exactly what Nordhougen said to Burdick is unknown. "It was something personal," said his Burdick's brother, Eugene. "It might have been that he was called a Communist or something like that. He didn't want anyone to attack his patriotism."[43] Tom Burgum, who arrrived at the Patterson within an hour of the incident, was more specific. "Orris came up and said, 'What are you radicals doing here?'"[44] Eugene also doubted the newspaper account about his brother's instant contrition. "No, I don't think he was [apologetic]," said Eugene.[45] Burgum also disputed the term "slap": "Burdick really didn't slap him. Orris thought he did." Years later Burdick told Burgum, "I really didn't hit him in the face. I just shoved him and knocked his hat off."[46]

When pressed to describe the incident, Burdick played with the question first before answering it:

> "Did you slap a legislator out in Bismarck in 1951?"
> "I did?" responded Burdick. "Which one was this?"
> "I was hoping you would tell me."
> "There was something in the Patterson Hotel. Oh yeh, yeh! Orris Nordhougen. Do you remember him?
> "Yes, the last name."

"He was a state senator," said Burdick. "He was aligned with the Leaguers, the Langer faction. I was a Leaguer, too, but not quite as Langerly as he was. The election had just been held and he was re-elected. He walked across the lobby and said, 'What do you guys want? You had better get the hell out of town — you Farmers Union guys.'"

Burdick continued, "I was the attorney for the Farmers Union at that time, and I bore all the brunt they had to offer. He staggered around and said, 'I want you guys to behave yourself.' Orris, I said, we're just down here at the opening of the session. We want to see what's on the table and see what we have to do. Anyway, the longer he stood there, the braver he got. Now what were the words he said that ticked me off?" With a little prompting, Burdick proceeded to describe the event:

> "He said something personal against you?"
> "Oh, yes!"
> "And then you hit him?"
> "Well, I didn't hit him very hard. Slap-hit. I didn't use full power on this guy. I thought he was a little bit older. But he rolled clear across the lobby, though, and I knocked his hat off is about all."
> "Did he get up and do anything?"
> "He said, 'oooooooh my heart, my heart!' after I slapped him."

"The newspaper clipping said that you made an apology."

"Hell, no!"

"No?"

"No, you're damn right I didn't. Why should I? I never saw heart problems develop so fast."[47]

The incident quickly reached Usher's ears in Washington. Moore, who was arranging congressional visits, tours and luncheons for the Farmers Union that month in Washington, recalled running into Quentin's father on the steps of the Capitol. "I never saw him dressed up quite like that," said a smiling Moore. "He had a hat on, boots, and was totally immaculate."[48]

"What's the occasion?" Moore asked Usher. "I just want you to know that I have become the father of the champion political fighter in North Dakota," replied the congressman. "Usher carried on and told me about this episode with Orris Nordhougen," said Moore. "Quentin in his younger days had a violent temper and he just hauled off and slugged him. He then immediately apologized, but the old man really got a kick out of it."[49]

In the small field of North Dakota politics, Burdick and Nordhougen's paths crossed again. It was a natural happenstance in a sparsely populated state with so many of the same few political characters participating in the game. In 1958, they ran against each other for the United States House of Representatives. There were four candidates, two of each party, running for two open seats. Burdick, running as a Democrat, and Don Short of Medora, North Dakota, running as a Republican, took the first two places. Republican Nordhougen ran a close third, while Democrat Dr. S.B. Hocking of Devils Lake, North Dakota, took a distant fourth. [50]

In later years, with Burdick safely in the United States Senate, their paths crossed once again. A recommendation came across Burdick's desk for Nordhougen's appointment to the North Dakota Wheat Commission. It was a routine appointment and one administered by Burdick simply out of courtesy. He could have objected, but he did not. "You know all Orris ever wanted to do was to come to Washington," said Burdick. "I don't think this appointment will hurt and he knows the subject. He's qualified."[51]

Although the FUPA officially lasted for only two years, its political agenda continued with a Farmers Union label. Talbott and the NDFU experimented with various other political strategies between 1949 and 1956. They established a variety of other short-term organizations and continued to get its members elected as delegates to both League and Democratic conventions. The ultimate goal, however, never wavered: create a major realignment in North Dakota's political structure. Patience, hard work and lots of money ultimately proved successful. The 1956 merger of the Nonpartisan League with the North Dakota Democratic Party was a major contribution of the Farmers Union to modern North Dakota political history.

The historical name most clearly associated with those who labored for realignment was "insurgent." It was a name first coined by Bill Allen, veteran reporter for the *Grand Forks Herald*, who covered the movement during those years. Later, of course, Lloyd Omdahl incorporated the term in the title of his 1961 book, which traced the complicated chronology of the successful merger. After 40 years, the beginnings of the insurgents remain crystal clear. It began, wrote Omdahl, in "1947 when the Legislature irritated the Farmers Union."[52] In other words, it began when Talbott created the FUPA and then chose Burdick to head it.

What remains in doubt about the movement centers on identifying the major insurgents. Memories and circumstances have changed between the 1950s and the 1990s. Nowhere is the historical record more cloudy than in evaluating the contribution of Burdick to the insurgents. Omdahl, for example, ends his book with a photo gallery of 52 major insurgents under the caption: "The Identifiable Circle." Among the stars are Burdick, Charles and Joyce Conrad, S.F. Hoffner, James Jungroth, Gorman King and Art Link. Talbott does not appear in the gallery, although Omdahl credits the Farmers Union as being the "impetus to the switch of the League into the Democratic Party."[53]

In 1961, the year the Omdahl book was published, Burdick stood as the symbol of the successful merger. He was a product of both League and Democratic traditions. He ran first as a Leaguer and lost. He ran later as a Democrat and lost. But he was the first to run on the newly combined Democratic-NPL ticket and win. Not only did Burdick win; he won big by winning a seat in the U.S. House of Representatives in 1958 and the U.S. Senate in 1960. For anyone such as Omdahl, who was associated with the new party, to in 1961 downplay the role Burdick played in the insurgent effort would have been simply politically incorrect.

In a 1995 interview with Omdahl, he viewed Burdick through a much different lens than he had 34 years earlier. Omdahl's point of view about Burdick had changed. So had a lot of North Dakota political history. The political imperative of 1961 was replaced with a more complete historical one. Burdick, of course, was gone and much had taken place in the Democrat-NPL family since 1961. No event was more important to Omdahl than the disappointing loss former Governor Bill Guy, his mentor, suffered at the hands of veteran Senator Milton Young in 1972. Guy's bitter defeat still stuck in Omdahl's craw.

He liked Burdick less in 1995 then he had in 1961 and he minced no words in saying so.

"Burdick was a peripheral person" among the insurgents, began Omdahl. "But as attorney for the Farmers Union and being a respected person among the insurgents, him just being in favor of the movement helped it." But Omdahl made no bones about Burdick being only a bench player among the insurgents. "The real work of the movement did not involve Quentin Burdick directly very much," asserted Omdahl. "He was not a leader in the movement. He was a supporter."[54]

Other insurgents challenged Omdahl's revisionism. "In the Insurgent Movement you would have to say that Quentin was the leader," stated Charles Conrad, a lifelong Burdick loyalist. "He was the one who really put our ideas over with Talbott. We used Quentin as the intermediary."[55] Even Gorman King, who urged Rep. Byron Dorgan to challenge Burdick in 1988, heaped praise on both Burdick and Talbott. "Talbott was the real architect of the Insurgent Movement," said King, and "Quentin was really the right-hand guy of Talbott and his top political operator."[56] Others spoke more bluntly. "Burdick was one of the few guys who was willing to stick his neck out and take a chance," said James Jungroth. "He recognized the fallacy of running on the Republican ticket because as soon as you were elected as a Republican, you start talking like Herbert Hoover and Burdick recognized that. He was very strong in moving us."[57] Moore, who viewed the movement from within the Farmers Union organization during those years, said that "Burdick did some of the same things in North Dakota that Hubert Humphrey did in Minnesota. You take two factors (farmers and labor) and you merge them."[58]

Burdick cut to the quick on his self-evaluation. He simply stated unabashedly: "That was my idea!"[59] Like Omdahl, Burdick's view had changed with time. From his perspective in 1992, he had every right to claim great personal credit for it. He was then 83 years old, and 36 years after the fact, still living and still serving in public office. He believed that he had not only originated the idea, but that he had come to embody it as well. He was the only successful symbol of the merger still exercising political power. "Burdick understood that the Farmers Union straddled both the NPL and the Democratic Party," noted Tom Burgum, "and with their manpower and aura, it was of critical importance. So he really courted the Farmers Union leadership, which was really an unusually able group then."[60]

The Wallace Phenomena

Henry Wallace represented to a young generation of liberals in the post-World War II era what Eugene McCarthy and George McGovern represented for a later generation of young liberals during the Vietnam era. He promised a liter ton of pure New Deal philosophy for farmers and unions during an adulterated mood of political change and compromise. He preached peace with the Soviet Union when most Americans were already shouting Cold War rhetoric. For a spell, his 1948 unsuccessful bid for the presidency as the Progressive Party candidate excited the country, gained the support of American Communists, scared the hell out of President Harry Truman and gave some encouragement to his Republican opponent, New York Governor Thomas Dewey. On Election Day, however, many Democrats abandoned Wallace and cast their votes for Truman, thus insuring Dewey's defeat. The results left Wallace's supporters distraught and disillusioned. What might have been never happened.

Among Wallace's 1948 supporters were two young Dakotans, Quentin Burdick, the lawyer from North Dakota, and George McGovern, the historian from South Dakota. They trusted his agricultural expertise and supported his anti-Cold War ideas. Both men later became critics of Truman's containment policy as members of the United States Senate. They agreed more often than not with critics of Truman's Cold War policies, who wrote:

> Henry Wallace was essentially right and Harry Truman was essentially and tragically wrong. Henry Wallace said that the United States could not purchase reliable friends. He said that the United States would end up supporting corrupt, incompetent, and repressive dictators all over the world. He said that the United States would not be able to stamp out revolution the world over. He said that the effort to contain communism would be costly in American blood and treasure. He said that a crusade against communism would lead to the repression of civil liberties at home. He said that American foreign policy would lead to militarism.[61]

Who was Henry Wallace? Why his attraction to the likes of Burdick and McGovern in 1948? It remains a tough historical question, producing many unresolved answers. As secretary of agriculture and Franklin Roosevelt's third-term vice president, (1941-1945) Wallace received copious analysis by key New Deal historians. William Leuchtenberg praised him as a brilliant plant geneticist and a first-rate economist. At the same time, he found Wallace's shy, reserve personality, his addiction to faddisms and even flights of mysticism confusing. "We are children of the transition," Wallace wrote in 1934. "We have left Egypt but we have not yet arrived at the Promised Land."[62]

Arthur Schlesinger Jr., the New Deal's court historian, characterized Wallace with sharp and penetrating prose. "Neither mysticism nor rhetoric could abolish the fissure, the emptiness, at the core of his own personality," wrote Schlesinger. "He rarely made contact with others, perhaps, because it was so hard for him to make contact with himself. His associates speculated whether he had any capacity for human affection. At times it seemed as if he had a greater sense of intimacy with plants. ... And, in his public life his inner division led to evasiveness and vacillation. Confronted by choice, he was always inclined to cut things in-half and split the difference, making eclecticism for synthesis. The quest for personal integration consumed him. It led him down strange byways in both religion and politics. In the end, neither yogis or commissars would produce a satisfactory answer."[63]

Wallace knew agriculture better than most. Leuchtenberg credited him with authorship and being the true architect of the New Deal farm programs. It was Wallace who embedded the concept of parity, not cost of production, as the cornerstone of American farm programs. He made farm subsidies, acreage, allotment and conservation practices part of American rural life and economic survival.[64] Schlesinger praised Wallace's deep understanding of agriculture, noting that Wallace was deft at explaining its unique problems, as opposed to other parts of the economy. "Business men, when confronted by reduced demand, could protect themselves by reducing output and maintaining price levels; farmers, when confronted by reduced demand, apparently have no choice but to maintain their individual output and watch prices collapse. 'In agriculture,' said Wallace succinctly, 'supply sets the price. In industry, price sets the supply.'"[65]

Wallace earned a spot in Truman's administration as secretary of commerce. He was the only continuity with the New Deal past, a political icon with respect and popularity. His persistent views, however, on a positive relationship with the Soviet Union caused consternation in the Cabinet. After a speech Wallace delivered to a large political rally in Madison Square Garden in September 1946, Truman fired him. "Henry is the most peculiar fellow I ever come in contact with," noted the president. "He wants to disband our armed forces, give Russia our atomic bomb secrets and trust a bunch of adventurers in the Kremlin Politburo."[66]

Historians of Truman predictably treat Wallace with a more critical eye than their New Deal colleagues. After the war, Wallace was simply out of the mainstream. He was a loose cannon in an atmosphere that demanded a hard line against events in Eastern Europe. He and his Progressive Party supporters stood on the extreme left wing fringe of the Democrat Party and "were tempting exasperated liberals with promises of a militant crusade for peace and justice preached in the rhetoric of the New Deal."[67] David McCullough, Truman's best-known biographer, wrote poignantly about him:

> Henry Wallace was one of the most serious-minded, fascinating figures in national public life. … He was an author, lecturer, social thinker, a firm advocate of civil rights and thorough New Dealer with a large, devoted following. With the exception of Franklin Roosevelt, he was the most popular Democrat in the country. Those who loved him saw him as one of the rare men of ideas in politics and the prophet of a truly democratic America. But he was also an easy man to make fun of and to these tough party professionals, Wallace seemed to have his head in the clouds. They had never wanted him for Vice President. He had been forced upon them in 1940, when Roosevelt threatened not to run again unless he could have Wallace as his running mate. Wallace was too intellectual, a mystic who spoke Russian and played with a boomerang and reputedly consulted with the spirit of a dead Sioux Indian chief. As Vice President he seemed pathetically out of place and painfully lacking in political talent, or even a serious interest in politics. When not presiding over the Senate he would often shut himself in his office and study Spanish. He was too remote, too controversial, too liberal — much too liberal, which was the main charge against him.[68]

Young Quentin Burdick could identify with Wallace on a personal level. He, too, carried the mantle of being too liberal — much too liberal. The label was the political albatross that hung around his neck in North Dakota. But other North Dakotans carried the liberal label: Glenn Talbott, the powerful president of the North Dakota Farmers Union, who was fighting hard to save their successful cooperative enterprises against a backlash of conservative Republican free enterprisers; Marietta, who read and agreed with much of what Wallace wrote in liberal magazines; brothers Charles and Gaylord Conrad and their spouses Joyce and Abigail Conrad; and still others, such as Charles Tighe, and Mart and Lois Vogel, who sought peace abroad as well as expansion of democracy at home, especially civil rights and an equal place for women. Wallace stood for what they stood for. They agreed foremost with his foreign policy stands, but trusted his agriculture and savvy labor views as well. For all of them, Truman was suspect while Wallace was trustworthy. He emerged as their political hero and they supported him unabashedly as their candidate for president in 1948. The Wallace candidacy was all about their dreams of liberalism in the years that followed war.

**Usher and Emma Burdick with
baby Quentin, summer of 1908.**
(University of North Dakota archives)

Baby Quentin, 1908.
(family photo)

Usher Burdick family. Back row: Quentin, Eugene and Usher. Front row: Grandma Robertson, Eileen and Emma. Circa 1924. (family photo)

Quentin Burdick in early 1930s.
(University of North Dakota archives)

Burdick as University of Minnesota football player, 1929. (University of North Dakota archives)

Quentin Burdick family photo around 1949. Left to right: Jon, Marietta, Jan, Jennifer, Jessica and Quentin. (family photo)

Chats with Usher on a typical North Dakota small town street, 1940s.

(family photo)

Stump speaking for Congress in 1958.
(North Dakota State Historical Society)

Burdick accepts nomination for Congress in 1958 in Bismarck.
(North Dakota State Historical Society)

A.J. Agard, Mrs. Grey Bear and Congressman Quentin Burdick, Feb. 1959.
(North Dakota State Historical Society)

Burdick's 1960 campaign slogan "Beat Benson with Burdick."
(University of North Dakota archives)

Congressman Burdick running for Senate in June 1960.
(University of North Dakota archives)

Sen. Lyndon B. Johnson and Congressman Burdick at Bismarck airport on May 31, 1960 during the Senate campaign. (North Dakota State Historical Society)

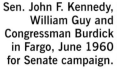

Sen. John F. Kennedy, William Guy and Congressman Burdick in Fargo, June 1960 for Senate campaign. (North Dakota State Historical Society)

Congressman Burdick, Rev. Grindlund and Gov. John Davis, 1960 Senate campaign. (North Dakota State Historical Society)

Sen. John F. Kennedy speaking at Burdick's 52nd birthday party in Fargo on June 19, 1960. (University of North Dakota archives)

Sen. Burdick and UND President Tom Clifford at UND football game, Sept. 1975. (University of North Dakota archives)

Sen. Burdick speaking
at groundbreaking for
Earth Science Building,
UND, October 1989.
(University of North Dakota
archives)

Gage Burdick, 1978.
(family photo)

Jocelyn Burdick.
(family photo)

The National Farmers Union organization, in general, and the North Dakota Farmers Union, in particular, shared a long-term relationship with Wallace. It began in the depth of the Depression when family farmers were leaving their farms in droves and Wallace as Roosevelt's secretary of agriculture was drafting new legislation to stop their exodus. The relationship was bolstered by a sweet deal between the Farm Security Administration (FSA) — a U.S. Department of Agriculture office — and Farmers Union Cooperatives. The deal authorized flexibility in FSA loans to farmers, which allowed them to purchase stock in local grain cooperatives. Farmers Union members bought stock in Grain Terminal Association (GTA) elevators, and the enterprise, run by the Twin Cities, grew tremendously as a direct result of the policy.[69]

The political climate changed significantly after the end of World War II. In Washington, Wallace remained a favorite of Farmers Union leaders and a majority of its members. He was the most knowledgeable national spokesman for American family farmers in the Truman administration. He stood solidly for Farmers Union programs and policies. Truman, on the other hand, was an unknown agricultural species. In North Dakota, the Farmers Union established a political action group and named Quentin Burdick to be its executive director. With the tremendous success of Farmers Union cooperatives, the political landscape had changed here as well. The Republican Party was ruthless in its attempts to thwart cooperative growth — even attempting to legislate it out of existence — forcing the Farmers Union to take a stronger political position.

When Wallace began to explore his presidential plans in 1947, he actively courted Farmers Union support. On May 30, 1947, Wallace made a one-day appearance in Bismarck, sponsored by the North Dakota Farmers Union. At a noon luncheon, he met with union leaders, including Burdick and other members of the newly formed Progressive Alliance. In the evening, Wallace gave a public address. He told the largely Farmers Union audience that the farm program, "which Roosevelt and I built with farmers' help," was now being systematically destroyed by "the hand of the Republicans." Heads nodded with approval as Wallace continued. They knew all about it. The same attack was well under way in North Dakota, too. Wallace closed his talk with reference to Truman. "If the Democratic Party becomes the war party and the party of reaction in 1948," said Wallace, "I shall take a Democratic vacation."[70]

In June, Wallace wrote about his North Dakota Farmers Union visit and its new political spokesman, Quentin Burdick. His comments were published in the popular liberal magazine, *New Republic*, where Wallace contributed a regular opinion column. He made several important points. The North Dakota Farmers Union in the 1940s was the heir of the first Nonpartisan League in the early

1900s. Under the talented leadership of Charles and then Glenn Talbott, the organization had far out-distanced the League memberships and enterprises. Thirty-five thousand of 57,000 farm families belonged to the Farmers Union. "They pay five dollars a family each year in dues," wrote Wallace. "For that they get a national, a statewide and even a county newspaper, and membership in one of the best organizations in the country."[71] The organization included 130 cooperatives that supplied farmers with oil, gas and farm machinery; more than 300 local grain elevators; 75 credit unions; and a shopping list of insurance programs.[72] Because of these factors, Wallace concluded that "the farmers of North Dakota are moving toward a new agrarian radicalism."[73]

Wallace heaped a bushel of individual praise on Burdick. Here was a bright and hard working attorney from a pedigreed, Progressive family working for the best state Farmers Union organization in the country. Here was the new leader of this agrarian radicalism in North Dakota. Wallace called Burdick "an outstanding young progressive" whose Progressive Alliance he heads "will support progressive men and issues, irrespective of party and will run its own candidates."[74]

Even before the Wallace visit, Burdick was searching for someone with pure Progressive credentials to support for president in 1948. He, like other liberals of his generation, put issues ahead of political parties. In May, Burdick raised doubts about the future of the country in a short letter to his father. "Truman is absolutely no good," wrote Quentin. "The Republicans are equally bad. So what can a Progressive do I ask?"[75] Although Usher did not write back, his son already answered his own letter. He would support Wallace. Progressive ideas were more important to him than anything else.

In the months ahead, Burdick moved further to the left than Talbott and the Farmers Union leadership. Many Farmers Union members, such as V.C. 'Hafey' Moore, Dickey County organization leader for the Farmers Union Progressive Alliance, urged Talbott to support Wallace. "Pressingly urge that the Progressive Alliance lend its utmost in support to Henry Wallace's courageous fight for peace and prosperity," Moore telegrammed to Talbott. "I am firmly convinced that the very existence of the Farmers Union Cooperative Movement organizations depends upon the success of Henry Wallace's fighting crusade"[76] Talbott demurred. He refused to sacrifice the power of the Progressive Alliance in North Dakota for a third-party endorsement of Wallace for president. In responding to Moore, he outlined his reasons. "It is obvious, I think, if the Farmers Union Progressive Alliance is to be successful in cleaning up the legislature and state offices here in North Dakota, which parenthetically is a 'must' if we are not to face liquidation in the next legislative session, we have no choice but to work through the columns of the Republican Party. With so many of our people wholly inexperienced in political action, we felt that forthright support of a third party, would so confuse the matter in the minds of thousands of our people here in North Dakota, that we probably would defeat our purposes here without being of substantial benefit to Harry."[77]

The North Dakota Progressive Party was established in spite of the decision of the Farmers Union not to officially support Wallace. It was a very small group of less than a couple hundred people. They were primarily liberals in their 30s or early 40s who were simply dissatisfied with the policies and practices of the Truman presidency. They believed Wallace could and would do better. Those with Farmers Union ties were backbone of the group, but the common denominator among all of them was "just basic liberals," said Gorman King, who liked Wallace, but voted for Truman.[78] Charles and Joyce Conrad echoed the liberal tag, casting their votes for Wallace because Truman "hadn't been liberal enough" and because "we were unalterably opposed to the loyalty oath. Our Wallace support was a reaction to Truman."[79]

There were other reasons, too. North Dakota Senator Kent Conrad recalled the close personal relationship that existed between the Burdicks and his parents, Gaylord and Abigail, who were killed in a tragic automobile accident in the early 1950s. Conrad recalled, "I can remember very, very clearly being in their house — I was younger than 5 years old, because my parents were still alive — the very close camaraderie. I mean you could feel it. You could sense it between them. They were real allies."[80] Years later Conrad talked to Burdick about the 1948 campaign and why he and his parents were so strong for Wallace. "I think it was this sense of his identification with the little guy," said Conrad. He continued,

> That here is somebody who is going to stand up for the little guy, and that the big economic interests always seem to have their allies. Wallace was secretary of agriculture, and Quentin was very interested in agriculture policy. He understood completely its importance to North Dakota because we are dominated by agriculture. If agriculture did not prosper, North Dakota was not going to. That went right on to the main streets, from the farm gates to the main streets of every city and town in the state. Here was somebody who cared. Wallace genuinely cared about agriculture, cared about farmers, understood their plight, and understood the enormous pressure they were under.[81]

Although the North Dakota chapter of Wallace's Progressive Party did not amount to much, it did accomplish its primary goal of securing Wallace a place on the North Dakota ballot. It also sought to send delegates to attend the Wallace convention in Philadelphia the last weekend in July. Delegate selections were not contested. It was difficult to find anyone who was available and who could pay his own expenses. A week before the convention started, a news release from the Wallace campaign headquarters announced that Burdick and Gaylord Conrad were selected from North Dakota to serve on the platform committee.[82] The selection was really more honorary than substantive. Select members of the committee who had met earlier in Chicago and other cities during the spring had already drafted the platform document. There were a total of 74 members eventually selected to the committee, but only 55 attended any meetings.[83] Burdick and Conrad would bless the final draft, but little else. The platform was alive and fully grown by the time they were appointed to the committee.

Two days after the news release, Burdick wrote a memo to Talbott. He informed him that he would take a portion of his vacation to be in Philadelphia at the time of the convention. He stated that the trip would be "at my own expense" and that he would "on no account attempt to represent the Farmers Union." At the same time, Burdick made it absolutely clear why he was taking personal vacation time to be there. "I believe it would be tragic if North Dakota, with its progressive background and present progressive organizations, was not in someway represented at the Wallace convention."[84]

By the time Talbott got around to answering the memo, Burdick was already back from Philadelphia. It really did not matter much. Talbott was fully aware of Burdick's intentions beforehand and believed his presence there would do more good than harm. In responding, Talbott was kind and supportive. He instructed Burdick not to take personal vacation time and that actual travel expenses should be charged to the Progressive Alliance. While not endorsing the convention per se, Talbott said Burdick's attendance was a way of "keeping yourself completely informed" and was "part of your job and responsibility as Director of the Progressive Alliance."[85]

In the meantime, Progressive Party colleagues, friends and associates always recalled Burdick's attendance with pride and maybe a touch of envy. "I knew that Quentin was a delegate in Philadelphia when Wallace was nominated," said Mart Vogel.[86] "Quentin went to Philadelphia to attend the convention for Wallace and supported him at that time," recalled Stanley Moore.[87] "Oh yes. He was a delegate to the convention," said Bob Vogel.[88]

The Progressive Party held its convention in the City of Brotherly Love in late July 1948. The convention began at an uptown hotel on Friday, July 23, and ended in a huge, outdoor rally at Shibe Park, the home of the Philadelphia Athletics on Sundays. "It was the darndest thing that ever happened," noted one account. "There were 3,240 delegates and alternatives selected to attend the convention. Journalists enjoyed contrasting the Wallace delegates with those who attended the Democrat and Republican conventions. They observed that the Philadelphia delegates acted differently in many ways. They slept in tents and trailers rather than hotels. Although they enjoyed less personal wealth, they still tipped better. They drank less beer and more Coca Cola. They walked more and rode less. They were unusually polite, seldom rude and carried themselves in a serene almost religious manner."[89]

The social profiles of the attendees read more like a list of delegates to a National Democratic Convention of the 1970s after adopting McGovern's new rules for delegate selection. Some were very old and some were very young. Michael Kennedy of Davenport, Iowa, 88, was the oldest delegate. Jack Hester of Omaha, Nebraska, 16, was the youngest. There were, of course, more men than women, but the 27 percent women's total was as significant as was the 40 percent who belonged to trade unions. Refreshingly, there were only two members of Congress among the delegates and a cache of editors, scientists, educators, artists and musicians. Most were under 60 years of age (60 percent were in this age bracket) and one delegate in five was a veteran. There were more professionals than business types and more business types than farmers, but all placed Philadelphia on their agenda. They came because they believed in Wallace and the issues he articulated.[90]

The convention drew small interest from the press. It was not a major news event of that summer. Most journalists who covered it were more critical than supportive. Wallace was more of a conversation piece than a viable presidential candidate. Yet, his speeches always made good copy. Rebecca West, the British novelist, covered the convention for an East Coast daily. "The youth at the Wallace convention was not intelligent," she observed. "It might have been staged as a presentation of the students most likely to flunk in 1949."[91] What prompted her attack on the young delegates was never explained. The *Detroit Free Press* waved the red, white and blue in big swaths: "Every type of crackpot, every known kind of malcontent, every species of hate-blinded neurotic, every element of anti-Americanism," editorialized the paper, "will be on hand to jeer and sneer at all this nation has ever stood for in its most exalted moments of service and sacrifice."[92]

The party platform, like the delegates, seemed out of place. The document was long (more than 6,000 words) and ahead of its time. It read more like a document of the '60s than the late '40s. It was visionary, controversial and too liberal for the mainstream of American voters. It blamed the United

States for the origins of the Cold War, called for the enactment of federal Civil Rights laws to end racial discrimination, supported constitutional amendments to guarantee equal rights for women and the right to vote for 18-year-olds, and a Cabinet position for education.

The farm platform read like a Farmers Union novella. It urged a graduated land tax, immediate flood control projects and universal electrification of all farms as soon as possible. The centerpiece of the farm plank, however, was the cornerstone of the National Farmers Union philosophy. It stated simply and powerfully that the Progressive Party affirmed support for farm families. "We stand for the family-type farm as the basic unit of American agriculture."[93]

There were two convention highlights: the nomination of Wallace and Democrat U.S. Senator Glenn Taylor of Idaho for president and vice president. These nominations occurred Saturday at the host hotel midst a wild demonstration of sign waving and song singing. A parade of placards with pithy political slogans such as "End Jim Crow," "Wallace or War," "Repeal the Draft," Why Tarry with Harry" and "Fooey on Dewey" marched through the crowd while folksinger Pete Seeger led the crowd with "Great Day."[94] Fred Stover, the president of the Iowa Farmers Union, nominated Wallace. On Sunday, Wallace and Taylor appeared at a rally in Shide Park before 32,000 supporters who bought tickets to support their campaign. When accepting, Wallace spoke almost entirely about foreign affairs and the call for the Allies to give up Berlin. "We can support — and we are supporting — armies during this cold war, but we cannot purchase suicide. We can buy governments, but we can't buy peoples."[95] Taylor, however, offered the best line: "I am not leaving the Democratic Party. It left me. Wall Street and the military have taken over."[96]

The 1948 presidential election proved to be a close one between Truman and Dewey. Wallace and his Progressive Party, however, took a terrible drubbing. They received less than 2 percent of the popular vote (1,119,032) and no electoral votes. It was a devastating defeat, labeled "one of the left's worse setbacks in recent American history."[97] There were few bright spots. Wallace did best in two urban centers, New York City and Los Angeles, and rural North Dakota. He captured 4 percent of the total votes in Burdick's home state (8,391) and did best in Burdick's home county, Williams (13 percent), and nearby Mountrail County (10.8 percent). Wallace carried five precincts in both of these northwestern counties. Dewey beat Truman, and William Lemke and Usher Burdick won two seats in the U.S. House of Representatives.[98]

Wallace did not visit North Dakota during the campaign. He gave his only address on agriculture issues at Moorhead, Minnesota, on October 10, 1948. His appearance was overshadowed almost entirely by his visit to the Twin Cities the next day and did not receive much media coverage. The only printed source seems to be Wallace's rhetorical one-liner: "Who stuck the pitchfork in the farmers back?"[99] The occasion was, however, a special one for Wallace supporters in Fargo. Many went to hear him and his appearance was not without controversy. "There was a good deal of feeling in the area about Wallace," recalled Mart Vogel, "and anyone who spoke a kind word about him."[100] In those years, Mart and Lois Vogel attended Fargo's northside Congregational Church. They vividly recalled what happened to their minister as a result of Wallace's appearance. "A minister who was asked to give an opening prayer and introduce Wallace in Moorhead cancelled. So our minister was asked to introduce Wallace and give the invocation. He did and the church congregation fired him."[101]

Burdick's participation in the Wallace campaign put another too-liberal notch in his North Dakota belt. He paid the price in personal slights and political defeats. In 1956, Burdick ran against incumbent Republican Senator Milton R. Young. As a decided Democrat underdog in the Age of Eisenhower, Burdick challenged Young to a debate. He hoped it would increase his stock to best Young, who was always uncomfortable in public speaking because of a speech impediment. Young ducked the challenge and pulled out the Wallace card. "I would refuse to debate him," said Young, "if he still supported three resolutions that he helped to draft for the 1948 Progressive Party platform."[102] The three planks (denouncing the FBI, requesting more military disarmament and insisting on no more financial aid to the Chinese Nationalist government of Chiang Kai-shek) were political hot potatoes in a heightened hysteria of anti-communism. Young's response caught Burdick off guard. He never responded directly to Young's question. Instead, he issued the following: "Since you won't debate the main issue of this campaign unconditionally, I offer to open the debate to include any and every issue in the campaign," said Burdick, "as long as I debate you and you alone."[103] There was, of course, no debate and Young easily won re-election.

Historians later pursued Burdick about Wallace. He did reply to Curtis D. MacDougall, the author of *Gideon's Army*, a copious three-volume work on Wallace and the 1948 presidential campaign. "It is my opinion," Burdick wrote to MacDougall, "that Wallace would have received a much greater vote, in fact a huge vote in North Dakota, but for one thing. The farmers were afraid they might lose their farm program and at the last minute they voted for Truman."[104] Ironically, MacDougall never mentioned the correspondence, writing instead, "In Fargo a young lawyer, Luther Burdick, was the most active Progressive," but he "refused to talk with MacDougall about their activities in the 1950s."[105]

Years later Burdick talked privately about the summer of '48 with Tom

Burgum, one of his closest Senate aides. Burdick said he took a July vacation that summer and ended up being stuck between trains in Philadelphia. He admitted planning it that way and that he was very interested in Wallace's candidacy. Once there, however, he began to change his mind. "I have never seen so many card-carrying Communists together in one place," he told Burgum, "and I left that place just as quick as that train would take me."[106] Burgum elaborated, "It had become very clear, very early to Burdick that Henry Wallace had bought some hard-line Communist stuff and was absolutely useless. He knew Henry Wallace. He never thought of him as a traitor. He just thought he was a man who was [in] way over his head and was being used by some not very nice people."[107]

During a 1991 interview with Burdick, the Wallace incident was broached again.

> "I was there as an observer," said Burdick. "I was there on my own. I wasn't elected as a delegate. I was just there to occupy a seat like anybody else. I didn't vote. I didn't have any function. I was working for the Farmers Union and we were interested in what was going to happen to a Progressive Party in North Dakota. I went there because I talked to the officers of the Farmers Union and they thought it would be a good thing if I did go there, so I got a leave of absence and I went down there for a day or two."[108]

Burdick's later recollections about his role in the 1948 Progressive Party convention took the historical bite out of his real enthusiasm for Wallace. He was on vacation, but a planned vacation to attend the convention. He, not the Farmers Union, initiated the trip and it was never described as a leave of absence. He was a participant in the 1948 North Dakota Progressive Party convention, and from all contemporary accounts, a delegate to the national convention. Whether he was elected or selected was only splitting hairs. As for the Communist disconnect, Burdick wanted to make it absolutely clear there was no relationship. "They had all kinds of interpretations on why I was there," Burdick said in reference to his political opponents who later pinned the red tag on his participation.[109] Time and circumstances had clearly altered his memory or interpretation. Burdick did not share the same fervor he held in 1948 when he wrote Talbott about the need to represent North Dakota Progressives in Philadelphia, although even a year after the convention, he was still wearing a tie that read, "Win With Wallace."[110] The Wallace phenomena had become a historical artifact in Burdick's consciousness. It was no longer relevant to the public career of Senator Burdick, but it had surely simmered during the summer of '48.

Run, Run, Run

Quentin Burdick ran three times for state office between 1942 and 1956 – the same number of contests he ran for in local Fargo offices before. The efforts unfortunately produced the same disappointing results: three more elections and three more defeats. In 1942, he ran as a Nonpartisan League-endorsed candidate for lieutenant governor in the Republican column. He won the primary contest, but lost to Democrat Henry Holt in the general election. In 1946, he ran as Democrat for governor against Republican incumbent Governor Fred Aandahl and lost. In 1956, he ran as a Democrat for the United States Senate against incumbent Senator Milton R. Young and lost again. Six political races and six political defeats in 22 years seemed enough even for Burdick.

Analysis of Burdick's three state races reveals changes in North Dakota's political landscape and his own political philosophy. He ran strongest as a Republican in his first race for lieutenant governor in 1942. He defeated his Republican opponent, Henry Holt, by a comfortable margin of 12,000 votes (60,258 to 38,199). As an NPL candidate, Burdick lost only five eastern counties (Barnes, Nelson, Pembina, Ransom and Walsh). The fall election loss to Democrats was very tight. Burdick lost by less than 3,000 votes (81,304 to 78,585). He carried 28 of the state's 53 counties, but none in the more populous Red River Valley.[111]

The 1942 election was especial noteworthy for the Burdick family, which made political history in that election. This was the first time that a father and son's name appeared on the same state ballot. Usher and Quentin were both nominated by the NPL for state office and each later won his June Republican primary contests. In Williams County, a third Burdick name also appeared on the ballot. The younger son, Eugene, sought a third term as state's attorney.[112] When the final tallies were counted in November, all three Burdicks carried their home county, but only Usher and Eugene won their races. The Burdick family made political history in 1942, but Quentin remained unelected.

Burdick ran weakest as a Democrat in his next two races against ROC Republicans.

In the1946 race for governor, he won the Democrat primary without opposition, but was crushed in the general election by Governor Aandahl. The final tally was 116,672 votes to 52,719. Burdick managed to carry only two counties – sparsely populated Bowman in the southwestern corner, and his home county, Williams. In the 1956 United States Senate race, he again won the Democratic primary without opposition but suffered another humiliating defeat at the hands of Senator Young (155, 305 to 87,919). This time Burdick failed to carry even Williams County or any other county for that matter.[113]

The political affiliation of the three races reflects Burdick's changing political philosophy. It was hard, very hard for him to shed his Republican clothes. He saw Progressivism through Republican tailors. He was born and raised a Republican. Although he never wore the three-piece suits, the old NPL'ers still wore clothes that bore a Republican label. Burdick ended his affiliation, however, with the NPL in August 1944. He stormed out of its convention in a fit of anger when the NPL refused to nominate his father as an independent candidate for the United States Senate against incumbent Senator Gerald P. Nye. Nye previously defeated Usher in the June primary contest in a closely contested race among Nye, Burdick and Fargo attorney Lynn J. Stambaugh.[114] Less than a year later, Burdick accepted the position of secretary of the North Dakota Democratic state central committee, promising to carry out the mandate to "establish a clear-cut difference between progressive or liberal interpretation of government policies and conservative or reactionary versions thereof."[115]

The election results also verified that a liberal did better in a Republican column than the Democrat column. This was simply the way it was in North Dakota, like it or not. At the same time, there was something uncomfortable, maybe even unsettling about the fit — the Republican garb simply did not match Burdick's political philosophy anymore. Burdick felt more comfortable wearing Democratic colors and donned them for the first time in 1946. The only problem was that the right colors painfully produced poor political results, with terrible political consequences. Burdick running as a Democrat was clobbered hard twice.

There were more insights. Burdick always did better in a race where his opponent was not an incumbent. In races against ROC incumbents Aandahl and Young, there was simply little chance of success. Burdick carried the state's most Republican and German-Russian counties (Emmons, Logan and McIntosh) when he ran with NPL endorsement in the Republican column, but throughout his later successful career as a U.S. Senator, he seldom did. Voters in those counties put party ahead of person even if it was the same candidate. Usher Burdick appeared on the same ballot in two of Quentin's three races (1942 and 1956) and won both. North Dakota voters liked Burdick the father, but not Burdick the son. There were no Burdick coattails for Quentin. Finally, the 1956 defeat was the nadir of Burdick's political career. "The loss of the U.S. Senate election to the incumbent Senator Milton R. Young was a heartbreaking event for Quentin and Marietta Burdick," said Myron Bright, a Fargo lawyer and staunch Burdick supporter.[116]

The depth of Burdick's despair during and after that election ran deep.

Gorman King recalled it began the very evening of Burdick's nomination. The Kings and the Burdicks were riding home in the same car. As they approached the Kings' residence in Valley City, Marietta began to cry. "Why do you people keep doing this to Quentin?" she asked King. Before King could respond, he looked first at Quentin. "It was the first time I ever saw tears in his eyes," said King.[117] Politically, the answer to Marietta's question was rather simple, but the emotions of the hour made a response impossible. "We knew Young was unbeatable and it was a sacrifice deal," King said later. "But Burdick was our strongest name and candidate. He did not want to run personally, but cleared it with Glenn Talbott ahead of time."[118]

The race was made even nastier by the presence of independent candidate Arthur C. Townley. Townley, the grandfather of the Nonpartisan League, was now a red-baiter in the era of Senator Joseph McCarthy of Wisconsin. Townley's committee was aptly named "The Citizens Committee for Better Understanding of the Communist Threat." The Communist threat was clearly the newly merged Democrat-NPL Party, and many North Dakota Democrats complained bitterly about Townley's entry into the race. One of the dissenters, P.W. Lanier Jr. of Fargo, complained bitterly after the election to the U.S. Senate Subcommittee on Privileges and Elections. "He lives out of a suitcase," wrote Lanier, "and it is difficult to say for sure where he can be located." He was "put into this race for the one purpose of vilifying and libeling the Democratic Party, both state and national, for the benefit of the Republican candidates," and has "directed his entire attack against Quentin Burdick."[119]

Other friends observed more of the same. It had been a tough race, with Burdick's patriotism called into question by Young and Townley because of his 1948 participation at the Wallace convention. In Fargo, Dr. G. Wilson Hunter hosted an election eve party in his northside home. Friends and political supporters hoped for the best, but all were preparing for the worst. The Burdicks, of course, mingled with the guests while trying to ignore the inevitable verdict. "It was a wake," said Bright. "Quentin and Marietta sat on the steps with a very sad look — one of the saddest I have ever seen. It was truly a sad day. Frankly, I never thought that Quentin would run again."[120]

Bright's observation was absolutely correct. Burdick's political career was finished. He was reconciled to it. The defeat left him and Marietta highly demoralized. Burdick kept much inside of him while Marietta was more vocal; she was hurt, angry and adamant that her husband would never go through another election defeat. The Burdicks reassessed their future. They enjoyed a steady income, were blessed with a growing family and shared a very close personal relationship. It was time for him to set politics aside. Enough was enough.

Let someone else shoulder the political burden. Burdick had carried the ball more than any other candidate in North Dakota history without scoring a single point. He was then 48 years old. He had been running for political office in North Dakota for 22 years. The voters said no to him in 1934, 1936, 1940, 1942, 1946 and 1956. Now it was his turn to say no to them. He was finished. He threw his political jersey away.

Years later in reflection, Burdick interpreted these defeats in a much different light. He acknowledged he was not "smart enough to quit," but then incorrectly repeated the same erroneous statement he made after losing the three Fargo elections: "If I was losing steadily or staying steady," said Burdick, "it might have been a different proposition, but I was gaining."[121] He was not. He also forgot that he had actually carried the three predominantly German Russian counties running as a Nonpartisan Leaguer in the 1942 election. "There are three counties I've never carried, but I gain each time. McIntosh is one, Emmons and Logan, but I didn't lose by much and I'm getting closer."[122]

Attorney

For all of Burdick's political work with the Farmers Union, it is easy to forget that most of his tenure with the organization was spent as a trial lawyer. He defended a great number of lawsuits filed against the Farmers Union Insurance Company in many North Dakota counties. The majority of these cases involved personal injury suits brought against the insurance company. Burdick represented the insurance company either by reaching pretrial settlements or by trying the case before a jury. He also became involved in the establishment of rural electric cooperatives and served as the attorney for one of the state's largest one in Cass County. On occasion, Burdick defended the Farmers Union from political attacks in North Dakota and even represented the Utah Farmers Union in a libel suit against the Utah Farm Bureau. Burdick's legal work for the Farmers Union was as important as his work as lobbyist, political organizer, insurgent and candidate for public office. He was a man for all seasons, but practicing law probably gave him the most satisfaction and the greatest sense of accomplishment during his Farmers Union days.

James Jungroth, longtime Jamestown attorney, knew more about Burdick's legal practice with the Farmers Union than anyone. "I traveled with him," recalled Jungroth. "I went to work for the Farmers Union in 1950 when I got out of law school. They called me an insurance adjuster, but they made me his flunky, which was a super job for me. Quentin tried almost all the lawsuits that the Farmers Union got into all over the state of North Dakota. We are talking about auto accidents for the insurance company. I did the legwork. I was with him on the various trials and I suppose we tried cases in two-thirds of the counties in North Dakota."[123]

Procedure for trying cases in North Dakota in those days stood in marked contrast from the rules that govern trials in the 21st century. "I would describe it as trial by ambush," noted Jungroth with a big smile and a chuckle. "You didn't reveal anything you had to the other side, nor were we required to do so. You didn't tell them your witnesses and vice versa."[124] The lack of shared information usually meant more trials and less pretrial settlements. Each side investigated the accident for its client and brought its secrets with it to court. The side with the most secrets often prevailed. There were very few depositions, the major exception being physicians' testimony, which both sides introduced to bolster their cases. In short, everyone went to court with his own deck and played his hand. "You had to be quick on your feet," said Jungroth, "because there were a lot of things that were going to happen."[125]

Jungroth described a typical insurance case. The trial would be set for Monday in most small-town county seats. "I would met with Quentin in the hotel room on Sunday afternoon and he would say 'tell me what the case is about,'" recalled Jungroth. "We would go through all of it and he had barely looked at it before that. I did all the investigating and I put it together, but in those days you didn't research like you do now, either."[126] Burdick would take handwritten notes and then would type them up because neither he nor Jungroth could read them the next day. A normal trial usually took three days and seldom went beyond five days or Friday, the end of the week. The first day centered on selecting a jury and making opening statements. Testimony for both sides consumed the next day or two. Testimony was followed by jury instructions and sitting around waiting for the verdict. "If you lost the case, it was seldom appealed."[127]

According to Jungroth, Burdick was a "very bright" person and a "super trial lawyer."[128] It was fairly common for Burdick to meet his main client the first day of the trial. The lack of personal contact required Burdick to make a quick assessment of his client's character and to decide almost instantly which potential jurors to select. Both lawyers agreed beforehand that if they were likely to lose the case, it was best to pick "conservative Republicans for the jury because they were tight with the dollar."[129] Once the trial commenced, there was no time for lengthy deliberations or delays. Burdick's physical appearance in the courtroom was daunting. He looked more like a strong farmer than a slick insurance lawyer. He moved deftly around the courtroom, always poised. He was especially adroit at examining evidence. Jungroth described his colleague as "a good public speaker" who demonstrated "convincing empathy with the jury and they related to him, too."[130]

At times, Burdick shocked his younger assistant with his repertoire of legal trivia. "On our first appeal to the North Dakota Supreme Court, we needed a supersedeas bond," recalled Jungroth. "Now I have been at this for 40 some years and I have never tried to memorize how to prepare a supersedeas bond. I pull out a form and I dictate it. Burdick picked up the machine and dictated the supersedeas bond. It's a fairly long bond and you have to have all the stuff in there!"[131]

"How and why the hell did you learn that?" Jungroth asked Burdick.

"Burdick replied that he had little else to do in Fargo, so he would memorize certain documents that he did when he was in his office."[132]

The two men developed a regular routine on their jaunts around the state. They always stayed in the cheapest hotels because Burdick insisted on it. They also ate Chinese cuisine whenever the opportunity presented itself. Every Chinese family who ran a cafe in North Dakota knew Burdick. "You would go in the front door and from the back someone would shout: 'Ah, Mr. Burdick!'" Jungroth liked to drink a lot more than Burdick, whom he described as "not much of a boozer." Simply translated, that meant Burdick on occasion would have a beer or two. So when Jungroth headed toward the bars, Burdick went back to the hotel room to call Marietta. "He made a zillion long distance calls to her."[133] On the road, Burdick would sometimes suddenly stop the car to pick buffalo berries and come back with a handful. He seemed to know where they were in many of the state's western counties. In their close association, which spanned a couple of years, Jungroth said Burdick never took himself too seriously. He was always "first on the shovel" to release a car from a snowbank. Burdick often gave his younger colleague good advice for being a good lawyer: "Take all the criminal cases because you get a lot of really good experience and they're damn near all guilty anyway, so it doesn't make a damn if you screw it up, and even if you do represent bad people, it doesn't hurt you any."[134]

Other lawyers who knew Burdick observed similar qualities. His brother, Eugene, noted that Quentin possessed a technical mindset of sorts. Quentin tinkered with cars and buildings almost his entire life. He was a self-taught handyman, proud of his work and never too daunted to fix anything that needed fixing. Working on machines was his way of blowing off steam, and he did it often. Although he never became a perfectionist like his brother, he could make most things work. Quentin not only understood the mechanical functions, he also knew what was possible and not possible when a machine broke down or caused accidents. In court, he was a formidable opponent. He did not require a textbook diagram to sustain his objection, and he could explain his reasoning in simple, layman's terms. Juries, which were often composed of tinkerers like Burdick, found his knowledge of mechanics convincing. In short, Burdick was a perfect attorney for the Farmers Union Insurance Company. "He knew what caused accidents," said Eugene. "I think he was a good defense lawyer for a jury. He could argue rather soundly."[135]

Loose trial procedures also fit Burdick's personality and work ethic. He disliked paperwork and the task of preparing testimony. He was never a paper lawyer. Burdick preferred to wing it, and with Jungroth doing the background, he enjoyed the daily combat of besting his opponent on the field of surprises. It was almost like playing football again. The game plan was always altered in some fashion by the players in the game. Burdick relished courtroom competition and the excitement of surprises and challenges. "In conversations with him," recalled his old college roommate, Morteer Skewes, "he told me that he did not really have a library. Most of the books he used were in the trunk of his car, but of course, the type of trial work was automobile cases, which didn't involve a lot of preparation. I don't think he was much on office work."[136]

Burdick improved his legal practice with the Farmers Union hire. It significantly broadened his exposure around the state. He came to know a lot more lawyers and found himself more comfortable practicing his craft in western counties than in Cass. Physical exposure did not, however, improve his personal standing among most members of the North Dakota Bar Association. He still carried the Burdick name. A 1956 incident in Grand Forks demonstrated once again the low opinion Burdick held among his peers. It was an election year and he drove to Grand Forks in hopes of putting in a political plug for his race against Senator Young at the annual convention of the Bar Association. He never received the slightest opportunity to make that appearance. "Members of the bar treated him terrible," noted Lois Vogel, who with her attorney husband, Mart, of Fargo, was in attendance. "They wouldn't even invite him to come in because he was a Democrat."[137] Her husband agreed. "I thought it was in poor taste."[138] The slight came as no surprise for the times. Most North Dakota lawyers were staunch Republicans who wholly supported Young, and those in charge saw no reason to invite Burdick to address the brethren. He was an attorney, yes, but one with an unacceptable liberal portfolio and a radical, anti-free-enterprise employer.

In court, Burdick sometimes appeared testy about his brand of politics and defensive about his employer. Those who crossed the line never forgot the repercussions, even when the lawyer making the statements was a personal friend and political supporter. "I remember one time in a final argument," recalled Mart Vogel, "in a case that Burdick was defending and I was for the plaintiff in a federal law suit in Grand Forks[,] I referred to something he had said in his closing arguments as 'just some more campaign oratory.' He never really forgave me for that remark. He did carry grudges."[139]

Myron Bright recalled a similar incident in a Lisbon, North Dakota, court-room. The two friends were opponents in a personal injury suit in Lisbon, southeast of Fargo. They drove down together in Burdick's car, probably to save expenses and talk about Democratic politics. Bright represented the plain-tiff, a young farmer, who had lost his right hand in a tragic combine accident. Burdick represented the defendant, the Farmers Union Insurance Company, with whom the farmer carried insurance and was seeking a settlement.

During the jury selection process, Bright ticked off Burdick. Since the jury pool consisted primarily of local farmers, Bright wanted to pick an impartial jury. So before potential jurors sat down, Bright would ask every one of them whether they were members of the Farmers Union. It was a fair question and he believed knowledge of it was important to his case. He also alluded to the fact that Burdick represented the organization through the Farmers Union In-surance Company. Bright's line of questioning nearly cost him a ride back to Fargo.

"He got so angry," recalled Bright, that "he refused to talk with me for the rest of the trial." Since Bright was totally dependent on Burdick for a ride home to Fargo, he called his Fritize, his wife, and told her the bad news. "I don't think Quentin wants to give me a ride back home to Fargo," he told her. Fritize, who had no intentions of driving to Lisbon, gave her husband specific instructions on what to do next. "Listen Myron," began Fritzie, "You'd better make peace with Quentin."

"So I went over to Quentin," said Myron, "and abashedly said, 'Well, Quentin, can I have a ride with you back to Fargo?'"

"'OK, Myron,' replied Burdick, with a wry smile. 'But don't you ever men-tion Farmers Union to me again!'"

"And, I didn't."[140]

Other lawyers who squared off regularly against Burdick nicknamed him the "deal maker." Burdick was less inclined by then to take every case to trial as he had earlier with Jungroth. Chub Ulmer, who began to practice law in Man-dan, North Dakota, after Jungroth left the Farmers Union, opposed Burdick often in western North Dakota district courts. "Our principle law practice mot-to," Ulmer stated, "was to comfort the afflicted and afflict the comfortable. We sued a lot of insurance companies, including the Farmers Union, who were heavily insured around here [Morton County]." Ulmer recalled that Burdick was a wily adversary who wanted to make a deal rather than go to court. He

characterized his method as being a cagey insurance lawyer who always preferred
to settle a personal injury suit with the other side rather than take a chance of
letting the jury decided the settlement.[141]

Ulmer recalled that the "call of the calendar," held a couple of times every
year in district courts throughout the state to list the dates of upcoming cases,
provided Burdick with a golden opportunity to make a deal. Every practicing
attorney in the district appeared that day because all of them wanted to find out
when their cases came up for trial. Burdick always showed up because he usually
had a heavy number of cases to try. It was always an important time for him and
he came prepared to do business. Ulmer elaborated on Burdick's next move.

"Quentin had a tendency to want to settle cases quickly and would say to
us: 'I will see you at the next calendar call.'

"The day would come and he would show up with all his files tucked under one arm. On one occasion he had a total of seven cases. 'I want to see you
guys for a few minutes,' Burdick said.

"We went over to him and he brought out his case files. 'This one. What's
your minimum? Well, $6,000. OK, fine. What do you want for this one? OK,
$700 fine.'

"He just took them bang, bang, bang. We were done in two minutes. We
never got him in court!

"Nobody was hurt by it," explained Ulmer. "We were satisfied. It saved a
trial and we got practically what we wanted. It's expensive trying a lawsuit. So
all we had to do was to have Quentin send us a check and we would send him
a stipulation of dismissal. That's it."[142]

Bob Vogel, another western North Dakota lawyer, observed many of
the same Burdick characteristics Ulmer did. "He was a lawyer that the other
lawyer[s] could talk to," noted Vogel. "You could talk settlement with him without getting into big arguments. It was the nature of his practice. You end up in
court a lot trying to keep the plaintiff from getting money out of your insurance
company." Like Ulmer, Vogel negotiated settlements with Burdick although he
never actually tried a case against him.[143]

Burdick's lawyer skills or lack of them did not always bring adulation. "My
father was a lawyer, my son and daughter, too," exclaimed Gorman King. "I
know I wouldn't hire Quentin as a lawyer because he was kind of lazy." King
maintained that Burdick had clients that most lawyers would not represent.
"The labor unions used him because he was connected to the Farmers Union
and it was hard to find a lawyer back then. It was kind of like trying to find a
bank in North Dakota that didn't vote Republican. It was pretty hard to find.
Quentin would rather stick his neck out and take one-third the salary as he was

very conservative financially."[144] Younger Democrats who knew a lot about his politics but not much about his legal talents opined the same. "He wasn't ever successful as an attorney, I don't think," said Jim Fuglie.[145] Vogel dissented. "Burdick knew the law. He knew his way around the courtroom. He was a good trial lawyer and he was a reasonable one."[146]

There were other aspects to Burdick's legal career with the Farmers Union. He was a legal watchdog for the Farmers Union against punitive and partisan attacks by Oscar Erickson, North Dakota's insurance commissioner. When politics crossed lines with the law, Burdick went to court to protect his client. One example occurred in 1949, when Erickson arbitrarily refused to renew the North Dakota license of the Denver, Colorado-based Farmers Union Life Insurance Company. Although the commissioner of insurance possessed the legal authority to deny a license renewal, the action was unprecedented, as all previous commissioners had approved the renewal routinely. Erickson's action was an extension of partisan politics after the Republican-controlled Legislature failed in its attempts to curtail all Farmers Union insurance programs by law.

Burdick took Erickson to court. He appealed his administrative ruling to the District Court in Bismarck. Burdick lost the case and appealed the decision to the North Dakota Supreme Court. The court heard the case on July 1, 1949. It ruled unanimously that "the district court must reverse the order or decision of the agency" because "the agency's findings of fact are not supported by the evidence."[147] Although the court recognized some accounting irregularities, it concluded that the policyowners were "adequately protected" and that violations cited by the insurance commissioner were "either approved by his predecessors in office or condoned by his examiners," and that as a result, Erickson's action was "too drastic a penalty."[148]

Fittingly perhaps, Burdick's most notable legal victory occurred in another state, but on an old topic. The location was the state of Utah and the issue the persistent theme of labeling someone a Communist. In this particular incident, the smear was made by the Utah Farm Bureau against the Utah Farmers Union. The charges were repeated during the 1950 elections and the facts were quite simple. Farm Bureau publications accused the Farmers Union of being Communist dominated. The Bureau did not refute making the charges, only that it was exercising its right of free speech in making them. When the Utah attorney who normally represented the Farmers Union dropped out of the case, the National Farmers Union dispatched Burdick to sue the Farm Bureau for libel.[149]

The case was tried twice; the Farmers Union won both times. Initially the Farmers Union sued in a Utah District Court for libel and won a verdict of

$25,000 in damages. The Farm Bureau immediately appealed the decision to the United States Court of Appeals for the Tenth Circuit and Burdick argued the case. The Appeals Court heard the case on June 4, 1952, and reaffirmed the lower court decision on July 25, 1952. Burdick argued successfully that to label someone a Communist in a time of Red Scare hysteria "places the plaintiffs beyond the pale of respectability and makes them a symbol of public hatred, ridicule or contempt." The court agreed with his reasoning.[150]

Fargo friends later reveled in the Utah victory. At a dinner party hosted by Mart and Lois Vogel, Quentin and Marietta wore smiles for a change. When light verse gave way to more serious discussion, all eyes turned toward the honored guest. "Quentin gave a rundown of what happens when you term somebody a Communist or Red," recalled Mart Vogel. "We were all fascinated by his account of that law firm because most of us were on the liberal side. Some of us more than moderately liberal. Some of us were pretty extreme. It was good to know that our champion had gone out to another state and had taught a newspaper a lesson."[151]

In 1956, a similar incident took place in North Dakota. Burdick again sued to protect the good name of the Farmers Union. On the evening of October 29, 1956, Arthur C. Townley, now advanced in years, appeared on WDAY Television in Fargo. He said in part that the "Farmers Union program fully carried out as planned ... would establish a Communist Farmers Union Soviet right here in North Dakota."[152] Townley was appearing on television as an independent candidate for U.S. Senator against incumbent Republican Senator Milton Young and his Democrat challenger Quentin Burdick. He did not have a chance in a million to win, but demanded that WDAY give him equal time. After reading Townley's script, WDAY initially refused him because it believed that certain statements were false and libelous. WDAY said it would proceed only if Townley demanded that the script be broadcast under Section 315 of the Federal Communications Act. Townley agreed and WDAY allowed the broadcast.[153]

Burdick represented the NDFU and sued WDAY for libel. Judge John C. Pollack Jr., Cass County District Court, dismissed the suit and Burdick appealed the case to the North Dakota Supreme Court. The higher court affirmed the lower court decision in 1958. The circumstances were different in this case than in Utah. Both North Dakota jurisdictions held that WDAY was protected from libel once Townley demanded the broadcast under the federal law. There was no such action taken in the Utah case. The bottom line, of course, was disappointing. It was legal under federal law to call the Farmers Union a Communist organization and get away with it.[154]

Burdick's long tenure for the North Dakota Farmers Union harvested a lifetime of invaluable experiences. "I guess we'd have to say that he was a person who was shaped a lot by the policies of the Farmers Union and [by] having been associated with the Farmers Union," said Lloyd Omdahl. "I think he did a lot of brainstorming with them, which an ordinary lawyer would not do, I mean, from a policy standpoint."[155] How true. From his employment first as an attorney for the Farmers Union growing insurance business, later as general counsel for the entire operation, and as executive director of the Farmers Union Progressive Alliance, Burdick sharpened his legal skills and honed his political proficiencies. The years of work for the state's most powerful farm organization provided him with excellent preparation to represent all North Dakotans when the majority of the electorate sent him to the House of Representatives in 1958 and the United States Senate in 1960.

Burdick's legal career is significant. He became a seasoned trial lawyer who traveled the roads of North Dakota trying hundreds and hundreds of personal injury suits. He learned the art of picking juries in virtually every North Dakota community and how to reach a settlement before quickly moving on to another courtroom. He learned the legal technicalities of running cooperative enterprises in a free-market economy. He researched and drafted all sorts of legal papers and gave personal advice to Glenn Talbott on a regular basis. When pests such as Townley and rival organizations such as the Farm Bureau painted the Farmers Union with a red brush, he sued them, and won, securing their First Amendment rights.

Burdick was among the first North Dakotans to understand the workings of the new federalism between the federal government and the individual states. He observed how federal agricultural programs worked and did not work in a farm state such as North Dakota. He memorized the names of the various U.S. Department of Agriculture agencies and the people who worked in them. He knew their policies, their likes and dislikes, and how to play the administrative game. He saw how important the legacy of the New Deal was for agriculture and how vital the secretary of agriculture and various congressional agricultural committees were for farmers. Finally, he knew instinctively that support for or against federal agricultural policies could make or break a North Dakota candidate running for Congress.

Most importantly, perhaps, Burdick learned how to play the political game in North Dakota, the Twin Cities and Washington. It was a combination of tasks and trials he toiled over for many years. The tasks included being the main lobbyist for the Farmers Union in Bismarck and political adviser on Grain Terminal Association and USDA matters. Burdick defended cooperative franchises against vicious attacks by private business while expanding them at the same time. His leadership role as executive director of the Progressive Alliance primed his political portfolio with the art of grass-roots organizing. He became adept at running meetings, drafting resolutions, stump speaking, circulating absentee ballots, developing convention delegate strategies, securing nominations and running statewide campaigns. His trials, among others, included years of in-house fighting and backbiting among Old Guard Leaguers, conservative Democrats, young Leaguers and liberal Democrats, and painful losses in statewide elections.

Quentin Burdick became a North Dakota Farmers Union man long before he ever became a successful politician. Although he never made his livelihood off of the land, he understood the meaning of the words written in 1929 by Gladys Talbott Edwards and practiced them for the rest of his life.

"The Farmers Union Creed"

Because I know that as an individual, I am nothing, but banded with my brother farmers, I am power, I pledge the work of my hands, the fruit of my soil and the loyalty of my heart to the Farmers Union.

I will keep my eyes on the goal and let no petty annoyances make me forget it.

I will attend my local meetings and let no personal animosities keep me from mingling with my neighbors for our common good.

I will support our business institutions with my entire production and our leadership with my utmost confidence.

And I will always remember that, greater than any man in it — worthy of any sacrifice — deserving of all faithfulness is the Union itself, built for me and by me — my own organization.[156]

When Quentin Burdick became Congressman Burdick in 1958, he donned his familiar black homburg, but wore suits with a Farmers Union label. He was the first North Dakota Farmers Union man elected to serve the people of North Dakota in Washington and he stayed there for a very long, long time.

Endnotes

1. Conrad and Conrad, *50 Years*, 10-11.
2. Ibid., 11-12.
3. Ibid., 3.
4. Ibid., 25.
5. Ibid., 12.
6. Ibid., 18, 22, 47.
7. Talbott, "The North Dakota Farmers Union and North Dakota Politics," *Western Political Quarterly* 10 (December 1957): 877.
8. Conrad and Conrad, 50 Years, 87.
9. Gorman King, interview with author, April 25, 1995.
10. Conrad and Conrad, *50 Years*, 93, 116.
11. Ibid., 29, 30-31, 53.
12. Ibid., 38.
13. Ibid., 50.
14. Ibid., 34.
15. Ibid., 21.
16. Stanley Moore, interview with author, Jan. 24, 1995.
17. King interview.
18. Arthur Link, interview with author, Jan. 25, 1995.
19. Eugene Burdick, interview with author, Feb. 28, 1995.
20. James Jungroth, interview with author, Feb. 2, 1995.
21. Ibid.
22. Lloyd Omdahl, interview with author, Jan. 15, 1995.
23. King interview.
24. Charles Conrad and Joyce Conrad, interview with author, March 25, 1995.
25. Moore interview.
26. Tom Burgum, interview with author, March 24, 1995.
27. Arthur Link interview. Quentin Burdick, interview with author, Jan. 6, 1992.
28. Conrad and Conrad interview, 134.
29. Ibid.
30. Conrad and Conrad, *50 Years*, 123-24; Talbott, "North Dakota Farmers Union," 880-81.
31. Talbott, "North Dakota Farmers Union," 878-79.
32. Omdahl interview.
33. Quentin Burdick interview.
34. Conrad and Conrad, *50 Years*, 126.
35. Talbott, "North Dakota Farmers Union," 882.
36. Omdahl interview.
37. Burgum interview.
38. Quentin Burdick interview.
39. Ibid.
40. Bob Vogel, interview with author, Jan. 10, 1994.
41. Quentin Burdick interview.
42. *Fargo (N.D.) Forum*, Jan. 9, 1951.
43. Eugene Burdick interview.
44. Burgum interview.
45. Eugene Burdick interview.
46. Burgum interview.
47. Quentin Burdick interview.
48. Moore interview.
49. Ibid.
50. *North Dakota Votes*, 161.
51. Burgum interview.
52. Lloyd Omdahl, *Insurgents*, 9.
53. Ibid., 236.
54. Omdahl interview.
55. Conrad and Conrad interview.

56. King interview.
57. Jungroth interview.
58. Moore interview.
59. Quentin Burdick interview.
60. Burgum interview.
61. Walton, *Henry Wallace, Harry Truman and the Cold War,* 194, 355.
62. Leuchtenberg, *Franklin Roosevelt and the New Deal,* 72, 347.
63. Schlesinger Jr., *The Coming of the New Deal,* 34.
64. Leuchtenberg, *Franklin Roosevelt and the New Deal,* 49, 77.
65. Schlesinger Jr., *The Coming of the New Deal,* 35.
66. McCullough, *Truman,* 517.
67. Matusow, *Farm Policies in the Truman Years,* 170.
68. McCullough, *Truman,* 294.
69. Pratt, "The Farmers Union and the 1948 Henry Wallace Campaign," *Annals of Iowa* 49 (Summer 1988): 351.
70. MacDougall, *The Components of the Decision,* vol. 1 of Gideon's Army, 163.
71. Ibid.
72. Henry Wallace, "Report of Farmers," *New Republic,* 116 (June 30, 1947): 12.
73. Ibid.
74. Wallace, "Report of Farmers," 12.
75. Quentin Burdick letter to Usher Burdick, May 17, 1947, in possession of Jennifer Burdick, Baltimore, Md.
76. V.C. Moore telegram to Glenn Talbott, Jan. 6, 1947, folder 23, box 8, Talbott Family Papers.
77. Glenn Talbott letter to V.C. Moore, Jan. 23, 1947, Talbott Family Papers.
78. King interview.
79. Conrad and Conrad interview.
80. Senator Kent Conrad, interview with author, March 27, 1995.
81. Kent Conrad interview.
82. *Fargo Forum,* July 20, 1948.
83. MacDougall, *The Decision and the Organization,* vol. 2 of Gideon's Army, 534.
84. Quentin Burdick memo to Glenn Talbott, July 22, 1948, Talbott Family Papers.
85. Glenn Talbott letter to Quentin Burdick, July 28, 1948, Talbott Family Papers.
86. Mart Vogel, interview with author, Jan. 19, 1995.
87. Moore interview.
88. Bob Vogel, interview with author, Jan. 10, 1994.
89. MacDougall, *The Decision and the Organization,* 458.
90. Ibid., 484; Young, "A Modern Isaiah: Henry Wallace and the 1948 Presidential Campaign," (PhD diss., University of North Dakota, 1992), 111.
91. MacDougall, *The Decision and the Organization,* 492.
92. Ibid., 491.
93. Ibid., 605-606.
94. Ibid., 488.
95. Lawrence, "Wallace Accepts Calling on Allies to Give up Berlin," *New York Times* (July 25, 1948), 1.
96. Peterson, *Prophet with Honor,* 103.
97. Pratt, "The Farmers Union," 349.
98. Ibid., 366; *North Dakota Votes,* 156.
99. Young, 144.
100. Mart Vogel interview.
101. Ibid.
102. Ibid.
103. *Fargo Forum,* Sept. 19, 1956.
104. Pratt, "The Farmers Union," 367.
105. MacDougall, *The Decision and the Organization,* 796.
106. Burgum interview.
107. Ibid.
108. Quentin Burdick interview.
109. Ibid.

110. Jungroth interview.
111. *North Dakota Votes*, 152.
112. *Fargo Forum*, March 15, 1942.
113. *North Dakota Votes*, 154-55; 160.
114. *Fargo Forum*, Oct. 25, 1958.
115. *Fargo Forum*, May 11, 1945
116. Myron Bright, interview with author, March 20, 1996.
117. King interview.
118. Ibid.
119. Bill Lanier Jr., letter to John P. Moore, Dec. 11, 1956, folder 16, box 2, David Kelly Papers.
120. Bright interview.
121. Quentin Burdick interview.
122. Ibid.
123. Jungroth interview.
124. Ibid.
125. Ibid.
126. Ibid.
127. Ibid.
128. Ibid.
129. Ibid.
130. Ibid.
131. Ibid. A supersedeas bond is a legal order that stays the proceedings of an inferior court.
132. Ibid.
133. Ibid.
134. Ibid.
135. Eugene Burdick interview.
136. Morteer Skewes, interview with author, April 15, 1995.
137. Lois Vogel, interview with author, Jan. 19, 1995.
138. Mart Vogel interview.
139. Ibid.
140. Bright interview.
141. Chub Ulmer, interview with author, April 25, 1995.
142. Ibid.
143. Bob Vogel interview.
144. King interview.
145. Jim Fuglie, interview with author, Feb. 6, 1995.
146. Bob Vogel interview.
147. *National Farmers Union Life Ass'n v. Krueger* 38 *Northwestern Reporter* (North Dakota 1949), 565.
148. Ibid., 576.
149. Mart Vogel interview.
150. *Farm Bureau Fed v. National F.U.S. Corp* 198 F2d20, 33ALR2d, 1193.
151. Mart Vogel interview.
152. *Farmers Educational & Cooperative Union of America, North Dakota Division v. WDAY, Inc.* 89 North Western Reporter, 2d Series (North Dakota 1958),104
153. Ibid.
154. *Farmers Educational & Cooperative Union of America*, North Dakota Division, 110.
155. Omdahl interview.
156. Conrad and Conrad, *50 Years*, 30.

- eight -

1958

Quentin Burdick's life changed dramatically in 1958. No single date before or after could compare with the events of that one, single year. It
was truly a chasm between two different landscapes — a year in which
his personal life hit rock bottom and his political career miraculously soared.
"I remember he really had sort of two lifetimes," recalled Jennifer Burdick,
his second eldest daughter. "Up until the age of 50, he had been an attorney,
political activist, a loser. His frame of reference was North Dakota. He really
hadn't left. Then in 1958, when he won his first election and spent a half to
three-quarters of his life in Washington, it became a very different existence.
It was like two different lives. Then he married another woman, and she was a
different woman from my mother. So in the chronology of his life, that age 50
is a watershed period."[1]

Jennifer's reflections accentuate the best of times of that remarkable year,
which included the stunning victory of winning a political office in North Dakota after six disappointing losses over two decades. Not only did her middle-
aged father win an office, he won a blue ribbon seat in the United States House
of Representatives. His victory made North Dakota political history. He was the
first Democrat in 69 years of statehood to be elected to that institution. After
traditionally electing Republicans time and time again, the voters finally elected
a Democrat to represent them in Washington. Quentin Burdick's capture of
"the House victory was so shocking," recalled Jerome Lamb of Fargo, "because
Democrats never won."[2] D. Jerome Tweton, respected North Dakota historian,
said simply that Burdick's 1958 victory in the state "symbolized the birth of the
Democratic Party."[3]

Unfortunately, the worst personal catastrophes followed his political celebration. Quentin's family experienced two devastating blows. In March, after

a long struggle with cancer, his beloved wife Marietta died. It was a personal loss of cataclysmic proportions. Her death left Quentin so distraught that his children feared for his future. His big, strong, physical frame sank into a list-less shadow of despair and disinterest. He sat around and stared into an empty world contemplating how he could survive without Marietta. The love of his life was gone. No words could comfort his grief or encourage hope. Eventually, when the first stage of his grief subsided, he faced the grim reality of a single-parent responsible for raising two teenage girls. The death of his wife preceded the shocking news that Jonathan, his only son, had suffered a complete mental breakdown. Not only was Marietta gone, but now the apple of her eye was spoiled with a mental disease that would plague him for life.

In the aftermath of death and despair, Burdick's daughters conceived a po-litical solution to ease their father's pain. They placed a last-minute telephone call from their home in Fargo to the Nonpartisan League convention being held in Bismarck. "Daddy will run," they said. He did. Their personal intervention rescued his political career. It was the only possible therapy they could come up with to put life back into their father's soul. Their plan worked, and their grieving father became Congressman Burdick. Life with Marietta ended, but Burdick's political life was reborn.

Till Death do Us Part

Many aspects of Marietta Janecky Burdick's short life bear remembrance. First and foremost was a combination of beauty, grace and elegance. Every friend, acquaintance and family member observed these external gifts. Marietta was simply stunning in appearance and intellectually beautiful in character. No one captured her presence better than Myron Bright, who recollected seeing Quentin and Marietta walk into a public gathering together:

> I saw Quentin Burdick the first time in the summer of 1947 at a North Dakota Bar Convention. I can still remember the occasion. My wife, Fritzie, and I were sitting in the ballroom of the Fargo Elks Club. I was a new lawyer just having come to North Dakota, and everyone was seated. In walked this curly haired, handsome man about 6 feet tall, escorting an absolutely stunning brunette woman dressed in white with a white turban. That was Marietta. I have never seen a more beautiful couple.[4]

Marietta was never strong physically — an aspect of her life that remained virtually secret from her friends and acquaintances. In fact, she experienced much pain during each of her 45 years of life. Scarlet fever stole strength from her heart as a child and left her susceptible to illness as an adult. Pregnancies extracted huge doses of energy from her and made her recoveries endless. She bore four children; the last birth nearly took her life. There were other, unsuccessful pregnancies. She miscarried several times and delivered one still-born child. She constantly fought off repeated attacks of pneumonia and adult mononucleosis.

In general, Marietta coped with her frailties. She kept a healthy regimen, opting not to drink any alcoholic beverages and resting frequently. Yet, like most human beings, she was not perfect: her vice was smoking. By all accounts, she was a chain-smoker, consuming between two and three packs of cigarettes daily. Her favorite brand was the deadly Pall Mall Longs, with its unblended tobacco, high nicotine concentration, and no filters to ameliorate its effects. In time, her endless smoking cast the final dart in a body already scarred with weakness.

Marietta's death left a devastated spouse, grief-stricken children and a family without a rudder. Amidst the storm of her dying was the mental breakdown of her only son, Jon, the hurried child, the embodiment of her life's dream and the living image of her own soul. Most said she was spared the knowledge of Jon's insanity, but her daughter, Jan Mary, who knew Marietta best, believed otherwise: Marietta knew. Perhaps in dying, Marietta spared herself the personal agony of losing Jon, which was a tragedy in her mind, far more devastating than her own death. In the winter of 1958, Marietta lost her life, but Jon lost his mind.

Marietta's three living children expressed different memories of their mother's illnesses. "My mother always seemed sickly," began Jennifer. "She had been very sick around the time that Jessica was born [1947]. She had a history of illnesses. She was hospitalized for mononucleosis, and in those days when adults would get mono, it was very serious."[5] Jan Mary, six years older than Jennifer, knew more about Marietta's miscarriages. "Mother was not well and lost several babies. I think she had a stillborn. I think she carried them quite far. I think she was RH negative. Between Jenny and I [born in 1938 and 1944], she lost two or three children. I remember her hemorrhaging in the Fargo house. She would also get pneumonia easily and she smoked very heavily."[6] Jessica, the youngest, recalled the least. "Because I was young when she died [10 years old], and she was sick for a good many of those years, I don't know much about her."[7]

The precise start of Marietta's terminal illness was obscured by her previous patterns of reoccurring illnesses. Because her sickness was daily, new onsets came as no surprise. Sometime, however, in the summer or early fall of 1957, Marietta began to experience sharp pains in her right arm. The pain became so

excruciating that she could barely lift a brush to comb her hair, and she reluc-
tantly withdrew from the adult painting class she enjoyed.[8] Marietta confided
often with her close friend, Marge Scott, about her pain, speculating about its
cause. The two women came up with nothing concrete — just concerns, doubts,
and reassurances.[9] Early medical consultations failed to pinpoint anything specific. "They told her it was nerves," exclaimed May Burdick "That's what they
told everybody. It's your nerves! She went home and it kept getting worse and
worse, and then they finally discovered the cancer."[10]

Marietta was diagnosed with clavicle cancer in late October or early November. The long search for medical answers had unfortunately rendered the
most devastating verdict. She was only 45 years old. Quentin and Marietta's
first response was to keep the diagnosis a secret from family and friends as long
as possible. Particularly concerned about how the news would affect their children, the Burdicks postponed informing them as long as possible. Since the two
oldest, Jon and Jan Mary, were away at college (Harvard and the University of
Colorado), the parents decided to say nothing until their children came home
for Christmas vacation. Quentin and Marietta did not want to affect Jan Mary
and Jon's studies by burdening them with any news about Marietta's illness.
As for the two youngest children, Jennifer and Jessica, the exact nature of their
mother's illness remained a mystery.

Events in December terminated the cancer blackout. During the first week,
Quentin and Marietta attended the annual Fargo Orchestra Ball. Although
Marietta was elegant as usual, she appeared tired to many of her closest friends.
In private, she spoke to some and confided to one, at least, that she was going
into the hospital again for further examinations. The ball was her last Fargo
public appearance.[11] Four days before Christmas, Quentin sat down and wrote
a letter to his father and two siblings. "I have some very bad news to give you,"
he began. "It has now been determined that Marietta has a malignant tumor
under the collar bone and X-ray treatments are scheduled to start in the morning, and some hope is held that they might be effective."[12] However, hope was
fading. On Christmas Eve, Quentin, distraught and beside himself, attended
the old Fargo First Congregational Church for services. Before he left, he told
his friends, Mart and Lois Vogel, "Marietta has been diagnosed with terminal
cancer."[13]

As Christmas approached at home, it was time to inform the children. Jan
Mary vividly recalled her response. "They did not tell my brother and I. So Jon
and I flew in at Christmas vacation and were immediately told that our mother
was in the hospital with cancer. Three months after the fact. I was very angry
about that. 'My mother is dying, and you didn't tell me!'"[14] The two youngest

children were told before their older siblings arrived home. "The first I heard of cancer," recalled Jennifer, "was December. Between that time and when she died, she was in the hospital almost all the time. I recall she came home for a few days at Christmas and I think she come home for a few days in January or February, but for the most part she was in the hospital the whole last two or three months of her life."[15]

Jessica shared two poignant memories about her mother. The first was visiting her in the hospital and being curious about what the patch was on her mother's upper chest, right below her throat. Marietta could hardly speak and Jessica did not recall any answer. When her mother came home for Christmas, Jessica thought long and hard about an appropriate welcome-home gift. "I gave her a cigarette pouch — something to hold your cigarettes in — one of those fancy leather things because she was a smoker. I thought that would be a nice gift. I didn't really have a lot of knowledge about a lot of things, and it was a rather stupid gift since her smoking is what caused the cancer or what a lot of people thought caused the cancer. And here I gave her something for Christmas that further supported her cancer."[16]

In fairness to Jessica, the medical verdict on smoking and lung cancer was still out in the 1950s. Some medical experts said, yes, there was a relationship, but other medical experts said there was no relationship. For example, in 1956, Dr. W.C. Hueper, head of the environmental cancer section of the National Institute of the U.S. Public Health Service, declared, "lung cancer probably was due chiefly to fumes, dusts, gases and chemicals in the air we breath," and that "lung cancer occurs more frequently in cities and industrial areas than in rural communities." Dr. Hueper downplayed the impact of smoking, stating that it seemed to play a "definite, but lesser direct or indirect role."[17] Yet, studies did confirm that death rates for all causes from cancer were 68 percent higher for smokers than nonsmokers; those rates rose even more with the numbers of cigarettes smoked daily. As for lung cancer specifically, there was "a spectacular relationship" between smoking and nonsmoking; the odds of developing cancer increased 15 times if one smoked one or two packs a day and 64 times if one smoked two or more packs per day.[18] Most studies done on the relationship between lung cancer and smoking, however, only centered on male smokers. But Dr. Ernest L. Wynder of the Manhattan Sloan Kettering Institute did predict that "because more women are smoking heavily today, they will be stricken by a sharp increase in lung cancer in 20 to 25 years."[19]

When chances of a medical recovery began to fade, Quentin and Marietta embarked upon more radical measures. "I mean they were going all over the country trying to find cures," recalled Jan Mary. "Terrible things. I guess when you're desperate, you do hills in Texas and all these things."[20] The most desperate measure they sought was indeed in Texas, at the Hoxsey Cancer Clinic in Dallas. Usher Burdick initially suggested a visit to the clinic. At first, Quentin rejected the idea. "No way. I'm aware of the suggestion you made about Hoxsey," he wrote to Usher. "Marietta and I have always considered him a complete fraud." Desperation, however, made them more receptive: "But — we could be wrong. If you have any definite evidence that he has successfully treated a thing like this let me know by return mail. I will do anything, and if necessary I would join the Republican Party if that would cure Marietta. Or if you could refer me to anyone who knows about the Hoxsey treatment, I would certainly follow it up."[21]

Harry Hoxsey established his Dallas Cancer Clinic in 1936, and he later established a second clinic in Portage, Pennsylvania. He was never a licensed doctor and listed himself as a certified naturopath. By the mid-1950s, popular magazines called him America's number one cancer quack, while the American Medical Association released a statement announcing there was nothing in his medicine that "has the slightest effect on cancer, except according to one investigation, to simulate its growth slightly."[22] Even with all these negative media attacks, Hoxsey's clientele continued to grow as people desperate to live went to see him anyway. His two-day treatment ran as smoothly as a modern assembly line. New patients were quickly interviewed, given blood and urine tests, and X-rays. Treatment centered on pills (containing potassium iodide) and a bottle of fig juice.[23] His practice made him wealthy, and so did his book, *You Don't Have to Die*. Hoxsey channeled profits into oil and real estate, and he bought a 588-acre ranch.[24] By 1956, the federal government put pressure on him. In April, the U.S. Food and Drug Administration issued a report calling the Hoxsey cancer cure "worthless" and "imminently dangerous."[25] In November, the government seized 500,000 pills from the Portage Clinic; two years later, the clinic closed its doors for good.[26]

Quentin and Marietta left for Dallas on January 30, 1958. This information was telegraphed by Marietta's mother, Mrs. Janecky, to Usher in Washington. No other information exists about their trip or their experience at the clinic.[27] Marietta never left the Fargo hospital after returning from Dallas. She died on March 11, 1958, without a voice — repeated X-ray treatments had badly burned her chest. She died two months short of her 46th birthday and a few days short of her 25th wedding anniversary. Marietta is buried in the Bohemian National Cemetery outside of Hutchinson, Minnesota, near her hometown of New Prague. "When my mother died," said Jessica, "they had a dual headstone and both names were put on it."[28]

Marietta's valiant struggle to fight a cancer without a cure was lost in the sorrow of her merciful death. "I think it's devastating for my sisters," said Jan Mary, "to not have a mother. It really is. You don't realize it. Jessie is still searching." Jan Mary's biggest disappointment, however, was that Marietta "never got to Washington because she went through so many, many defeats."[29] Among Marietta's close friends, however, remained an image of beauty that even death could not extinguish. "I can see her with her hats and her very dramatic, flamboyant clothes," recalled Marge Scott, 37 years later. "You enjoyed just looking at her and seeing her. She was like a magnet."[30]

Within hours of the burial, Quentin turned immediately to a second family tragedy: Jon had suffered a serious mental breakdown. Quentin found no escape from anguish. In 1958, he committed Jon to the Jamestown State Hospital. Jamestown was the most logical placement for long-term care and for a family that could ill afford a more expensive environment. Meanwhile, the family made one other adjustment: Jan Mary transferred from the University of Colorado to the University of North Dakota in Grand Forks at the start of the second semester. "I'm not bragging or complaining; I just kind of took over. I had to. So I would come home every weekend from Grand Forks. We'd get housekeepers, and Jenny would proceed to fire them all. That little stinker! We'd get people to come in, and I'd come home on Friday and there'd be nobody there. I'd say, 'There's nobody here with a 13-year-old,' and Jenny would say, 'I couldn't stand her!'" Jan Mary also felt responsible for the care of her father. "I mean, he was just out of it. He was really, really out of it. This was the loss of his life. I think if I cry, it's for him. He was just so lost."[31]

The Hurried Child

Jon Burdick was born in Fargo in 1936. He was the oldest child and only son of Quentin and Marietta. In many appearances, he was a clone of Marietta — her appearance and mannerisms reborn in a male body. He was tall and thin, sensitive and gentle. His eyes, identical to Marietta's, were perhaps the most appealing aspect of his physical appearance. He was a brilliant student; his love of learning appeared to be his only recreation. Sports bored him, although his long frame made him a graceful, if not natural, swimmer. For team sports, Jon was not well coordinated; contact sports repulsed him. He was unlike his father — neither aggressive nor physical. Jon Burdick preferred studying French to playing high school football. He seemed always to be his mother's child and seldom his father's.

By all family accounts, Jon was a hurried child. He was raised in a milieu of heightened interest in child psychology by well-read parents who relied on Freudian influences. Psychologist David Elkind coined the term *hurried children*, which also became the title of his 1981 book. Elkin wrote, "Hurried children are forced to take on the physical, psychological, and social trappings of adulthood before they are prepared to deal with them," and that parents of hurried children put enormous pressure on them "for early intellectual attainment," especially to read early. This pressure, Elkind concluded, "reflects parental need, not the child's need or inclination."[32]

By educational standards, there was no escaping the fact that Jon was indeed a hurried child. He ran through the Fargo public schools, skipping several early grades. He far excelled his older peers in academics and graduated from Fargo Central High School at age 16. He was senior class president, a straight A student, a member of the National Honor Society, and vice captain of both Debate and Science clubs. Despite his expressed apathy for sports, he participated in track and swimming, and went out for football, wearing the jersey with the unlucky number 13. His outstanding academic record earned him a full ride to Harvard University. He was clearly Marietta's prodigy —not Quentin's — and everyone in the family accepted that fact.[33]

In his race to learn, however, Jon missed other important aspects of growing up. He never learned to enjoy himself or to be with young people his own age. The pressures to learn obviated time to re-create. Jan Mary recalled that her brother never went on a date. Instead, he used to sit in his room on the weekends, studying and waiting for her to come home. "I dated all the time," said Jan Mary, and "the first thing I would do would be to go to Jon's room and tell him about my date. He never went to these things, so I think there was a kind of sadness there that maybe socially he was completely inept." She recalled on one occasion when Jon was president of the senior class that a girl did ask him to go to the senior prom and how difficult that was for him. "She was 18 and he was 16. That's tough!"[34]

The exact circumstances of Jon's mental breakdown remain sketchy. Sisters all agree that something happened to him at Harvard. Something so horrific that he was labeled a paranoid schizophrenic. "I don't know what it was," said Jan Mary. "Something happened in his years there that he was ... exposed to something, [or] it might have been something that was latent. I don't know that [the cause of his mental distress] came out. I really don't know why [he became ill] because I just know that Jon was a normal person growing up — besides being brilliant. I just don't think he socially ever adapted because he was so young."[35] Siblings repeat the same story. "It started when he was about 20 or 21, after he graduated from Harvard, first year of law school," said Jennifer. "He was hospitalized and I don't know when I learned of the official diagnosis."[36] Jessica, the youngest, knew the least. "All that I know about my brother and his illness I have received from my sisters. It was always something that I never understood. I never knew what happened. He went away to school and was never quite the same again."[37]

Jon's sisters knew little about circumstances of his breakdown, but his Uncle Eugene knew more. He expanded on the Harvard experience with greater detail. "There was an episode where he was able to take a test on a certain day, and he had the wrong day, so he didn't show up for the test and they gave him an F. It was the first F he'd ever received." This academic failure, the first in Jon's life, seems to have triggered his problem, and then he was "diagnosed as a schizophrenic" and "suffered from delusions."[38] Eugene Burdick recollected these facts, and he offered his own interpretation. In short, Quentin's lack of support contributed to his only son's mental breakdown. Why? Just as Quentin lacked the personal skills to be supportive of his younger brother, he was unable to support Jon's accomplishments. "I don't recall Quentin passing out any compliments to anybody on anything," began Eugene. "He lacked the capacity to express admiration — I don't know about love, but certainly admiration or any compliments for success. He was unable to do it, and I think this may have affected Jon because he was an excellent student, and maybe he didn't get enough positive support from Quentin. It kind of created a gulf there that didn't quite close, at least that's what the psychiatrist thought."[39]

Jan Mary refuted her uncle's interpretation. She believed that her father knew that Jon was favored by her mother, and although that bothered him, he also let Marietta have free rein on that. In fact, everyone in the family knew it and accepted it. As for any disappointment about Jon's lack of athletic ability, she downplayed it. "I think his problems go much deeper than that. I think Jon felt a disappointment, but I never had the feeling that Dad pushed him into anything. I could be wrong on that, but I don't have the feeling that Jon was being pushed." In conclusion, she stated: "If people want to blame it on Dad and stuff, I don't see that."[40]

Finally, Jan Mary alone maintains that while Marietta was dying, she knew of Jon's illness. "Oh, I think she knew," began Jan Mary. "I think she knew. She couldn't talk at the end, but I think she knew that. Mother knew. That was her pride and joy. She had such high hopes for Jon because Jon was brilliant. She gave a lot of time and attention to him and I think she knew. He was spacey, so I can't imagine Mother not knowing something was wrong with her child, but she never said."[41]

Family friends shared their thoughts about the father-son relationship. "It was difficult in a strange way," said Marge Scott. "Their interests were differ-ent. Jon wouldn't worry about the football team. This was something Quentin couldn't understand — that your own children aren't in your shape or form or feelings."[42] Myron Bright recalled that Jon's mental illness affected Quentin deeply, and although he tried to help his son in every way possible, their rela-tionship always "seemed somewhat estranged."[43]

Life for Jon Burdick did not end at the Jamestown Hospital, but he was never the same person again. After the death of their mother, Jan Mary re-mained the closest family member to him. "I'd go down to Jamestown and try to communicate with him because he and I were very close," she recalled. However, each visit confirmed the stark reality that the brother she knew and the relationship they enjoyed in the past no longer existed in the present. "It was gone. It was just gone. He resented me and [our old relationship] never came back."[44] Incredibly, after years of treatment, Jon made substantial prog-ress in his fight against mental illness. As Jennifer stated, "something worked," although "there were relapses and subsequent hospitalizations over the years."[45] Jon eventually left the hospital, but never without his medication, and he re-turned to Harvard Law School, where he earned his law degree. He became a lawyer, married and fathered two children. He worked for the U.S. Department of Agriculture until his rapid and unexpected death from liver cancer in 1994. "But the adult that he was when he died," said Jan Mary, "is not the brother I knew growing up. He became a different person, and I didn't have the closeness to him in his adult years."[46] Despite the changes, Jon Burdick made a remark-able adjustment. "I think that it couldn't have been easy to fight those demons in him that were always talking to him, and he somehow fought them off and was able to function," added Jennifer.[47]

Realignment

The year 1958 was climatic for Burdick personally, and so was the 1958 election for most North Dakota voters. There was, as noted in the song by rock singer Jerry Lee Lewis, "a whole lotta of shaking goin' on." The stage was set two years earlier, when the Nonpartisan League (NPL) merged with the North Dakota Democratic Party after a 40-year association with the Republican Party. The political realignment created a political void in North Dakota politics last-ing until the 1960 election. Only then did voters seem comfortable electing Democratic-NPL candidates to state office rather than regular or NPL Repub-licans. But during those few years, political loyalties were divided, fluid and uncertain. Some senior members of the NPL, such as Senator William Langer and Congressman Usher Burdick, protected their incumbency by remaining in the Republican family. They repeatedly told their constituents that they were simply too old to switch, which was perhaps true, but also that they were born Republican and that they would die Republican. And, of course, both did.

Usher stayed a Republican, but like an old bull, he strayed often. He voted like a Democrat and caught hell from both sides. "You know, in Washington they accuse me of voting with the Democrats 60 percent of the time," Usher told a full house of his constituents gathered in 1956 at the Civic Center in Parshall, North Dakota. "I tell you they are dead wrong. I vote with them 90 percent of the time!"[48] Two years later, Usher took aim at the North Dakota Farmers Union for treating him like a political enemy rather than a friend. "I have never wavered in my support for progressive legislation and am not different now from what I have always been," he wrote to Mrs. H.C. Williams in June. "I am amazed at the attitude of the Farmers Union. For eighteen years, including this year, I have supported that organization with no exceptions, but since I would not file as a Democrat, they now find fault with my record. If I had joined the Democrats, the Farmers Union paper would have gloried in my record."[49]

Others made the switch and found the transition traumatic. Two examples suffice. One was Ralph Dewing, a state legislator from Divide County in the northwest corner of the state. He served in the North Dakota House for one term (1949-1950) and two terms in the Senate (1951-1959). Dewing represented a hotbed of NPL constituents and always ran on the Republican ticket. The merger of the NPL and the Democrats occurred during Dewing's last term in the Senate. He was elected as a Nonpartisan League Republican in 1956, but when the Legislature organized in 1957, he was chosen minority leader of the state Senate as a Democratic-Nonpartisan Leaguer. "I was the only one in North Dakota, probably in the nation," to experience that, claimed Dewing. "It was kind of confusing." Dewing quickly added, "Only in North Dakota could that happen."[50]

The other example was the familiar Burdick name, which continued to appear on the North Dakota ballot. It was always present, and not surprisingly, under both party labels. Usher, the father, always ran as a Republican — sometimes against NPL candidates in his early career and often with NPL endorsements in his later years. Although he voted more often than not with Democrats in Washington, he never ran as Democrat in North Dakota. Quentin, on the other hand, started running for office as a Republican, but then switched his loyalty to the Democrats. If North Dakotans were unsure about which column or which candidate to vote for in 1958, they found continuity in the name

Burdick. No surprise. There it was again. The same name, and in this instance, even seeking the same office. It really did not matter if it was a Burdick with a different first name or a different political party.

The Kid is Honest

Former Governor Art Link tells a wonderful campaign story about the 1958 election. The story arose from an autumn evening at the Cartwright, North Dakota, community hall. Cartwright is located in western McKenzie County, the state's largest county in one of the state's tiniest unincorporated villages. The county was named for Alexander McKenzie, the notorious railroad boss of early North Dakota political history.[51] Most of the voters, however, became early supporters of the NPL and later the North Dakota Farmers Union. Cartwright, a reasonable drive from the family ranch, was also the birthplace of Grace Johnson Link, Art's beloved wife. The Cartwright community hall was always a favorite watering hole for the region's ranchers, serving a hamlet with few markings and only a handful of residents. The town originally began as a farm post office, and then moved slightly to just a short distance from Fairview, Montana, thereby becoming the farthest west station of the Great Northern Railroad in the whole state.

The hall was packed on this particular evening. The people came to hear Quentin Burdick speak. He was, of course, a candidate for Congress with good credentials and Farmers Union connections, but nevertheless he still wore a Democrat hat. As the evening progressed, it was announced that Quentin's appearance was canceled. He was held up somewhere back east, and Cartwright was a long distance from anywhere back east, even in North Dakota. In his place appeared the familiar frame of Usher, his father. He was a well-known figure in those parts, a Williams County neighbor, a fellow rancher, their elected Congressman, and like most of them, a lifelong Republican. Usher showed up like he always did, in sloppy clothes, moving about slowly in a friendly manner. He knew many of those present by their first names and spent the majority of the evening just chatting. No politics. When it became time for him to speak, he moved easily to the front of the hall with no fanfare. His remarks were brief and the words unmistakable. "I want you to know," he began, "that I am a Republican and Quentin has filed for this office as a Democrat. I want you to know that the kid is honest."[52]

That was all Usher had to say. Everyone got the message and all knew exactly what those words meant. There was comfort in the Burdick name and understanding of the change in party affiliation. More importantly, perhaps, was the comfort and security in what the father had said about his son. As Link drove home that evening, Usher's words stuck. "I thought those four words told it all," recalled Link. "What better endorsement could a young candidate have than for his father, who is on the other side of the political aisle, to say, 'the kid is honest.'"[53] Link's vivid recollection of those words almost 40 years later is testimony to the powerful message Usher Burdick gave in Cartwright that night. It is also noteworthy that Link referred to Quentin as a young candidate. He was 50 years old, but always the younger Burdick.

The part Usher played in Quentin's 1958 election was almost as important as the role played by his daughters who nominated him in the first place. At age 79, Usher retired before the political season opened. He was old, naughty, and lacked support from the newly reorganized North Dakota Republican Party. His withdrawal provided an open seat for Quentin to run for the same office, although under a different political logo. Quentin won the open seat and never lost another election in his lifetime. Burdick, the son, replaced Burdick, the father. Together they served a total of 53 years in the Congress of the United States.

There was more to Usher's involvement in Quentin's candidacy. It may in hindsight seem insignificant to many, maybe to most, but not to Usher. It was very important to him that Quentin enter the race, and that he support Quentin's candidacy without Republican reprisals. In order to accomplish those twin goals, Usher hatched a plan in the spring of 1958. Usher believed his plan would upset Quentin so much that he would change his mind and enter the race, while at the same time allowing Usher to provide political cover, enabling him to campaign for Quentin without criticism from many of his Republican friends. Usher precipitated an incident — a personal snub — by the North Dakota Republican Party convention officials, who denied his personal request to address the convention. He just wanted to say goodbye to the Grand Old Party. His political days were behind him. But Usher's request was for some unknown reason denied, and what followed was a personal performance that tore at the hearts of many Republicans who liked the old man (Usher was hard not to like) and saw no reason whatsoever why he should not be allowed to speak one last time.

"I think Usher deliberately set it up so they would not let him speak," asserted Tom Burgum. "I can't prove it, but I would put a lot of money on it." Why the assertion for such an incident? Because if "Usher retired with full honors and laurels, he really could not go out and work for Quentin, and so he deliberately set it up so they would not let him speak." Burgum's evidence is circumstantial but convincing. It comes from two sources — first from his father, Leslie Burgum, North Dakota's Republican attorney general (1956-1960) and close friend of Usher's, and second from Quentin himself many years later when Burgum served on his senatorial staff. "I asked Quentin about it," stated Burgum, "and he said, 'Oh, by the way, I forgot to ask you about the Garrison appropriation.' So I suspect that Usher knew he was going to retire."[54]

After the snub, Usher held court in the Patterson Hotel in Bismarck, where many of the delegates roomed during the convention. When Leslie retired to the hotel after the day's proceedings at the convention, he found Usher moping about in the lobby. When he approached Usher, the older man began to cry and and blurted out, "They wouldn't even let me speak!" When Burgum told the incident to his son, Tom expressed instant disbelief. "Usher with tears in his eyes? Excuse me! That's like Jim Eastland crying. Then Usher went out and worked hard for Quentin."[55]

Mark Andrews, an old family friend of Usher and also a Republican delegate, witnessed the second half of the plot. Andrews was really upset about how the party mistreated Usher that day. "He had been a totally good soldier for the Republican concept in North Dakota," Andrews began, "yet they wouldn't even allow him to make a 10-minute speech — a farewell speech, really, at the convention. I thought that was the bottom and absolute lack of grace." Andrews left the convention, walked back to the hotel with Usher, and later recalled what transpired next: "I was sitting in the hotel when he called Quentin — 'Quentin, you've gotta to run for my house seat. You have no idea what these blankety-blanks did to me.'"[56]

Senator Milton R. Young, although not in attendance, heard immediately about the incident. It quickly became a major topic of conversation among many old-time Republican regulars. Young, too, found the incident rude and unwarranted. "I think that one of the most unkind things that happened to Usher Burdick was at the last Republican convention he attended," said Young. "He had some trouble with his marriage at that time and that maybe was one of the reasons they didn't give him an opportunity to speak, but I don't know why yet." Young never did find out who precipitated the snub, but recalled that "Usher took this very hard and became very bitter about it." He also conjectured that if the convention had recognized Usher, Quentin might not have run. "A lot of little things can change history," said Young.[57]

After the Burdick family won an unprecedented double in the 1958 elections, Usher, as the political godfather of the clan, could barely contain himself. It seemed almost unfathomable that both his son, Quentin, and his son-in-law, Robert Levering, would simultaneously be serving in the U.S. House of Representatives. It was almost too much for him to imagine and even more amusing for him to contemplate that both Burdicks would take their seats as Democrats. The leader of the House of Usher wrote philosophically about new life being propagated from old stock: "So while the old tree went down, two new sprouts came right up so the reactionaries are in worse position than they were when I was here alone."[58]

Although Usher acknowledged the importance of the Burdick name in Quentin's victory, he downplayed the notion that a political clone would succeed him. "I am sure that the name Burdick didn't hurt Quentin any in the campaign," he wrote in one letter.[59] At the same time, he asserted his son's political independence in another letter. "I am not sure that Quentin will follow in my footsteps, and the reason for it is that he is a Burdick, and none of them can be hog-tied. He will probably just figure the thing out for himself."[60]

Daddy Will Run

Usher's two-pronged plan proved only half successful. He certainly earned the sympathy of many Republicans for the slight, and this advantage provided him with the excuse he felt he needed to go out and campaign for Quentin. There was only one hitch — Quentin made it quite clear, even against his father's pleadings, that he was not going to run for any political office in 1958. "As you know," said Andrews, "Quentin replied to his dad that Marietta had just died and the last thing in the world he wanted to do is run for office."[61]

When the North Dakota Democrats and the NPL merged in 1956, they kept separate organizations. In short, they wanted to hold their own political conventions and nominate their own slate of candidates, who would pair off against each other in the June primary in the Democratic column. The winners, whether they be Leaguers or Democrats, would then run against Republican primary winners in the November general election. Maintaining separate conventions was a merger concession to the NPL, which sought to continue its 40-year-old tradition to endorse its own slate of candidates. The only difference in 1958, of course, was that the Leaguers were now realigned with a small but growing number of liberals rather than sticking with a much larger, but slightly declining, number of conservatives.

In March, the NPL and the Democrats hosted their own conventions in Bismarck. They were held a week apart, with the League convention meeting first. These conventions came right after Quentin Burdick's two family tragedies. His mind was preoccupied with family matters and far removed from political ones. At the same time, his daughters, who were concerned with his future, urged him to make an appearance and to stay politically involved because they knew his life would always be happier with politics than without.

Burdick drove from Fargo to Bismarck to attend the NPL convention. He saw many familiar faces and experienced a warm reception. When asked about running, however, he said in no uncertain terms that he would not accept a nomination to run for Congress. With that message off his chest, Burdick immediately left the convention, jumped in his car and drove home to Fargo. The decision was permanent and based on his belief that family now came first. His political life collapsed with Marietta's death and Jon's illness. Enough was enough. It was time to be a father. Period.

Little did he know that putting family first was out-and-out rejected by his children. When he arrived home and told his daughters about his decision, they objected strongly. The family caucused, argued and argued some more. When he repeated his decision not to run, they broke down and cried. All pleaded with him to reconsider his decision, but he said, "No." Jennifer, of the three, continued the debate and refused to accept her father's decision. She kept after him relentlessly and simply wore his patience down. Finally, to end the discussion, he said, "OK. Do what you want." It was not a declaration of candidacy, but an olive branch of peace or surrender. He was tired of badgering and wanted peace. He did not want to hear any more arguments from any of them on the matter, and so to promote harmony, he said, "Yes." Little did he know what Jennifer would do next.[62]

Jennifer, 14, immediately went to the telephone and asked the operator to call the NPL Convention. She impatiently told the operator the call was "an emergency," and soon found herself talking with Jim Jungroth, a Jamestown attorney and chair of the convention. She uttered six words to a surprised Jungroth: "My Daddy will run for Congress." Jungroth wanted collaboration, so he asked to speak to her father; Quentin confirmed his daughter's message. With the balloting already in progress, Jungroth returned to the podium and placed the name of Quentin Burdick in nomination for Congress. Quentin won the nomination on the first ballot.[63]

Jennifer's call changed her father's life and rescued his political career. Mart Vogel reflected on what had happened. "I know when he ran for Congress, Marietta was dead, and he said, 'I think I'm finished with trying to get a political office.' But his daughters had a different idea. Had they not done so, he would not have accepted the nomination and that probably would have been the end of his political career."[64]

One week after capturing the NPL endorsement, Fargo supporters asked Burdick to seek the the Democratic endorsement. He gave the green light, and the Fargo crew headed to Bismarck. Myron Bright delivered his nomination speech, and the convention seemed receptive. Burdick ran strongest on the first ballot before eventually losing to S.B. Hocking and Harold Morrison after several more ballots. Internal factors dictated his defeat rather than anti-Burdick sentiment. Although Burdick was personally disappointed in the results, he was still an endorsed candidate in the June primary.[65]

In retrospect, it is hard to fathom what actually occurred. Burdick said, "No" to the NPL convention, but his daughters nominated him anyway. He then won easily on the first ballot sitting at home in Fargo. Though he agreed to be nominated at the Democratic convention, he failed to win the endorsement after some effort. Burdick, the old, beaten-up Leaguer who turned Democrat only to be slaughtered in races for them, now saw his political fortune revived by the League instead of his own party.

Finally a Winner

Burdick's strategy in the June primary was quite simple: he did not campaign. When pressed by some of his Fargo supporters to go out and campaign, he explained his reasons for doing nothing. "Listen, if I can't win the primary on my own merits without campaigning, I'm not going to win the general election."[66] Burdick's reasoning was well-founded. Unlike any of the other three candidates, his name was well-known throughout the state. In fact, it was the only familiar North Dakota name among all of the 11 candidates running in the June primary for either party. In addition, he had run less than two years ago in a losing race against Senator Milton R. Young. Moreover, in the Democratic primary, there were four candidates running for two seats, not just one. If the Burdick name could not prevail and win one of these two open slots, there was really no chance for him to win in November. Burdick did not believe, however, that he would lose. He firmly believed this race was not only his last opportunity to win, but his best chance as well. Staying home was the right call for his seventh run for public office. John Kelly, a Fargo attoney and lifelong Democrat, concluded, "I think he realized in 1958 that that was the first time he had a real chance to win, at least for statewide office."[67]

The primary results confirmed Burdick's strategy. He garnered 43 percent of the ballots, totaling 38,131 votes in the Democratic primary, and he placed first among the four candidates. He collected more than double the number of votes of S.B. Hocking of Devils Lake, who received 19 percent of the vote, or 17,256 votes. Burdick carried 52 of the state's 53 counties, losing only Oliver County, a sparsely populated county northwest of Bismarck. The votes in the Republican primary, however, reinforced the historical fact that North Dakotans still cast far more Republican votes than Democratic. Orris Nordhougen of Leeds, Burdick's old sparring partner, and Don Short, a Badlands rancher, ran far ahead of Burdick, receiving 54,130 and 47,302 votes respectively.[68] The preseason event was a wash, and Burdick won easily without exerting much effort. The big game in November would be far more challenging.

By today's standards, even the general election proved to be a low-key affair. Burdick spent a total of $3,500 on the race. Two-thirds of the money came from his Fargo supporters. "The contributions were small, not over $100 in any case," recalled Myron Bright, who was then the county chairman of the Cass County Democrats."[69] Lois Casavant, one of the Fargo supporters, added: "I remember in 1958 when he ran that he had so little money — simply because there wasn't many Democrats, and none of us had a lot of money. He wasn't in the right party for money."[70]

Burdick spent most of his money on newspaper ads. He ran reversed ads, i.e., 1-inch ads in all the county newspapers that were white on black rather than black on white. The advertisements read "Be for Burdick" in capital letters. According to Bright, the ads drove the Republicans wild "because they claimed it meant that many in North Dakota would be voting for Quentin thinking they would be voting for his father, Usher."[71] Their concern, of course, was well-founded.

In addition to the newspaper advertisements, Burdick worked hard to get Democratic voters to the polls. "I think he went to every Democrat meeting when he was running in 1958," said Casavant, "because I figured he just needed every live, warm body he could get there."[72] In those meetings, Burdick talked almost always about the farm issue. He criticized the federal farm programs of the Eisenhower administration and their chief architect, Secretary of Agriculture Ezra Taft Benson. Burdick also promoted the need for the Missouri Diversion, or the Garrison Diversion, as it soon became known.[73]

The November general election for two open House seats proved a tight race. It was a close election even though it was of short duration and neither extremely partisan or personal. "You know what I recall when Quentin ran for Congress in 1958," said May Burdick, is "that there wasn't this horrible animosity. It wasn't this nastiness. I think it was because the Republicans didn't think he had a chance, so they weren't out fighting."[74] All four candidates received between 21 percent and 27 percent of the votes. Burdick, the Fargo Democrat, and Short, the Medora Republican, prevailed. Burdick finished first, polling 99,562 votes, while Short polled 97,862 votes. Nordhougen garnered a close third with 92,124 votes, while Hocking was further back with 78,889 votes.[75]

It was almost entirely a northern victory for Burdick. He ran first in 32 counties, an area comprising nearly the entire top half of the state, except for Divide County in the west and Pembina and Grand Forks County in the east. He did the poorest in the southern German-Russian counties such as Logan and McIntosh. Short, on the other hand, won 17 counties located primarily south-central as well as the populous urban counties of Burleigh, Cass and Grand Forks — all traditional Republican strongholds.[76]

Of the many factors that contributed to Burdick's first win for elective office, first and foremost was the Burdick name. "I know that a lot of people thought they were still voting for Usher," noted Jack Zaleski, veteran North Dakota journalist.[77] "One of the reasons Quentin finally won," added longtime Fargo supporter Helen Pepple, "was the name — his father's name — that carried through."[78] Others were more blunt. "If Burdick would have had to start from scratch without the benefit of the Burdick name," stated Lloyd Omdahl, "Burdick would not have been elected to Congress and would not have been elected to the Senate. I think in 1958, when Usher practically silently moved out and Quentin moved in ... that there were a lot of people that thought that Burdick is Burdick regardless. Burdick won on the Burdick name."[79]

The second reason centered on the strength of the candidates running in this particular election. None of the candidates running for the two open seats were incumbents. It is hard to beat an incumbent anywhere in this country, but it is even harder to beat an incumbent North Dakota Republican. History, until recent years, proved it. Although there were two Republicans running in this race, neither of them enjoyed the job security of incumbency or the popularity of name recognition. They were still favored to win, but the odds of victory diminished when challenged by the Democratic candidate bearing a popular Republican surname.

The third reason for Burdick's success derived from the deep changes occurring within North Dakota's political landscape. Stanley Moore, president of the North Dakota Farmers Union, said it best: "The League-Democrat merger had never elected anybody. I think there was an awful lot of structure change during this period of time. There is no question about the fact that when the Republicans dumped his Dad, that brought over a whole bunch of unannounced people over to Quentin's side."[80] Fellow Democrat, Joyce Conrad of Mandan, described the situation more broadly: "There was no one reason. It just all came together."[81] Jim Jungroth added: "Everybody wasn't just voting in the Republican column anymore. The NPL had moved to the Democratic column, and the time had come to do that."[82] On the flip side, the weakness of the Republican ticket appeared. "The Republicans kind of blew it," said Mark Andrews. "Don Short was an admirable candidate," but the other candidate,

"Orris Nordhougen, on a statewide basis, didn't have the same kind of appeal that Quentin had. They, in a sense, made the opening."[83] The opening, however, was not big, and both Republican candidates ran a strong race against a Democrat with a Republican following. But the gap was just wide enough for Burdick to run through, and he took advantage of it.

The Quentin Burdick victory was ever so sweet. In Williston, his home town, the western Burdicks parked themselves around a newly purchased television in Eugene and May's comfortable home. They were anxious to watch the results. That election eve was really the very beginning of television election results in the nation and North Dakota. Usher, at first, seemed more intent on winning a game of solitaire than watching the election results, although he kept one eye on the tube, too. Suddenly, however, when the regular show was interrupted with an election update and reports of several county tallies, Usher broke the silence; looking up from his cards, he said, "We won."[84] Some 500 miles away, a Burdick victory party was in full swing at Bill Thompson's Fargo home. The winner soon appeared, and Bright, one of his strongest supporters, said the look on Burdick's face will always be etched in his memory; at the moment of victory "his face carried a rather pensive and sad look, and in his eyes you could see him silently saying, 'Marietta, I made it, but it's a hollow victory without you.'"[85]

North Dakota Democrat leaders were quick to lose their moment in history. Their past track record was dismal. The last time they had sent anyone to Washington was when Governor John Moses went to the U.S. Senate in 1944. Moses died, however, in the spring of 1945, and Governor Fred Aandahl appointed Young, who served until his retirement in 1981. On the House side, North Dakota Democrats were winless, never electing anyone to the U.S. House of Representatives. "I grew up with the mentality," said state Senator Corliss Mushik of Mandan, "that Republicans always won. You know, because that's the way it was."[86] The Burdick victory was a first, and the Democrats wanted to build on this win and gain recognition among the national Democratic Party.

"As you know, we elected our first Democratic Congressman in the history of North Dakota," began Daphna Nygaard's letter to Katie Loucbbeim, vice chair of the National Democratic Committee. Nygaard was a longtime fixture in North Dakota Democratic circles, serving as the state's Democratic committee woman. She opined that as a result of Burdick's victory, Democrats "have made the break from the idea of a traditionally Republican state," and "we would like to elect some more Democrats and now possibly we [will] do just that." She concluded by writing, "Mr. Burdick is a real Democrat and has always been a promoter of the Democratic philosophy."[87]

David Kelly, her male sidekick as North Dakota's national committeeman, wrote to former President Harry Truman. They were old friends and although Republican Senator William Langer campaigned for Truman in 1948 and Usher was a good personal friend, there was not much good news about North Dakota Democratic Party successes to share with national leaders of the party. The Burdick victory changed all of that, and Kelly wanted the president to know. He also wanted to make sure the election was not a fluke. "Now that we have our feet in the door," began Kelly, "it is extremely important that everything be done to insure Quentin's reelection in 1960 and, if possible, a Democratic senator and congressman." Kelly asked Truman to secure an appointment for Burdick on the Committee for Internal and Insular Affairs. Kelly reasoned that joining the newly elected congressman with support for the Missouri River Basin would guarantee longevity for both."[88]

The last nine months of 1958 were pivotal in the life of Quentin Burdick. In March, he lost his wife and institutionalized his son. In June, he won the primary, and in November, he captured a seat in the U.S. House of Representatives. It was his first victory after six defeats and the first time that North Dakota Democrats prevailed in a House election. New-found political success ameliorated deep sorrow for family tragedies. Burdick became an office holder — not just an office seeker. Family concerns, however, did not disappear with his November win. Jan Mary sought her freedom after being totally burned out from trying to keep tabs on her sisters. The younger girls were quite independent, especially Jennifer. The most pressing family issue centered around what would a 50-year-old freshman congressman do with two young teenage girls. The solution was for their father to pull them out of Fargo schools in January of 1959 and take them with him to Washington. At first, there were some concerns about their adjustments, but the six months they spent with their father proved to be some of the most memorable in their young lives. "We were there from January to June," recalled Jessica with pride, "and in that time period, I saw a lot of places, a lot of historical sites."[89]

The girls' accompanying Quentin to Washington was a short-term fix. The solution fit the moments of sorrow and joy of 1958, but not the future. In the summer of 1959, the girls returned to Fargo and Quentin went back to Washington. No one, certainly not the congressman or his daughters, could imagine the changes that lay ahead. The past was still too tender and the future too uncertain.

Endnotes

1. Jennifer Burdick, interview with author, March 26, 1995.
2. Jerome Lamb, interview with author, Jan. 20, 1995.
3. D. Jerome Tweton, interview with author, April 17, 1995.
4. Myron Bright, interview with author, March 28, 1996.
5. Jennifer Burdick interview.
6. Jan Mary Burdick Hill, interview with author, May 25, 1995.
7. Jessica Burdick, interview with author, Jan. 28, 1996.
8. Jennifer Burdick interview.
9. Marge Scott, interview with author, Jan. 22, 1995.
10. May Burdick, interview with author, March 1, 1995.
11. Lois Vogel, interview with author, Jan. 21, 1995.
12. Quentin Burdick, letter to Usher Burdick, Dec. 21, 1958, folder 4, box 34, Usher L. Burdick Manuscript Collection [hereafter BMC].
13. Vogel interview.
14. Hill interview.
15. Jennifer Burdick interview.
16. Jessica Burdick interview.
17. "Cancer in the Air," *Newsweek*, Nov. 26, 1956, 102.
18. "Smoking and Health," *Time*, June 7, 1957, 40.
19. "Cancer and Women Smokers," *Time*, March 5, 1957, 71.
20. Hill interview.
21. Quentin Burdick, letter to Usher Burdick, Jan. 18, 1958, folder 4, box 34, BMC.
22. "Great Humilation," *Time* 64, Aug. 9, 1954, 65-66.
23. "Things Get Hotter for Hoxsey," *Life*, April 16, 1956, 125.
24. "Great Humilation," 65-66.
25. "Hoxsey and his Cure," *Newsweek*, April 1956, 89.
26. *New York Times*, Nov. 16, 1956, 10, and Oct. 31, 1958, 31.
27. Mrs. Janecky, telegram to Usher Burdick, Jan. 30, 1958, folder 4, box 34, BMC.
28. Jessica Burdick interview.
29. Hill interview.
29. Scott interview.
30. Hill interview.
32. Elkind, *The Hurried Child*, xi-xii, 6, 11, 32.
33. Hill interview; *Cynosure*, Fargo Central High School 1953 Annual, 26.
34. Hill interview.
35. Ibid.
36. Jennifer Burdick interview.
37. Jessica Burdick interview.
38. Eugene Burdick, interview with author, Feb. 28, 1995.
39. Ibid.
40. Hill interview.
41. Ibid.
42. Scott interview.
43. Bright interview.
44. Hill interview.
45. Jennifer Burdick interview.
46. Hill interview.
47. Jennifer Burdick interview.
48. Austin Engel, interview with author, Feb. 9, 1995.
49. Usher L. Burdick, letter to Mrs. H.C. Williams, June 22, 1958, folder 24, box 17, BMC.
50. Ralph Dewing, interview with author, Feb. 9, 1995.
51. Wick, *North Dakota Place Names*, 32, 224.
52. Arthur LInk, interview with author, Jan. 25, 1995.
53. Ibid.
54. Tom Burgum, interview with author, March 24, 1995.
55. Ibid.

56. Mark Andrews, interview with author, April 19, 1995.
57. Milton R. Young, interview with D. Jerome Tweton, folder 29, box 794, Milton R. Young Papers.
58. Usher Burdick, letter to A.J. Biewer, November 1958, folder 14, box 36, BMC.
59. Ibid.
60. Usher Burdick, letter to Judge Eugene Worley, Nov. 20, 1958, folder 20, box 34, BMC.
61. Andrews interview.
62. Hill interview.
63. *Fargo (N.D.) Forum*, Nov. 5, 1958, Section E.
64. Mart Vogel, interview with author, Jan. 19, 1995.
65. Bright interview.
66. Ibid.
67. John Kelly, interview with author, Jan. 22, 1995.
68. *North Dakota Votes*, 161.
69. Bright interview.
70. Lois Casavant, interview with author, Jan. 23, 1995.
71. Bright interview.
72. Casavant interview.
73. Thorson, "The Campaign and Election of Quentin Burdick 1958," (master's thesis, University of North Dakota, Grand Forks, N.D., 1963), 57.
74. May Burdick interview.
75. *North Dakota Votes*, 161.
76. Ibid.
77. Jack Zaleski, interview with author, Jan. 23, 1995.
78. Helen Pepple, interview with author, April 1, 1995.
79. Lloyd Omdahl, interview with author, Jan. 18, 1995.
80. Stanley Moore, interview with author, Jan. 24, 1995.
81. Joyce Conrad, interview with author, March 25, 1995.
82. James Jungroth, interview with author, Feb. 5, 1995.
83. Andrews interview.
84. Ardell Tharaldson, interview with author, Jan. 25, 1995.
85. Bright interview.
86. Corliss Mushik, interview with author, Feb. 9, 1995.
87. Daphna Nygaard, letter to Katie Louchbbein, Dec. 10, 1958, folder 3, box 3, Daphna Nygaard Collection.
88. David Kelly, letter to Harry S. Truman, Dec. 11, 1958, folder 10, box 2, David Kelly Papers.
89. Jessica Burdick interview.

- nine -

1960

958 proved to be the watershed in Quentin Burdick's life; 1960 evoked a second year of equal significance — the former for great changes, and the latter year for an equally powerful continuity. Though 1958 produced personal pain and political success, 1960 produced personal happiness and a bright, if not almost unbelievably vibrant political future. As in 1958, there were two major events in 1960 that transformed Burdick's life. In June, the newly elected Congressman Burdick became Senator Burdick when he defeated Republican Governor John Davis for the unexpired term of the late Senator William Langer, who died in November 1959. In July, Burdick married an attractive Fargo widow, Jocelyn Birch Peterson (Jocie to family and friends). Widower and widow became man and wife. Two single parents united two separate families under one southside Fargo roof. North Dakota's first Democratic congressman shockingly became North Dakota's first Democrat United States senator in 15 years by winning the special election for the four remaining years of Langer's term. In winning a second statewide election in less than two years, Burdick never repeated his many earlier losses. He won five more Senate elections quite handily in 1964, 1970, 1976, 1982, and 1988. From 1960 until his death in 1992, Quentin and Jocie developed a strong personal union matched by an equally vibrant political relationship. These two North Dakota Republican children raised in very different homes under very different circumstances matured into the leading man and the first lady of the modern North Dakota NPL Democratic Party. Theirs proved a union of commitment and loyalty. Two mature adults, robbed of a longer life with spouses of early choices, found in the tranquility of Fargo and the halls of Congress a second life with unexpected happiness — 32 years of marriage with all the honor and prestige of being Senator and Jocelyn Burdick.

Jocelyn Birch Burdick

Jocelyn Birch Burdick and Fargo seem almost one and the same. Their paths cross so often and at so many important junctures that it is hard to separate her from the city. Albert Birch and Magdelina Carpenter, her parents, arrived in Fargo as youngsters with their families to seek a better life in North Dakota's most promising city. Jocie, born in 1922, and Antoinette, her older sister by seven years, were born in Fargo. Parents and children alike all attended Fargo elementary schools and all proudly graduated from Fargo Central, the city's only public high school. Jocie married twice in Fargo, first to Kenneth Peterson in 1948, and then to Quentin Burdick 12 years later. All of her children — Leslie (b. 1951), Birch (b. 1955) and Gage (b. 1961) — were born in Fargo. All the siblings followed their maternal grandparents and their mother through the same Fargo public schools. Leslie, unmarried, divides her time between Fargo and Washington, D.C.; Birch, married, was elected Cass County state's attorney in 1998 on his very first attempt. Gage, who died tragically in a freak accident at home in 1976, is buried in Fargo. Perhaps the strongest bond between Jocie and Fargo remains the modest Birch house at 1110 South Ninth Street, her long-term residence since 1944, and the summer Birch family cottage, built by her father on the shores of Lake Melissa in 1929, an hour's drive east of Fargo in the land of 10,000 lakes.

Jocie's parents nurtured a secure and idyllic childhood for their two daughters. Albert provided the family with financial security even through the difficult years between the two World Wars. Magdalene added a strong feminist and literary pedigree. Her conversion to one of America's unique religions, Christian Science, also left an indelible mark on her youngest daughter's life and those of her grandchildren. The Birches lived comfortably on Fargo's near south side. Until 1944, they resided on the more prestigious Eighth Street, but during the war, moved a block west to the present Ninth Street location. The cottage-looking structure was smaller, cheaper to heat, offered a first-floor bedroom for Albert's aging parents, and required much less upkeep for Magdalene, who was left on her own while Albert was busy with construction work. The dwelling attested to the family virtue of frugality. There was no evidence of wealth or any demonstrative signs of ostentation. Although the Birches, like most of their neighbors, were traditional Republicans, they never appeared or acted partisan. "They were not outspoken Republicans or hidden Democrats," said Marge Scott. "They were just even-keeled people."[1] Personal life and politics resided privately in the family. "The importance of voting had always been stressed in our family," recalled Jocie, "because of my great-grandmother and her fight for women's rights and all that sort of thing."[2]

The Birch family had moved south from Manitoba to North Dakota in the late 19th century. Albert's parents were Canadians, but he and his brother, Fred, were born on the American side of the Red River Valley of the North. They first lived in Pembina, an important border stop on the Red River between the two countries. Here Albert's father, Steven, launched a small family business, which eventually became known as S. Birch and Sons, a construction firm devoted primarily to sidewalk and street improvements. In the summer of 1893, the family moved farther south and upriver to Fargo. The city, destroyed by the infamous fire of June 7, offered a boom era for builders. The fire's path destroyed more than 31 blocks of business, scores of residential homes and miles of wooden sidewalks.[3] "They came to Fargo after the fire to rebuild the town," recalled Jocie with pride.[4]

The Birch family enterprise expanded rapidly and later split into two parts. Steven and Albert stayed permanently in Fargo, while Fred moved to Great Falls, Montana. Fred incorporated the business in Montana because of the state's favorable tax laws. The Fargo firm concentrated on city and street improvements and experienced two years of no new business in the early 1930s, but shared significantly in the New Deal work projects, which filtered down to state and local communities by the mid-1930s. The Montana portfolio expanded to include the building of bridges and dams, and it, too, benefited from federally funded infrastructure projects after World War II. The increased business made for bigger profits, but often took Albert away from home.

The Carpenter family arrived in Fargo nine years after the Birches' arrival in 1902. Two family branches — Gage and Baum — leap off the pages of Jocie's family tree. They help to explain her strong stand on women's issues and her lifelong pursuit of intellectual interests. She is most proud of the heritage of her maternal family name, Gage. The standout in the family was Matilda Jocelyn Gage, Jocie's great-grandmother, who was a leading New York suffragist. Jocie preserved the family name by naming her and Quentin's only son, Gage, in 1961. The Baum connection is equally important but for quite different reasons. Maude Gage was a sister of Julia Jocelyn Gage, Jocie's grandmother. Maude married Frank Baum, the American journalist and writer who became most famous for his children's books, *The Wizard of Oz* series. Maude and Frank lived for a time in Aberdeen, South Dakota, before Baum became rich and famous and moved to Hollywood, California. Although Frank Baum died before Jocie was born, she recalled vividly her first meeting with her great Aunt Maude. "I'm your Aunt Maude," she told an excited and attentive little girl, "and I'm your best friend." Jocie, who was only 4 at the time, never forgot the message or the messenger. She said that she always felt the same way toward her Aunt Maude, who lived to be 97 years old. Jocie also knew most of the Oz characters by heart and passed those stories on to her children.[5]

Jocie's parents became good friends in high school. Magdelina and Albert were active and popular students engaged in a variety of extracurricular activities. Albert, although short of stature, was an outstanding athlete and captained football and basketball teams for Fargo Central. Magdelina, Albert and her brother held "all of the offices in the school" and "were editors of the paper." Albert later attended the University of Wisconsin at Madison, where he played on varsity teams. Their love for Fargo, the traditions of Fargo Central, and the importance of investing in social capital were legacies of their formative years growing up in Fargo before the First World War.[6]

Illness, however, disrupted Magdelina's life; she contracted tuberculosis before Jocie was born. The search for a cure consumed much of the family's energies, leading them down several roads. When the illness worsened, Magdelina went west for extended stays in California sanitariums in attempts to prolong her life. She spent one year in Palm Springs and another in Victorville. The climate gave her added strength but no cure, and the doctors gave her only a short time to live. With patients dying all around her, the Baums, who made regular visits to see her in California, suggested another course. Why not try Christian Science, a religion which emphasized healing through spiritual means as an important element of Christianity? "She did," recalled Jocie, "and had a remarkable healing. They didn't expect her to live, and they said she couldn't go back to North Dakota and that she could not have any more children. With the help of Christian Science, she did all three. When I was 16, she and I went back to see the man who was head of the anti-tuberculosis unit in southern California, so he could meet the daughter she was never supposed to have had. She lived 32 years after they told her she had no hope to live, and that was our beginning interest in Christian Science."[7]

The new religion and the healing it brought exerted a significant influence on Magdelina and later on Jocie. Mother and daughter became devout and lifelong members of Fargo's Christian Science Church. Through the years, they gave financial support and countless volunteer hours to the church. Both women believed their very life came from their contact with the church. Although Albert strongly supported his wife's religious choice and began to attend church regularly, he never officially became a member. Jocie passed her religious beliefs on to her children, who were also raised within the church that had exerted such a powerful influence over their grandmother and mother.

Security and spontaneity best describe Jocie's childhood. Jean Mason, who later became Jean Guy, the first lady of North Dakota, grew up in the same southside Fargo neighborhood. "Jocie had been a friend of mine since I was in the second grade," recalled Mason. "We went to Hawthorne School and she was a half year ahead of me ... we played together as very young girls." The girls especially enjoyed playing with dolls after school often at the Birch home. When the Birches took their annual extended winter health trips to California, Mason looked forward to her girlfriend's return. Jocie was "never unpleasant" or "hard to get along with" and was "always very smart," said Mason. Even today, she remembers Jocie as a little girl with long curls, whose wealth never seemed important to the Birch family or their daughter.[8]

Those long curls of her school-girl days were not forgotten by Jocie, either. "I got to be the queen of third or fourth grade at Hawthorne Grade School," recalled Jocie, "not because I was so pretty, but because I had long curls. It was so funny because my friend, Freddy Green, was the king. Now, Freddy was not very tall, and I was tall, so they had a crown on his head which was about 4 inches high. He stood on a book so he would be taller than me for the picture."[9]

Jocie's popularity expanded as she grew older; she was as well-liked among the boys as she was with the girls. She dated often and with lots of young men. Nothing serious. She preferred to be no one's particular special girl, opting instead to be everyone's. She was always fun to be with, and Jocie stood out among her peers. There was the Erickson lad, for example, the son of the Island Park grocer who owned the neighborhood candy store, who became her first boyfriend of sorts. Erickson's father's store was a frequent stop for Jocie and her girlfriends after school. The glass cases of the store overflowed with dozens of varieties of penny candy, and Jocie, to the delight of her classmates, often picked up the tab. The practice continued until Mr. Erickson called her mother to see if she had given her daughter approval to charge at the store. After his call, the charging abruptly stopped. Jocie later dated Bruce Dalrymple, a member of one of Fargo's oldest and most important families. The relationship proved more serious. Both were older by then, and Dalrymple was several years older than Jocie. In the end, however, college away from home cooled their dating.[10]

College choices for Jocie came, in part, from two close southside friends, Peggy Black and Mary Lemke. Both girls carried famous North Dakota Republican names. Peggy's father was Norman D. Black, the publisher and owner of the *Fargo Forum*. The *Forum* was the state's pre-eminent newspaper, and its editorials became the standard-bearer of the North Dakota Republican Party. The Blacks lived on Eighth Street, and their large home symbolized personal wealth and Hoover economics. Mary's father was William Lemke, the notorious Nonpartisan League attorney general, who was recalled in 1921 and who later became one of the nation's most outspoken critics of monied interests. He served in the United States House of Representatives from 1933-1941 and 1943 until his death in 1950. In 1932, Lemke ran as the state's only presidential candidate on the Union Party ticket. The home also stood on Eighth Street, but on the opposite side and paid for by quite different wealth. Critics of the League, including the *Fargo Forum*, painted the house as an example of corrupt state Socialism. Lemke's home was never debt-free, and Fargo cabbies gave free rides to anyone who wanted them to tell the story of those rotten days of North Dakota Socialism.[11] Although Peggy and Mary's families were both Republican by name, anyone remotely aware of the intense hatred between conservative Republicans and the Nonpartisan League in those years knew they shared nothing in common.

Peggy Black shared an almost unbelievably long and close friendship with Jocie. "We walked to school together every day for 12 years," Jocie fondly recalls. "She went to St. Anthony's for the last half of the fifth grade and the first half of the sixth grade. We started 15 minutes before Hawthorne, so I could walk to St. Anthony's with her and then walk over to Hawthorne afterwards."[12] They graduated together from Central and later became classmates and sorority sisters (Gamma Phi Beta) at Northwestern University in Evanston, Illinois. They still keep in touch today. Loyalty to her friends is one of Jocie's strongest character traits.

Mary Lemke was a year older than the other two girls. She was not as close to Jocie as was Peggy, and certainly their friendship paled in contrast to the intensity and longevity of the other one. However, Mary still exerted much influence in Jocie's choice of a college. When Jocie was a high school senior, Mary invited her to spend a weekend with her at Prinsipea College in Elsah, Illinois. The small liberal arts college was located on the bluffs of the Mississippi River 35 miles north of St. Louis, Missouri. It offered a small, private liberal arts atmosphere with a strong Christian Science connection. The visit confirmed Jocie's choice of colleges as well as continuity with Fargo and, of course, with her religion. She attended Prinsipea for two years and took primarily liberal arts classes while demonstrating both a talent and an interest in communications. Seeking a better school to pursue her career, she transferred to Northwestern in Evanston, Illinois, for her junior year. The transfer reunited her with Peggy, who had transferred there a year earlier from St. Mary's College, the sister school of Notre Dame at South Bend, Indiana. Jocie graduated in 1943 with a speech major and then she returned to Fargo.[13]

The war years brought new challenges and a sudden, almost pressured urgency to live life to the fullest. The years between 1941 and 1945 were uncertain for many young adults, who turned to each other for support, companionship and marriage. "I went with several boys before the war," said Jocie. "Then I went with Don Schollander. I was engaged to him, but he was killed in the war."[14]

Donald Arthur Schollander was the same age as Jocie, a neighborhood friend and a fellow graduate of Fargo Central. She graduated in 1939; he graduated one year later. His school annual photograph, academic accomplishments and long list of extracurricular activities epitomized an all-American boy. He was clean-cut, tall, blond, intelligent, and as popular among his peers in Fargo as Jocie. He was heavy on civic participation in the Boy Scouts and demonstrated natural athletic talent in high school, American Legion summer baseball and college. He spent two years at North Dakota State University before transferring north to Grand Forks and the University of North Dakota's law school. He was commissioned a second lieutenant in June of 1943 and sailed for France on December 5, 1944, arriving 15 days later. Within one month's time, he was killed in action – January 10, 1945 – in the Battle of the Bulge, Germany's last offensive of the war. It was a brief war stint for a young man in the bloom of his life.[15] Schollander, along with 1,938 other North Dakotans, laid down their lives to make the world a safer place.[16] Schollander's remains lie in a cemetery full of fellow soldiers in Epinal, France, marked inconspicuously by only a small marker in Plot A, Row 15, Grave 16.[17]

Mason experienced those war years, too. Fargo just did not seem the same place as before the war. The atmosphere tensed as families, wives and fiancées made themselves busy to avoid the worst as they waited for news from the war. "You know," recalled Mason, "there were no men around here, so the girls would get together frequently and have hot suppers and [do] things together." She was a classmate of Schollander, and the news of his death, along with a number of young men from the Fargo area killed in the same engagement, brought the war closer to her. As for Jocie, "It was a very traumatic time for her." William Guy, Mason's husband, served in the Pacific as a naval officer, but he was more fortunate. Guy, unlike Schollander, made it home.[18]

With a return to normalcy after the war and the death of her fiancée, Jocie, then 23 years old, began to concentrate on a professional career in communications. She spent the next three years working hard in a couple of interesting jobs. She interviewed for a job in New York while visiting the city. "I went to a number of plays," recalls Jocie. "I just thought I was in seventh heaven, but I didn't want to live there. I loved to visit, but I wanted to come home."[19] Fargo would always be her base for family and now for work.

With a communication degree, Jocie tried to get a job in radio. She interviewed first with WDAY, the premier Fargo-Moorhead station, but came up dry. They were not interested in her. She then turned to secretarial work, which seemed more acceptable for the time and her gender. She easily secured part-time work with Kelly Girls, but quickly admitted she was not really cut out to be a secretary. "I was a disaster. My handwriting was a disaster," said Jocie. Undaunted, however, she decided to take a shorthand test to secure a permanent position. The exercise proved embarrassing. When asked to take dictation for one letter, Jocie simply froze. After a long pause, which seemed like forever, she handed back a blank piece of paper. She could not remember anything and was quickly dismissed with a curt, polite, one-liner that they would get back to her.[20]

Jocie, however, still pursued work in her chosen field. She soon landed a job with KNOX radio, a smaller and less popular Fargo-Moorhead station. She worked at KNOX for two years, enjoying a great variety of work and the opportunity to use her training in communications. Manny Marget, her mentor, was a dapper little man with a wonderful radio personality. He became the voice of Red River Valley sports for decades. His live coverage of Fargo Central, Moorhead High School and later Shanley High School games garnered a large audience and good revenue for the station. "I really adored him," said Jocie. "I had a lot of fun there. You're a jack of all trades in a small station, a little bit of everything. I did the same as everyone else, write news and everything. I think there were no other women announcers at that time in this area"[21] This career opportunity would have most certainly pleased her great-grandmother.

When a national position became available with Gamma Phi Beta Sorority, Jocie resigned her job at KNOX. The new position appealed to her for a variety of reasons. First and foremost, she was a Gamma Phi, active in the sorority as an undergraduate and now as an alumnus. She was eager to work for the organization that meant so much to her personally. The position also gave her a wonderful opportunity to be on her own, to write more and to just be free. "I traveled around the country," recalled Jocie. "I was their entertainment chairman and was compiling a booklet of party ideas that they used at the different schools. Then I got married."[22]

Several factors contributed to Jocie's decision to marry in 1948. The first was that society expected women of her generation to marry. Marriage was the fulfillment of their adulthood. Now in her mid-20s, with a professional career that was unusual for her sex, Jocie was still without a husband and a family. Many of her friends were married and the children they bore became the focus of their lives. War's end added an aura of normalcy to build families once again. North Dakota, like the rest of the country, shared in the wealth of a war economy, rain versus drought, and better than cost-of-production returns for farm products. The children born in the '20s and raised in the '30s saw their lives change with the war years. Now it was over. The times seemed different, especially for those who lost loved ones. On the flip side, Jocie, for the boys who came home, was an attractive catch in this new milieu. She was not only beautiful and talented, but also available.

At first glance, Kenneth Peterson seemed an unlikely suitor — a second choice, perhaps. In some ways, because of the war, he was. He was, for example, not counted among one of the boys who came home; he never went in the first place. He flunked his physical because he was born with a weak heart. The heart condition, however, did not prevent him from either work or play. He earned good wages as the roundhouse foreman for the Great Northern Railroad when Jocie married him. He was described as "handsome and quite athletic." He was one of the best, if not the best, of Fargo's many fine figure skaters. "He was a darling," recalled Marge Scott. "He was as lovely as Quentin's first wife and a beautiful skater. Theresa Powers [her father owned the Powers Hotel] and I were very good friends and we would deliberately go down just to watch Kenny Peterson skate. We just thought he was out of this world. If he would have been a dancer, he should have been in the Zigfield Follies."[23] Jocie remembered that Ken always wanted her to go skating, but admitted that she was a terrible skater. "When Mary Jane Danovick [a close friend] came up and saw us on the ice, she said, 'It's obvious you didn't fall in love on the ice.'"[24]

Ken and Jocie were married in 1948. His heart condition posed no problem. "I knew about it when I married him," recalled Jocie, "but it didn't seem to hamper us in any way." With the death of Jocie's mother the same year, the young couple moved into the family home to be with Albert. "He [Dad] didn't know how to boil water," said Jocie, "and I was married, so my husband and I rented from my Dad and stayed here."[25]

Marriage ended Jocie's working career. It was another reminder of a traditional role for women in those years. "In that day and age," said Jocie, "and I think this is so funny now, it didn't enter my head that I would work after I was married."[26] With Leslie and Birch both born in the quiet of the '50s, life seemed fulfilled and normal. The children were raised as Christian Scientist because Ken was not a church-goer and because "whatever I wanted was fine with him." said Jocie. One of Fargo's leading daughters was now raising a family during the Age of Eisenhower. It all seemed so simple, and it was until, as Jocie abruptly put it: "He dropped dead in 1958."[27]

Love and Marriage

"Love and marriage, love and marriage, go together like a horse and carriage. This I tell you, brother, Ya can't have one without the other." Do you remember the song? The lyrics were written by Sammy Cahn and sung by the likes of Doris Day and Frank Sinatra in the mid-1950s. It was a very popular song, and the words captured the essence of marriage in popular verse. The lyric also underlies an understanding of the marriage of Quentin and Jocelyn Birch Peterson on July 7, 1960. It is accurate and certainly not unkind to suggest marriage for both of them came before love. The characterization is not a condemnation of their 32 years of love and marriage; rather it is an observation that second marriages often begin with reality and not infatuation.

The Petersons and the Burdicks ran in different Fargo social circles. The Burdicks were a generation older, and if they went anywhere, it was seldom publicized. The Petersons were better off financially and far more active socially. For example, they belonged to a Fargo dance club that included William and Jean Guy. They also occasionally took skiing trips north of Duluth, Minnesota. Jocie knew Marietta better than she did Quentin. Both women were active members of the Drama Section of the Fargo Fine Arts Club, which met often in the club's residence near Fargo's Island Park. Jocie and Marietta also ran into each other on occasion at school functions. Both Jessica Burdick and Leslie Peterson attended Hawthorne Elementary School, which was within easy walking distance of both family homes. Although Jocie knew Quentin by name and could recognize him at a glance, she never enjoyed any direct contact with him until after the death of her husband. Her recollection more than 35 years later was quite vivid.

"He wrote me a note when I lost Ken and expressed sympathy," said Jocie. "I wrote back and thanked him. Eventually, he called and left word with my baby sitter, Mary Lou Bilmer, who had baby-sat for me for years. She gave me the telephone number and said that Quentin Burdick had called. I thought that was amazing. I wondered what he wanted. I called him up, and he said, 'Oh, I didn't mean for you to call me.' I reminded him, 'Well, you left your name!'" Jocie recalled his explanation: "Well, what he wanted to know was if I would like to go to the Symphony Ball [giggle]. I thought that would be nice." Jocie further described the ensuing events. "Later I was over at my friend's, Margie Crow's, and we got to talking about the Symphony Ball. 'You know,' I said. 'I'm going to go to the Symphony Ball.' 'Who with?' she asked. She was very surprised when I told her. My sister's reaction was: 'Why did he ask you out? He's going to marry Bunny Hector Smith.' Later on I told Quentin about this, and he said that was those coffee clutches getting together and deciding. Quentin and I were married in July of 1960. He gave me a diamond in Florida when I was down there with the two kids. Quentin came down and spent a weekend down there, and he bought me a diamond at that time. Myron Bright was horrified when he heard about it because he was masterminding Quentin's campaign for the Senate against Governor John Davis. I remember this all so well because I told him John's sister was one of my best friends. 'Heavens. She is?' said Quentin. Yes. We had known each other since we were little girls. We went to Hawthorne together. Myron Bright thought then Quentin would get a sympathy vote because he was a widower, and he knew he needed every vote he could get. He was horrified that we had become engaged. He told Quentin to tell me to wear the ring around my neck. 'You tell him to forget it,' I told Quentin. 'I'm going to wear it.' We set it up to be married on July 7. I think the election was June 27. For a while, I thought I was the consolation prize because it was a long time before we found out who won. When we did, it was by a very small margin, slightly over a thousand votes."[28]

Jocie's recollection omitted one small detail. In 1952, she and Quentin appeared on the same platform in a contentious Fargo debate over fluoridation for the city's water. The public forum was sponsored by the League of Women Voters. Quentin spoke in favor of fluoridation and Jocie spoke against it. In time, Quentin's position won, but the debate was prolonged and split the Fargo community deeply. "Years later, I kidded him," recalled Jocie. "You know the poor people voted for me then. The silk stocking district voted for you. The people with means wanted it for the benefit of the poor, but the poor people were against it."[29] So was Jocie!

The couple were married privately on July 7, 1960. The ceremony took place at the Birch residence, a location that came as a surprise to no one who knew the bride. Siblings of the bride (Bonnie) and groom (Eugene) stood in as the maid of honor and the best man. Jocie's children, who still remember the day with great excitement, participated in the ceremony. "I was in the wedding," recalled Leslie. "It was in our house!"[30] Birch remembered holding the ribbons with his older sister as his mother and new father walked through them.[31] Quentin's two youngest daughters shared no thoughts about the occasion. It was not a particularly happy day for them. The marriage meant big change – change they did not want. Jan Mary, the older sister, looked at her father's remarriage differently. "I was very happy," she recalled. "Delighted. Someone else was going to take care of those two girls [laughter]."[32]

A public reception and a private party followed. The formal reception took place at the Graver Hotel in downtown Fargo. It was then one of the great hotels of the city and a grand place to celebrate such an occasion. The wedding, after all, was a public event of sorts. It is not every day that a newly elected United States senator gets married, and even more rare that a North Dakota Democrat marries one of Fargo's most attractive Republican widows. The reception was uneventful until the newlyweds, with some trepidation, called on Usher to make a few remarks. Their fears were not unfounded. With Usher in control, the noisy ballroom suddenly grew quiet waiting for anything to happen. No one was disappointed. With his booming voice and the wit of the Chautauqua speaker he used to be, Usher lifted his glass and proposed a toast to his oldest son and his new bride. His opening line: "Unaccustomed as I am to speaking at weddings," evoked a tense moment of silence followed by a roar of laughter. Jocie said those were the only words she could remember before "everyone just collapsed!"[33]

A private party, hosted by Dave and Marge Scott, commenced later that evening on Broadway's north side. They were, of course, among Quentin and Marietta's dearest friends and strongest political supporters. This was the end of a long and eventful day for the bride and groom, as well as family members and friends. As the evening progressed, Eugene started to ask his father some questions about the old days. Usher, still in rare form, required no prompting and quickly found a comfortable perch on a living room window seat before launching into his reminiscences. "It was the most amazing conversation between Eugene, his father and Quentin," recalled Mart Vogel. "I think Usher was very proud of Quentin."[34] This was one of the last conversations between Usher and his two boys together. It was a poignant recollection of the past forever lost to history except in the memories of those present.

There was some discussion but little debate about where the two newly combined families would reside. "Right from the start," said Jocie, "I thought it would be better for me to stay home and for him to commute."[35] This meant, of course, that Jocie preferred to manage the two families under one Birch roof and that Quentin would divide his time between Washington and Fargo. She would spend a few weeks in January at the start of each session of Congress in Washington, and he would come home to Fargo on the weekends and recesses. Summers were divided between Fargo and the Minnesota lake cottage. This routine remained the same until after Gage's death in 1976, when Jocie began to spend more time with Quentin in Washington. "They would talk for indefinite periods of time on the telephone," recalled Birch Burdick, and there were "disagreements about my father spending money on anything." The new family consisted of three adults and four children; on the Birch side: Jocie, her father (Albert) and her two children (Leslie and Birch), and on the Burdick side:

Quentin and his two youngest daughters (Jennifer and Jessica). Jonathan (out of college) and Jan Mary (in college) never lived in the Birch home. Discipline was never in doubt. "My mother was the parenting force in the house," said Birch.[36]

Everyone who joined the household viewed the arrangement differently. Jocie jumped into her new role with a firm resolution and her always positive approach to everything. Her challenges were never small. Her new spouse was a public figure with a demanding job in Washington most of the year, and any return was greeted with equally demanding constituents in North Dakota. She observed, however, that she thought the transition was easier for a widow than for a widower. "A woman has things to do in her home and with her children," but "for a man there are a lot of things he is not used to doing that he has to do or get done, some way or another, for his family."[37] As the years passed, Jean Guy once asked Quentin how things were going in his marriage. Quentin replied, "Just wonderful. You know Jocie took two broken families and made them into one happy family."[38]

Although Quentin never expressed any thoughts about the adjustments, some were obvious. He was first and foremost married again. He wanted that. He liked being around women and his new spouse was an attractive and vivacious woman to be around. She offered him love, loyalty, companionship, a stable environment for his two teenage girls, and a higher degree of financial security than he had ever experienced. Jocie recalled him bringing only two physical possessions with him into the marriage. "I'm the only one in history to inherit a washing machine and a dryer from their husband," she quipped.[39] Quentin immediately transported the laundry equipment to the lake cottage and installed it in the boathouse. There were also other signs of happiness. Quentin's high blood pressure receded. The marriage "was the best thing for him," said May Burdick, "because he was grieving so for Marietta. When he met Jocie, it was a whole new life. She was an entirely different type of personality. She was more athletic and all that."[40]

Leslie and Birch, the youngest of the new family, were full of excitement. Change for them was seen as only positive. In part, because so little of their lives actually changed. They remained in the same house of their maternal grandfather, the only house of their lives. They did not have to move anywhere. The same mother who bore them was still there every day to nourish them. Moreover, they were gaining a new father. Since they could recall few memories about their natural father, there was no guilt about welcoming a stepfather. Their new circumstances all seemed wonderful and upbeat.

"I was getting a Dad and that was really one of the greatest things that

happened out of this for me," said Leslie, "and he was a fun Dad." Leslie, however, never came to call her new father Dad. It was not out of embarrassment
for her, but rather the result of a new peer pressure. Leslie put it this way. "I
have two older sisters — teenagers!" But when the Burdick girls arrived in her
house, they refused to call her mother or mom. They always called her Jocie. So
young Leslie immediately took note of it and always referred to her new Dad
as Quentin.[41]

Birch, the youngest at five, expressed only bewilderment with the new
circumstances. "The house that I had been living in had suddenly grown a bit,"
he said, "and I had no idea who these people were." He remembered that it
took him about a year or two before he called Quentin Dad. He did so finally
because it was for him the most natural thing do. "He was the only father I
knew." There was some peer pressure placed on Birch's shoulders, too. But
unlike Leslie, it came from his neighborhood male friends. His new father,
unlike his peers, appeared as some sort of a foreign, Fargo species. Birch's new
father was a Democrat! "I had friends in the neighborhood. I mean Fargo is not
particularly a Democratic stronghold, but I grew up at a good time," explained
Birch. "There were a lot of kids all within a block that were all my age, and they
would ... pile on top of me and make me promise to say that I was, in fact, a
Republican and not Democrat [chuckles] because their parents were. I would,
of course, refuse that."[42]

Quentin's children viewed events in 1960 quite differently. There were
many reasons. First and foremost, they were a lot older than Jocie's offspring,
with vivid memories of their own family. They were also by nature, age and
experience more independent. The two oldest, Jan Mary and Jonathan, never
moved into the Birch residence. The two youngest, Jennifer, age 16, and Jessica,
almost 13, had no other choice. Jennifer, a rebel, never came to accept her new
home. Jessica, who lived there longer and was by nature less outspoken, was
more tolerant and accepting. Both severed their relationship with their new
family as soon as they graduated from high school, choosing colleges in Wisconsin and Maine. Behind all of their doubts, of course, stood intense loyalty
to Marietta. But she was gone.

Perhaps Quentin could have handled the transition from widower to
spouse better, but circumstances narrowed his choice. He was busy — busy at being a first-term congressman, and since January of 1960, even more busy planning to run for an open Senate seat in June. His political career stood in the
winner's circle and losing again was to be avoided at all costs. Frequent appearances with other women during this time brought few verbal objections from his
daughters. At times, they viewed it as sort of a game where politics more than

romance randomly picked his next date. Dating was harmless because it did not alter the status quo of their newly found independence, nor did it change their relationship with their father. Quentin understood the difference, especially his daughters' loyalty to their mother, but he also came to acknowledge that he was unable to provide for their daily needs or his own. The Washington experience in 1959 played heavily on his mind. At the same time, he feared facing them when his dating focused on marriage because he knew he would pay holy hell! So he became a no-show when the event was announced.

Each daughter recalled Quentin playing the dating game. Jan Mary, who was about to graduate from college at UND, said she was "anxious about him," yet "so delighted" to learn that her father was dating.[43] Jennifer remembered that her father was always being matched up with somebody at a dinner party. That was OK with her, too. Just good fun.[44] Jessica blamed others for putting pressure on her father to date. "He dated women because his friends wanted him to date women, and he dated some interesting women!"[45] This arrangement seemed satisfactory to her as well. It was sort of an exciting game to see who would be his next date.

None of the daughters recalled the exact circumstances of the engagement. But their anger was unmistakable. "I didn't know her," exclaimed Jan Mary. "I mean, he didn't tell us. We found out like two months before the marriage. It was almost like he was embarrassed to tell us, which is fine."[46] Jennifer was more blunt. "My opinion was not asked," she said loudly. She and Jessica were invited over to dinner at the Birch residence, where Jocie showed them her engagement ring. "I don't even think he was even there."[47] Jessica struggled with the specifics while trying to be philosophical about its inevitability. "I think it is very unfair to compare — two marriages, two wives and two loves — because they are different kinds of love. They loved their first spouses in a different way. That's part of life."[48]

When Quentin went back to Washington after the wedding, Jennifer and Jessica joined the stable Birch family. Their comments bear testimony to just how different their lives suddenly became. "I always felt like a visitor," exclaimed Jennifer. She entered this new environment with a chip on her shoulder and resentment in her heart. She saw no need for another mother for her or for Jessica. In fact, she even believed that she could take care of her father probably for the rest of his life. Her first impression remained her last impression. "It was different than most merged families," she recalled, "because Daddy wasn't around. Here I was with somebody I barely knew, and it was a very different life style. Very structured."[49]

Jennifer never adjusted to the Birch routine. "There are certain things you do at certain times," she observed almost in total disbelief, "just like dinner at six." It was all very different than anything she had ever experienced in her entire existence. "It was like clockwork. Jocie knew exactly how many flowers to plant in the garden every summer. Same color. Same order. It happens."[50] While life was so different, there was also recognition of Jocie's strength and virtues. She was a remarkable woman, and in so many ways unlike Marietta.

As the years passed, Jennifer's respect for Jocie grew. She acknowledged Jocie's devout religious beliefs and loyalty to family first. Jennifer admired her close friendships, especially with her girlfriends from college years, and her archival habits of mounting everything in scrapbooks. Jocie loved bridge and playing charades, a game she excelled in. Jocie never seemed interested in material possessions. Although she dressed well, there was never anything about her clothes that were extravagant. Above all, Jocie ran her life and her household by tight schedules that Jennifer understood but never accepted.[51]

When Jennifer graduated from Fargo Central High School in June of 1962, she was ready to leave North Dakota. She accepted the reality that her life, like that of her father, had permanently changed. She also observed that he was happy again. Love and marriage had became one. Jocie catered to Quentin whenever he was with her. Quentin, on the other hand, enjoyed teasing Jocie, and she soon learned to banter back. "I was real glad that college came quickly," said Jennifer, "but I knew that he was happy, and I also knew that I was going to be gone."[52] Jennifer spent the next four years at Beloit College in Wisconsin. She graduated in 1966 with a degree in art, much to the chagrin of her father, who urged her to get a degree in education.[53]

Jessica shared many of her older sister's observations. Yet, she was younger, more innocent, and she lived in the Birch residence for five years — the last three without Jennifer. There was more continuity in her life than her sister's. For starters, she remained under Jennifer's tight control, as she explained it: "Whatever Jennifer told you was probably correct." Left on her own, however, she developed a closer relationship to Leslie, and they became "quite good friends." She warmed to Albert Birch, whom she described as "a beautiful man, very gentle, very kind, and a very loving man as well as a wonderful role model for Birch."[54] She adjusted to Jocie with less difficulty and passed fewer judgments.

On the other hand, she held many doubts about her new family. "We kind of liked the way it was," admitted Jessica. "We didn't want to change. We didn't want to move. We weren't necessarily close to Jocie. We had met her. It wasn't anything negative. We just didn't want to go through this change in life."[55] Like Jennifer, she felt uncomfortable about Jocie's attitudes toward medicine and doctors. She also knew that her sister was more unhappy than she. "It was not a good time for her," Jessica observed. Perhaps, more than anything, it was "a very hard time because I don't remember a lot." However, Jessica became accepting and always less judgmental. "I'll tell you those five years were not easy," she began, "and I don't think the two families ever really came together because of the age differences. There wasn't really a way to bridge that gap and that probably just happens with step-families."[56]

Jan Mary, the oldest, and on her own before the marriage, enjoyed a good relationship with Jocie. She admired her intelligence and her achievements. "She was a very strong-willed person," she noted, "another one of the strong-willed women associated with Quentin Burdick." But there was something unsettling about her younger sisters moving into the Birch home. "The Eighth and Ninth Street people were out of our class," she said, and Jocie "was country club." That distinction hurt. "Did you know that Quentin and Marietta tried to get into the country club and were rejected?"[57]

The birth of Gage Burdick on July 7, 1961, contributed substantially to the dynamics of the two families. "Surprise," smiled Jocie. "It really was funny. I can remember when I told my father that I was expecting a child. He looked around the breakfast room and said, 'My, we are going to be quite a crowd!' Oh, bless his heart! All the children were excited about him and they thought it was wonderful. We had many, many happy times."[58]

Gage's presence brought immediate joy to his parents. He symbolized the essence of their relationship and the fruit of their love and marriage. He brought them closer together and gave new focus to his siblings. Above all, perhaps, he touched his father in a very special way. "Oh, he was a delight," said Jan Mary. "He really was. He was rambunctious and Dad adored him. I'd say that in Gage, he had the son that had the relationship he might not have had with Jon. I'm saying that as an outsider, because I wasn't raised with Gage, but he was a delight."[59]

Gage bonded naturally with the youngest siblings and those who remained in the household the longest. By age and gender, he was most attached to Birch, who was six years older. They shared the same mother, the same grandfather and the same bedroom. "We were roommates for a long time," said Birch, "and longer than we needed to be." Gage was less attached to his older sisters. Jennifer, who lived there the least amount of time, said bluntly, "I honestly did not know him."[60] Jessica, whose bedroom was next to his, knew him better. Each of the sisters recalled his outgoing personality, rebellious nature and prowess in sports. He was "very athletic," said Leslie, and a "beautiful swimmer."[61] It was a talent, Jennifer said, "My Dad liked."[62]

A Senate Race

As in 1958, historical circumstances gave Congressman Quentin Burdick another political opportunity. The November 1959 death of North Dakota's senior United States senator, William Langer – a scion of the Second Non-partisan League, and a perennial office seeker for almost a half century – left the political door ajar for Quentin. Langer's death, although not unexpected, suddenly turned North Dakota politics on an unpredictable course. Langer was the fourth U.S. senator from North Dakota to die in office (Martin Johnson, 1909; Edwin Ladd, 1925; John Moses, 1945). Political change blew across the prairie as political parties and candidates began plans to take advantage of the circumstances. An open Senate seat in 1960 was as rare as two open House seats in 1958. Burdick seized this second opportunity more forcibly than the first because he stood in a stronger position to do so. He was on a roll, a political winner rather than a political loser. He was an incumbent congressman, with political capital, the first of his party to hold that office in Washington. He wanted to run for Langer's seat and he did.

Langer's death, however, provided Republican Governor John Davis with the first opportunity to shape the Senate contest. On November 19, 1959, he selected former Governor C. Norman Brunsdale of Mayville, North Dakota, to serve as Langer's replacement until August 7, 1960. Brunsdale was 68 years old, and Davis's predecessor as governor (1951-1956). In selecting Brunsdale, Davis ultimately selected himself. Brunsdale would serve as a caretaker, not an office seeker in his own right. The lame duck appointment gave Davis time to plan his campaign. He, too, wanted to run for Langer's seat, even though the Brunsdale interim choice leveled the playing field. Davis had no other choice because appointing himself would be political suicide. The special election was to be held on June 28, 1960.

The Burdick-Davis race proved to be one of the most interesting and tight-ly contested political races in modern North Dakota political history. Nation-ally, it came at the end of the Age of Eisenhower and the beginning of the Age of Camelot. The race was as much a referendum on the agricultural policies of U.S. Agriculture Secretary Ezra Taft Benson as it was about Congressman Burdick and Governor Davis. In the end, Burdick's slogan, "Beat Benson with Burdick," prevailed. Burdick had defeated Davis by beating Benson. But the election results went undecided for several days. When the final votes were certified, Burdick defeated Davis by 1,118 votes (The final tally was 104,593 to 103,475.).[63] The Senate win, coupled with Quentin's marriage to Jocie, made 1960 quite a year. The best of times. He recognized the difference between a two-year term in the House and a six-year term in the Senate, based on experience from his father's political career and his own short House tenure. There were huge differences between being a congressman and a senator. The open Senate seat provided him with a once-in-a-lifetime opportunity to be the latter. "You strike when the iron is hot," he recalled in interviews in 1992. "Don't you? Now this was a death. It's much easier to run when there is no incumbent, isn't that the smart thing? I did it."[64] Usher, the perennial contrarian, opposed his decision. "I told that damn kid to stay where he is," Quentin recalled of his father's advice. "I don't necessarily agree with my father. Hell, by example, he got me into this trouble in the first place."[65] Actually, Usher told the press that "Quentin had better stay where he is. ... I think he could succeed himself there. I think Quentin is making good there. But it looks like he is getting ambitious."[66]

Soon after the Langer funeral, Burdick turned to his Fargo Democrat friends. They were instrumental in his 1958 success and were vital to a victory again in 1960. The discussions centered on strategy, not on running. According to Myron Bright, Burdick's mind was already made up. He seemed as eager to run in 1960 as he had been to play quarterback in the old Minnesota days. His team won the coin toss and he was determined to score on the opening drive. "Myron, I will never have a better chance. I don't want to stay in the House for the rest of my life, and I'm going to make a run for it. I will either make it or I will lose and go back to practicing law."[67]

Bright, in 1960, was encouraging and supportive. The political landscape was much improved. Although the Democrats failed to endorse Burdick in 1958, his victory assured him of their support this time around. The convention would be upbeat, absent of rancor or the presence of challengers. Burdick would receive their endorsement with enthusiasm and unanimity. North Dakota Democrats wanted to elect Representative Burdick to Senator Burdick. "He was kind of a light in the darkness," said Lloyd Omdahl. "He was our greatest hero. He had to run for the Senate."[68] In other words, supporting a winner usually comes easier than supporting a loser. Yet, victory was far from certain and it would prove to be much more difficult than winning a House seat. There were several reasons. The two obvious obstacles were the race itself and a strong opponent. A Senate race was "the big time," and the funds required to compete were significant. "This wasn't going to be any $3,500 election campaign," like 1958, said Bright.[69] The other difference was the opponent, a sitting North Dakota governor. "I just remember Governor John Davis as being sort of the standard Republican," recalled Jerome Lamb, another Fargo Democrat, "like Warren G. Harding, you know, look[ing] good."[70]

John Davis, at 47, stood at the apex of a promising political career. The future looked even brighter, in part, because his past seemed almost perfect. His biography stood in stark contrast to his older opponent. Davis was born in Sheridan County, a grassy, rolling Great Plains region of the state, due north of Burleigh County and Bismarck, the state capital. His father, James Ellsworth Davis, served as Republican state senator (1909-1916) from Goodrich, the town of John's birth in 1913. Davis graduated from UND with a degree in business in the middle of the Depression. He returned from World War II having served with distinction on the European front at the rank of lieutenant colonel. He was a decorated war hero and a wounded soldier. He earned the Silver Star, the Bronze Star, four battle stars and the Purple Heart. His social and economic profile matched his military medals. He was an Elk, Lutheran, Mason, Shriner, banker, rancher and insurance director.[71]

Davis' political career rose rapidly after the war. He served as the mayor of McClusky (1948-1956), state senator (1953-1956), and was completing his second term as governor in 1960. He was the third and last of ROC Republican governors who successfully wrestled control of the GOP from the Nonpartisan League and helped chase it into the Democratic fold in 1956. Davis was handsome, although somewhat aloof. He symbolized for the majority of North Dakotans what President Dwight Eisenhower symbolized for the majority of Americans — a return to normalcy and prosperity after two decades of Depression and four years of war.

Below the surface, however, ran tensions of Republican discord. After 16 years of hegemony, schisms were more pronounced. Lloyd Omdahl, the Democrat, and Mark Andrews, the Republican, shared their street smarts about these Republican tensions, which existed prior to the Burdick-Davis Senate race, especially at the 1956 and 1958 Republican state conventions.

In 1956, the issue centered on the Republican nomination of Clarence P. Dahl of Cooperstown, North Dakota, to be governor. Dahl, or C.P. to most everybody, was a Republican loyalist whose turn to be governor had arrived. He had served for three terms as lieutenant governor (1945-1950) under Fred Aandahl and two terms (1953-1956) under Brunsdale. C.P. was a fine, old-time Republican known for his folksy manner and his old car, which he drove proudly in every local parade. Davis and his supporters, however, who represented a younger generation in the party, dumped Dahl and nominated Davis. "There was continuous resentment between the Davis people and the Dahl people over that, which was not healed up in the four-year period," observed Omdahl.[72]

Mark Andrews saw more tensions at the 1958 Republican State Convention. Specifically two blunders: first, they nominated Clyde Duffy, a Devils Lake, North Dakota, lawyer, over incumbent Senator William Langer, for the U.S. Senate. Second, they refused to allow retiring Congressman Usher Burdick to address the convention. "Had Davis been able to deliver for Langer, that group would have been solidly behind him later," noted Andrews. The second mistake issued from the first. "If Usher had spoken and been treated the way he should have been treated, Quentin would never have run in 1958, and if Quentin hadn't run, there would have been two Republicans elected to the House and there would have been no competition for Davis when he ran for the Senate in 1960."[73]

Andrews also noted an institutional difference between North Dakota Democrats and North Dakota Republicans in "party structure" and "the way they do things." For example, Democrats would leave their convention and say: "Aren't we fortunate that we were able to get Quentin to run for us. Now, by gosh, we are really going to have to go out and work for him because he's really given us a great shot of confidence by being our candidate." The Republicans, on the other hand, would leave their convention and say: "Well, by God, we gave Davis the endorsement. He owes us! What is he going to do for us? If he doesn't come around and kiss our ring, then the hell with him."[74]

The 1960 Senate race, however, was a pretty low-key contest. It never approached a heated, partisan battle or a contentious, personal one. Both candidates were gentle warriors, who after receiving the blessings of their party's faithful in April, began to campaign. The final sprint was a short, compact race of six weeks sandwiched between spots of spring and scents of summer. The political contest fit North Dakota's uncertain months of April and May, mixed with hopes and fears. Ranchers are busy with newborn calves and farmers are busy with preparations for seeding. Spring is a waiting game. The Burdick-Davis race flowed with the natural rhythms of nature. It was void of partisan rancor or huge war chests. This was just a typical North Dakota spring with a normal June primary slightly heightened by a Senate special election.

At the same time, two political clouds blew across the North Dakota prairie. The first was a search to select the next president of the United States. A candidate who could fill the shoes of the beloved Ike while aspiring to lead this nation into a new decade. The Republican front-runner, of course, was Vice President Richard Nixon, a national crusader against communism. The Democratic choice was less apparent. Of many aspirants that spring, only one, Senator John F. Kennedy of Massachusetts, emerged as the leader of the pack and odds-on favorite to win his party's nomination for president. Their brief footprints on North Dakota soil added drama to the June primary and seasoned the results.

The second occurrence was strictly a North Dakota happening. Who would be the next governor of North Dakota? Although the June primary was only a preliminary bout, the nominees of both political parties also appeared in the limelight. North Dakotans were as curious about who would be their next governor as they were about who would be their next president. The contrast between the two nominees could not have been more stark than farming with horses or tractors. Finally, C.P. Dahl got his turn to be the Republican nominee for governor. Dahl represented the past and continuity. He looked, dressed and talked with the images of a previous era, not unlike Burdick in some ways. The Democrat nominee was Bill Guy. Guy represented the future and change. He looked, dressed and talked with images of a future era, not unlike Kennedy in some ways. Thus, while most North Dakotans focused on electing a new senator, many voters were also paying some attention to the presidential races and sizing up the two candidates for governor. What happened in North Dakota's June primary would portend November's choices as well.

The tight outcome of the Burdick-Davis contest invites closer scrutiny. The mere fact that Burdick prevailed raises the historical possibility that some of his strategy proved sound. That Davis lost raises equally relevant speculation that his strategy proved unsound. It is impossible to ascertain which factors ultimately contributed to Burdick's narrow victory or Davis's narrow loss; nevertheless, much is remembered about this important election by key participants of more than 45 years ago.

Of the many key players in Burdick's camp, three stand out. Lloyd Omdahl served as Burdick's press secretary and political adviser for the campaign. He spent the entire six weeks prior to the election campaigning daily with Burdick. Omdahl was also the Democratic-NPL candidate for secretary of state in the June primary. Myron Bright planned the single, biggest event of the campaign — a highly publicized Fargo birthday party for Burdick. Finally, there was Joseph Miller, a nationally paid consultant from organized labor (COPE), who was assisting in the planning for various Democratic senatorial campaigns in 1958 and 1960. These three individuals alone were not solely responsible for Burdick's surprise victory, but their recollections provide invaluable insights into the inner workings of the campaign.

"The Burdick campaign in the spring of 1960 was the beginning of the modern campaigns in North Dakota," said Omdahl. This was a rather startling comment to make, but considering the campaign's comparison with previous ones, Omdahl's statement makes sense. Before this campaign, statewide candidates usually spoke at small-town rallies preceded by local party workers plastering storefronts and poles with fliers. Advertising concentrated on standard newspapers while ignoring highway billboards or the power of television. In 1960, new campaign strategies were applied for the first time in a North Dakota statewide campaign. These techniques included the use of outside consultants such as Miller, reliance on an array of mass communications strategies and a national target of voter dissatisfaction, which in this case was the unpopular farm programs of Secretary of Agriculture Benson.[75]

Senate Majority Leader Lyndon B. Johnson of Texas dispatched Miller to North Dakota to work on the Burdick campaign. "Go to North Dakota," ordered Johnson, "we can pick up a seat there." Before dismissing Miller, Johnson leaned back in his chair and gave a brief lecture about Great Plains politics and Congressman Burdick's attributes. "The only difference between Texas and Dakota is climate," opined Johnson. "Our politics are the same, only the Civil War made us Democrats and them Republicans." As for Burdick, Johnson expressed some reservations about his desire to win because "the Burdick boy isn't much of a campaigner, the kind his Daddy was."[76]

Miller just showed up one spring day in Omdahl's Bismarck advertising agency. He presented a cache of ideas about how to successfully run a Senate campaign; Omdahl quickly incorporated many of his suggestions into Burdick's campaign. Omdahl was especially keen on dummy advertising makeups and blank press items that could be filled in with Burdick's name while on the road. The labor organizer also secured badly needed campaign funds. The estimate for running the campaign was approaching $100,000, an unheard of sum to run a statewide campaign in North Dakota. To make matters worse, the party was in the red to a tune of about $30,000. To hide labor money, Miller established an account in the Riggs National Bank in Washington under a bogus name, "D.C. Committee for Civil Rights." Money from organized labor was then funneled into this account unreported.[77] As one Burdick loyalist put it, "Joe taught the North Dakota Democrats how to raise money."[78]

Miller sized up the two candidates. He toyed with Johnson's earlier assessment of Burdick, but quickly added his own. "He was remarkably naive," said Miller, but also "almost excessively shy and self-effacing, devoid of an up-front ego that earmarked most politicians." Yet, there was something attractive and unusual about his physical stature. Miller soon came to the conclusion that Burdick's greatest political assist was his face, which he described as "a craggy, lived-in face that shone with an open optimism." As for Davis, Miller simply referred to him as "a silver-haired charmer."[79] He knew his type.

Miller and Omdahl shared ideas and planned strategy. They began by conducting a political poll. With funds Miller secured from AFL-CIO, they hired a national firm (Harris) to survey North Dakota voters. The poll produced three significant findings. First, Burdick was unknown to 44 percent of the state's voters. Second, Davis was known to 83 percent of the voters. But there was a kicker: 10 percent of the voters regarded Davis as "weak and ineffective." Finally, a majority of North Dakotans strongly disapproved of Secretary of Agriculture Benson and his soil bank program. Benson was public enemy number one during the spring of 1960.[80]

The Burdick campaign built its foundation on the poll results. If many North Dakotans did not know Burdick, they soon would, and name identification from the start became a major component of the race. They decided to print huge billboards and place them on strategic highways in and out of major population areas. It would be impossible to drive on main roads in North Dakota without seeing a Burdick billboard. The billboards made Burdick bigger than life. The focus was on Burdick's greatest asset, his face and pugilistic chin, and below the image was a simple but powerful message: "Burdick will make a strong U.S. Senator."[81] As Omdahl remembered it, "We created an image because there was no image. You could start from scratch. I think this was kind of the beginning of the idea in people's minds that Burdick was a much more aggressive leader than he really was."[82]

The campaign wasted little time attacking Benson. Omdahl created one of the most effective four-word bumper stickers in North Dakota political history: "Beat Benson with Burdick." At first, Omdahl ordered a run of 10,000 stickers, but they went like hot cakes supporting the poll that Benson was the boogieman of this election. So he ended up ordering 80,000 more. "Benson did as much for Burdick as any of us who were working on the campaign did for Burdick, and as much as Burdick did for Burdick."[83] When Burdick formally kicked off his campaign in Fargo in May, he paid special attention to the secretary of agriculture. "If a man who has fought Benson for seven years is elected, it will be heralded all over this country as a defeat for Ezra Benson and his policies, and what we decide in North Dakota will have a profound effect upon the platforms written by Republican and Democratic parties."[84]

The campaign implemented other forms of mass communication, including television, radio and newspapers. The most effective television production was a 30-minute documentary on Burdick's life. It was later edited to a 15-minute segment and aired again. Both television and radio were supplied with 60-second spots that centered on issues. The newspaper blitz came 10 days before the election. It included a four-page insert in the state's daily newspapers and smaller inserts in the most widely read county weeklies. For the most part, these media presentations focused on the image of Burdick and stressed the same billboard message that Burdick would be a strong U.S. senator for North

Dakota.[85]

The focal point of the campaign centered on Burdick's birthday party. June 19, 1960, was both Father's Day and Quentin's 52nd birthday. The event was hatched early in the campaign, the brainchild of Myron and Fritzie Bright and John and Rosemary Murphy to accomplish two purposes. The first agenda was to negate potential last-minute negative campaigns that Burdick was a "pinko." This epithet was an old Republican charge leveled against Burdick for his support of Henry Wallace in the 1948 presidential race and his work for the North Dakota Farmers Union. There was nothing new about Burdick being soft on communism, but it was used most recently in Senator Milton Young's drubbing of Burdick in the 1956 senatorial race. In order to diffuse the issue, the campaign strategy was to invite the nation's most widely respected anti-communist Democrat, Senator John Kennedy, to come to North Dakota on Burdick's behalf. Burdick approached Kennedy soon after he announced his intention to seek the Senate seat, but no specific date was set.[86]

Fargo Democrats decided to combine the promised Kennedy appearance with the Burdick birthday party. Together, Kennedy and Burdick would symbolize new leadership for the 1960s. Plans for the birthday party consumed much time. The three Burdick daughters went to work addressing invitations, which were mailed to every household in Fargo and West Fargo. The Brights and the Murphys concentrated on working out the details and publicity for the event. "He's coming to wish Daddy a happy birthday," said Jan Mary, and "we asked Senator Kennedy not to say anything political."[87]

Fargo Democrats were up early the morning of June 19. Kennedy's airplane arrived at Hector Field around 2:30 p.m. A motorized train then took Kennedy and Burdick and Jennifer Burdick from the airport to the Red River Valley Fairgrounds. The fairgrounds were packed with Democrats from all over the state, Fargo supporters, well-wishers and the curious. Everyone was served cake and ice cream. "The Indians put on a powwow," recalled Bright. "It was wonderful. That event exceeded all our expectations and I think it was the frosting on the cake that possibly made the difference in the election."[88]

Many left the fairgrounds that afternoon humming these words to the music of *Slattery's Irish March*:

> B for Burdick
> B for Burdick
> We support him everyone.
>
> He's the man of the people.
> And the one we've chosen to run.

We've selected him.
And we will elect him.
And our senator he will be.

B for Burdick
B for Burdick
For a smashing victory.

Oh, the NPL and the Democrats
are going all the way.
To put Quentin Burdick in the Senate
of the USA.

We respect him.
Will elect him.
And our senator he will be.

B for Burdick
B for Burdick
For a smashing victory.[89]

Election results remained uncertain when North Dakota polls closed Tuesday evening. In 1960, elections were almost exclusively a hand-to-hand operation. Voters marked paper ballots and election workers counted every one of those paper ballots by hand and then recounted them again by hand. It was a laborious and time-consuming process. Many officials worked all night and some were still recounting and double checking the next morning. By Wednesday morning, however, the Associated Press began to report the first results. They showed Burdick trailing Davis by a substantial margin. At Burdick headquarters in Fargo, tired workers wore long faces as optimism began to slip away. "I was a wreck," recalled Bright. "My wife was a wreck. Quentin was a wreck. The Democrats were a wreck. We were all a wreck."[90] Jocie, his bride to be, said she felt for a while that she would be the consolation prize.[91]

Later Wednesday, results brought heartburn rather than relief to the Burdick forces. A tired Burdick and a tired Bright caucused around noon. The agenda was short and the mood somber. They discussed only one item — concession. After discussing the pros and cons, Burdick told Bright to draft a concession statement. But the writing was suddenly interrupted by a call from a Democratic observer camped at the *Fargo Forum*. The call, for the first time, contained some good news. The newspaper had just confirmed a 2,000-vote tabulating error. The Davis lead shrunk to 300 votes. Bright quit writing the release. There would be no concession statement, yet. But by late Wednesday afternoon, Davis's lead climbed back to 700 votes. Burdick grabbed a much needed nap. Bright went home to bed. A couple of hours later, a second tele-phone call came from Rosemary Murphy, one of Burdick's close Fargo support-ers. She told Bright in an excited voice that "Quentin has just gone 50 votes ahead. The Indians had come through."[92] Concession talk was no longer on the table. Burdick was ahead for good.

Several patterns emerge from an analysis of the votes. The first pattern is Davis's disappointing performance in the Republican-dominated Red River Valley. Historically, the Valley yields a huge plurality for Republican statewide candidates. Margins so deep that smaller loses in other parts of the state cannot offset the big eastern lead. However, such an advantage did not occur in this election. Although Davis left the Valley with a 3,674-vote lead, winning five of the six counties (except for Walsh County), Burdick ran much stronger than expected. For example, he lost Grand Forks County by only 695 votes and Cass County by only 2,375 votes.[93] These results were good news for Burdick and not so good news for Davis.

A second pattern developed along the southern route west on Highway 10 (Interstate 94). It became a close contest of county checkers with Davis winning one county and Burdick the next. For example, Davis carried Barnes County by five votes and Burdick carried Stutsman, the next county, by 25 votes. Davis, as expected, beat Burdick by 1,780 votes in Burleigh County, but Burdick defeated Davis in the next county, Morton, by 1,405 votes. The same pattern repeated itself on the northern route across Highway 2. Davis took Ramsey County by 68 votes, but Burdick won the next three counties — Ward by 642 votes; Mountrail by 1,015 votes; and Williams, his home county, by 1,405 votes. Other similar patterns emerged. In heavily populated German-Russian counties, Davis won handily, but Burdick offset those gains by capturing three Native American counties (Benson, Rolette and Sioux) by some 1,500 votes.[94]

The overall county breakdown demonstrated just how tight the race end-ed. Davis won 29 counties, most in the lower half of the state. Burdick won 24 counties, with all but four counties in the northern half of the state. Davis won five of six counties adjacent to Minnesota, but only three of six counties touching Montana. Burdick won six of eight counties bordering Canada, but lost six of eight counties bordering South Dakota. The final margin of 1,118 votes equaled less than one vote per precinct. In the primary races for governor, Bill Guy added shock to the hegemony of the North Dakota Republican Party. He out-polled C.P. Dahl by 732 votes (87,632 to 86,900).[95] This outcome was unprecedented. North Dakota Democrats had not only captured a Senate seat, they now stood favored to win the governorship in November. Burdick, by all accounts, ran an aggressive campaign. Omdahl, who spent the entire last six weeks traveling with him as his press aide, marveled at his stamina. "He was tireless," said Omdahl. "We would start at 8 a.m. in the morning, and we would go until 11 p.m. If there was some public thing, like after a rally, that he knew about, he'd want to go there. He shook hands and he met people well." After a couple of weeks of 15-hour days, Omdahl ran out of gas. He simply could not match Burdick's energy. "He would be going down the street, and I would just not be going down the street." Instead, Omdahl said he developed his own formula for the rest of the campaign. "The higher the office, the more energy, because I wasn't going to work that hard."[96]

There was never much variety in the Burdick message. He gave one speech —the same speech — at every stop. "I traveled around with him," recalled Gorman King, "and he had the same speech no matter where he was. I can quote it word for word; that was basically it."[97] The speech centered on five issues:
- Preservation of the family farm
- Elimination of the soil bank program
- Acceleration of the Garrison Diversion project
- Lower interest rates
- Expand Social Security to include medical aid for the elderly[98]

Two important North Dakota personalities hit the campaign trail for Burdick. His father, Usher, took the Indian trail. He made frequent stops at each of the state's four Indian reservations. His message was low-key and unpublicized. He just went visiting to remind the elders, as he had done so many times in the past, to vote for Burdick again. Glenn Talbott, Burdick's old boss, took a more publicized road. Speaking to many Farmers Union locals, he gave the familiar hard-hitting stump speech he was famous for: "You're nuts if you're not for Quentin Burdick and you're nuts if you don't vote for him." If that did not get a rise, Talbott hit another chord. "Burdick needs money; he needs your support. You can get it. Dig down. If you haven't got it, do what I did. Go out and borrow it at 6 percent."[99]

Other operatives worked the Burdick campaign, the most noticeable being the appearances of Bill and Jean Guy, who seemed to be everywhere during the campaign. "Jean and I put a large gold sign wired to the roof of our car with black letters — 'Burdick' on it on both sides — and headed across the state," recalled Guy.[100] The Guys joined the campaign effort after a request from the state office, which saw in them a real chance to help Burdick and an excellent opportunity to gain exposure for the November general election. The Guys' contribution came at great personal sacrifice because they stopped renovation on their old farmhouse, hired a nanny to stay with their children, and hit the campaign trail in heavy 10-day stretches until Election Day. They crisscrossed the entire state visiting every Democratic district. "We were helpful to Quentin" and "we were helpful to ourselves,"[101] said Jean Guy. Mark Andrews, their neighbor, believed in the later interpretation more than the former. "Bill Guy wouldn't have been elected at that point in time if Quentin hadn't been on the ticket."[102]

Explanations for Burdick's victory and Davis's defeat are many. Few historical events occur because of one single factor. In 1958, North Dakota voters replaced a Republican Burdick with a Democrat Burdick for Congress. The momentum and the name carried the election again in 1960. Lloyd Omdahl, who probably knew the inner workings of the campaign better than anyone else, maintained that the single most important factor was the power of the Burdick name. "If Burdick would have had to start from scratch without the benefit of the Burdick name, Burdick would not have been elected to Congress and he would not have been elected to the Senate."[103]

The Omdahl thesis downplays the contributions of the candidates themselves. Burdick wanted to win this election more than Davis. It was his stamina and will to win that ultimately made the difference. Davis, by contrast, was an easy Republican winner in every previous race. He did not know how to win a tough election contest because he had never been involved in one. He believed he would win easily again by doing all the same things done in the past, which was just talk to the same crowd and make the same stops around the state. Burdick knew better. His 1958 victory after six defeats gave him momentum and confidence. He knew what it took to win because he had tasted defeat so many times before. Winning meant lots of work. This different campaign work ethic between the two candidates played an important part in the results.

Modestly, Burdick placed more emphasis on Davis losing than in him winning. "He didn't like to campaign," began Burdick. "He liked to campaign with people he knew. You have to campaign with people you didn't know. He would come to town and stay in the American Legion Club all day. I know. I was in town passing out cards when he would be inside visiting."[104] Several Burdick cohorts agreed with his interpretation. James Jungroth noted that the only campaigning Davis ever did in Jamestown was to visit the American Legion and VFW clubs. "He didn't understand that he had to go get votes other than those he already had."[105] Fargoan Mart Vogel offered a concurring opinion: "Quentin was a much better campaigner that Davis, who was somewhat reticent. He was a much milder guy, and even though he had been governor of the state, he didn't have the abilities that Burdick had."[106]

The election also centered on strategy and planning. In this effort, the Burdick campaign (especially Omdahl's and Miller's contributions) injected new techniques into a statewide campaign. The use of a national poll, clever advertising methods, access to labor money, Senate campaign experts and a national focus on agricultural discontent all contributed to success. And according to Bruce Hagen, longtime Democratic public service commissioner, "the slogan 'Beat Benson with Burdick' was a lot better than 'Beat Davis with Burdick.'"[107] From a national perspective, Benson was the key. "The big Burdick vote was striking evidence of farmer discontent with the administration's farm program," wrote the *New York Times*. "A decade ago a Democratic candidate for the Senate would have done well to get a fourth of the vote in this state."[108]

In close elections, little things mean a lot. In this election, the vote of the four Indian reservations proved invaluable. "Basically that campaign was won by the Indians," said Jungroth.[109] Burdick agreed. "I almost got a 95 percent vote on the reservations. It did it!"[110] Certainly, the Omdahl interpretation had merit in this factor. "Usher Burdick was very popular with the Native Americans, and I think that transferred to Quentin, so he ran very strong."[111]

Bill Guy, who worked hard for Burdick and his own candidacy, painted a broader canvas. "I think the people of North Dakota had Republicanism for so long, and the Republicans had been in office so long, and had not, in my judgment, kept very clean skirts and were vulnerable in many of the electors' eyes."[112]

Finally, the pinko smear never materialized. It was there all the time, but it never became a major issue in the campaign. Credit the Fargo Democrats, especially Myron Bright, for keeping the lid on it and getting the endorsement of John Kennedy in the crucial stretch of the campaign.

In July, Senator-elect Burdick addressed the Democratic National Convention in Los Angeles. In doing so, he became the first North Dakotan of either party to address a national political convention on television. Burdick spoke briefly during a lull in the convention, but his remarks brought applause from those present. "The North Dakota election proves," he began, "without a shadow of a doubt that no area in this country remains within the exclusive domination of the Republican Party."[113] After Burdick left the podium, the North Dakota delegation went wild. In fact, in years past, they did not have much to celebrate. They began waving their state banner as other states joined in the demonstration. The band with no cue or clue started playing *The Old Gray Mare*. By then Burdick was no longer in sight and when the music stopped, Senator Frank Church of Idaho, the temporary chairman, told the delegates that Burdick was not only the newest member of the Senate, but the most modest because he missed an ovation for himself.[114]

Burdick was sworn in on August 8, one day after he resigned his House seat. At age 52, Burdick was then the junior senator of North Dakota. He would never again face a close race or suffer a political defeat. The results of the June 28 special election made Burdick a senator for life. In November, Richard Nixon carried North Dakota, but John F. Kennedy won the presidency. Bill Guy bested C.P. Dahl again and won the governorship. If the decade of the 1950s belonged to the Republicans, the decade of the 1960s would belong to the Democrats even in Republican strongholds such as North Dakota. Clearly times had changed with the election victories of Kennedy, Burdick and Guy. North Dakota was no longer exclusively a Republican state.

Endnotes

1. Marge Scott, interview with author, Jan. 22, 1995.
2. Jocelyn Birch Burdick, interview with author, April 18, 1995.
3. A Century Together, 53.
4. Jocelyn Birch Burdick interview.
5. Ibid.
6. Ibid.
7. Ibid.
8. Jean Mason Guy, interview with author, Jan. 20, 1995.
9. Jocelyn Birch Burdick interview.
10. Ibid.
11. Author's recollection of stories told to him as a young boy growing up in Fargo.
12. Jocelyn Birch Burdick interview.
13. Ibid.
14. Ibid.
15. Spectrum (Fargo, ND), Feb. 1, 1945.
16. Robinson, History of North Dakota, 429.
17. Register of North Dakota Veterans. World War II, 1941-1945 and Korean Conflict, 1950-1953, p. 1323.
18. Jean Mason Guy interview.
19. Jocelyn Birch Burdick interview.
20. Ibid.
21. Ibid.
22. Ibid.
23. Scott interview.
24. Jean Mason Guy and Jocelyn Birch Burdick interviews.
25. "Jocelyn Speaks," Grand Forks Herald, Oct. 2, 1993.
26. Jocelyn Birch Burdick interview.
27. Ibid.
28. Ibid.
29. "Jocelyn Speaks."
30. Leslie Burdick, interview with author, March 28, 1995.
31. Birch Burdick, interview with author, April 18, 1995.
32. Jan Mary Burdick Hill, interview with author, May 25, 1995.
33. Jocelyn Birch Burdick interview.
34. Mart Vogel, interview with author, Jan. 19, 1995.
35. Jocelyn Birch Burdick interview.
36. Birch Burdick interview.
37. Jocelyn Birch Burdick interview.
38. Jean Mason Guy interview.
39. Jocelyn Birch Burdick interview.

40. May Burdick, interview with author, March 1, 1995.

41. Leslie Burdick interview.

42. Birch Burdick interview.

43. Jan Mary Burdick Hill interview.

44. Jennifer Burdick, interview with author, April 26, 1995.

45. Jessica Burdick, interview with author, Jan. 28, 1996.

46. Jan Mary Burdick Hill interview.

47. Jennifer Burdick interview.

48. Jessica Burdick interview.

49. Jennifer Burdick interview.

50. Ibid.

51. Ibid.

52. Ibid.

53. Ibid.

54. Jessica Burdick interview.

55. Ibid.

56. Ibid.

57. Hill interview.

58. Jocelyn Birch Burdick interview.

59. Hill interview.

60. Jennifer Burdick interview.

61. Leslie Burdick interview.

62. Jennifer Burdick interview.

63. *North Dakota Votes*, 162.

64. Quentin Burdick, interview with author, Jan. 6, 1992.

65. Ibid.

66. *Fargo (N.D.) Forum*, Nov. 20, 1959.

67. Myron Bright, interview with author, March 26, 1996.

68. Lloyd Omdahl, interview with author, Jan. 18, 1995.

69. Bright interview.

70. Jerome Lamb, interview with author, Jan. 20, 1995.

71. *Who's Who in North Dakota*, 72.

72. Omdahl interview.

73. Mark Andrews, interview with author, April 19, 1995.

74. Andrews interview.

75. Omdahl interview.

76. Joseph Miller, unpublished manuscript, Chapter Five: "A State That Forgot Time," 1960, 1-2.

77. Miller, 11.

78. Tom Burgum, interview with author, March 24, 1995.

79. Miller, 9.

80. Ibid., 6.

81. Ibid.

82. Omdahl interview.

83. Ibid.

84. *Fargo Forum*, May 22, 1960.

85. Miller, 11.

86. Bright interview.

87. *Fargo Forum*, June 7, 1960.

88. Bright interview.

89. Ibid.

90. Ibid.

91. Jocelyn Birch Burdick interview.

92. Bright interview.

93. *North Dakota, Secretary of State, Compilation of State and National Election Returns, 1946-1964.*

94. Ibid.

95. *North Dakota Votes*, 162.

96. Omdahl interview.

97. Gorman King, interview with author, April 25, 1995.

98. *Fargo Forum*, June 26, 1960.
99. Ibid., June 19, 1960.
100. Bill Guy, interview with author, Jan. 20, 1995.
101. Jean Mason Guy interview.
102. Andrews interview.
103. Omdahl interview.
104. Quentin Burdick interview.
105. James Jungroth, interview with author, Feb. 5, 1995.
106. Vogel interview.
107. Bruce Hagen, interview with author, April 25, 1995.
108. *New York Times*, June 30, 1960.
109. Jungroth interview.
110. Quentin Burdick interview.
111. Omdahl interview.
112. Bill Guy interview.
113. *Fargo Forum*, July 13, 1960.
114. Ibid.

- ten -

Guy and Burdick

B ill Guy and Quentin Burdick represented the pinnacle of success for the
modern North Dakota Democratic-NPL Party. In 1960, at age 41, Guy
became the state's fourth Democrat to be elected as governor following
in the footsteps of John Burke (1907-1912), Thomas Moodie (1935) and John
Moses (1939-1944). In 1958, at age 50, Burdick became the state's first Democrat ever elected to the U.S. House of Representatives, and in June 1960, he
became the state's fifth Democrat to be elected United States senator following
William Roach (1893-1899), Fountain Thompson (1909-1910), William Purcell
(1910-1911) and John Moses (1945). Both Guy and Burdick, however, served
longer than any of their Democrat forebears and significantly out-performed all
of them in party building. It is not an exaggeration to state that Guy demonstrated to the people of North Dakota that a Democrat could run state government as well as a Republican and that Burdick could vote liberal in Washington
and still get elected in North Dakota.

In the years between 1960 and 1972, Guy and Burdick exerted much influence over the growth and development of the Democratic-NPL Party. Guy
believed the governor was and should be the head of the party. He exercised
maximum political control whenever possible, made stellar appointments to
fill vacancies in state government (Bruce Hagen as public service commissioner
in 1961 and Byron Dorgan as tax commissioner in 1969), and pushed for the
building of the Kennedy Center in Bismarck as a symbol of the state Democratic-NPL Party headquarters. Burdick believed that his position as U.S. senator
made him the titular head of the party. "He was kind of the prophet of the religion," said Lloyd Omdahl, "rather than one of the functionaries."[1] He became
the standard-bearer in elections, poured huge amounts of campaign contributions into party coffers for voter surveys, and surrounded himself with young

and bright advisers such as Scott Anderson, Tom Burgum, Kent Conrad and David Strauss. Guy identified with the establishment, while Burdick associated with those less powerful. "I heard of Burdick through others," recalled Tom Matchie, a Fargo legislator (1977-1986), "especially through Herschel Lashkowitz, as a real defender of the underdog, of somebody who had something to say and didn't go along with the system. Burdick was a great supporter of people like that."[2]

The 1974 senatorial race between incumbent Republican Senator Milton R. Young and Guy was a highly important election in North Dakota political history. Young was at the nadir of his long Senate career, which began as an appointment in 1945 following the death of the recently sworn-in Democrat John Moses. He was in his late 70s and still smarting from an inner-party challenge from Republican Mark Andrews that never materialized. He was not in the best of health, but he was determined to run for one more term. In 1974, Guy was no longer governor, but clearly he was a viable and popular candidate and 20 some years younger than his Republican opponent. The election proved to the closest senatorial election in state history. Young defeated Guy by 186 votes. The entry of independent candidate James Jungroth, a Jamestown attorney and former state chairman of the Democratic-NPL Party, complicated the contest. Jungroth ran on environmental issues and captured 6,739 votes, which proved crucial in such a close election. The election recount added another variable by discounting ballots where voters had mistakenly voted for both Guy and Jungroth. In victory, Young angrily tore Cass County from his North Dakota office map after Guy carried the state's most populous county by 7,000 votes. In defeat, Guy blamed everyone but himself, but especially Burdick, for not helping him, or worse, for aiding Jungroth.

In interviews with both Guy and Burdick, each blamed the other for the outcome of the 1974 senatorial race. Guy remained convinced that Burdick refused his help when he desperately required it. Burdick maintained that Guy spurned his early offers for support (he did second Guy's nomination) and when the race appeared lost, asked him to attack Young in the waning days of the campaign, a request that Burdick flatly refused.[3] Beneath the burnout of the 1974 election, however, smoldered an older animosity between these two giants of the modern Democratic-NPL Party. Bill Guy and Quentin Burdick, although members of the same political party, had not liked each other for a very long time. It should come as a surprise to few that Republicans and Democrats do not like each other at election time, but most of the time they get along better with each other than they do with themselves. Bill Guy the Democrat and Quentin Burdick the Democrat were no exceptions to that overview.

National events coincided with the reigns of Guy and Burdick and proved important for North Dakota Democrats who prospered from the two presidential campaigns of John F. Kennedy and Lyndon B. Johnson in the '60s. As the United States entered the new decade, Kennedy offered the country a youthful and energetic image. He was articulate, bright and attractive. He gave inspiring speeches full of catchy phrases and clever alliterations. His broad smile and quick Irish wit made him the darling of the television media. Jackie, his younger and stunning spouse, and two small children came to symbolize family values and new beginnings in the Age of Camelot. Kennedy, like most Democrat presidential candidates, failed to carry North Dakota in the 1960 election. He lost to Richard Nixon by 30,000 votes. His candidacy, however, bolstered Bill Guy's surprise 13,500-vote victory over his much older opponent, Lieutenant Governor C.P. Dahl of Cooperstown.[4] With the young Kennedy family in the White House and the young Guy family in the North Dakota governor's residence, both the nation and the state seemed posed for new frontiers; the Democrats were in charge.

Johnson's victory in 1964 did even more for North Dakota Democrats than Kennedy's effort four years earlier. He was, of course, after the Kennedy assassination the sitting president. He carried the mantle of the Kennedy presidency and the promise to make it complete in legislation as well as rhetoric. His opponent, Senator Barry Goldwater, represented the victory of conservatives over moderates in the Republican Party. He was really a candidate of the '90s, not the '60s, and his candidacy scared too many voters on too many issues. He even jolted the loyalty of North Dakota voters, who gave Johnson an unprecedented 41,000-vote margin over the Arizona senator.[5]

The Johnson victory was a presidential revolution in North Dakota elections. Johnson was the first Democrat in 28 years to carry the state. He was also the last. Only Woodrow Wilson's victories in 1912 and 1916 (by small margins) and Franklin Roosevelt's victories in 1932 and 1936 (by landslides) produced Democrat wins in North Dakota. After Roosevelt's second term in 1936, North Dakota voters returned to support Republican candidates for president. They stayed there until Johnson's smashing victory in 1964, and there they have remained ever since.

Johnson's victory spun long coattails for North Dakota Democrats. It carried Burdick and Guy to easy re-elections. Burdick won his first six-year term by thumping Tom Kleppe with a lead of more than 40,000 votes, while Guy, after winning a close election against Mark Andrews in 1962, easily defeated Don Halcrow, his Republican opponent, by 30,000 votes. Burdick and Guy were probably predictable winners without the Johnson landslide, but they benefited enormously from voters staying in the Democrat column after voting for president. Burdick was seen as most vulnerable in 1964 and Kleppe seemed a viable opponent to unseat him. Burdick's margin of victory, however, ended most speculation about his vulnerability. The full six-year term gave him voter immunity from stressful elections that swallowed the remainder of the decade, especially in 1968. Guy won his third term as governor and the state's first four-year term after voters amended the constitution and changed the term of constitutional offices from two years to four.

Johnson's coattails extended beyond Burdick and Guy. Voters in the west stayed in the Democrat column and gave Rollie Redlin of Minot an upset victory over two-term West District Congressman Don Short of Medora. Redlin was only the second Democrat in state history to be elected to the U.S. House of Representatives. In the East District, George Sinner of Casselton almost made a Democrat sweep by narrowly losing to his Mapleton farming neighbor, Mark Andrews, by 6,000 votes. There was more to the Democrat landslide as voters also elected four new Democrats to constitutional offices. They chose Charles Tighe as lieutenant governor, Walt Christensen as treasurer, K.O. Nygaard as insurance commissioner and Lloyd Omdahl as tax commissioner. They also kept Bruce Hagen on the Public Service Commission after his appointment in 1961 by Guy. These Democrat victories were unprecedented in North Dakota elections, and the changes in terms of office assured the positions for Democrats until 1986. Three of the 1964 winners — Christensen, Omdahl and Hagen — remained as Democratic-NPL standard-bearers for many years after their first election victories.

Significantly, Johnson's coattails reached even lower than state offices. Democrats won the House of Representatives for the first time in the state's history and elected Art Link of Alexander, North Dakota, speaker. After the 1962 elections, Republicans held a 53 to 43 majority in the House and a 37 to 12 majority in the Senate. Then came Johnson, and North Dakota awoke to a 65 to 33 Democrat majority in the House and a slimmer Republican-controlled Senate of 29 to 20.[6] New Democrat faces soon became long-term ballot winners. Among new House Democrats, for example, was a young, 29-year-old schoolteacher from Minot: Wayne Sanstead. He would later serve in the Senate, two terms as lieutenant governor (1973-1980), and is still serving as superintendent of public instruction since 1985.

Bill Guy grew up in a different garden than Quentin Burdick. Born at Devils Lake, North Dakota, in the fall of 1919, he was a decade younger than Burdick. He was the middle son of William and Mabel Guy, both proud graduates of the North Dakota Agricultural College (North Dakota State University since 1960). His father was a county agricultural Extension agent who began his career in Ramsey County but soon transferred to the more populous Cass County. In 1925, the family moved to Amenia in rural Cass County when William Guy Sr. became the manager of the Carrie T. Chaffee estate, a legal name for the Amenia Seed and Grain Company. It was the remnants of one of the nation's largest bonanza farms of the late 19th century. In the shadow of corporate farming and Farm Bureau philosophy, Bill Guy Jr. and his two brothers, Jim and John, participated in myriad 4-H Club activities, especially raising sheep. Bill stared as center on the Amenia High School basketball team and played the saxophone.[6]

Three themes dominated Bill Guy's formative years — years that were quite different in both existence and meaning than Burdick's. The themes include a deep respect, almost reverence, for NDAC, an avowed career in agricultural economics, and service in the Second World War. Guy adored the Fargo institution and followed in his parents' footsteps on the eve of the war. He was a popular man on campus, clean cut and handsome, busy with extracurricular activities (manager of the college year book), and active in the Sigma Alpha Epsilon fraternity. "I followed him in afterwards, and everybody spoke about Bill Guy like God had just left the campus in those days," recalled Chub Ulmer, who belonged to the same fraternity and later became executive director of the North Dakota Rural Electric Association.[7] As an upperclassman, Guy became a persistent suitor for a beautiful and charming freshman coed, Jean Mason of Fargo. Guy enrolled at the University of Minnesota in the fall of 1941 to pursue a graduate degree in agricultural economics. The war altered his studies. He was commissioned an ensign in the U.S. Navy and married Mason in early 1943.[8]

Patriotism ran deep in the Guy family. Guy Sr. served as chairman of the Cass County Draft Board and all three of his sons enlisted in the U.S. Navy. Two sons made extraordinary sacrifices for their country. Jim, the eldest, gave his life. He died of starvation in a Japanese prison camp. Bill Jr. was more fortunate, escaping death in the last months of the war. His destroyer, the USS William D. Porter, was sunk in the South Pacific on June 10, 1945, a causality of a Japanese kamikaze attack. The crew, however, were immediately rescued by another ship.

Like most men of his generation, Guy returned from the war eager to resume a normal and productive life. After being so close to death in war, living a fuller life in peace became imperative. He first finished his M.S. degree in agricultural economics at Minnesota and dabbled in various agricultural-related enterprises (most unsuccessful) before he and Jean decided to make a go on the 820-acre family farm near Amenia.[10] In the ensuing years, Bill and Jean Guy threw themselves into a disciplined, energetic routine of building a new home for themselves and their five children, all born between 1946 and 1958. When the United States ended the Age of Eisenhower, the young Guy family symbolized a new generation of North Dakota family farmers eager to work hard and make a success of their labors for family and community.

Political participation flowed as a natural course of life after war years. Making a better society at home was now as important as making the world a safe place. Political action presented itself as a civic responsibility or community service, not as any crusade for either left- or right-wing ideologies. Guy, like fellow Democrats S.F. Buckshot Hoffner of Esmond and Dick Backus of Glenburn, turned to the Democrat Party as brighter and more open than the staid Republican Party of their ancestors. They were younger sons who changed farming from horses to tractors, and they wanted to be as independent in politics as they were modern in farming. "I'd always considered myself a Republican, having grown up in a Republican family," said Guy, "but my experience in graduate school and looking at President Franklin Roosevelt's record convinced me that the Democratic Party stood for more of the ideals than the Republican Party, so I became a Democratic precinct committeeman in 1950 and attended my first Democratic convention."[11]

Initially, belonging to a political party was more important than winning, but Guy was ambitious as well as civic minded. He took the political plunge four times in the 1950s and won only once. It was a rude awakening to be a Democratic challenger and to lose consistently against less qualified Republican candidates. Guy ran twice for the state Senate in 1952 and 1956 and lost both races. He accepted the proverbial sacrificial lamb offering in 1954 for commissioner of agriculture and labor and received the proverbial pounding, losing by 65,000 votes to incumbent Republican Math Dahl, the quintessence of political mediocrity and Republican invincibility. Finally, in 1958, Guy won a seat in the North Dakota House of Representatives, a seemingly unlikely step to the governor's residence two years hence.

Quentin Burdick could not remember when he first met Bill Guy. The encounter was not an important event in his experiences. It really did not matter. Guy, on the other hand, recalled clearly the first time he met Burdick. It did matter. It was an important event and made a lasting impression. "It happened when he and his wife were part of a panel at the Little Country Theater at NDAC and I discovered that this man, Quentin Burdick, and his wife were pacifists," recalled Guy.[12]

What exactly did Guy mean by using the word *pacifist* to describe Quentin and Marietta Burdick? When asked to expand on its meaning, he did so in clear and unmistakable language: "I'd lost a brother in a Japanese prison camp," began Guy. "I'd been on a combat patrol in the Navy and had survived the sinking of the destroyer ship I was on. ... [Pacifism] wasn't something that I was violently in disagreement with, but I just didn't agree to their approach to it."[13]

Quentin Burdick was a Henry Wallace Democrat living in a Truman Cold War world, is what Guy really meant. As a war veteran, Guy did not trust Burdick's stand on neutrality, and in the years that ensued, took issue with the macho ex-football player who did not join the war effort. As Guy personalized it: "I've always questioned how Senator Burdick was able to avoid serving in the military. He points to a football injury in one of his knees, but I met many people in the service who, through one disability or another, were serving, but not necessarily in combat positions. I think in the back of my mind this troubled me a little bit when I saw this big, husky man telling us what a great football player he was, but how he was physically unable to be in the military."[14]

Guy harbored doubts about the loyalty of Burdick. If his pacifism brought criticism, Fargo talk about Burdick's other alleged anti-American activity scared the living daylights out of Guy. Pacifism was one thing, but communism was quite another. When NDAC administrators dismissed physics professor Daniel Q. Posin and others for so-called pinko activities in the early 1950s, both town and gown took sides. Posin was anything but a card-carrying member of the Communist Party. He was a dapper little man with a dark moustache and a Ph.D. from the University of Chicago. He was also the entertaining WDAY-TV weatherman, whose scientific explanations may have contributed to his dismissal because he might have known how to make the bomb.[15] Burdick and other town liberals defended the right of free speech and academic freedom, and on some occasions criticized the firings.

Burdick's alleged Communist affiliation for supporting Henry Wallace, foreclosed farmers and striking truck drivers in the 1930s surfaced often in Fargo social circles. The assumed association accounted, in part, for his social exclusion by the city's conservative elite. The Burdick name (father and son) was too radical for Fargo. Jerome Lamb, a member of one of the oldest North Dakota Democratic families, and a long-time Fargo intellectual, recalled one such discussion after Burdick's 1960 Senate win. "It was the liberal establishment of Fargo," said Lamb. "They were at a party and Bill Guy was there [Burdick was not present]. Something came up about Burdick and someone said, 'Well, he was a Communist!' Bill Guy [who was then running for governor] bristled, but the person continued, 'Well, he was.'" Lamb observed, "We all knew that. I mean, a lot of us were in the same boat, and Quentin was a Communist. Who knows what it means? It's like saying you're a Catholic. Nobody knows what it means. But Burdick did escape from that and that probably would have done him in."[16]

Differences

Bill Guy and Quentin Burdick were serious sorts walking the fields of North Dakota. They never appeared jaunty. They took themselves and their politics with frank and deadly seriousness. They could and did demonstrate controlled humor at times, which was really nothing more than an ability to repeat a joke in public. But they seldom engaged in a spontaneous burst of uncontrolled laughter. They could laugh at themselves if necessary, but neither man wore a smile naturally. Guy smiled easier and probably was more humorous than Burdick, but neither could be described as funny or ever full of humor. "Guy certainly had no sense of humor," observed Senator Young, who got along well with most Democrats. "He was not the kind of person that you could visit with, at least, I couldn't."[17] As for Burdick's humor, Jocylen Birch Burdick expressed some frustration in defending it: "He always told things with a perfectly straight face and I spent most of my life explaining to people that didn't know him that he was kidding."[18] Laughing at either a Guy or Burdick joke often was compensatory for their positions — not their lines. Facial anatomy softened Guy's smile. His face was smooth, with few angles, and his hair was cropped short like a fresh-cut field of sweet clover. Burdick always appeared more unkempt. His hair, especially in midyears, ran wild and seemed out of control, while his pugilistic jaw shot out for confrontation rather than greetings. It was harder for a fighter to smile than an economist, although few agricultural economists come across as comedians.

Both men exercised control from different experiences. Guy plowed detail at every turn. He was an academic economist who crunched numbers and wrote up the reports. He was an empiricist and his point of view was that of a social scientist. In 12 years as governor, Guy probably wrote more memos than all of his predecessors and most of his successors combined. He strove to modernize state government, and during his tenure made many improvements, especially in reorganizing executive departments under the jurisdiction of his office. His grand attempt to rewrite the state constitution, however, flopped. North Dakota voters supported his efforts to reform state government, but they were unwilling to change the state's charter, which included many perks, privileges and freedoms. Guy probably never understood the true meaning of its defeat. He often seemed inflexible and overly sensitive to those who did not agree with his recommendations. They were, after all, empirical in nature and thus true in scientific fact.

Burdick detested detail in any form. It drove him nuts. He became immediately impatient, then incensed, and finally rude when presented with it. This three-step reaction to detail seldom took more than a minute or two, and most presenters got the message even sooner. But throughout his life, Burdick always operated on the basis of orderly procedure. It was the lawyer in him that incubated his sense of control and the absolute need for order. He probably never took a deposition in his entire legal career, but he was quick on his feet and could read a jury with the very best of the state's trial lawyers in his time. He wanted to get to the point of the matter with great dispatch, like a blocker opening a hole for the trailing running back. He was not interested in lots of detail or extended explanations. "What's the point?" was Burdick's opening statement and his political trademark. Yet, for all his disdain of detail, he was a stickler for words. He loved words, exact words, and tight, proper grammar. If records existed, he probably would rank among the best crossword puzzle players who ever served in the US Senate.[19]

Religion also contributed to their differences. Guy was a Presbyterian. He believed in a hierarchical organization. God made some individuals born leaders and some natural followers, and planetary life soon revealed who was who. Churches required bishops. States required governors. As one, Guy preached and practiced this vertical religious organization in a political context. There was always an Old Testament tone to his reign. He was the preordained leader and the party faithful were his preordained flock. Although he married a Congregationalist, Guy remained a Democratic practicing Presbyterian. In another age, he would have been made a strong Protestant duke or even a king. In the American experiment, however, he appeared too imperial. His religion assumed that some Christians were born with perfection and some were born without it. Guy knew the score. As governor, he stood among the elect, not the damned. The political allies who surrounded him carried his mandate with equal superiority. They reinforced his own beliefs, and together they divided the party faithful between Guy soldiers and Burdick soldiers. There were good Democrats and bad Democrats. Bill Guy was as moral, stern and uncompromising a governor as was another Presbyterian — Woodrow Wilson — as president.

Burdick, in contrast, was pedigreed American Protestant. He was a Congregationalist. He rejected any form of hierarchical authority. It was a remarkable and uniquely American institution horizontal in organization and democratic in religious beliefs. Each congregation and every member stood equal before church and God. No one gave religious orders and no one took religious orders. Religious autonomy was sacrosanct. Religious beliefs came from personal interpretation, not papal bulls or bishop letters. Although Burdick married an atheist and later a Christian Scientist, Congregationalism remained a cornerstone of his political creed. This religion made him more democratic and tolerant of others' beliefs. In another age, Burdick would have burned at the stake. In the American landscape, however, he prospered as a true Jeffersonian. Freedom of religion and freedom of speech must always be granted and always defended. The doctrine of Congregationalism preached equality and a democratic approach to government as well as religion. Congregationalists made more friends than their Presbyterian Protestant cousins because they believed everyone was equal in the eyes of God and in the eyes of man. There were no good Democrats and bad Democrats in Burdick's mind. They were all Democrats.

Jean Mason Guy, who attended a Congregational Church in Fargo, explained the core essence of this Protestant tradition. "Well, I'll tell you, one reason that my parents liked the Congregational Church so much was that there was no form," recalled Jean Guy. "I shouldn't say no form, but there were no bishops or anything like that. It's a very democratic church with no frills. The first ministers that I remember stood up in front of the church in dark blue suits and conducted the service and preached. There were no clerical collars and no robes. ... The next minister wore a robe. That upset my parents very much because they thought that was too much form or too much formality in the church."[20]

Other institutional influences also broadened Burdick's political philosophy. He was active in the Nonpartisan League, the North Dakota Farmers Union, the establishment of rural electric cooperatives and the defense of Teamster union locals. Each of these organizations operated on an organizational model similar to the Congregationalists. Each political district, each farmers local, each rural electric cooperative and each union local made its own decisions and then took them forward to higher levels. When they made a decision, it was done by majority vote, and once made, every member was obligated to support it. Burdick never separated himself or stood above the wishes of the majority. He sought support from the people before he announced his own candidacy. More importantly, for his entire political career he supported every endorsed candidate and every item on the platform. He believed the decision of the majority, not the hierarchical instructions of just a few, who dictated the political covenant, and he was only the representative of that process. Burdick's politics grew from the soil. They were not handed down from the mountaintop.

Bill Guy, on the other hand, never experienced these core North Dakota institutions. He was never really a Nonpartisan Leaguer, an active Farmers Union farmer, a rural electric organizer or a Teamster. His background was academic and scientific agriculture — authoritarians who told farmers what to do because they knew better. Majority rule in the Guy formula was never a substitute for the superiority of a classroom lecture, an agricultural Extension bulletin or an executive order. Rules descended from the top, never from the bottom. When Guy became governor, he took that philosophy with him into state government and the Democratic-NPL Party. If he did not like a particular endorsed candidate, he publicly refused to support the person. Imperial decrees were always more important than majority rule or platform planks passed in an emotion-filled convention. As a boy, Bill Guy never heard the cries of the NPL slogan, "We'll Stick. We'll Win." sweeping across the Chaffee corporate fields. And as governor, he never practiced it, either.

In historical narrative, Burdick appears as a son of the Depression, while Guy appears as a veteran of the Second World War. These sharp differences in time contributed into sharp differences between the two in matters of human beings and public institutions. The Depression seared Burdick. It made him more frugal, if that was really possible. He internalized the suffering of others and that knowledge made him compassionate toward his fellow man. He saw the world of the Depression in various shades of gray. He refused to pass judgment on those who held different points of view. Economic survival was more pressing than ideological supremacy. Radicals were not the source of the Depression and the ideas that they espoused would never be the solutions. Burdick supported economic programs that assisted those who truly needed assistance. He was less interested in building monuments to the past than in rearranging the economic ladder of the *haves* and the *have-nots*. The cost of production and cheap electricity for farmers or defending striking truck drivers was always more important to him than building party headquarters, constructing a Heritage Center or rewriting the state constitution.

Guy wore navy white in another decade. The significance of his participation in both the Atlantic and Pacific theaters yielded a much different perspective. The Second World War was a titanic struggle between democracy and totalitarianism. It was truly a biblical global engagement between the forces of good and evil. The results demonstrated perhaps in a predetermined message the superiority of one ideology over another and the absolute importance to maintain it throughout the Cold War. Guy, the young naval officer, always saw the world in terms of black and white. He was less tolerant of other points of view, and anything that challenged American institutions or values were deemed dangerous. There was no gray in Guy's world. It was imperative to stay on the correct side of life as a matter of principle. In seeing death so often on water, Guy strove to celebrate life with brick and mortar on land. The Democratic-NPL Party needed a building, the state needed a Heritage Center and the people of North Dakota must have a modern constitution.

Through the years, specific issues heightened their basic differences. "I can't pick a single issue where [their differences] would have been as pronounced as the corporation farm issue," recalled Stanley Moore, longtime president of the North Dakota Farmers Union.[21] Guy, weaned on Farm Bureau grain, supported the idea of changing North Dakota's anti-corporation farming law. Burdick, indoctrinated on Glenn Talbott teachings, steadfastly opposed it. "I don't want to say that Guy was a conservative," said Tom Burgum, "but Guy's whole social and political agenda was much more conservative than Burdick's." And what did each think of the other? "Guy thought Burdick was too liberal, too radical," and Burdick "always thought Guy was a political wuss. He wasn't strong enough for labor. He wasn't strong enough for the working man or the common man."[22]

Finally, Burdick and Guy exhibited varying styles of campaigning. Burdick liked personal contact. Guy opted for more formal settings. Burdick roamed small town streets like a middle linebacker stalking an option quarterback. He seldom missed a house or a hand. Guy concentrated more on one-to-one meetings with the small-town elite. Burdick was pumped and shook everybody's hand. Guy was more reticent and selective. If there was a parade, a horse to ride or a ski slope to descent, Burdick participated. One might see Guy in a parade, but never on a horse or skis.

The party faithful recognized the personality differences between the two men. "Burdick was like an old shoe. Comfortable," recalled Betty and John Maher, longtime Democrats. "We were a young couple, we lived in Bowman, and you thought you should feel a little uptight with somebody like that coming, but when Quentin came, it was just like somebody's good friend in the family came. He'd come in and wanted to know if there was any soup in the kettle and if you had a bed he could sleep in."[23]

Up north in Bottineau County on the Canadian border, some of the Democrats tabbed Guy "old turkey neck." Walt Erdman, a longtime Nonpartisan Leaguer and Democrat, and one of the party's true gentlemen, explained the nickname: "I'll tell you a little story about Bill Guy. I liked him but I can name you any number of guys here in town that used to call him 'old turkey neck.'" When asked, "What does that mean?" Erdman replied simply, "Well, he had a long neck!" When further pressed for details, Erdman added that the nickname meant "they didn't think too much of him," finding Guy to be a stuffed shirt.[24]

These sharp differences in life experiences and political philosophy predated any personal conflicts that Bill Guy and Quentin Burdick engaged in later. The background, however, is vital to understanding why they viewed the building of the Democratic-NPL Party and the election of 1974 so differently.

Party Building

Organizer and energizer best describe the unique personal contributions made by Guy and Burdick to the modern North Dakota Democratic-NPL Party. Guy was a natural-born organizer. He breathed in detail and breathed out organizational models. Burdick was the antithesis of a good organizer. Instead, he stood as the symbol of the party's first significant victory, and in time, as its longest serving member. He brought inspiration and energy to the party. "Guy and Burdick really grounded the two-party system," noted Lloyd Omdahl, "but they each contributed in their different ways."[25]

George Sinner, a Guy protégé and a Burdick admirer, saw the contributions of party building in both men's approaches. Sinner confessed, however, that when he served as governor, he felt uncomfortable exercising dual duties as head of state and head of party. It violated his American Roman Catholic sense of separation of church and state. Guy, the Presbyterian, saw no conflict in wearing both hats. "Bill Guy felt that he was head of the party," said Sinner, "and he worked very hard and did a lot of really good things to build the party. ... He was much better at that than probably Quentin and I were, or Art Link for that matter, although Link was very good at it, too."[26]

If Guy built the church, Burdick delivered the most stirring sermons. Sinner recalled an incident of Burdick's inspiration during his tenure as governor. The party was vacillating over some women's issues and Burdick was speaking before a party rally in Bismarck. He was old and his reading of a prepared text was going rather poorly. The audience seemed as lost as he was. Suddenly, in the middle of his speech, he stopped, looked up and raised the index finger of his right hand above his head and shouted in a strong voice: "Don't you dare vote against the women in the Legislature. That issue you are dealing with is a woman's issue and you don't dare vote against women!"[27]

The place awoke, but then fell silent as a whisper. This was vintage Burdick. "It was a remarkable testimony of the man he was," said Sinner. "He didn't care about whether it was popular. He just said it and that was the Populist in him."[28] Jim Fuglie, who served a long tenure as executive director of the party, saw this Burdick characteristic work among the party faithful again and again. "He was the rallying point. He was the party statesman. He energized the party faithful and the potential Democrat voters."[29]

Guy, the good organizer, wanted to build a headquarters for the party. "I felt that the party needed to have a focus," recalled Guy, "and so one way to do that would be to establish our own headquarters in Bismarck so that we could operate 12 months out of the year instead of four months before the election out of some vacant storefront somewhere."[30] Burdick, of course, opposed the idea. He "referred to it as a waste of money," said Gorman King Sr.[31] House Leader Dick Backus was more critical of Burdick's motives: "He didn't want that money going in there because it would take away from his campaigning."[32] Fuglie noted that through the years, Burdick actually flip-flopped on the Kennedy Center. When he knew it was going to be built, he pushed for a Fargo site. When party coffers ran deficit numbers, he later proposed selling it.[33]

"Quentin was adamantly opposed," stated Guy. "Adamantly opposed to it! He not only refused to have anything to do with fundraising, he wouldn't contribute anything himself to it. ... although there is a $1,000 credit to his account in the Kennedy Center that was given shortly before he died by David Strauss handling the senator's residual campaign funds."[34] In fairness to Burdick, his largest financial contributions to the party came in his later years after the building of the center "because our resources were so substantial," said David Strauss, and "we were able to give money to legislative candidates and other state candidates," and equally important, "we bankrolled the operation at the Kennedy Center" for voter turnout surveys.[35] Austin Engel, who served as the executive director of the party in the early 1970s, stated that most Democrats who worked in Bismarck looked to Guy as the party leader because he was there and Quentin was kind of off on his own as senator, but after Strauss came on board, Burdick played a greater role in party matters.[36]

Burdick sometimes surprised both legislative and state candidates with personal contributions. "I don't remember what year, but I got a campaign contribution of $100 from Quentin," recalled Tish Kelly, a Fargo Democrat who served in the Legislature for 20 years (1975-1995). "Based on his reputation, I was really quite stunned. It turned out, I think, I'm not exactly sure about this, but, at least, all the Democrats that ran in Fargo that year got that sort of contribution." Kelly quickly added with a smile, however, that Burdick's contribution was "a one-time thing."[37]

Earl Pomeroy and Nicholas Spaeth both approached Burdick for money in the fall of 1984. They were running for the first time as state candidates — for insurance commissioner and attorney general. They were caught in tight races with polls showing excellent chances to topple their Republican opponents. But like most rookie state candidates in the stretch drive, they ran out of funds. They caught up with Burdick and his aide, Tom Stallman, somewhere in a cheap motel somewhere in North Dakota. Stallman woke the sleeping Burdick in the adjacent room as the two young hopefuls waited nervously for their opportunity to speak. They were faced with the difficult task of making a pitch for money to the frugal half-awake senator, who was obviously not pleased with their interruption. "Representative Dorgan has all the money!" roared a sleepy-eyed Burdick. "Dorgan is raising money all the time from those PACs and I just have a little money in my sock. If you want money, go see Dorgan."[38] Burdick did, however, end up contributing to their campaigns and both men won the elections.

Guy and Burdick approached endorsement of party candidates differently. Guy did not associate with Democratic officials and candidates who drank too much and showed up at party events with evidence of their sins. Guy was very adamant in this regard. When time came for his endorsements, he asked the *drys* to stand up while ignoring the *wets*. Tom Burgum, the son of Leslie Burgum, former Republican attorney general (1955-1962), was the Democratic-NPL candidate for attorney general in 1968 and later became one of Burdick's top Senate aides. Guy did not approve of Burgum's drinking. Burgum, in return, did not approve of Guy's disapproval. "Put it this way," stated Burgum. "Guy was a ruler. What he would do is they would have all the candidates there, and Guy would have three stand up and he would endorse them." Later at the governor's residence, Burgum challenged Guy after he asked all the candidates, "What can I do to help?" Burgum responded, "Why don't you endorse all of us or none of us?"[39]

Guy passed moral judgments on other Democrats. He insulted one of the party regulars — Hank Kelly, a Park River, North Dakota, newspaper editor. Guy told Kelly face to face: "Hank, you should change brands of whiskey."[40] Guy particularly disliked Jamestown attorney Jim Jungroth for his drinking habits. "I remember when we were having a Democratic executive committee meeting," recalled Larry Erickson of Minot. "Jim had been drinking the night before. He was chairman and obviously hung over, maybe even a little intoxicated that morning. Bill Guy turned to Jungroth in front of everybody and said, 'Why don't you go to your room, take a bath and come back and we'll start over.'"[41] As governor, Guy took specific steps to punish Jungroth for his sins. He ignored his water expertise in policy matters and offered the state hospital legal portfolio to David Nething, a Jamestown Republican. Finally and most humiliating, when Guy came to Jamestown, he would contact Jungroth's law partner to drive him around town, although Jungroth was state chairman of the party.[42]

Burdick took no interest in punishing someone else's sins. He never drank much himself and never on the job. He always enjoyed a beer with the boys in the labor hall and through the years probably snuck a few past Jocie, especially in the later years when doctors said he should not drink beer. But to punish fellow Democrats for drinking too much probably never crossed his mind. It was counterproductive and impossible. There were too many of them in those years, and to choose between wet Democrats and dry Democrats weakened the party and created future enemies for any standing politician. Prohibition was a dead horse in the nation and the bars of the North Dakota Democratic-NPL Party.

Selective endorsements for any philosophical or political motive were never part of Burdick's creed. He believed that every endorsed candidate reflected the will of the majority and should receive the support of everyone in the party. Selective endorsements were undemocratic and reflected an elitist viewpoint. Burdick was neither. By endorsing every candidate, Burdick endeared himself across the entire political spectrum, and by respecting the opinions of others even when in disagreement, Burdick became the senior partner of the party. His support was always there and his opinion was respected without reprisals.

For all their disagreements, Guy and Burdick took the party from infancy to maturity. "I think it is absolutely true that it was Quentin Burdick and Bill Guy that built the Democratic Party in the state," said Chuck Fleming, longtime Democratic legislator and Sinner's chief of staff. Fleming saw two stages in the party's development: "Burdick led the movement and brought a lot of liberals into the party," and "afterward Bill Guy deserves more of the credit following his election."[43]

Many Democrat veterans, however, concede that Burdick led the way. "I think Quentin Burdick's early successes in 1958 and in June of 1960 contributed to Bill Guy's election in November of 1960," noted Associate Supreme Court Justice Herb Meschke, a former Minot Democratic legislator (1965-1970).[44] "I don't think we would have a party without him," said veteran Public Service Commissioner Bruce Hagen. "Would we have done it without him? I don't think so. Not at all."[45] "He was the first to win and to stay," said Helen Pepple, an early Fargo supporter who worked many years for Burdick in Washington.[46] "Bill Guy never, in my estimation," however, "reached the hearts of the people of North Dakota like Quentin Burdick did. In order to build a political party, you have to reach the hearts of a lot of people. Bill Guy never did that and Quentin Burdick did, so that factor alone gives Burdick far more importance to the party than Guy," concluded Jack Zaleski, longtime North Dakota journalist.[47]

Republicans shared the same viewpoint. "Burdick was the one who really got the Democratic Party re-established," said Senator Young. "He was elected to Congress and that paved the way for Guy. The candidate we put up for governor in 1960 was a fine fellow, C.P. Dahl, but the train had gone by him. It was fairly easy for Guy to make it, but Guy claims credit for reorganizing the party. He probably did more than Burdick after he was elected governor, but I think Quentin Burdick really got it established."[48]

The mainstay of the North Dakota Democratic-NPL Party centered on the constitutional offices. In that sense, the Guy model worked. The tall and slender state capitol, a bastion of Republican mastery since its occupancy in 1934, became a captured Democratic fortress. The governor's office held the biggest key to the fort, and Democrats Bill Guy (1961-1972), Art Link (1973-1980) and George Sinner (1985-1992) held those keys for 28 years between 1960 and 1992.

Political influence from that office emanated to others in the tower. Slowly, surely and steadily, Democrats by appointment and election began to replace the Republican knights who resided in the vertical tower. The party never gained control of the three-member Public Service Commission, but Bruce Hagen (1961-2000) remained its anchor, Nicholas Spaeth of Fargo became the first Democratic attorney general in 1985, and Jim Kusler became the first and only Democratic secretary of state in 1989 and served one term.

The second most powerful Democrat knighthood, however, came from the office of tax commissioner. Technically observed as a no-party office with a low profile, it grew into the second most influential position in state government. Byron Dorgan (1969-1980), Kent Conrad (1981-1986) and Heidi Heitkamp (1986-1992) turned it into a policy-making political office. Dorgan, for example, lead the party's fight for a high severance tax in the bitter, partisan legislative sessions of 1975 and 1977 and bested the Republican's most powerful figure, House Majority Leader Earl Strinden of Grand Forks. Conrad played a key role in Sinner's upset victory over Republican incumbent Governor Al Olson in 1988.

State voters rewarded the work of all three tax commissioners, *the only elective one in the entire nation.* It seemed ironic that the position of tax collector in North Dakota became the people's most public ombudsmen. Dorgan and Conrad went to Washington — Dorgan in 1981 to replace Rep. Mark Andrews, who won Young's seat, and in 1992 to the U.S. Senate to take Conrad's unexpired seat. Conrad slayed the most powerful Republican, Andrews, in 1986 — the greatest upset victory in all of the Democrat's successes — and ran for Burdick's unexpired term in 1992 and is still there. Heitkamp followed Spaeth as attorney general in 1993, serving two four-year terms.

Since its creation, the party experienced few schisms and few heretics. Guy preferred Republican candidate Richard Larsen of Grand Forks for lieutenant governor in 1968 over incumbent Democrat Charles Tighe. Larsen won. Maverick Byron Knutson defeated the party's endorsement for public service commissioner in the 1974 primary, but he failed to win the seat in the general election. He did win the office of insurance commissioner in 1976 and labor commissioner in 1982.

The independent candidacy of James Jungroth in 1974 hurt Guy in his unsuccessful bid to defeat Senator Young. What followed hurt the party less than the final separation of its two longtime standard-bearers. Allegations by Guy and denials by Burdick on who did what for whom in that election exacerbated their long held differences and made permanent scars on each other's record as senior partners in the party. Younger Democrats knew the allegations but preferred not to take sides. "It was before me," said Fuglie. "It was never repaired. It's not something the Democrats talked about."[49] And, "All I know is heresay," noted Heitkamp. "Lloyd Omdahl knows the truth."[50]

The most serious schism occurred in 1992. Attorney General Nicholas Spaeth, defeated for the office of governor at the convention, challenged and defeated Senate Majority Leader Bill Heigaard of Langdon, North Dakota, in the primary. The party nomination was an overwhelming mandate for Heigaard. A surprised Spaeth lost badly. Party regulars knew the work of Heigaard and strongly supported his candidacy. Voters in the primary who knew Spaeth better selected him by a wide margin and disappointed Heigaard. Crippled by party division, Republican Ed Schafer easily bested Spaeth in the general election. The 1992 schism turned the valuable key of the governor's office back to the Republicans. An important key the Republicans still have today with Schafer winning a second term in 1996. Spaeth and Heigaard, hurt by the struggle and defeated at the polls, retired from politics. With their departures, the party lost two popular and capable men. In the struggle, Guy and Sinner supported Spaeth, the challenger. Burdick supported Heigaard, the party's nominee.

The 1974 Election

North Dakota elections tend to be free-flowing events. Jeffersonian ideas about participatory democracy encourage voter mischief and high voter turnout. It is easier to vote in Cogswell, North Dakota, than it is to register to vote in Chicago, Illinois. North Dakotans stand pat on open-range principles when it comes time for election roundups. State statutes prohibit voter registration and guarantee open primaries, as well as establishing a minimum number of signatures for either a political party or a varmint to get on the ballot.

Oddly enough, however, the state sanctioned a Hamiltonian ballot. The

Republicans, who maintained their legislative hegemony while forfeiting executive control of state government, seized the first column on the ballot. They created a party ballot rather than an office ballot and punished the Democrats by placing their candidates in a second column below the Republicans. Finally, and most Hamiltonian, they lumped all other illegitimate party or independent candidates on top of one another in a third column. A federal court ruled this party ballot unconstitutional in 1979, when Harley McClain, a Valley City folk singer, running as a candidate for the Chemical Farming Banned Party, successfully challenged it.[51] He was an independent candidate for the U.S. House of Representatives in 1978.

North Dakota elections also harbor family feuds. The longest lasted for 40 years (1916-1956) and pitted progressive Republicans (NPL) against conservative Republicans (IVA and ROC). Never content with just a primary fight, losers from either Republican faction then refiled as independent candidates in the general election. Round two produced unpredictable results. The votes were split three ways, accounting for either the defeat of the primary winner or the victory of the primary loser, or sometimes even a stunned Democrat in the fall election.

"Wild" Bill Langer perfected this form of election strategy. If he did not win in the primary, he filed again in the general election. For example, he lost Republican primary fights for governor in 1936 and for the U.S. Senate in 1938. He won the governorship while losing his Senate bid to unseat incumbent Senator Gerald P. Nye in the ensuing November election. Lynn Stambaugh, a Fargo attorney, lost in the 1944 Republican primary to Nye, but refiled again as an independent candidate in the general election. Stambaugh lost again, but he took 45,000 votes from Nye, which ensured his defeat and the election of Democrat John Moses.

The 1974 U.S. Senate race was a humdinger. It was a classic North Dakota election contest that combined past habits and new trends. It went in all sorts of directions because of democratic election privileges and changed the outcome because of a Hamiltonian ballot. National pundits saw it as a referral on the presidency of Richard Nixon. North Dakota voters were supposed to punish senior Republican Senator Milton Young for the sins of Watergate. Former Democratic Governor Bill Guy would be the beneficiary of this referendum and join fellow Democrat Senator Quentin Burdick in the Senate. If successful, Democrats hoped that even the unbeatable Republican Congressman Mark Andrews might also fall prey to the challenge by Tax Commissioner Byron Dorgan. North Dakota Democrats would then hold a full house in the state's congressional delegation.

The cast of characters of this title bout would fill the pages of a Shakespearian tragedy or comedy, maybe even a Mel Brooks film. Bismarck car dealer Robert McCarney — best known for his tax referrals and unabashed dislike of Guy — filed in the primary as a Democrat. James Jungroth, a damned Guy Democrat, announced his plans to run as an independent candidate in the general election. Democrat deacons Lloyd Omdahl and George Sinner lined up behind Guy and hired young David Strauss, later a Burdick staffer, to coordinate Guy's campaign. Scott Anderson, who helped Guy's successful bid for governor in 1960 and later worked for Burdick, cut campaign films for Young while working for a Washington public relations firm. Senator Burdick fired Senate staffer Mike Mullins for working on the Guy campaign after Young threatened to file a complaint with Senate authorities. In the meantime, however, Young's staffer, Bill Wright, a former Jamestown sports writer and good hunting buddy of Jungroth, silently gave comfort to his campaign and did not get fired. The featured fighters, Guy and Young, shared little in common except a personal friendship with Strasburg, North Dakota, native and champagne music maker Lawrence Welk. Guy ran a moral campaign against the evils of seniority rather than attacking Young personally. Young, at one point in the campaign, brought the house down by calling Guy "a far-out liberal," the best overstatement line in the entire drama.[52] Jungroth entered the race on environmental issues because he detected no differences between Guy and Young on them. He excited a committed number of young Democrats to work on his behalf and Guy spurned them. The election was so close that Guy, a loser by a hair, requested a recount, which then took weeks to complete. District judges supervised the process and discarded almost 2,000 votes because voters, mislead by the ballot, cast two votes for the Senate candidates. It was easy for voters to vote for either Young or Guy in one of the first two columns, but when voters saw two independent candidates, Jungroth and Ken Gardner — a Drayton, North Dakota, social studies teacher — in a third column above each other, some voted a second time. During the weeks of the recount, a young UND law student from Valley City — Earl Pomeroy — studiously watched the proceedings and impressed everyone with his acumen.[53]

Continuity, not change, proved the short-term result of the election. Voters gave Young one more term and sent Guy to the sidelines. Jungroth did not win, but the 6,000 votes he garnered helped to defeat Guy and ensure the recount. Andrews won with less difficulty, spanking Dorgan with the only loss of his highly successful political career. Senator Burdick remained the only North Dakota Democrat in Washington. In losing, however, Guy opened the Washington seats to other Democrats. Had he won, the North Dakota delegation would have remained Burdick, Guy and Andrews for years to come. Instead, the Young victory postponed for only a short stint the eventual change that would come to North Dakota's congressional delegation. In 1980, Andrews won Young's Senate seat and Dorgan won Andrews's House seat. The combination of Guy's 1974 loss and Kent Conrad's upset victory over Andrews in 1986 established the change that brought more North Dakota Democrats to the Washington table. In defeat, Guy ended his own political career, but he ensured the ultimate success of other Democrats. Had he won in 1974, Dorgan, Conrad and Pomeroy would not be serving in Washington today.

The reasons for Guy's loss and the historical analysis of Burdick's involvement in the election deserve more discussion. The answers reveal more about the egos of these two giants of the modern North Dakota Democratic-NPL Party than anything else. Guy did not lose the 1974 election because of Burdick's lack of support for him or because of his alleged support for Jungroth. Burdick's position that Guy lost the election because he refused his help does not fly, either. What Burdick did not do for Guy or what he did for Jungroth becomes the final act in the drama of Guy and Burdick.

From the bleachers, the 1974 episode plays petty and insignificant. In many ways it was petty, but never to the two protagonists. When a 20-game winner disappointedly loses the big one, every pitch is replayed. In losing, Guy pointed his finger at the bullpen and asked where was Burdick. The answer came back loud and clear. Burdick was in pinstripes all the time. At the beginning of the game, Guy kept him off the mound and refused to use him, but when the bases got loaded and the contest started to slip away, he made the call for Burdick. The instructions on the mound were simple. Burdick was told to pitch a bean ball at Senator Young, but the wily old politician refused. The game went to extra innings and Guy eventually lost the contest.

Upon reflection years later, both men recalled the events differently. "I started with a number of good, sharp spots [taped advertisements] for Bill Guy from Washington," recalled Burdick. "I sent them to North Dakota but not one damn one of them was used."[54] Tom Burgum supported Burdick's recollection but gave the incident another twist. "Burdick got ads for Guy because he was aware that if Jungroth ran, it would look bad for him."[55] Guy refuted that Burdick ever sent him the tapes in the first place. Others close to him during the campaign agreed. "I was doing the booking," said Omdahl, "and I don't remember having anything from Burdick."[56]

When the election tightened, Guy did ask Burdick to cut some campaign tapes. "We cornered Quentin at the dedication of the new sugar beet refinery at Hillsboro," recalled Guy, who went on to describe the conversation:

"Well, Quentin" [said Guy], "Will you please, now that you are back in the state, please cut some positive statements for our campaign?"

"We will," replied Burdick. "I've been thinking about it and I've got the statement I'm going to make right here in my pocket."

"That' fine," said Omdahl. "We're set up for Monday morning at 8:00 a.m. at WDAY."

"That suits me fine," replied Burdick.[57]

Burdick, however, according to both Guy and Omdahl, never showed up at the Fargo television studio on Monday. Moreover, their repeated attempts to pin him down and reschedule another taping session produced the same results. Burdick presented an entirely different story. He stated that the only call he received from Guy came very late in the campaign. "The day or two before the election Guy called somebody on my staff," said Burdick, "and said: 'We want Burdick to go on the air and just tear Milton Young from limb to limb. Just do a hatchet job on him,' and I said no."[58]

When Guy heard Burdick tell that story on a television interview shortly before Burdick died, he became quite upset. "That was so untrue," said Guy. "It just rankled me because one of our campaign strategies (Milt Young was an expert at bleeding in public) and if you started charging him with doing, or being too old, or doing something wrong, he would come out and sob in front of the public. We didn't want that to happen, so our strategy was not to ever mention Milt Young. Not to criticize his work or some of the questionable things he had done during his Senate career, like his trips abroad with his secretary and things like that. We didn't touch any of that stuff."[59]

Beneath the tapes lay a deeper issue: motive. "I had the feeling that Quentin was afraid that I might win because he was afraid," said Guy, "and that with two Democratic senators in the U.S. Senate from North Dakota, one of the two senators might have trouble getting re-elected."[60] Burdick posed the motive question from his viewpoint: "Why didn't Guy use me?" He then proceeded to answer his own question. "I had helped some other people and I was ready to help him, but not the way he wanted me to. He was sitting comfortably in some poll he had taken and thought he was in good shape. My surmise is that I don't think he wanted to be indebted to me and that's why he didn't use the spots."[61]

So which man is telling the truth? The answer is complicated because virtually all of the communication between Guy and Burdick during the 1974 election was indirect. People on Guy's campaign staff talked with Burdick staffers and vice versa, but Guy and Burdick did not directly communicate with each other. Little help came from Burdick because sitting politicians seldom assist other sitting politicians, especially in this case. Although Guy held no political office in 1974, he was still the most visible force in the North Dakota Democratic-NPL Party in the state. Burdick knew that and assumed that Guy would continue to be a force for many years to come. Guy, on the other hand, really did not want Burdick's help. It pained him to ask and it pained him to provide the senator with any political IOU. Guy and Burdick did not join hands in the 1974 senatorial election because they simply did not trust one another.

Two key staffers gave more insights into the controversy. "I think, in 1974, the relationship with Burdick was probably mismanaged to some extent," said David Strauss who was Guy's campaign coordinator, "and that Guy and Burdick were never close."[62] Strauss confirmed that in the early stages of the campaign "Burdick had taped some positive tapes that weren't used," and that in the late stages "they were looking for Burdick to cut ads attacking Milt Young." When polls showed the election was beginning to slip away from Guy to Young, "the groundwork had not been laid properly to Burdick," but "all the virtue isn't on one side or the other."[63]

"A Bill Guy victory in 1974 would have changed much," added Tom Stallman, Burdick's top staffer in North Dakota. "I wanted him to win."[64] But the demands put on Burdick during the last week of the campaign by the Guy forces "were unreal. They wanted him to really personally attack Senator Young. That's not the norm and not before the last few days before the election." In fairness to Guy, however, Stallman conceded: "I don't think Bill Guy knew what his managers were doing up to that point."[65]

The James Jungroth imbroglio was far more complicated than the case of the missing tapes. He was a longtime Burdick friend and a longtime Guy enemy. His Jamestown drinking and hunting buddies, Scott Anderson, Tom Burgum and Bill Wright, were associated with both North Dakota senators. Jungroth's strongest supporters were young committed environmentalists and old Progressive Party Democrats. The moment Jungroth entered the race, the Guy-Burdick relationship was destroyed permanently. When Jungroth polled more than 6,000 votes in the closest North Dakota senatorial race in history, more fingers were pointed at what Burdick did for Jungroth than at what he had not done for Guy.

"I thought he was a man who looked after the folks," said Jungroth of Burdick. "This is why I regarded myself as a friend of his and why I admired him."[66] Their friendship covered a quarter of a century back to 1950, when Jungroth went to work for the North Dakota Farmers Union straight out of law school. For the next couple of years, Burdick and Jungroth were a presence in the towns of North Dakota, together trying insurance cases in two-thirds of the state's 53 counties. They represented the Farmers Union Insurance Company against personal injury suits in a hostile political climate of conservative ROC Republican politics that detested the entry of the Farmers Union into the private insurance business.

By nature, Jungroth was a true political believer. He was raised on Non-partisan League political values and saw the merger of the League with the Democratic Party as the only way to achieve political success in North Dakota. Aside from Guy's stern, moral judgment against his personal behavior, which personally hurt Jungroth a great deal, he took Guy as a political interloper in the whole political process. "The only way Bill Guy got elected is that four of us picked him because we thought he could win," asserted Jungroth. "Gorman King, Charles Tighe, Charles Conrad and myself picked him! He was a Navy veteran from Cass County and almost looked like a REPUBLICAN."[67] If Guy hated Jungroth, so did Omdahl, his most faithful adviser, who historically ignored Jungroth's contributions to the merger of League and the Democratic Party. "He didn't like me very well," conceded Jungroth. "He never mentioned me in his book *The Insurgents* although I was there all the time. That is why I suspect researchers."[68]

It would be convenient to dismiss the Jungroth candidacy as a Burdick plot to keep Bill Guy in North Dakota. North Dakota politics, however, are never quite that singular. The Jungroth candidacy became a catalyst for Guy haters, environmentalists and Progressive Democrats such as Charles Tighe, who envisaged a new beginning for the North Dakota Democratic-NPL Party. All these factions came together — angered by Guy's party elitism and pro-growth stand on coal development — and reached the same verdict: Six more years of Senator Young was decidedly better for the future of North Dakota politics than 20 more years of Bill Guy.

The anti-Guy factor, however, cannot be separated from the other issues. Yet, neither can it be established as the only issue. The Jungroth candidacy and what it represented was far more complex than just hating Guy. Those closest to the Jungroth campaign remain quite clear on their primary objective without ever denying their disdain of fellow Democrat Bill Guy. "I hated Bill Guy," said Ardell Tharaldson, Jungroth's campaign coordinator. "Charles Tighe hated Bill Guy. Jim Jungroth hated Bill Guy. But it wasn't the dominant reason. If we didn't think that coal development was the reason, we'd never [have] done it."[69]

The anti-Guy card was also played by those who sought a new direction for the party, especially Tighe. He stood first among Guy Democratic haters because the governor shafted him in the 1968 lieutenant governor's race, which he lost to Republican Dick Larsen. He never forgave Guy for that act of political betrayal. "Charles Tighe," said Tharaldson, "cared more about Bill Guy losing than Jungroth and I did."[70] Beneath the personal hatred, however, burned a bright plan for the future. Tighe gave the group another positive goal for defeating the former governor, which he repeated throughout the campaign. His message was straight up: "The new generation of Democrats will never come if we don't get rid of these guys. We've just got to clean them out."[71]

Burdick felt more at home in the anti-Guy camp. He felt the sting of Guy's instructions to do this or to do that and his repeated moral messages of the elect and the damned. Jungroth knew better than most just how testy the Guy-Burdick relationship had become. "Burdick didn't like Guy and Guy kept making it worse," said Jungroth. "For example, Guy would write him the damnedest letters basically telling him this is how you run that thing down here and you better to do this."[72]

Before Jungroth announced his candidacy, he went to his old friend, Burdick, for advice and support. A meeting was arranged in Jim's loft in Jamestown and included Burdick, Jungroth, Scott Anderson, Harlan Severson and Ardell Tharaldson. The gathering was informal, but everyone present knew the true purpose of the discussion. The five participants circled the wagons before they lit the fire. Finally, the question was simply put to Burdick: What would you do if Jungroth announced as an independent candidate for the U.S. Senate race? Burdick first paused and then gave an oblique sort of response. Tharaldson recalled that it sounded almost Oriental in tone: "If you were to run," said Burdick, looking away from the others, "... and I believe one has the right to run against anyone if they want to, in Democratic politics it's fair to do it — and if you wanted to run, Jim, I wouldn't oppose it. I'll try to help you and I'll try to raise money for you."[73]

The Burdick promise to assist Jungroth never materialized. The sitting senator did for Jungroth what he had promised to Guy. Nothing. Burdick was never heard from again. "I wish they would have been involved, but they weren't," recalled a disappointed Tharaldson.[74] Burdick later ran into Karl Limvere, another local Jamestown Democrat and Farmers Union man. "I basically said to Burdick," Limvere recalled, that "Bill Guy was going to win the election." Without even a discernible pause, Burdick replied, "I'll take that bet."[75]

Others associated with Burdick, however, did assist the Jungroth campaign. The main player was Scott Anderson, another Jamestown Democrat with ties to both Burdick and Jungroth. Although Anderson was not on Burdick's staff in 1974, he was a trusted adviser and a close personal friend. When Anderson made any political moves, which was often if not daily, those who followed his trail tried to trace it to the Burdick camp. Kevin Carvell, who covered the Senate race for the *Fargo Forum*, identified Anderson as a key player in the Jungroth campaign.[76] So did Larry Erickson, a state Democratic-NPL chairman from Minot. "Scott Anderson was always a worm in the ointment," said Erickson, "and he was deeply involved in this."[77] Guy, too, pointed a finger at Erickson and added without mentioning names that "there's a couple of young fellows in Washington who had free access in and out of Quentin's office while the Jungroth campaign was targeting me."[78]

Tying Anderson directly to Burdick was another matter. Even Omdahl and Guy remained cautious in pointing a finger at Burdick for supporting Jungroth. "There was a conspiracy in terms of the Jungroth candidacy," stated Omdahl. He went on to state that Burdick was indirectly involved in the conspiracy; he qualified his accusation by stating, "at least, he was fully aware of what was going on because he and Jungroth were always very close."[79] Guy was hesitant to say even that much. "I've avoided making any allegations because I don't want to get sued for libel."[80]

Burdick, while attempting to please Jungroth and placate Guy, maintained a cordial working relationship with Young. He sent clever smoke signals to members of Young's staff that he was not going to take sides in the fray. "He let it be known early on that he liked, as he put it, the number three license plate," recalled Chris Sylvester, Young's chief of staff. Later, after Guy's endorsement, Burdick told Sylvester, "I'm going to have to make the usual statements for the Democratic ticket, but that's all it is going to be."[81] Burdick's lukewarm support for Guy was less common than not attacking Young. "Hubert Humphrey never came to North Dakota to campaign against Senator Young," said Sylvester, "and every campaign he was invited to come over[,] and he never once came over."[82]

There was, however, one altercation between Burdick and Young during the campaign. It centered on the political activity of Mike Mullins, a Burdick staffer assigned to the Senate judiciary committee of which Burdick was a member. Burdick fired Mullins because he hosted a fundraiser for Guy's campaign. The event was in violation of Burdick's specific instructions to his staff and to anyone working on the judiciary committee. When Young discovered the activity, he became very angry. He gave Burdick hell and an ultimatum to clean the matter up in 48 hours or "I'm going after you and to ask for a Senate ethics investigation."[83] Burdick promptly fired Mullins. There was a bit of political irony to the Mullins matter; he was probably in line for a good position with Guy's Senate staff, but had been hired, in part, by Burdick through the recommendation of Jungroth.[84]

Bill Guy lost the closest senatorial election in North Dakota history. It was a bitter defeat for one of the state's most popular governors and a satisfying climax to Senator Young's long Senate career. "The Democrats tried to discourage me from running," noted Young in an interview in 1977, "as well as some in my own party. A lot of them thought I couldn't win. That became a real challenge. I thought I could and I did win, but not by very much."[85] In defeating Guy, Young completed the cycle of being the only Republican to beat both Guy and Burdick in separate Senate elections.

The closeness of the 1974 Senate election makes it difficult to evaluate why Guy lost or why Young won. There are, however, in retrospect a few key factors that stand out. By every poll, Guy blew a big early lead in the race. The election from day one seemed to be his to win or lose rather than Young's, but in the final weeks of the contest, Guy squandered his lead. Astute Republicans credit Guy's overconfidence as a major factor in his defeat. "Guy got ahead of himself," said Mark Andrews, neighbor and a close loser to Guy in the 1962 governor's race, "and tripped over his own ego more than anything else."[86] The winner echoed Andrews's assessment. "I think where Bill Guy made his mistake was in the overconfidence he had," said Young. "He was so sure he was going to win!"[87]

North Dakota Democrats agreed with Andrews and Young. Those close to the North Dakota Farmers Union noted that Guy was so overconfident that he made no attempts to even ask the organization for support against Young, who was always attacking Farmers Union politics for being too radical. "How can a Democrat of North Dakota win without the Farmers Union?" asked Charles Conrad, "even if you are Bill Guy?"[88]

A second factor was the independent candidacy of James Jungroth. In a close contest, Guy needed every Democrat vote. Jungroth offered anti-Guy Democrats an alternative and enough of them jumped the party ship for a variety of reasons, some political and some personal. Jungroth also offered those interested in opposing significant coal development in North Dakota a clear choice for their views. Those inside the Jungroth campaign dispute this interpretation. "I'd like to think we're the reason why Bill Guy lost," said Tharaldson, "but I don't think we were."[89] Bob Vogel, a child of the Nonpartisan League and a longtime Democratic activist, took an even more contrary position. "I don't think Jungroth deserves all the blame or maybe not any of it," argued Vogel. "I checked the process of where Jungroth's votes came from, and they came from areas where Young was strongest, not where Bill Guy was."[90] With due respect for these positions, it seems improbable that Bill Guy would not have garnered at least a couple hundred votes from Democratic voters without a challenge from within his own party.

The third factor was the Hamiltonian ballot. The North Dakota ballot gave Young an unconstitutional advantage over Guy and the two independent candidates in the race. He, as a Republican, appeared in the first column on all election ballots, while Guy, as a Democrat, was in the second column. Even more unfair, the ballot punished the two nonparty candidates by lumping them together in a separate column. If the ballot had listed all four candidates in one column under the heading, "U.S. Senate race (vote for one)," Bill Guy, not Milton Young, would have won the 1974 senatorial election in North Dakota.

The recount became a second election contest. The results demonstrate that the party ballot helped significantly in the defeat of Guy, especially in the paper ballot in rural counties. "I personally sat through every precinct that was recounted," stated Herb Meschke, who worked for the Democratic-NPL Party on the recount in the state's northwest corner counties. "There were literally hundreds of ballots that had a vote for both Bill Guy and James Jungroth that were spoiled and were all thrown out, but seldom a spoiled ballot for Senator Young."[91]

Bill Guy and Quentin Burdick contributed significantly to the building of the modern North Dakota Democratic-NPL Party. They were the standard-bearers and the most visible symbols of Democratic success in a traditionally Republican environment. Guy served 12 years as governor, the longest tenure of the state's 32 governors. Burdick served 32 years as U.S. Senator, second only to Milton Young.

Guy and Burdick shared little in common. They were born in different eras and grew up in equally different environments. Guy never accepted the aloof and non-complimentary nature of Burdick's complex personality. Burdick showed impatience and disdain for Guy's superior organizational skills. Their negative behavior toward each other during the 1974 election confirmed their personal and political differences rather than the unity of the Democratic-NPL Party. "They carried on a pretense well," rooted Chub Ulmer, "but they were a couple of bulls in the same pen and they kept their distance."[92]

Unfortunately, the 1974 election defeat left Guy bitter and Burdick non-plussed. Opinions of each other grew further apart as they entered their senior years. They never enjoyed the warm personal friendship that John Adams and Thomas Jefferson shared in their final years. Interviews with both were pained with their unwillingness to speak in positive terms about each other. When asked to characterize Burdick, Guy replied: "Well, I think you want only favorable responses, but not all of my experiences with Quentin would I classify as positive."[93] He concluded the interview by stating: "I never feared the senator as a competitor within the party, but I think he always feared me as a competitor that might some time challenge him in an election. So whereas I got along with Quentin and never had any quarrel with him, there was never the close feeling that comes when two people depend on one another, you know."[94] Burdick dismissed Guy in fewer words. "I don't have any hard feelings. We don't see each other as much as we should. Bill Guy is here. I'm in Washington."[95]

Observers of both men paint different images after 1974. "Bill Guy is not a happy man politically," said journalist Jack Zaleski, "you kind of want to say to the man: 'Get over it. That's done. It's history. Now enjoy your retirement.' He doesn't seem to be doing that and that's too bad."[96] At the heart of Guy's unhappiness is a personal fault to not forgive. "I know that there were just people that Bill Guy wouldn't forgive," said Jerome Lamb. "It turned him into a bitter old man. He could never forgive!"[97] Burdick remained on Guy's permanent list of the unforgiven. "I don't think Bill Guy will ever forgive Quentin Burdick," said Rep. Earl Pomeroy.[98] "I have never heard Quentin Burdick say nasty things about Bill Guy," recalled Chuck Fleming, "but I have heard Bill Guy say derogatory things about Quentin Burdick in private."[99]

Sometimes winning or losing politically makes all the difference in how individuals deal with each other. The 1974 senatorial race ended Guy's political career. Burdick carried on winning three more Senate terms in 1976, 1982 and 1988. A year or two after his defeat, Guy asked Burdick if he was planning to run again in 1976. Guy explained to Burdick that he was interested in running for his seat should he want to retire. Burdick's response does not appear in print, but the answer was loud and unmistakably clear. No one took Burdick's seat short of death, especially Bill Guy and later Byron Dorgan.

Endnotes

1. Lloyd Omdahl, interview by author, Jan. 18, 1995.
2. Tom Matchie, interview by author, April 17, 1995.
3. William Guy, interview by author, Jan. 20, 1995; Quentin Burdick, interview by author, Jan. 6, 1992.
4. *North Dakota Votes*, Grand Forks, UND Bureau of Governmental Affairs, 165
5. Ibid.
6. Guy, *Where Seldom was Heard*, 1-8.
7. Chub Ulmer, interview by author, April 25, 1995.
8. Guy, *Where Seldom was Heard*, 9-14.
9. Ibid., 14-24.
10. Ibid., 25-33.
11. William Guy, interview by author, Jan. 20, 1995.
12. Ibid.
13. Ibid.
14. Ibid.
15. Ibid.
16. Jerome Lamb, interview by author, Jan. 20, 1995.
17. Milton R. Young, interview by D. Jerome Tweton, folder 29, box 794, Milton R. Young Collection.
18. Jocelyn Birch Burdick, interview by author, April 18,1995.
19. Burdick interview
20. Jean Guy, interview by author, Jan. 20, 1995.
21. Stanley Moore, interview by author, Jan. 24, 1995.
22. Tom Burgum, interview by author, March 24, 1995.
23. Betty and John Maher, interview by author, April 26, 1995.
24. Walter Erdman, interview by author, Jan. 17, 1995.
25. Omdahl interview.
26. George Sinner, interview by author, Jan. 19, 1995.
27. Ibid.
28. Ibid.
29. Jim Fuglie, interview by author, Feb. 6, 1995.
30. Guy interview.
31. Gorman King Sr., interview by author, April 25, 1995.
32. Dick Backus, interview by author, April 27, 1995.
33. Fuglie interview.
34. Guy interview.
35. David Strauss, interview by author, March 30, 1995.
36. Austin Engel, interview by author, Feb. 9, 1995.
37. Tish Kelly, interview by author, Jan. 22, 1995.
38. Earl Pomeroy, interview by author, March 24, 1995.
39. Burgum interview.
40. Ibid.
41. Larry Erickson, interview by author, Feb. 9, 1995.
42. Burgum interview.
43. Chuck Fleming, interview by author, April 25, 1995.
44. Herb Meschke, interview by author, Feb. 10, 1995.
45. Bruce Hagen, interview by author, April 25, 1995.
46. Helen Pepple, interview by author, April 13, 1995.
47. Jack Zaleski, interview by author, Jan. 23, 1995.
48. Young interview.
49. Fuglie interview.
50. Heidi Heitkamp, interview by author, Jan. 27, 1995.
51. *Harley McClain v. Ben Meier and Allen Olsen* 612F.2D-349, 8th cir. 1979.
52. Young, "Race of the Century: Guy vs. Young 1974 U.S. Senate Election," (master's thesis, University of North Dakota, 1989), 45.
53. Young, "Race of the Century," 124.

54. Quentin Burdick, interview by author, Jan. 6, 1992.
55. Burgum interview.
56. Omdahl interview.
57. Guy interview.
58. Quentin Burdick interview.
59. William Guy interview.
60. Ibid.
61. Quentin Burdick interview.
62. Strauss interview.
63. Ibid.
64. Tom Stallman, interview by author, fall 1996.
65. Ibid.
66. James Jungroth, interview by author, Feb. 5, 1995.
67. Ibid.
68. Ibid.
69. Ardell Tharaldson, interview by author, Jan. 25, 1995.
70. Ibid.
71. Ibid.
72. Jungroth interview.
73. Tharaldson interview.
74. Ibid.
75. Karl Limvere, interview by author, Jan. 24, 1995.
76. Kevin Carvell, interview by author, Jan. 23, 1995.
77. Erickson interview.
78. Guy interview.
79. Omdahl interview.
80. Guy interview.
81. Chris Sylvester, interview by D. Jerome Tweton, folder 10, box 796, Milton R. Young Collection.
82. Ibid.
83. Burgum interview.
84. Ibid.
85. Young interview.
86. Mark Andrews, interview by author, April 19, 1995.
87. Young interview.
88. Charles Conrad, interview by author, March 25, 1995.
89. Tharaldson interview.
90. Bob Vogel, interview by author, Jan. 16, 1995.
91. Meschke interview.
92. Ulmer interview.
93. Guy interview.
94. Ibid.
95. Quentin Burdick interview.
96. Zaleski interview.
97. Lamb interview.
98. Pomeroy interview.
99. Fleming interview.

- eleven -

The Quiet Senator
(1960-1992)

The title of this chapter about Quentin Burdick's tenure as a United States senator was a gift from the late Senator Mike Mansfield (D-MT), who died in 2002 after a remarkable career as history professor, congressman (1943-53), senator (1953-1977), including 16 years as Senate majority leader, and ambassador to Japan (1977-1988). He proposed the title. This is how it occurred.

During an interview in his Washington office on an early March morning, Mansfield began by noting the discussion would take only a couple of minutes. When politely asked if he was short on time (the interview had been scheduled to last 30 minutes), he replied, "No. I just don't have much to say." Mansfield's premonition proved correct. When asked to characterize Quentin Burdick, the senator, he answered crisply and concisely that "He was the quiet senator. Probably said less than anyone else I've ever known in the Senate, and in the process, accomplished a great deal for North Dakota, and that's about all I know about Quent."[1]

The power of Mansfield's analysis hit home immediately. In a short phrase, he captured the essence of Burdick's long Senate career. It was a perfect title for this chapter and a perfect theme to discuss the historical significance of the last 32 years of Burdick's life. Mansfield made only two additional comments, both of which emanated from his first statement. First, in comparison to Burdick's loquacious father, Usher, Quentin was the exact opposite. This comparison, of course, was not a new discovery and remains a constant theme in this biography. For Mansfield, however, this observation was key to his analysis of Quentin. The contrast between father and son was so noticeable that the word *quiet* became a perfect characterization of the son.

Mansfield elaborated a bit further on the meaning of the word. He wanted me to know and for history to remember that although quiet is an unusual adjective to describe any United States senator, it should not be interpreted negatively. "A quiet senator," Mansfield explained, "is a standout among the hundred up there. I say that with comprehension and with understanding and with the recognition of the fact that, in that sense, he was unique."[2]

With that clarification, Mansfield chatted a while about other subjects — history, especially that of the Great Plains, and the Westerner's support of women. Mansfield then pulled out and lit his familiar pipe and sipped warm tea. The whole conversation took about 25 minutes. At the end of the interview appointment, he shook hands and said, "It took more time than I thought it would." It is fortunate that it did, for Mansfield, in his terse but historical sense, proffered a great title and an accurate theme for Burdick's Senate years.[3]

Not much will be said here, either, about Burdick's long Senate career. Just one chapter — no more, no less — and no apologies for only one chapter to cover such a long time frame. The significant historical years of Burdick were seeded and harvested before his Senate years. They were born and damaged in Williston. They were further damaged by a huge disappointment in a promising but shortened football career on the Minnesota gridiron. There were moments of satisfaction in the labor halls of Fargo and in building the North Dakota Farmers Union into a powerful economic and political organization. Political victories, however, never materialized, and the love and death of his beloved Marietta and the mental breakdown of his son, Jonathan, made him even quieter.

This chapter centers on several themes that best explain Quentin Burdick, the Quiet Senator. They include a historical overview, elections, the Welk project, Gage, aging and his state funeral.

Historical Overview

The United States Senate changed more between 1960 and 1992 than did Senator Quentin Burdick. He entered a Senate that was quite private, assisted by small staffs, and to a large extent, a body that seldom appeared every day in the public eye. Most senators were tied to their office, committee work and their constituents back home while spending little time raising campaign funds. Recess sessions were longer and partisan bickering more infrequent. Burdick preferred this old Senate atmosphere to the highly contentious new Senate. He felt comfortable working behind the scenes, depending on strong personal friendships to secure his modest legislative goals. He was a pretelevision senator and he tried to stay that way. He seldom spoke on the Senate floor, and when he did speak, he read from a written text with no visual aids. The thought of using large colored charts or enlarged comments from a newspaper never entered his mind. He hated press conferences so much that he avoided having them most of the time. He loyally attended his committee meetings, which drew the support of the chairs who appreciated his attendance, and he absolutely hated to miss a single roll-call vote. Most unique perhaps, and unlike many of his younger peers, he never showed the slightest interest in running for president. "He was not a senator for the '90s," said Senator Mark Andrews, his colleague and friend, who knew him well. "I think he was a senator for the '50s and '60s, and it was a totally different operation in those days."[4]

For Burdick, the western bond of a man being as good as his word was the essence of the old Senate, and he never abandoned it. When he gave his word, he always kept it, and he expected those who promised their word to him to do the same. It did not always happen. Sara Garland, one of Burdick's loyal staffers, told about one such incident that she wanted included in Quentin's biography. The event took place one day on the Senate floor when she was sitting next to Senator Burdick. There was an important vote before him on whether to reduce or eliminate funding for the Garrison Diversion project. He sat right up front where the senators had to come in and vote. "It's called the well," said Garland, "and, of course, by sitting there, you make it very uncomfortable for your colleagues who are coming in to vote against you. On this vote, Senator Bill Bradley (D-NJ) came in, walked by Burdick, and voted for the funding, but later, as the votes were counted, he changed his vote to "No." As he came past Senator Burdick, he said to him, "I'm sure you understand why I had to do that. I wanted to make sure that you got over 50 votes, but I'm getting a lot of pressure from the environmentalists to oppose this. Senator Burdick just smiled and nodded his head, and as Bradley walked away, [Burdick] turned to me and said, 'that son of a bitch.'"[5]

Senator Russell Long (D-LA) also knew the difference between the old Senate and the new Senate. "I liked the old Senate," said Long. "I liked the fact that senators talked to one another and knew one another, especially those who *were* there as long as Quent. He had good discretion. To tell you the truth, he was just a noble gentleman."[6]

Quentin Burdick was also the last member of North Dakota's congressional delegation to live in the state. He went home every weekend whenever possible and spent his recesses in either his Fargo residence or the Lake Melissa cottage. All his children attended public schools in the state. He lived in a modest apartment within walking distance of the Capitol and never purchased a home in the D.C. area for Jocie or any of the children. He was part United States senator and part Fargo resident. In his later years, he could not wait to leave his office and get on a plane back to North Dakota; returning after recesses became increasingly more taxing. He never took part of Washington social life. "He was a homebody," said his friend, Senator Daniel Inouye (D-HI). "When he wore a black tie, he looked like a waiter!"[7] He regularly changed his own car oil (a 1968 Cadillac with a #2 North Dakota license plate) in the Senate parking lot, always keeping a case of oil and a pair of coveralls in the trunk. He was also frugal about turning back portions of his allocated staff money. In 1983, when he was moved from the old Senate office building to the new Senator Hart building, he refused $147,000 in new office furniture. "I carried furniture over from the other office," he told the press. "I'm well situated. I don't need any more furniture."[8]

There are some important historical legacies to this quiet senator from North Dakota, the first being longevity. He served the people of North Dakota in the United States Congress for 33 years, seven months and seven days. His record of service was second only to Senator Milton Young, who served two years and almost three months longer. Nationally, the Library of Congress in 1991 ranked Burdick 105 among 173 individuals who had served 30 or more years in Congress. This was from a total number of 11,230 people who had served in Congress since 1789.[9] This was a remarkable record of longevity made even more remarkable because he was half a century old when he began his congressional service. There is one important footnote to his longevity — it is his spotless record of clean government. "I think the greatest thing about him is that there was never a scandal about anything he was ever involved in or ever did," noted Larry Erickson, a longtime Minot Democrat. "He was very honest, very forthright, and a man who really had the people's best interests at heart."[10]

Burdick was a loyal but low-key supporter of the Democratic liberal agenda throughout his entire career. He seldom strayed although he followed rather than led. "He was a Democrat!" shouted Lucy Calautti. "He did not wander off the reservation. He was an absolute team player and absolutely devoted to the Democratic cause. He voted for the average person. He voted his conscience. He was a true liberal in the best sense of that word, and he voted that way and that was the most important contribution he could make in the U.S. Senate — to vote his principles, and he did."[11]

For his entire congressional service, Burdick cast and compiled a continuous Democratic voting record. He supported civil rights, opposed conservative Republican nominees to the U.S. Supreme Court, supported President Johnson's social programs and the right for a woman to have an abortion, but voted against the Vietnam War. He asked little in return. He sought a vote here and there for Garrison Diversion, for example. But when President Jimmy Carter listed the project in his budget as one of the nation's worst environmental projects, Burdick bolted and voted against the treaty turning Teddy Roosevelt's Panama Canal over to Panama. Even a visit paid by Vice President Walter Mondale met with no success. "I got mad as hell," roared Burdick. "I really exploded! My letters from North Dakota are running 4,000 to 10 against the Panama Canal Treaty, and now they won't even give me a water project, in any shape, that could do some good for North Dakota. I'm damn mad and I've had enough of this. From now on, I'm a free person."[12] The incident was a rare exception, and for many it was not even a liberal agenda issue.

David Strauss knew the nuts and bolts of Burdick's liberal legislative agenda. He said Burdick had core values that never changed. His values included support for working people and organized labor, seniors, family farmers, agriculture and the rights of women. "He was very ahead of his time in terms of his commitment to women and the right to choose an abortion." For Strauss, what was even more remarkable about his agenda was Burdick "being able to remain steadfast in terms of those core values and survive politically representing a state like North Dakota. That's not to be underestimated."[13] Burdick never bragged about his liberalism back home.

Burdick also served in Congress under eight presidents from 1959 to 1992 — three Democratic presidents (John F. Kennedy, Lyndon B. Johnson and Jimmy Carter) and five Republican presidents (Dwight D. Eisenhower, Richard M. Nixon, Gerald R. Ford, Ronald Reagan and George H.W. Bush). Despite his longevity in Washington, Burdick was never a White House regular and seldom participated in the busy social life of the Washington establishment. He rated Johnson "the most impressive" and Reagan "the least impressive" of the presidents he served under. He gave high marks to Kennedy, whom he believed understood agriculture better than the others. He also gave passing grades (C's) to all of the others with the exception of Ford, who earned an incomplete because "he wasn't there long enough to rate." He was unimpressed with most of the Republican nominees for the Supreme Court with the exception of Anthony Kennedy. He clearly disliked Carter for supporting a host of Republican programs, but mostly for trying to kill his favorite project, Garrison Diversion.[14]

A Big Fish or a Little One?

Invariably one must ask the question of whether Senator Burdick was an insider with lots of power in Washington or whether he was an outsider who primarily represented North Dakota in the halls of Congress. The answer is mixed. Those who knew him least blew him off, especially the Eastern establishment in their annual publications about who really runs Washington. Those who knew him best, his staff, fellow senators and some executive officials, make the case that Burdick wielded much more power and influence than he was ever given credit for by others.

The *Almanac of American Politics* annually evaluates members of Congress. The 1982 publication states that Senator Burdick had never "sought to play a leadership role on major national issues." The assessment is supported with Burdick statements: "I just want to be a good North Dakota senator. I try to represent the people of my state and hope their interests coincide with the national interest."[15] Two years later, the almanac continued the same earlier theme: "Burdick is not a real power broker in the Senate." The authors concluded that the reason was really one of personal choice and character: "He simply does not possess the ambition and the desire to dominate that animate so many other Senators," and "that in turn is what makes him so attractive to North Dakotans, who tend reflexively to be suspicious of people in power."[16] Two years later, the almanac authors accused Burdick of running from Senate power by changing committees, in this case giving up a seat on the Senate Judiciary Committee with earned seniority for a lower seat on the Senate Appropriations Committee. Burdick gives "up his membership on several committees just as he was being asked to assume responsibility for managing them."[17]

By 1988, the elder Burdick was treated more as a folk hero. Criticism was replaced by admiration. "For years Burdick has been quiet in Washington, with his rumpled clothes, and au shucks manner, and beat up old car, he cut a modest social figure indeed." At the same time, the almanac showed some interest in the possibility of a challenge in that year for his seat from fellow Democrat, Representative Byron Dorgan. The threat brought out of Burdick "a recurrent motif in North Dakota politics" and that was simply an "old Senator, jealous and mistrustful of a popular young politician in his own party."[18]

Burdick himself was modest about his own legislative legacy. He once said he could not care less about what happened in Albany. That was, of course, his way of saying that issues outside of North Dakota were less important to him. He always pointed to Garrison Diversion as his greatest Senate accomplishment, which is a rather humble and revealing view of one's accomplishments for serving so long in the Senate. When pushed for more accomplishments, he added modestly: "This may sound a little corny, but I tried to respond to the needs of the ordinary person, mostly poor people. I think my record would hold that out. I haven't been a corporation supporter, but I gave them a fair break, and I'm for the family farmer and for all family situations. I have been a great friend of the Native American Indians."[19]

The case for Burdick being an influential senator comes from those who knew and worked with him on a more personal basis. One of his staunchest defenders was Bob Bergland, a fellow resident of the Red River Valley. Bergland represented northwestern Minnesota in the U.S. House of Representatives and later served as secretary of agriculture in the Carter administration. Bergland worked with Burdick for a quarter of a century and was adamant in his assessment of him as an influential member of the Senate. "He was an insider. He was a senior fellow as senators go. He was totally honest. He was the keeper of secrets. He could not be pressured into changing his mind. He just wouldn't quit." Burdick served as Bergland's mentor when he first came to Washington. Bergland called Burdick "the rock" and dismissed those who wrote that speaking on the Senate floor was in any shape or form a mark of leadership. He also shared Burdick's dislike of President Carter. "I don't think Carter had any political principles," said Bergland. "He was always kind of a wimp."[20]

Tom Burgum addressed the charge that Burdick practiced committee switching. He did not deny the fact that this was the case, but he offered some real insights into the motives. At the beginning of his Senate career, Burdick had great difficulty obtaining good committee assignments. There were a couple of major obstacles. The first impediment was Senator Lyndon Johnson, who was the Senate majority leader when Burdick arrived in the Senate. Earlier in 1960, Burdick had supported Senator John Kennedy for the Democratic nomination for president over Johnson. This was still fresh in his memory when Burdick started searching for committee assignments and Johnson was not interested in giving him good assignments. There was a second factor. Some other Southern senators in leadership positions shared doubts about Burdick for other reasons. According to Burgum, those doubts developed "because the story got around that Burdick was a Communist," and that Senator Young, a good friend of those Southern Democrats, "had helped to preach the rumor."[21]

Burdick finally got assigned to the Judiciary Committee in 1962. But he found himself stuck behind two young Democratic senators, Ted Kennedy of Massachusetts and Birch Bayh of Indiana. Both had been appointed to the committee a year earlier. Finally, after 14 years on the committee and still behind Kennedy and Bayh on the Judiciary Committee, Burdick unbeknown to virtually anyone in his office or other senators, switched to the Appropriations Committee. He was appointed in the eleventh hour by the retiring chair of the committee, Senator John McClellan (D-AR), one of those southern Democrat Senate leaders who earlier shared doubts about Burdick.

Burdick based his decision to leave Judiciary on two political realities. First, because the committee was preoccupied with two sensitive issues — abortion and school prayer — which Burdick believed were important but not key issues for North Dakota; he also believed that the Appropriations Committee was more important for him and his constituents. There was a second reason to leave the Judiciary Committee. He would never move up in the committee because he was always stuck behind Kennedy and Bayh. Ironically, within two years, both men were gone from the committee — Bayh was defeated and Kennedy switched to the Labor Committee.[22]

Burdick enjoyed the support and friendship of many senators. Unfortunately, many of them have taken their stories to the grave. Burdick had to scratch his head when asked for a list of his closest Senate friends. They're "all gone," he replied, "I'm Rip Van Winkle!"[23] Three colleagues did, however, share some personal insights into their working relationship with their friend, Senator Burdick.

Senator Russell Long began his interview by comparing the states of Louisiana and North Dakota. He said the two states had much in common. They were both located in the two poorest regions of the country, the West and the South. Although the two states and the two senators were separate on issues of race, they were together on issues of water. North Dakota lacked adequate water and Louisiana suffered from too much water, with most of the water flowing from north to south. "If there was a dam in North Dakota that was important to Quent, I know I voted for it," said Long. When asked about Garrison Diversion, the senator sat up in his chair and admitted he knew very little about it except "that is up in North Dakota and Quent wanted it. If that's what he wanted, I was going to vote for it."[24]

Senator Howell Hefflin (D-AL) established a different but equally warm relationship with Senator Burdick. The two states shared a common tradition. Alabama and North Dakota were farm states, and supporting farm programs were essential to those who served them in Congress. "I didn't know much about sugar beets," admitted Hefflin, "but I always tried to help him because he'd help me with peanuts." As for the Garrison Diversion project, Hefflin admitted he knew very little about it. "I just depended on Quentin."[25]

Senator Daniel Inouye and Senator Burdick were close friends. The two states of Hawaii and North Dakota had less in common than the bond of friendship, which existed between these two senators. When Inouye first arrived in the Capitol in August of 1959, the first person to greet him was Congressman Quentin Burdick, wearing his familiar black homburg. "He introduced himself, and we became fast friends," recalled Inouye. "He guided me through the strange byways of Congress, and as a result to this day, I support activities that have very little, if any relevance to the state of Hawaii — like REA." Burdick often got his friend to attend morning breakfasts with farmers. This was no small feat because Inouye detested eating early in the morning. But when the REA or North Dakota Farmers Union came to Washington and all wanted an early morning breakfast, he joined them. As for Garrison Diversion, when asked whether Burdick ever got his vote on the project, he smiled and answered emphatically, "always." Then he paused and added with a smile and chuckle: "Don't ask me what it was!"[26]

Neither North Dakota colleagues Senator Kent Conrad or Senator Byron Dorgan bought the insider spin. "He was a loner," said Conrad, "and he was not somebody to organize coalitions or to engage in a lot of behind-the-scenes putting together a plan. I can only remember one time that he spoke in caucus."[27] Dorgan agreed. "He was a loner, but he also was well-liked. He was a quiet part of the club — steady and consistent and people liked him, but he didn't call the shots."[28] Governor Art Link did not believe he was an insider, either, but added, "I don't think he was lazy."[29]

Senator Inouye made one additional observation that reveals a different Senator Burdick. "For example, we have a separate men's room for members of the Senate, and in that men's room they usually have two men, usually African-American men, to assist you there with towels and shining shoes. He was very generous with them because he knew that these men were receiving minimum wage and they all had families. He was treated like royalty. So at least in the men's room, Quentin Burdick was KING. They loved it because he would tip them very generously after the shoeshine. Where most of us would give a quarter or 50 cents, he would give much more than that. He was very, very generous."[30]

Elections

Quentin Burdick could not win any election in North Dakota before 1958. He ran six times and he lost six times. Ironically, Burdick could not *lose* an election after 1958. He ran seven times and he won seven times. This dramatic change in his political fortune should not be glossed over. It was more than a personal testimony to his stamina — it was also a close-up of the continual changing nature of North Dakota politics after 1960. Who would have believed that Burdick, in the years after 1960, would spend 32 years in the United States Senate? Who would have predicted that North Dakota's entire congressional delegation would be Democrat and not Republican? Who then would credit Burdick for becoming the standard-bearer of the North Dakota Democratic-NPL Party until his death in 1992? The answer then was probably no one; certainly Burdick did not make any such prediction.

Burdick never experienced a close election after his razor-thin victory over Governor John Davis in 1960. Although North Dakota Republican strategists held firm to their beliefs that Burdick could be beat, it never happened. They never even came close. In 1964, at the end of Senator William Langer's six-year-term (of which Burdick served the last four years), Republicans nominated their strongest candidate, West District Congressman Thomas Kleppe of Bismarck. Kleppe was a strong candidate and a formidable opponent to challenge Burdick. A greater historical force, however, intervened and ultimately determined the outcome. The assassination of President John F. Kennedy only a year earlier remained on most people's minds, and President Lyndon B. Johnson's leadership was positive. Moreover, in nominating Senator Barry Goldwater of Arizona to challenge Johnson, most voters supported the president. The war in Vietnam was in its infancy, and Goldwater's conservatism scared many who normally voted Republican. Johnson became only the third and last Democrat (Woodrow Wilson in 1912 and 1916, and Franklin Roosevelt in 1932 and 1936) to win North Dakota in a presidential election. Johnson defeated Goldwater by 41,577 votes and Burdick beat Kleppe by 40,583 votes, carrying 43 of the state's 53 counties.[31]

Republicans urged Kleppe to try again in 1970. They argued that 1964 was a Democratic fluke in North Dakota. The state was still Republican and Burdick was just plain lucky. He had won the primarily on the coattails of President Johnson's unprecedented victory. The White House also put pressure on Kleppe as President Richard Nixon added Burdick's name to his personal hit list of vulnerable Democratic senators. With mounting pressure and lots of money, Kleppe agreed to run against Burdick again. He, too, probably shared the belief that Burdick was weak and that he could be beaten. It did not happen. Burdick crushed Kleppe, topping him by 51,523 votes. Burdick won 50 counties while Kleppe managed to carry only three traditional rural Republican counties: Logan, McIntosh and Sheridan.[32]

After Burdick's impressive victory in 1970, other factors emerged. The first was the default of strong candidates against him in the next two elections. Republicans scratched around everywhere but without success to attract formidable opponents to run against Burdick in 1976 and 1982. A "great thing that makes you look good and win elections," said Chuck Fleming, "is when they run poor people against you, and they never mounted any challenge that I can remember that was really strong."[33] In other words, North Dakota Republicans were experiencing the same problem Democrats faced in nominating strong candidates to unseat Republican Congressman Mark Andrews. In 1976, Republicans nominated State Senator Robert Stroup of Hazen to run against Burdick. The result was a good old-fashioned political whipping. Burdick beat Stroup by 72,306 votes. He won 50 counties again. Stroup managed to win just three: McIntosh, Sheridan and his home county of Mercer. In 1982, Republicans recruited an out-of-stater, Gene Knorr, with more ties to Virginia than his home state. The results proved even worse. Burdick beat Knorr by 75,569 votes, again winning 50 counties to Knorr's three: McIntosh and Sheridan repeats and Billings.[34]

There was more disturbing news for North Dakota Republicans. In 1976, Burdick received more votes in the Democratic primary than Stroup did in the Republican primary.[35] Until that election, there were always more votes cast in the Republican primary than in the Democratic primary. Not after 1976. Burdick and other major Democratic office holders surpassed their Republican opponents in total votes cast in both the primary and the general election. North Dakota then counted more Democratic voters than Republican voters in some, but not all, statewide races. Equally important to Burdick winning was the fact that Democrats across the board fared better in the years that he ran. He was a party candidate and getting out the vote for everyone on the ticket was very important to him. With the exception of 1970, party leaders noted that the party did better with Burdick running.

Finally, although no strong Republican opponents emerged, there was a potential Democratic challenger to Burdick. This, of course, was Democratic Governor William Guy, who served 12 years as governor (1961-1973) and was the loser in a close race for the United States Senate against Senator Milton R. Young in 1974. Although Guy never sought public office after his bitter defeat in 1974, speculation often surfaced that he would challenge Burdick. He never did, even though personal relations between the two Democrats continued to deteriorate. Guy wanted Burdick to retire and so did the Republicans. Neither got their wish.

The Last Campaign

In many ways, Quentin Burdick's last campaign proved to be the most interesting of his long Senate career. He was old and in poor health. Family, staff and everyone who came in contact with him knew it. Privately he knew, too, but to acknowledge it would be a concession to his own mortality, which was a road he avoided traveling. He was also incredibly stubborn and unwilling to leave the Senate and the life he experienced since 1960. In feeling so, he was not unlike many of his older constituents who still lived in farmhouses, small towns or city neighborhoods. Many North Dakotans saw in their senior senator a mirror image of themselves, with neither appearing the same as they did 20 years earlier. Burdick looked and acted older and so did so many of them. Nor was his unwillingness to retire unlike his North Dakota Senate peers, especially William Langer, who ran in 1958, or Milton Young, who ran in 1974. All three of them understood, like many of the great Southern senators of the 20th century, that seniority was the only game played in Washington. So they played the game and stayed too long to serve their constituents well.

With Burdick's age and poor health more apparent, political talk about a possible cast of characters to run against him increased significantly. At first glance, speculation centered on whether the senator, at age 80, would even seek a sixth term. His decision would one way or another drive the election. Clearly, if Burdick chose to retire, the field would be enlarged and the election would become more engaging. The Democratic candidate most certainly would be Congressman Byron Dorgan, who was completing his fourth term in the U.S. House of Representatives. Dorgan coveted Burdick's seat — then more than ever after North Dakota Tax Commissioner Kent Conrad, his friend and colleague and six years his junior, upset Senator Mark Andrews in 1986. The Republican challenger was less certain and less likely to win than Dorgan, although an open seat often produces more and sometimes surprise candidates. The most likely were Andrews, House Majority Leader Earl Strinden of Grand Forks, and Public Service Commissioner Dale Sandstrom. If, however, Burdick decided to run, all bets were off, with the possible exception of Dorgan, who might emerge as a challenger within the party.

There is little evidence to suggest that Burdick ever gave serious consideration to retirement. In fact, the anecdotal evidence appears so compelling that the "R" word simply did not appear anywhere in his vocabulary. Stanley Moore, longtime North Dakota Farmers Union president, recalled a telephone call he made to Burdick after he won his fourth term in 1976. "I called up to congratulate him and I said facetiously, 'I want to congratulate you on your election for your last term in office,' and he hung up the phone."[36] David Strauss, who ably served Burdick in his last three campaigns, philosophized that "Burdick associated his job in the Senate with his own immortality. I think he thought if he leaves the Senate, he dies. That was his core character. He was so hell-bent on running. There was never any doubt in his mind from 1983 on that he was going to run again in 1988."[37]

Burdick's position, however, did not obviate some of his supporters from urging him to step down. "I think it was the challenge of somebody telling him," said former Governor Art Link. "Burdick had a stubborn streak in his makeup and, by God, nobody was going to tell him not to run."[38] Tom Burgum tried to talk the senator out of running and Burdick "exploded."[39] Burdick himself circled the topic. "I think the best way to approach aging is not to think about it," and then he added in a more testy voice, "I don't worry about clinging to a hospital bed the last few hours of my life. I don't think about things like that!"[40]

Dorgan operatives pursued a plan to promote his candidacy before Burdick got around to making his decision to retire. The group was loosely organized. It included state Senators Rick Maxiner of Bowman and Rollie Redlin of Minot, as well as North Dakota Education Association spokesperson Willis Heinrich of Bismarck, and some old-timers such as Gorman King Sr. The group was pro-Dorgan more than it was anti-Burdick. They believed that Burdick's time was up and that by pushing Dorgan early, they might force him out of running again and also get a head start on Republican challengers. The group circulated a letter and met in private to discuss strategy and build more Democratic support for Dorgan's candidacy. Dorgan promised the group nothing but played the game with them for about a year.[41]

Privately, Dorgan and his staff remained frustrated by Burdick's unwillingness to retire. "He should have stepped down," exclaimed Dorgan. "He knew, and I think everybody else knew, that he was staying too long, but it is hard not to. Young stayed too long. Quentin stayed too long, and I hope no one ever says that about me."[42] Dorgan's staffers were more critical of Burdick. "He didn't show enough leadership in the Senate, not nearly enough," said Lucy Calautti, Dorgan's chief administrative head.[43] While Kevin Carvell, Dorgan's Fargo coordinator, said Burdick was just plain jealous of Dorgan. "You can see some uncomfortableness about this rising star coming up along side of you and eclipsing you."[44]

Some leading Democrats agreed with Dorgan, but kept their opinions to themselves. "I believe there is a time to quit," said Governor George Sinner, "that Dorgan had the courage, or in Quentin's point of view, the haughtiness to suggest that time had run out, I mean that is too bad."[45] Austin Engel, former executive head of the party, agreed. "I think he hung in far too long. It would have been much better to have retired gracefully and leave the field open."[46]

The Dorgan challenge did not go unnoticed. North Dakota is a sparsely populated state with many people who have big ears, especially among those involved in politics. It did not take very long for the Burdick staff to hear about the Dorgan moves. Jim Fuglie, North Dakota tourism director and former executive director of the party, recalled just how clever the Burdick people were in tracing the opposition:

> This group (I think Rick Maxiner was the leader) called a meeting at the Peacock Alley in Bismarck of people whose names were not on the letter to feel out the sense of Bismarck Democrats for whether Byron should run for the Senate or not. A lot of people said a lot of things. These were all Dorgan people, but Burdick had a spy there. I don't know who it was. The next morning, David Strauss called me and repeated almost verbatim the remarks of everyone in the room. I don't know who was there, but I wish,you know, that I'd thought to look around. I assumed that it was all Dorgan people there because everybody there was encouraging Dorgan to run, but someone wasn't [laughter]. It was great sabotage! Somebody was either taking really good notes or had a really great memory because I said like 15 words and David knew all 15 of them. He called me first to let me know, but he wasn't angry with me because I wasn't vociferous or anything, but he was really pissed at some of the people."[47]

In the meantime, Dorgan supporters proceeded on different fronts. Arly Richau, a Bismarck attorney, organized a statewide group called "North Dakota Citizens for 88." It was really a Dorgan for Senate committee, headed by a person closely identified with Dorgan. Richau's group attempted to shut the campaign funding faucet off for Burdick. They did so by writing hundreds of letters around the country to various PACs. Their letters carried the same message: Do not invest your PAC money to support a Burdick campaign because Rep. Dorgan is considering a challenge and the polls demonstrate that he enjoys a commanding lead over Burdick in a hypothetical race.[48] Dorgan stayed way ahead of Burdick in other polls throughout 1987 and early 1988.

As Democrats prepared for their 1988 spring state convention, many Burdick loyalists became aware of another strategy. Dorgan had already begun lining up his supporters to be delegates to the convention and had taken control of the Credentials Committee. When Sarah Vogel went to her District 49 convention in Bismarck, she discovered a stacked deck: "I mean, the slates of candidates had been thoroughly cooked up behind the scenes and my folks were not on the list and it was awful."[49] Arvin Kvasager, a longtime Burdick supporter and labor leader in Grand Forks, discovered the same operative in his district. He went to Dorgan and told him: "If you've done that, count us out. We'll sit and watch from the sidelines."[50] Perhaps most damaging to the Dorgan supporters was their treatment of former Governor Art Link, who also was passed over as a delegate.

Burdick's decision to run probably surprised no one who knew him in either the state's Democrat or Republican parties, although he might have surprised Dorgan. Earl Pomeroy, then commissioner of insurance, dubbed Burdick's last campaign as "The Lazarus Project." He called it "one of the greatest political comebacks in North Dakota history when Quentin was polling 15 percent to Dorgan's 70 to 80 percent."[51] Inside the Burdick camp, the senator's reaction was predictable and volatile. "It pissed him off greatly," said Mary Wakefield, who was Burdick's chief administrative head from 1988-1992. She added that the senator was accommodating most of the time, but "if he thought he was being taken advantage of or if somebody was cutting into his jurisdiction or his press or whatever it was, there would be hell to pay."[52] Geraldine Gaginis, Burdick's personal secretary, was more tactful, simply adding that the senator was "incredibly competitive."[53] Sara Garland, Burdick's longtime staffer, put the Dorgan challenge in a broader perspective. "Senator Burdick felt that Byron Dorgan should wait his turn. He was a traditionalist in that this is the way the system works."[54]

The much-expected Burdick-Dorgan showdown never occurred. It was one of the great what-ifs of modern North Dakota politics. The best explanation as to why Dorgan did not challenge came during a rather brief and uncomfortable interview: "As I began to prepare to think about it, I realized that what I was going to have to do in the districts in the party was going to be so gut-wrenching for the party that I thought it would benefit me at the expense of the party, and I just decided not to do it." Dorgan added that there were other factors as well. "I had just gotten remarried the previous April, and I just didn't want to commit myself to what that was going to be either in terms of time. But mostly, [I] saw what it was going to do to my friends." Dorgan, however, minced no words in predicting what would have been the outcome of his challenge to Burdick. "I'm convinced I would have beaten him and convinced I would have beaten him in the party."[55]

Burdick, when asked about Dorgan's decision, replied: "Why didn't he run?" and then, "He wouldn't have won."[56]

David Strauss opined more than Burdick. "Dorgan was a very formidable politician and would have given Senator Burdick a real run for his money ... but we had plenty of resources and Burdick was the incumbent." As for Dorgan's assertion that he would have won the party's nomination, "I disagree with that," said Strauss. "I think our strength was the base. We had a better labor record, we were more liberal and more pro-choice. We would have kicked his butt at the convention."[57]

Whether pro-Dorgan or pro-Burdick, supporters of the men had strong opinions about the results in that hypothetical 1988 showdown. "Dorgan is a wire walker," stated Tom Burgum, a Burdick loyalist. "He doesn't like to get a hold of [one] wire until he makes sure he has a hold of the other one."[58] Jon Lindgren, longtime Fargo mayor and Burdick supporter, said the senator "knew Dorgan was a waffler" and that "he knew how to deal with that one."[59] Ardell Tharaldson stated, "Dorgan underestimated Burdick. When he got somebody to run the flag up the pole to see what happened, he had no idea just how tough the game gets played. Loyalty is a commodity that you cannot change."[60] Jim Fuglie, on the other hand, conceded that "Dorgan might have won, but given enough time, David Strauss would have raised a few million dollars and just beat the shit out of Dorgan."[61] In the end, Fuglie believed that it was Dorgan's good friend, Senator Kent Conrad, who ultimately talked him out of making the race. Lloyd Omdahl probably said it best from the Dorgan side: "I would have voted for Dorgan," but "Burdick would have run the race."[62]

History can record all kind of reasons why Representative Byron Dorgan stepped back from his 1988 challenge to unseat Senator Quentin Burdick. Some reasons play well; some do not. Certainly the political well-being of the North Dakota Democratic-NPL Party was spared a major blood-letting. Dorgan's decision on this factor comes across as magnanimous. Party first and Dorgan second. Other reasons pale — like citing personal reasons to save a third marriage and, of course, the long-term reason not mentioned: Dorgan's decision not to challenge in 1988 meant waiting then in order not to lose later.

In the final scene of the personal confrontation between these two powerful politicians, only one conclusion stands. On the day of the game, only one candidate, an old but gentle warrior, showed up. He was ready, even primed, to defend a Senate seat for which he had worked to win and retain. On the other side of the line, no opponent came forth. Representative Dorgan, for whatever personal reasons and political considerations, was absent. He was, in the political box score of North Dakota political history, simply recorded as a "no show."

Somehow that final scene with the old politician standing alone with his rumpled uniform of seniority, still eager to fight to the death, and the young

Turk dressed in Washington Bond, fit, trim, hairpiece and all, yet unwilling to take the ultimate risk of his political career, symbolizes the major character difference between Quentin Burdick and Byron Dorgan.

The Earl of Strinden

Earl Strinden, a Republican member of the North Dakota House of Representatives from Grand Forks, influenced a great deal of North Dakota politics for almost two decades between the mid-1970s and the early 1990s. He did so by wearing two uniforms, which afforded him statewide contacts and tremendous political influence. His first uniform came embroidered with an elephant logo. It symbolized the Republican Party and his masterful control of it as majority leader of the House of Representatives from 1975-1991, minus the 1983 session, when he was reduced to the minority leader. In Grand Forks and elsewhere, Strinden proudly wore a green blazer, which represented his position as the executive vice president of the University of North Dakota (UND) Alumni Association. In his Bismarck office in the state Capitol, Strinden singularly controlled the legislative branch of government. He worked as the only full-time legislator of either party in a state proud of having only a part-time citizen legislature. In his UND Alumni House, Strinden effectively administered one of the largest and most influential statewide organizations. With a wardrobe consisting of these two well-known uniforms, Strinden combined power and controversy, both of which soon earned him the title: The Earl of Strinden.

Strinden exerted more political influence when North Dakota elected a Democratic governor. Unfortunately for North Dakota Democrats, this occurred far too often, and in all but Strinden's four years of House leadership when Allen Olson served one term as governor (1981-1985). Strinden forced Democrats to play defense even when they controlled the governor's office. He repeatedly pontificated that the Legislature was the policy branch of state government (and he was the policymarker), and most Democrats seemed to agree with his sermon. Instead of playing offense, they almost always resorted to defensive measures. In 1975 and 1977 sessions, Democrat leaders regularly asked each other: "What is Strinden going to do?" instead of simply planning what they were going to do.

Strinden relished his role as the Democratic spoiler, but especially to those who were elected from his hometown of Grand Forks. He never could accept their presence after 1974, when UND students elected several of them in a multicity Senate district and then again in single-city Senate districts. He was particularly vindictive to Representative Eliot Glassheim, who served in the

1975 session and later sessions, and to Judy DeMers, who was first elected to the House in 1982 and later served many years in the Senate. Strinden was protective of his Grand Forks hegemony while the Democrats, by winning elections on his home field, were energized. They tried to embarrass Strinden as much as he worked to undercut them. There was never love lost between all North Dakota Democrats and Strinden, their Republican nemesis. Among Grand Forks Democrats, however, there was only contempt and political war. Their mission, although never successful, was to dethrone the "Earl of Strinden" and chase him out of his kingdom. Unfortunately, the more they tried, the more unsuccessful they became. Strinden was aided by Jack Hagerty, the Republican editor of the *Grand Forks Herald*, whom Strinden fed regularly with his spin on every issue; Hagerty ended up publishing most of it.

The strongest challenger to Strinden during the governorship of Art Link was then North Dakota Tax Commissioner Byron Dorgan (1969-1980). Although he was 11 years younger than Strinden, he became the strongest voice of the North Dakota Democratic-NPL Party in the bitter and deeply contentious partisan fights over coal development in the late 1970s. Both men drew from equally supportive constituencies, and both engaged each other in political debate in Bismarck and at UND on the complex issues of the coal severance tax and reclamation. In 1980, both warriors seemed poised to fight each other for the state's one U.S. House seat, left vacant by U.S. Representative Mark Andrews' announcement that he would be a candidate for the U.S. Senate seat left open by the resignation of aging Senator Milton Young. Would both Strinden and Dorgan now run for Andrews' open House seat?

The 1980 Strinden-Dorgan U.S. House race never materialized. It remains as another one of the great *what-ifs* of contemporary North Dakota politics. In the end, Republicans gave Dorgan a free pass to Washington by nominating State Senator Jim Smykowski of Cayuga, North Dakota. Dorgan easily put the ultra-conservative legislator away by 41,653 votes (166,340 to 124,707).[63] Strinden explained his decision as a missed opportunity and one that he simply could not mount at that time. "In 1980, there was a lot of pressure on me," said Strinden, "to run for the House seat. Milt Young was very, very adamant that I absolutely had to run for the open Andrews seat. The timing wasn't good for me. I still had kids at home and in school and maybe I just didn't want to go through all you have to go through. Not being financially in a position to put very much on the poker table of politics, either, but anyway, I turned that down."[64] Strinden had more to say about the 1980 race against Dorgan. "Timing is everything," repeated Strinden. "I think I could have won that. It was a Ronald Reagan year, a good Republican year. Yes, I could have won that and that would have changed a lot of things for me. I would have liked to run against Byron."[65]

Eight years later, Strinden was still a powerful legislative leader. But he was not as popular as he was in 1980. In politics, eight years is a long, long time, and although he remained at the center of most state political issues, his aggressive posture made him more unpopular. On television, Strinden's nasty style of belittling his opponents came off poorly. Yes, he was still effective, but he was less likable. By 1988, Strinden enjoyed high statewide name recognition as well as high negative ratings. He was, in the public eye, just simply hard to like. At 58 years of age, Strinden appeared near the end of his long legislative career. He had served for a long time and he looked for one opportunity to run for statewide office before he pulled the plug completely. The opportunity came in 1988, when his party encouraged him to run against North Dakota's senior senator, Quentin Burdick, who was 22 years older, not in good health, and with a huge war chest to ward off any Republican challenger.

Strinden accepted the draft without any illusions. This was a tough race and he was the clear underdog. Yet, he was a good soldier and always a loyal member of the Republican Party. His children were older and his personal financial situation better. This year was also like 1980 – a presidential one – and no Republican had failed to carry North Dakota since 1964. After eight years of the Reagan presidency, most North Dakotans were supportive of turning his legacy over to Vice President George H. Bush. These were important factors that contributed to Strinden's willingness to enter the race. But there was one overriding reason that made the race worthwhile, and that was the age and health of his opponent. As Strinden explained, "I knew that the only opportunity I had to win was for the people of North Dakota to realize that Quentin was no longer in the kind of health that should or would allow him to serve anymore in Washington." But it would be a tough sell. "It was very tough. There were so many instances and a lot of people knew that. They had protected Quentin. We knew that Quentin would get lost in the Senate office building, we knew that he would get up and try to get on the wrong airplane, and we had all kinds of firsthand stories about Quentin showing that he just really didn't remember what was going on or understand what was going on. We knew that his physical condition was also quite serious and that he had a number of problems, but how do you establish that?"[66]

The health gambit failed. Strinden never established the support of most North Dakotans to have him replace the aging senator. Burdick crushed Strinden, defeating him by 58,962 votes (171,899 to 112,937). Burdick won 50 counties. Strinden won only three counties: Dickey, McIntosh and Sheridan. The ultimate defeat, however, came in Grand Forks County with Burdick beating Strinden by 5,469 votes (14,821 to 9,352). In addition, Burdick received 5,000 more votes than presidential winner Vice President George Bush, and Strinden garnered 14,000 fewer votes than presidential loser Michael Dukakis.[67] "In 1988, it wasn't even close," said Burdick, "and they said it was going to be. It turned out so well out there in Grand Forks, I couldn't believe it."[68]

In retrospect, Strinden attributed his loss to several factors. One of the primary reasons was external. The Republican Senatorial Campaign Committee, headed by Senator Rudy Boshkowitz of Minnesota, put a leash on Strinden's campaign. It instructed him from day one to avoid personal attacks on Burdick. Its power was absolute because Boshkowitz controlled the purse strings. "So my campaign was way too much controlled out of Washington," said Strinden. When Strinden began to run strong ads attacking Burdick, Boshkowitz "pulled [them]."[69] Although Strinden did not come right out and state that the Senatorial Campaign Committee doubted that Burdick could be defeated, it was clear that it was not interested in investing lots of money in a strong negative campaign against him. Strinden's candidacy from Washington was a long shot, and it simply was not interested in going to the wall to make a real contest out of it.

Equally important in Strinden's game plan was Burdick's health. The strategy failed, not because of anything that Strinden did wrong, but because Burdick was hospitalized for prostrate cancer. At that instance, the entire focus of the campaign shifted to daily reports about his condition and recovery. Suddenly Burdick's recovery became the major focus of the campaign, and North Dakotans showed sympathy for him rather than support for his opponent. Burdick's poll numbers went higher while Strinden's poll numbers went down. "Can you imagine people getting called about this brave man fighting cancer," asked Strinden, "and then they get a telephone call about who are you going to vote for, and we could never ever recover — and we never did recover in the campaign."[70] In the final analysis, Strinden acknowledged that the lack of support from Washington, the attack ads against him by Burdick and the health issues backfiring accounted for his defeat. Privately, Strinden quipped that his biggest nightmare in the whole election was that Burdick would die and he would still beat him.[71]

North Dakota Democrats obviously interpreted the election results quite differently. After being routed regularly by Strinden's ruthless style of politics for more than two decades, there was finally political justice. At last, a Democrat got into the ring with the Earl of Strinden and whipped him badly. The fact that the trouncing came from the oldest living Democrat holding office in the state made no difference whatsoever. The joy in their ranks was unmistakable. "My advice to Republicans in 1988 would have been to spend a lot of time cultivating and searching for somebody who is young and charismatic," observed Lucy Calautti, "but they didn't have a lot of those."[72] Ardell Tharaldson, a long-time Democratic activist, was more brutal. "I'm convinced that Earl Strinden is the only man he could have beaten at election."[73]

History will most remember only two debates during the last week of October 1988 as the focal point of the election. The first debate occurred in Fargo on Sunday, October 24. According to newspaper accounts, Strinden came out swinging. He took the offense from the opening bell and never relented, even chiding his opponent to prolong the fight and to continue the debate beyond the previously agreed time limits. Burdick was slow in responding and often used prepared notes, which clearly upset his adversary. Burdick seldom landed a direct punch to his more aggressive opponent, and although his counterpunches were lacking in strength, they did prove effective. Burdick had handled the onslaught with a passing grade and, although slouched at the conclusion, he was still on his feet.[74]

Mike Jacobs, the young editor of the *Grand Forks Herald* who replaced Hagerty and whose columns and editorials were widely read, analyzed the first debate. Although at times Jacobs remained an admirer of Strinden's legislative prowess, he opined what many North Dakotans took away from the first debate. "Strinden," wrote Jacobs, "just doesn't click with North Dakotans. He seems too strident, too impersonal and too mean. His emphasis on debates with Burdick, designed to show the senator's frailty, had the opposite effect, and Strinden came out the loser because it emphasized his image of meanness. Burdick's buoyancy reflects it."[75]

The second debate quickly eclipsed the first. It took place on Friday, October 28, at the North Dakota Heritage Center in Bismarck, again before a statewide television audience. This was Strinden's last chance to make an impression and Burdick's last opportunity to demonstrate he was physically fit to serve another term. The main bout was for the most part a repeat of the previous one. Strinden, again without notes, took the offense from the start and continued punching away at his older opponent for the entire debate. Burdick again responded by reading from his notes. Same scenario. Same ending. No knockouts.

Not quite. In fact, what took place after the debate came to symbolize the entire campaign. It was only a few memorable seconds caught on television forever. As the two came together to shake hands, Strinden turned to Burdick and said something like: "You did a good job of reading" your notes. Burdick immediately jerked Strinden off balance and responded, "You're damn right!"[76] That was it, or in singer Peggy Lee's words, *Is That All There Is?* Yes, that was all there was. The old man with the still steel grip of his former youth, embarrassed the most powerful Republican in North Dakota by literally pulling him off balance. It was Burdick's last physical demonstration of strength. The Gentle Warrior was still alive. The incident received more press than any other single issue in the campaign.

When asked about the incident in 1922, Burdick recalled:

> Strinden came up to me and said: "want to congratulate you. You read that speech awful well."
> I said: "You're damn right," and I just pulled him off balance.
> When asked if the incident was planned, Burdick replied angrily, "Hell, no!"[77]

After the debate in Grand Forks, Democrats took to the streets in celebration. "The turning point in the debate," said Eliot Glassheim, who was then in charge of Burdick's Grand Forks office, was when the senator pulled Strinden off balance after the debate. "I saw it on television. It was just wonderful!"[78] In Glassheim's eyes, this was the moment he was waiting for, this was the moment Grand Forks Democrats were waiting for, the embarrassment of Strinden before the eyes of the state. Other Democrats around the state joined in the celebration. "The impression was he almost fell down," observed Sarah Vogel, "and Senator Burdick was just grinning — sort of like — call me an old man!"[79] Chuck Fleming, Governor George Sinner's right-hand man and a former legislative foe of Strinden, said what most Democrats will never forget about the debate and the election and that final incident: "I'm still around and I'm King of the Hill!"[80]

Strinden pooh-poohed the impact of the debates. "The debates didn't make any difference. There was certainly a lot of concern, though. David Strauss was on pins and needles. He was sitting there mouthing and giving more signals to Quentin." As for the handshake incident following the last debate, Strinden was adamant that it had no impact whatsoever in his defeat. None. "At the very end of the debate," according to Strinden, "I said to Quentin: 'You read that well.' The debate was over and we still had our microphones wired to our ties and I leaned over to shake hands with Quentin. Quentin grasped my hand and tried to pull me over so he pulled me a couple of steps and of course that was reported as feisty and showing what a feisty fighter he was, but really, I looked on it as childish and probably a sign that Quentin had slipped some."[81]

Not everyone in Grand Forks supported Burdick or the incident at the end of the second debate. "I knew Earl Strinden personally," said Suezette Bieri, "and I felt sorry for him having to run against this legend and knowing that it was just this incredible uphill battle. I didn't think that Burdick should have run for re-election." As for the debate incident, Bieri agreed completely with Strinden. "I though it was a cheap trick. It gave the impression that he was physically in control and if he was physically in control, he was mentally, too. That's not true."[82]

Power, Pork and Welk

When the Democrats regained control of the United States Senate following the 1986 congressional elections, Senator Burdick entered a second and more scrutinized phase of his Senate career and one that would remain with him until his death in September of 1992. After 26 years of being a "quiet senator," he emerged as the chairman of the Senate Committee on Environment and Public Works and the chair of the Senate Appropriations Subcommittee on Agriculture. He had been a member of the Appropriations Committee since 1979, but he had never served as chair of any subcommittee. This sudden departure from obscurity did not go unnoticed in the national press. "The jovial, gentlemanly Democrat from North Dakota has quietly and effectively served the interests of his native state," wrote Philip Shabecoff of the *New York Times*, "but he has never been chairman of a full Congressional Committee, no major laws bear his name, and he has conducted no headline grabbing investigative hearings."[83]

Burdick went on to explain to the *Times* reporter why it took him so long to become chair of Senate Committee in a Senate controlled almost his entire career by Democrats. Starting with a sports analogy, Burdick responded that "the ball bounces in strange ways." On a more serious note, Burdick tried a historical approach. He commented that Senator Milton Young, who had served longer in the Senate from North Dakota than he had, had never held a chairmanship. Although this was true on the surface, the reporter did not pursue it deeper by noting that the Republicans seldom held control of the Senate for all the years Young served in the Senate.[84]

Burdick's work as chair of the Environment and Public Works Committee was by all accounts low-key. He was the senior Democrat and he did chair the committee. Yet, he delegated substantial power to four Democratic members on the committee: Senators George Mitchell of Maine, Daniel Patrick Moynihan of New York, Frank Lautenberg of New Jersey and Max Baucus of Montana. Committee work centered on two main issues — a clean air bill and reauthorization of the Federal Highway Program.[85] Clean air, under Mitchell's leadership, became law, and even overcame a presidential veto by the first President George Bush; Burdick's role, except to protect emissions from coal generating plants in North Dakota, was minor. The new federal highway formula proved very beneficial to North Dakota, but again the committee work was accomplished by others, most notably David Strauss, who moved over to become the chief of staff for the entire committee. Still, North Dakotans appreciated Burdick's contribution. "He did well for North Dakota," recalled Dick Backus, longtime House Democratic leader and the state's highway commissioner from 1989-1993. "It was a formula change so that the rural states got more back than they put in. He did tremendously, exceeding well, and better than I ever dreamed."[86]

Reed Karaim, who worked for Knight Ridder newspapers on Capitol Hill, covered Burdick's chairmanship for the *Grand Forks Herald*. He characterized Burdick as being "the most carefully scripted Senate committee chairman" he had ever seen in Washington. To prove his assessment, he recalled the following incident: "I was at a hearing of the Environment and Public Works Committee once when they had to adjourn because of a vote. Burdick looked down at a sheet of paper that David Strauss slid in front of him and announced, 'We will now adjourn for 15 minutes.' When the senators had left, I wandered up to the desk and looked at the piece of paper that Strauss had slid forward. It was still sitting on the desk. On it, in big capital letters, was written: 'WE WILL NOW ADJOURN FOR FIFTEEN MINUTES.'"[87] Karaim believed unequivocally that Strauss was the single most important person who made the committee function. "It was David who handled the day-to-day mechanics that kept all the subcommittee chairman satisfied, that saw that things got done and that the press got taken care [of]. It was an amazing feat of organization and detail work."[88]

Others closer to Burdick and more loyal to him saw his chairmanship quite differently. Gary Holm, active in North Dakota Young Democrats in the '60s, chatted with Burdick on a regular, monthly basis between 1985 and 1990. Holm worked elsewhere in Washington, but Burdick usually found time to spend with him. At first blush, Holm noted a dramatic change in Burdick's dress and behavior. "It was like he metamorphosed. This guy all of a sudden has new blood, new energy, new suit and a new sign." A few weeks later, however, old North Dakota habits returned. "I don't remember when it was," said Holm, "but not too far down the road, the old desk plate was back to Quentin Burdick, and all of a sudden the suits started to look like they were getting more wrinkled again. Before too long, he was back into the old Burdick routine."[89] As for his chairmanship, Bruce McKay, who worked for Burdick from 1986-1992, took aim at those who made light of his tenure. "No. Burdick was not a young dynamic committee chairperson who ruled with an iron fist. No one would argue that, and neither would he. Instead, Burdick did what many senior committee chairs did. He organized the meeting, took care of his home state interests, kept the agenda moving and never tried to run the committee."[90]

Work as chair of the Agriculture Appropriations Committee was less public. Burdick felt more at home with members of the parent committee (who were far less partisan than the other committee) and with the various U.S. Department of Agriculture heads he had learned to know and respect through the years. This was home turf and Burdick knew the landscape. There was a sudden rush and a new open-door policy for North Dakota institutions and agencies to submit funding proposals through Burdick's office. It was almost always easier to hide a little pork in an appropriation bill than anywhere else. Now it was North Dakota's turn.

It is difficult and unnecessary for the purposes of this work to determine the total federal dollars channeled through Burdick's Appropriations Agriculture subcommittee for North Dakota. In the larger scale, it was peanuts compared to Alaska or West Virginia but very significant for a small rural state. David Strauss recalled that in 1992, there was $100 million more in Senate appropriations bills for the state than House appropriations. "I mean, we are talking about tangible benefits for North Dakota," said Strauss. "Burdick had his own style in terms of how he related to his colleagues. He was able to accomplish a lot because he had a style that worked well and his relationships with his colleagues was extremely important."[91]

A couple of illustrations with North Dakota agencies demonstrate in more detail just how this worked. The first example was the University of North Dakota. President Tom Clifford contracted with Sara Garland, a UND graduate and former longtime Burdick staffer (1977-1988) who was then a private consultant, to shepherd UND projects through Burdick's subcommittee. She was the perfect choice, and although UND was not her only client, it was an important one to her. She also had access to Burdick that few, if any, lobbyists ever enjoyed. "She was fantastic," exclaimed Clifford. "There was no one like Sara Garland, and there was no one who had the affection that Burdick had for Garland. She was a daughter." Clifford gave her high marks for the structuring of grants for medicine, aerospace and energy that went to the university from 1988-1992.[92]

A second example centered on a master plan for North Dakota tourism — an ambitious vision to secure substantial funding for Fort Union, Fort Lincoln, Knife River and the north unit of Theodore Roosevelt National Park. The impetus for these projects came from Jim Fuglie, North Dakota tourism director, and Doug Eiken, director of state parks. The real driver, however, was Fuglie, the former executive director of the North Dakota Democratic-NPL Party who maintained close ties to the entire North Dakota congressional delegation. There were many stages to the plan, and some were channeled through the efforts of Senator Mark Andrews and Senator Kent Conrad, who defeated Andrews in the 1986 election. Soon after Burdick assumed chair of the Appropriations Agriculture subcommittee, all North Dakota tourism-related projects were funneled to his committee through Fuglie and Eiken. There was also a gentlemen's agreement between them and the heads of smaller city and county organizations to work through Fuglie and Eiken to get to Burdick. "We agreed that we would continue this forever. That we would continue to put a couple of million dollars a year on the Park Service budget to do these kinds of projects," said Fuglie. But Fuglie was insistent that "all tourism projects seeking federal dollars must first come to him or Eiken and they would approach Burdick for the money."[93]

Initially, everything worked according to plan. Everyone played the game the way it was supposed to be played and the projects continued to receive federal funding through Burdick's subcommittee. That is until a lone rider by the name of Gary Saturn rode into town and upset the gravy train. Saturn was a freelancer who ignored the gentlemen's agreement and went directly to Burdick. His proposal was to secure $500,000 in federal funding to complete the renovation of the Lawrence Welk home in Strasburg, North Dakota, and to construct a Germans from Russia Heritage Center adjacent to Welk's birthplace. Saturn's idea got full support from those in Strasburg, as well as from others in the state who were deeply involved in the preservation and dissemination of North Dakota Germans from Russia heritage. And, guess what?

To the surprise of almost everyone, especially Fuglie and Eiken and even Strauss, the whole $500,000 appropriation mysteriously appeared on a markup of a bill reported out of Burdick's subcommittee. "We've really been screwed here," Fuglie told Eiken. "This is not good because it wasn't anywhere on our priority list."[94]

If state officials expressed anger about the Welk project, the other two members of the North Dakota congressional delegation were caught completely off guard. "I was flabbergasted by it," said Senator Conrad. He recalled in great detail being informed of it by Representative Dorgan, who called him while he was eating lunch in the Senate dining room. "Do you know there's $500,000 in this Appropriation bill for the Welk museum?" Conrad replied, "No" and he explained to Dorgan that he had only requested $50,000. "I wonder if this is a numerical error," he asked his friend, did "somebody put in another zero?" Dorgan said he had no idea what happened, but that he would immediately try to reduce the amount "because this will be highly controversial and could cause a backlash." Conrad agreed, and after finishing his lunch, returned to his office. Dorgan called again. "You aren't going to believe this," he told Conrad. "The $500,000 amount is still in!," explaining that "they were afraid if they took it out [on the House side] Quentin would take something of their's out."[95]

Welk's music soon played to a full audience in the winter of 1991. For some, it became a national symbol of unnecessary waste in government, or pork, if you like, that must be curtailed. For others, it revealed the unchecked power of senior members of Congress to hide funds for their pet projects in larger appropriation bills without debate and usually without public exposure. In truth, there was nothing unusual about the Welk project at all. Every state promoted similar projects, and if known to the public, would produce the same criticisms. This session was no different. There were dozens of pork bills marinating in both houses of Congress, put there by members of both political parties who expected most of them to be approved. None seemed to matter except one: a little tenderloin of $500,000 for a Lawrence Welk museum in North Dakota, put there by its state's senior senator, Quentin Burdick.

Dorgan's fears about the Welk appropriation came true. In early February, Rep. Jim Slattery (D-KS) quickly gathered 60 co-sponsors in the House to rescind the Welk project. Although his amendment included other pork bills, no one seemed to pay attention to any of them except the Welk item. It was too good a story to leave alone. The *New York Times* editorialized that "such excesses flow from a budget process that permits powerful lawmakers to quietly insert their pet projects, however marginal, in funding bills without real debate or scrutiny by the appropriations committees."[96] In fairness to the *Times* editorial, it did quote an unidentified North Dakotan who quipped: "If they are going to throw money away, we might as well get some of it."[97]

North Dakota, however, did not receive the money. On March 8, the House approved the Slattery motion and repealed the entire $500,000 appropriation. The federal government was not going to spend money on these pet projects, at least not one with the name of Lawrence Welk attached to it. Slattery's Kansas Democratic colleague, Rep. Dan Glickman, expressed a sigh of relief after the vote. "No issue caused us more grief," he said. The House then moved on to approve other appropriations bills, which included a $650 million package in aid for Israel and $4.3 billion supplemental appropriation bill to pay some of the domestic costs of the Gulf War.[98]

The whole episode hit a final chord four days later when Adam Clymer of the *Times* took a parting shot at Burdick's bill. He wrote that the Welk appropriation "was scorned outside of the capital as the epitome of selfish pork barrel spending at a time when the poor, or even the military were not being suitably taken care of." Clymer also opened his column to remarks by Rep. Silvio Conte (R-MA), a fiscal watchdog of federal spending for Garrison Diversion over the years. Conte mixed political scorn with popular culture rhetoric, and with a one, and a two, and a three, asked sarcastically: "What will they do for an encore? Earmark funds to renovate Guy Lombardo's speedboat? Or restore Artie Shaw's wedding tuxedo?"[99]

Many North Dakotans blew off the Eastern spin like a tumbleweed blowing down Highway 2 in the spring. They knew from past episodes that writers from the East knew nothing about the northern Great Plains, and those who faked they did often confused what was in South Dakota, such as Mount Rushmore, with North Dakota. For New Yorkers, the music of Lawrence Welk was regional at best and inferior to the music of the streets of New York. "This is a class thing," said Suezette Bieri of Grand Forks. "I think if Burdick had tried to get $500,000 to build a museum in Jamestown for Peggy Lee, there would have been no outcry at all because Peggy Lee is respected as a musician among the people who consider themselves 'intelligencia.' Peggy Lee can go on Broadway and be accepted. Lawrence Welk represents the polyester suit crowd, the mechanics, the farmers, and has always been seen as a hick."[100]

Senator Daniel Inouye, one of Burdick's closest Senate colleagues, echoed Bieri's assessment. He recalled that he and Burdick had discussed the Welk appropriation after the national press roast. "Lawrence Welk was not the music of Manhattan or Berkeley or Hollywood or places like that," began Inouye. "It was the music of Iowa, Nebraska and the Dakotas. I can almost see the corn silk and those things floating around. I'm a lifelong member of the musicians union, but that doesn't make me an expert on music, but I happen to know that there is a place in America for Leonard Bernstein and for Lawrence Welk."[101]

Aside from the cultural bias was the argument of the nature and amount of the appropriation. By any standards, this grant was small potatoes and minuscule to the huge amounts that went to other states. "Half a million for Lawrence Welk is probably no worse than $4 million for Warren Harding," said Jerome Lamb of Fargo sarcastically. "That sort of thing goes on all the time. It just happens that Lawrence is a little bit more funnier."[102] Historian D. Jerome Tweton noted that if you peeled off the label, "it was purely economic development for a rural part of North Dakota."[103] Nothing more. Nothing less. Yet, others, such as Karaim, maintained that it was not a bum rap. It really boils down to whether the federal government should play a role in paying for cultural sites, or whether Lawrence Welk rises to a level of national historical significance to qualify for the spending of taxpayers' dollars to honor him. However, as Karaim conclud-ed, "certainly it represented pork barrel politics of the most local kind."[104]

Both Lawrence Welk and Quentin Burdick died in 1992. In the measure-ment of historical significance, however, one is more bound to the other. The champagne music of Lawrence Welk is still enjoyed by millions who watch week-ly reruns of his popular television program. As for Burdick's legacy, it seems forever linked to his one piece of legislation honoring Lawrence Welk. "I feel ... sad about the fact that after 30-some years in the Congress and all the thing's he'd achieved, not just for his state but on a national level, that was the thing that people remembered him by," said Sara Garland about her mentor.[105]

Gage

The birth of Gage Burdick on July 7, 1961, brought joy and excitement to Quentin and Jocelyn Burdick. Although Gage would be their only child, he nestled into a much larger family consisting of a kind maternal grandfa-ther and four older half-siblings — two from each parent. His first name bore the surname of Matilda Jocelyn Gage, his mother's great-grandmother and an ardent feminist of her time. His own surname, of course, placed his genealogy within one of North Dakota's oldest political families and with a father who carried the title of a United States senator. Life was usually good growing up on that quiet street on Fargo's south side in those years. As for the future, well, although it was way too early to know, the limits were endless. Gage Burdick, by genes and environment, appeared to have a bright future. Certainly, he would make a difference someday.

All this suddenly changed in the last week of May 1978. On Wednesday, May 24, Gage was accidentally electrocuted holding an electric drill while stand-ing on an aluminum ladder outside his Fargo home.[106] Death came quickly and snatched the life of a young and vigorous boy soon approaching his 17th birthday. In March, Jocelyn's father had peacefully passed away at the age of 90. This second family death within two months, however, was unexpected as well as tragic. It shook the entire family and severely tested Jocelyn's strength and personal faith. The loss of his son simply devastated Quentin. At first, he blamed himself, and later he retreated into painful memories of past family tragedies. For days, he simply sat silently in a chair and stared at nothing. He simply could not face the loss of another loved one. On that May day, Senator Burdick became an old man. He was never quite the same again.

What happened?

In nontechnical terms, father and son were doing some minor repairs on the house. It was late in the afternoon and supper was to be served soon. Gage was finishing stripping old paint off a window frame on the south side of the house. He was standing on an aluminum ladder, holding in one hand an aluminum-cast electric drill with a cord at the bottom of the grip. Quentin was busy with other work and would periodically change the receptacle for the extension cord, which was connected to the drill. At some point, the wire at the grip of the drill became bare and disconnected; with one random twist of wire, Gage was electrocuted.

Quentin's brother, Eugene, without notes and not missing a word, explained in greater detail what Quentin told him later:

> As it turns out, the wire had run from underneath the living room window. There was a receptacle in the wall, but not a grounded receptacle, and the drill was not one of these insulated types. A lot of tools of that nature today are only two-prong, but they're built in such a way that they're insulated. They can't short across and get to the outside, but this was not one of those. Whether it was a three-prong wire originally, I don't remember. Anyhow, it wouldn't have made any difference because it was plugged into a two-wire receptacle. The wire ran underneath the sill and outside through some bushes and then up to the ladder. The ladder was on the south side of the house. He was stripping against this oriel [window], some people might call it a bay window, but it was like an oriel. He was on the left side of the oriel. He was on that aluminum ladder and as he was stripping it, reaching the flails of this — the wire flails [wire brushes] that you [would attach to] a drill — the flails were [turning]. When you see one of those flails, you don't see the outside area, you see kind of the heart of the thing, but you don't see the tips of the flails. Well, it was the tips of the flails that caught this wire — caught the very wire that feeds the drill, so that it took the wire and wrapped it around the tool. He still has a hold of it and has his hand on the ladder. He let out a yell. "Help" first of all, and then when Quentin came around to the scene, he said, "Don't touch me!" He knew he was being electrocuted. Quentin didn't know where the wire was because the wire had kind of disappeared in the bushes through the window, so it was a matter of seconds before Quentin had to go around back to where he came out to go into the living room and to pull the plug. His best estimate on that was that it took about 45 seconds. By the time he got the plug pulled, Gage had fallen off the ladder and was in the bushes. The lady next door, Mrs. Davies, was a nurse and came immediately over there and started giving CPR. Someone else called the ambulance. They got his heart going, and they got him to the hospital. The heart continued

to function for about 20 minutes and then stopped because the brain had overheated in those 45 seconds. That's what killed him. He was grounded on that ladder, and the ladder made sufficient contact with the ground to take the current. It went through his left arm and through his upper frame and on down through the feet on the ladder, which made a complete round. Even if he'd had the presence of mind to leap away from it — but he couldn't have done that because there was too much slack in the wire. He was too close to where the wire came out of the dining room. Of course, Quentin was sick about it. He said the wiring of the house wasn't modern. It was an old house. Dangerous stuff from electricity."[107]

Gage, by all family accounts, had quickly emerged as the son Quentin always cherished and never really experienced with Jonathan. The two boys were as different as night and day. Jonathan, by build, temperament and interests, was unmistakably Marietta's son. Gage looked and acted like his father. Jonathan was tall, skinny and intellectual. Gage was shorter, more compact and very social. Jonathan spoke fluent French. Gage lifted weights. Jonathan was shy with no close friends. Gage was outgoing and very popular. Jonathan dismissed sports, while Gage could not get enough of them — although both were good swimmers. "I'd say that maybe in Gage he had the son and the relationship he might not have had with Jon," said Jan Mary.[108]

One early incident shared by Jessica, who lived with Gage for his first four years, captured a glimpse of her younger brother's zest for living. It occurred one afternoon when she returned home from school. She found Jocelyn beside herself with worry because, Gage, who was then 3 years old, had mysteriously disappeared. He was nowhere to be found, and the more places she looked, the more concerned she became. Where was Gage? She instructed Jessica to take the car and cruise the neighborhood to see if she could find her little brother. "I had no idea which direction to go," said Jessica. "So I just turned on Eighth Street and about five blocks down I came to a stop sign and there was Gage on his little tricycle. I don't know where he was going, but he was going as fast as he could to get there."[109]

Birch, who was six years older, knew Gage best. They shared a bedroom for many years until Birch was halfway through high school. They were finally separated because Birch had earned his privacy and sought nuisance protection for his new stereo. "He was a good kid," recalled Birch. "He was fun loving and had a lot of good friends in the neighborhood."[110] Sports became Gage's avocation, especially swimming. Birch called Gage a "driven swimmer," and he became a valuable member of the Fargo South High School swimming team. Later, when Birch would return from college, he noticed how much Gage was pumping iron and the huge development of his chest and arms. Gage was becoming a strong and powerful athlete.[111]

At times, Gage exercised magical power over his frugal father. This was a feat unmatched by any of his siblings. "I was forever in awe of him," said Birch, "because he was able to do something that I was unable to do, which was to convince my father to get a new speedboat for the lake."[112] Quentin seldom owned anything that was new, and a bigger speedboat was not on his list. Gage persisted, however, convincing him that more speed and power were essential for water skiing. When the new boat appeared at the family cottage on Lake Melissa, the family watched in disbelief. "I was absolutely astounded," exclaimed Birch. "Talking my father into buying something was quite a trick."[113] Jan Mary, who had experienced more poverty and less wealth when she was growing up, appeared miffed — maybe even angry. "We didn't have TV. We were one of the last families in Fargo to have a television. He refused to buy one!"[114]

Senator Burdick postponed his return to the Capitol after Gage's death. He was not ready to resume his pubic posture. He spent several days replaying the incident and trying to determine in his own mind exactly what caused his son's death. He was not afraid. He just felt alone, so he avoided the inevitable as long as he could. When he did return, his staff tried in every way possible to console him and make him happier; fellow senators dropped by his office to pay their respects. All the personal attention and endless condolences weighed on his grief and probably made him more uncomfortable. He was still alone. No one could really say or do anything to comfort him. Gage was gone. If anyone had given him comfort through this entire ordeal, it was Jocelyn. Jan Mary said that with Jocelyn's strength and religion, her father somehow had survived.[115]

Still the change was obvious to those who worked in his office. "He really sort of lost his fire," recalled Gaginis, his loyal and longtime personal secretary. As the days went by, the senator began to talk privately with her about the accident. He recalled how Gage had looked at him and had uttered his final words: "Dad, don't touch me, I'm hot." As time passed, even years, he would repeatedly tell her "there isn't a day that goes by that [I don't] hear those words." After a pause, Gaginis continued. "It was so sad. He loved Gage. I mean, he was sort of the apple of his eye. He was probably a little more like him, a little more rebellious. He was a smart kid. He got into a little trouble. Good athlete. Senator Burdick never missed a swimming meet. He packed out of here to get home to Fargo. Those meets were Friday night at the Y and he never missed one if he could help it. He just adored him."[116]

Jan Mary put this final tragedy of her father's life into perspective. Although she never lived with Gage, she felt that the impact of his death deeply affected her aging father. "He was never the same again," she stated. "I mean, that was one blow too many. There was a part of him that was gone."[117] She recalled how her father had changed once before in his relationship to her after he lost Marietta and Jonathan on the same day. "He became a totally different person. He went from being a father and a husband to a politician. And then I think with he and Gage a little bit of that warmth came back, a little bit of that feeling, that joy in life, he had through Gage. He adored Gage. And I think the door just shut, and I think he shut it to all of us. He didn't mean to, but I think he did. I think politics became his entire life and that he just couldn't be hurt one more time."[118]

Aging

Aging will always be a democratic process. It is never a stage in which any person wants to participate, yet the bottom line is that no one has any choice in the matter. It happens to every human whether they are Democrat, Republican or Independent. It occurs to every one of us regardless of the color of our skin, our gender, or our wealth or lack of wealth. In most cases, aging remains thankfully a highly personal journey. Family, doctors and health-care providers handle aging and illness – which often occur together – quietly at home or in nursing home facilities. Seldom does a serious medical problem of any person become a public issue. News about someone's aging is shared privately, and then publicly in a published obituary.

Is the question of aging for a biography about Quentin Burdick different? Does the exposure of the aging process for a public official differ from that of his constituents? This is an essential question, but the answer to what extent Burdick was physically and mentally capable of performing his duties as United States senator remains incomplete for several reasons. First, Burdick and his family and his Senate staff believed strongly that the issue was private. No one from the Burdick camp really wanted to discuss the subject, and when pressed, their answers were brief and to the point. David Strauss, for example, stated unequivocally, "Jocie and I both agree on this and will swear to this to our dying day that he never lost his wits. He always had his wits about him. He knew who I was till his dying day."[119] Second, the health records of Senator Burdick are private; examination without permission of the family was simply out of the question. The option was never negotiable. Third, the strong opinion of Mike Jacobs, editor of the *Grand Forks Herald,* is not complete. He was the major proponent in the state saying that Burdick's health was a public issue, and that Burdick was not always in control. In other words, Burdick had lost his wits.

Although Jacobs graciously agreed to be interviewed, he declined — for reasons only known to him — to sign the oral history release form that would allow the use of his interview for this publication. He was the only interviewee in research for this book to refuse, and as a result his perspective, though valuable, is absent.

Other members of the media were more generous. Jack Zaleski, editorial editor of the *Fargo Forum*, did agree with Jacobs on this issue and said so. "I think Burdick handled it as well as any proud, strong, elderly person can," said Zaleski. "The difference, of course, is that the man was a U.S. senator, and there is a difference between Joe getting old and Senator Joe getting old."[120] On the whole, however, only members of the North Dakota media — and not all of them — agreed with Jacobs and Zaleski. Karl Limvere, for example, a longtime spokesman for the North Dakota Farmers Union and who himself had serious health problems, flatly disagreed. "I don't think that health is a public issue. Not even for a U.S. senator."[121]

Although Burdick's health record is incomplete, there is some evidence and anecdotal records. Burdick's diet and exercise routine added to his longevity. He was a picky eater, a nonsmoker and only an occasionally a social drinker, less so after his marriage to Jocie, who was adamantly opposed to any alcohol consumption whatsoever. Burdick was a strong swimmer and a lifelong daily walker. He never lay around and was always physically active working on his car, his Fargo home, and the Lake Melissa summer cottage or working out in the Senate gym. He remained mentally active working crossword puzzles and was an avid cribbage player. Leisure never meant doing nothing. Doing nothing for Burdick meant not living or simply being lazy.

Senate peers were well aware of his physical strength. He probably was one of the Senate's most physically fit senators for much of his tenure. Many knew about his Minnesota football career and that he preferred contact sports over golf, squash or tennis. It was never anything he ever bragged about, but it was a characterization of him that was observed by many who served with him. A couple of these impressions are most memorable. Senator Inouye, whom Burdick picked up at Washington National Airport when Inouye first arrived in Washington, knew a lot about Burdick's football career and his physical presence. "You should have seen him then," recalled Inouye. "He looked gentle and kindly, but underneath, he had rippling muscles."[122] Senator Hefflin often watched Burdick work out in the Senate gym. "I used to work out in the Senate gym with him. I'd watch him. He wasn't as young as he had been earlier, and he'd lift weights. He'd do various and sundry exercises and other things. You could see those muscles on him pop out. He had tremendous strength."[123]

Tom Burgum recalled an incident in the late 1970s, which further attests to Burdick's physical stamina. It centered on a weekend project involving Burdick, Burgum, Scott Anderson and Vern Weaver, a handyman from West Virginia. Burdick wanted help in clearing some small mountain hardwoods, which had grown up all over a small piece of land owned earlier by Burdick's father, Usher, close to the West Virginia border and seven miles west of Leesburg. The trees were small in diameter, 1 inch to 1½ inches, but they were "little trees with a skin as tough as steel."[124] The four of them began taking turns using a two-man saw brought along by Weaver. Anderson pooped out within a short period of time and was done. Burdick worked one end of the saw for the rest of the day, while Burgum and Weaver took turns on the other end. They worked from 8:00 a.m. to 4:00 p.m., with an hour lunch break. Burdick nearly worked the two of them to death, yet showed no sign of physical exhaustion. He was in his early 70s, some 20 years older than the other two.[125] Fargo Mayor Jon Lindgren, who often chatted with Burdick when he came back on weekends, told a similar story. Well into the 1980s, Lindgren would find him working on some kitchen appliance, dressed in his grubbies and lying on the floor.[126]

Aging is also an evolutionary process. It is seldom triggered by a single event to mark either mental or physical change. In Burdick's life, however, the tragic death of his son, Gage, in May 1978 clearly affected him more than any other single event in his later years. In physical terms, 1987 and 1988 proved challenging and difficult for him. In December 1987, Burdick slipped on the ice while boarding a charter plane to Jamestown and had to be hospitalized. Some passed it off as only a concussion, while others whispered the "S" word for stroke. Reed Karaim, a Washington journalist, observed that Burdick "lost much of his physical and mental vitality" after the fall. The next year proved even more difficult. In July, doctors removed noncancerous polyps, and a month later, took 18 inches of his colon. He lost 15 pounds and never regained much of it. Yet, Burdick bounced back and again perked up. When Karaim visited him in the hospital, he found the senator wearing a sweatshirt that read, "I blocked for Bronco Nagurski."[127]

Burdick began serving his last term in January of 1989. He was then third in Senate seniority; only Senators Strom Thurmond (R-SC) and Robert Byrd (D-WV) had served more years. Burdick's final four Senate years were marked with increased physical and mental frailties. When fellow senators joined in June to celebrate one of his last birthdays, many came away with the sobering conclusion that Burdick had deteriorated considerably. "I remember being shocked [at] how small and frail he seemed standing in the middle of the room," wrote Karaim later. "He'd clung to an appearance of physical vitality long after his mind began to slip and it was strange to see him looking like a weak old man bent like a question mark, unsteady on his feet."[128]

Some senators came to his aid in those final years. Senator Inouye, who was a member of the leadership and on the Rooms Committee, took the initiative and instructed that a private room be reserved for his old friend, Senator Burdick. "I used to tell Quentin: 'Why don't you just stay home or go to the hospital.' But he would reply: 'No, I've got work to do!' So I said: 'If that's the case, we're going to put a bed in here for you.' Inouye then called Burdick's staff and told them: 'I don't know who it is, you assign someone to be with him, but he should be here under the best of auspices."[129]

Kindness toward Burdick was not exclusively a Democrat response. Senator Steve Symms (R-ID), who served on Burdick's Committee on Environment and Public Works, returned from one of the committee meetings, called his key staff together and closed the door. He told his staff, "I've always liked Senator Burdick. He is now in some distress. You may think it is funny, but I would advise you not to tell jokes about him in this office, at least not where I can hear you. And if he needs something from us, a vote or something you don't think we can give him, it's not your decision. In this case, it is mine."[130]

The only member of the Senate to poke fun at Senator Burdick publicly was Senator Alan Simpson (R-WY). He, too, was a member of the Environment and Public Works Committee and was quoted as saying that all "Senator Burdick did as chairman was to gavel the committee together."[131] The backlash to Simpson's comment was immediate and spirited. "Alan Simpson lived to regret that," said Jocie, with a slight rise in her voice. "He apologized to me every time he saw me and to Quentin for years after he had said that. He finally told people that 'I think the Burdicks have forgiven me, but the staff has never forgiven me.'"[132] Simpson was probably correct about that observation. His remark hurt Burdick personally, and Burdick confided to Senator Inouye that what hurt most was that it showed the beginning of the breakup of the institution of the Senate.[133]

Two members of the North Dakota congressional delegation who saw him most often observed Burdick's last years. Although Dorgan was never close to Burdick, he talked about how sick and frail he had become and still, "even then you would see him plodding through the airport alone. This is ... Quentin at age 80, shuffling along and having real health problems, no assistant and carrying a little bag by himself, shuffling through the Minneapolis airport all alone."[134] Burdick was personally much closer to Senator Conrad. "At the end it was pretty tough," admitted Conrad. "It was pretty tough. He was not well at the end. ... Clearly, his body was under assault for those last several years. In fact, I had thought several years before that he would die and he didn't and he didn't. Then I begin to think he wouldn't die. That he was going to last out his term. I really changed my mind. For a numbers of years there, I thought he is going to die and he could die next month, but after I saw him just keep going, I kind of concluded he was going to last out this term. He is determined to live through his term. I was surprised that he died."[135]

Staffer Bruce McKay, who loved Burdick as a father, shared his thoughts on Burdick's final stages. "Until the day he died, he liked to talk about Bronco Nagurski and his blocking days at the University of Minnesota. He still thought of himself as a rugged guy. He thought very highly of the opposite sex. Until the day he died, he always found women very attractive and appealing. He wanted to think until he was gone that he was quite a catch. He loved to flirt."[136]

Senator Burdick did not live to complete his last term in the United States Senate. He died from a heart attack on the 8th of September 1992, the day after Labor Day and during Senate recess, in a Fargo hospital. North Dakota's Gentle Warrior passed away peacefully in his sleep. He was tired. He had wanted to die with his boots on and he did. "I think if he'd have left before he died, he would have died when he left," observed Lloyd Omdahl. "I think that life to QB was being in the Senate. And when you ask him to step down, you're asking him to go up on a hill and die."[137]

A Senate Funeral

The Senate, Jocie, and members of his staff wasted no time preparing a memorial service for Senator Burdick. The details were basically arranged among the Sergeant of Arms Office in Washington, Jocie, her daughter Leslie in Fargo and David Strauss of Burdick's staff. Senate staffers arrived a day early to assist in the many details of the service. Strauss took the delicate responsibility of asking Senate Majority Leader George Mitchell of Maine and Minority Leader Robert Dole of Kansas to give eulogies on behalf of the United States Senate. There was some disagreement on whom should be asked, but Strauss insisted that the two best choices were Mitchell and Dole. Jocie and friends selected the Fargo Holiday Inn near Interstate 29 and the Fargo airport to host the memorial service, although Leslie was horrified at her mother's choice. The Holiday Inn could handle 1,500 guests and was most accessible for those who came either by plane or automobile.

The Burdick family asked the Reverend Nelson Stone, pastor of the First Congregational Church in Fargo, to preside over the service. The senator was a longtime member of the Fargo church. The television media approached Stone

about the content of the service. He gave almost the same answer that Senator Mansfield relayed about Burdick. Stone said the service would be "quiet,
simple and straightforward," because "Quentin was a very simple man."[138] How
ironic that the one word, quiet, had become both a beginning and an ending
to Burdick's Senate career.

The memorial service for Senator Burdick was held at 2:00 p.m. on Friday, September 11, 1992. Approximately 1,300 people attended the service,
including family and friends, North Dakota state officials, and members of the
United States Senate from both sides of the aisle who flew to Fargo to pay their
respects to their friend and longtime colleague. Senior senators such as Robert
Byrd (D-WV), Daniel Patrick Moynihan (D-NY), Ted Stevens (R-AK) and John
Chafee (R-RI) were in attendance, as were conservatives such as Senator Or-
rin Hatch (R-UT) and liberals such as Senator Paul Wellstone (D-MN). Others
came who seldom went to funereal occasions. "I don't go to all funerals," admitted Senator Inouye. "I went to Quentin's because I think old buddies should
say goodbye and say, 'We'll see you later, buddy.'"[139]

Many Native Americans from North Dakota also came to the service.
They, like the Hawaiian senator, were old Burdick buddies. Outside, they beat
their drums and chanted songs. They also brought the riderless horse. Later,
Eugene Burdick implored them all to come inside, and after the service, the
Three Affiliated Tribes presented Jocie with a woven quilt.

Inside, the two Senate leaders gave short and meaningful eulogies. "His
presence in the Senate," began Senator Mitchell, "was a daily reminder to all of
us that the basic purpose for which our nation is founded is the well-being of
the people. He believed and acted as though government exists for the benefit
of the people, not the other way around." As he ended, Mitchell turned to the
Burdick family and said goodbye to his colleague. "Today Quentin Burdick
comes home for the last time. Home to his God, home to the Plains and the
people of North Dakota he loved so much and served so well. Goodbye, Quentin. May God bless you and hold you in his arms forever."[140] Senator Dole,
in his usual deadpan presence and frank tone, complemented the remarks of
the majority leader. "North Dakota is a better place for Senator Burdick having lived there," and "The Senate is a better place for Senator Burdick having
served there."[141]

With the formal service completed, friends and guests joined together in
a reception that allowed many of those who knew Senator Burdick a time to
chat and remember. The memorial service was a tribute to the Senate, Senator
Burdick and family, and the people of North Dakota. "I thought it was again
indicative of the camaraderie that develops after years. Here was Robert Dole

standing up there and eulogizing Quentin Burdick," said former Fargo Mayor Jon Lindgren. "The top brass of the United States Senate were there. It was very impressive to sit there with those people."[142] Soon, however, the big buses pulled up in front and the senators one by one began to board for the short hop back to the airport. One-third of the Senate had taken a day off to pay tribute to Senator Burdick. Now they had work to do. "I don't know if people understand that back home," said Gaginis, "but a senator dying in office reflects on the Senate. I mean, it's Senator Burdick. Yes, but it's more than Senator Burdick. It's the institution as well. But all you do is invite other senators and they only come because they want to come. They all liked Senator Burdick."[142]

No burial service followed; none was planned. Oddly, perhaps no one bothered to ask, not even the state's media: Where is Senator Burdick to be buried? The answer, of course, was private. No one in the Burdick family wanted to talk about it. It was a very sensitive issue. Quietly, after her father's body was cremated, Jan Mary took the ashes in their small container, placed them in the trunk of her car and drove home to her Twin Cities residence. The ashes remained there for several days. Later, she drove to the Bohemian National Cemetery outside of Hutchinson, Minnesota, where it was then time to bury her father's remains.

The Williston boy, the Gopher footballer, the Fargo loser, the North Dakota Farmers Union organizer, the Democratic-NPL Party builder and the senator from North Dakota was privately and peacefully laid to rest on Minnesota soil beside his beloved Marietta, where a dual headstone with both their names waited for his presence. Separated far too soon, they were then joined again forever.

Endnotes

1. Senator Mike Mansfield, interview with author, March 28, 1995.
2. Ibid.
3. Ibid.
4. Mark Andrews, interview with author, May 19, 1995.
5. Sara Garland, interview with author, March 22, 1995.
6. Senator Russell Long, interview with author, March 22, 1995.
7. Senator Daniel Inouye, interview with author, March 22, 1995.
8. *Grand Forks (N.D.) Herald*, Sept. 27, 1983.
9. Amer, *Members of the U.S. Congress Who Have Served Thirty Years or More*, 1, 14.
10. Larry Erickson, interview with author, Feb. 29, 1995.
11. Lucy Calautti, interview with author, March 24, 1995.
12. *Grand Forks Herald*, Feb. 6, 1978.
13. David Strauss, interview with author, March 30, 1995.
14. Quentin Burdick, interview with author, Jan. 6, 1992.
15. *The Almanac of American Politics 1982*, 920.
16. *The Almanac of American Politics 1984*, 897.
17. *The Almanac of American Politics 1986*, 1168.
18. *The Almanac of American Politics 1988*, 908.
19. Quentin Burdick interview.
20. Bob Bergland, interview with author, Jan. 27, 1995.
21. Tom Burgum, interview with author, March 24, 1995.
22. Ibid.
23. Quentin Burdick interview.
24. Long interview.
25. Senator Howell Hefflin, interview with author, March 31, 1995.
26. Inouye interview.
27. Senator Kent Conrad, interview with author, March 27, 1995.
28. Senator Byron Dorgan, interview with author, March 27, 1995.
29. Art Link, interview with author, Jan. 25, 1995.
30. Inouye interview.
31. *North Dakota Votes*, 165.
32. Ibid., 167.
33. Charles Fleming, interview with author, April 25, 1995.
34. *North Dakota Votes*, 169, 172.
35. Ibid., 169.
36. Stanley Moore, interview with author, Jan. 24, 1995.
37. Strauss interview.
38. Link interview.
39. Burgum interview.
40. Quentin Burdick interview.
41. Jim Fuglie, interview with author, Feb. 2, 1995.
42. Dorgan interview.
43. Calautti interview.
44. Kevin Carvell, interview with author, Jan. 23, 1995.
45. George Sinner, interview with author, Jan. 19, 1995.
46. Austin Engel, interview with author, Feb. 9, 1995.
47. Fuglie interview.
48. *Grand Forks Herald*, Feb. 26, 1987.
49. Sarah Vogel, interview with author, Feb. 7, 1995.
50. Arvin Kvasager, interview with author, Jan. 26, 1995.
51. Representative Earl Pomeroy, interview with author, March 24, 1995.
52. Mary Wakefield, interview with author, March 30, 1995.
53. Geraldine Gaginis, interview with author, March 30, 1995.
54. Garland interview.
55. Dorgan interview.
56. Quentin Burdick interview.

57. Strauss interview.
58. Burgum interview.
59. Jon Lindgren, interview with author, Jan. 21, 1995.
60. Ardell Tharaldson, interview with author, Jan. 25, 1995.
61. Fuglie interview.
62. Lloyd Omdahl, interview with author, Jan. 18, 1995.
63. *North Dakota Votes*, 171.
64. Earl Strinden, interview with author, Feb. 3, 1995.
65. Ibid.
66. Ibid.
67. *North Dakota Votes*, 174.
68. Quentin Burdick interview.
69. Earl Strinden interview.
70. Ibid.
71. Kvasager interview.
72. Calautti interview.
73. Tharaldson interview.
74. *Grand Forks Herald*, Oct. 25, 1988.
75. Ibid., Oct. 28, 1988.
76. *Grand Forks Herald*, Oct. 29, 1988.
77. Quentin Burdick interview.
78. Eliot Glassheim, interview with author, Jan. 29, 1995.
79. Sarah Vogel interview.
80. Fleming interview.
81. Strinden interview.
82. Suezette Bieri, interview with author, Jan. 17, 1995.
83. Philip Shabecoff, "Now the Environment According to North Dakota," *New York Times*, Jan. 9, 1987, I-16:3
84. Ibid.
85. Ibid.
86. Dick Backus, interview with author, April 27, 1995.
87. Reed Karaim, letter to author, Oct. 26, 1995.
88. Ibid.
89. Gary Holm, interview with author, Jan. 29, 1995.
90. Bruce McKay, interview with author, March 28, 1995.
91. Strauss interview.
92. Tom Clifford, interview with author, April 14, 1995.
93. Fuglie interview.
94. Ibid.
95. Conrad interview.
96. *New York Times*, Feb. 10, 1991, IV 16: 1.
97. Ibid.
98. Ibid., March 8, 1991, A 11:3.
99. Clymer, "Congress Stumbles on Honors for Welk," *New York Times*, March 12, 1991, A: 18:1.
100. Bieri interview.
101. Inouye interview.
102. Jerome Lamb, interview with author, Jan. 20, 1995.
103. D. Jerome Tweton, interview with author, April 17, 1995.
104. Karaim letter.
105. Garland interview.
106. *New York Times*, May 25, 1978, A:19.
107. Eugene Burdick, interview with author, Feb. 28, 1995.
108. Jan Mary Hill, interview with author, May 2, 1995.
109. Jessica Burdick, interview with author, Jan. 28, 1996.
110. Birch Burdick, interview with author, April 18, 1995.
111. Ibid.
112. Ibid.
113. Ibid.

114. Jan Mary Hill interview.
115. Ibid.
116. Gaginis interview.
117. Jan Mary Hill interview.
118. Ibid.
119. Strauss interview.
120. Jack Zaleski, interview with author, Jan. 23, 1995.
121. Karl Limvere, interview with author, Jan. 24, 1995.
122. Inouye interview.
123. Hefflin interview.
124. Burgum interview.
125. Ibid.
126. Lindgren interview.
127. Karaim letter.
128. Ibid.
129. Inouye interview.
130. Burgum interview.
131. Ibid.
132. Jocelyn Birch Burdick, interview with author, April 18, 1995.
133. Inouye interview.
134. Dorgan interview.
135. Conrad interview.
136. McKay interview.
137. Omdahl interview.
138. Fargo WDAY television video in possession of author.
139. Inouye interview.
140. Fargo WDAY video.
141. Ibid.
142. Lindgren interview.
143. Gaginis interview.

- twelve -

Afterword

Three singular events transpired after the death of Quentin Burdick that deserve discussion in his biography. The first and most significant was the surprise appointment of Jocelyn Birch Burdick as an interim successor to her late husband in the U.S. Senate until a special election could be called in North Dakota. Democratic Governor George Sinner made the appointment on September 16, 1992, eight days after Quentin's death. Jocelyn served 90 days until December 14, 1992, thus becoming the first woman in North Dakota to serve in the Senate.

The second and third incidents were scraps compared to the Senate appointment. Both events, in quite different ways, related to Burdick's relationship with the U.S. Department of Justice. One brought surprise and controversy. The other brought public acclaim and honor. Neither event altered the major themes presented in this biography. Both raised, however, the proverbial speculation biographers entertain about their subjects. No one, of course, will ever know what Burdick's reaction would have been to either of these incidents. Still, it is intellectually stimulating to guess with some hindsight and historical evidence.

The first of these two minor events occurred unexpectedly in September 1993. It was the partial release of an FBI file on Burdick and a related news article in *Roll Call*, a Washington political publication. The news story claimed that Burdick had made FBI Director J. Edgar Hoover's infamous un-American list. It caught family, colleagues and North Dakotans by surprise. Historically, however, no surprise was warranted. These post-death revelations simply restated old charges that had dogged Burdick in the years before his first political victory in 1958. The fact that the latest revelation came from the FBI rather than North Dakota Republicans, or even some Democrats, evidently made for greater excitement.

The second event occurred in Fargo on July 29, 1998. This was the long awaited dedication of the new Quentin Burdick wing of the federal courthouse building. The new portion of the U.S. Courthouse was an impressive four-story addition adjoining the original federal building, which had been constructed in 1931. Although Burdick had been instrumental in obtaining the original funding for the addition, the cost amount faced repeated reductions and delays before finally being approved for $15 million. The Burdick building houses the U.S. District and Bankruptcy Court systems, the Eighth U.S. Circuit Court of Appeals judges' chambers, a large law library and the U.S. Marshal Service. The addition also includes a Burdick Education Center, which offers information about North Dakota, the judicial system and the senator. The whole structure is wrapped with a very sophisticated security system and state-of-the-art technology equipment.[1]

The two Justice Department events contained elements of historical hypocrisy. The first, the FBI file, reveals that Burdick was under suspicion for years by one branch of the federal government for alleged communist activities. The second, the dedication of the new wing to the federal courthouse – by the same branch of the federal government – honored the same man in the name of justice for all Americans.

A Sinner's Penance

Political skies darkened over the Washington offices of North Dakota Democrats in the fall of 1992. The party's control of the state's congressional delegation appeared in some jeopardy. Gone were its two U.S. senators – the elder by death and the younger by choice. The third member of the party, Congressman Byron Dorgan, stood eager to run for Senator Kent Conrad's vacated seat. The identities of candidates to fill the other two offices remained in doubt. In this milieu of political uncertainty, pressure mounted on Democratic Governor George Sinner to protect the party's power in Washington by quickly naming a successor to Senator Burdick's seat.

Governor Sinner wasted little time in making the decision. His choice, however, surprised many political observers. He appointed Jocelyn Birch Burdick to succeed her late husband. In accepting the appointment, she became the first woman in North Dakota history to serve in that body and only the fifth person to be appointed (Fountain Thompson, 1909; William Purcell, 1910; Gerald Nye, 1925; and Milton Young, 1945).

"I was amazed when Governor Sinner contacted me," exclaimed Jocelyn, "because I had been very mad at George Sinner, and I thought how amazing that he would ask me. You understand, I like George and had liked him for years, but when he said this thing about [how] if he were Quentin he would resign — well, I thought, 'You just had a heart attack and you didn't resign!'"[2]

Others shared Jocelyn's reaction. Lloyd Omdahl, Sinner's lieutenant governor, said he was "astounded" when Sinner made the appointment. He simply could not believe it. When reason prevailed, he offered some insights into Sinner's philosophy and the political significance of the decision. He knew that the Burdicks were very upset when the governor made his public statement that Quentin should resign and that he had caused hard feelings among Burdick loyalists, too. "I think the governor felt guilty," opined Omdahl. "He didn't mean to hurt anybody. Governor Sinner is basically a priest. He really is in his makeup and values."[3] From a theological perspective, Joceyln's appointment was Sinner's penance for his political sin against Quentin Burdick. The appointment also proved to be politically astute. "It kind of was a way of holding the seat until something could be straightened out," said Omdahl. "It made everyone feel good about it and she took it."[4]

Sinner, a thoughtful and kind person, talked freely about the pressures placed on him to make the appointment. "It was not a happy week," confessed Sinner, who took life more seriously than most. "It was one of the toughest weeks I had because I couldn't understand some of the feelings that were about."[5] He also acknowledged that from the very moment that he had learned about Quentin's death, he knew he would have to make the appointment and began to think about whom he would appoint. It was largely a personal decision, and he consulted no one in his office.[6]

Three main factors guided Sinner's appointment. The first was the jackal factor, which was to say "No" to a chorus of applicants who began to call his office. Although Sinner declined to name any of them, he was highly critical of all of them. "I was frankly almost sick to my stomach at the scavengers who wanted the job before the man was scarcely cold and I said so in that interim before his burial. I didn't mean to be critical to the people who couldn't avoid thinking about it, but there were some outrageous suggestions."[7]

The second factor was futuristic and it centered on the political career of Kent Conrad. After his upset victory over Senator Mark Andrews in 1986, he promised not to seek a second term if the federal budget was not balanced. True to his word, he announced that he would not seek re-election in 1992. His decision nevertheless was a terrible political blow to the North Dakota Democratic Party. Sinner felt deeply about Conrad and what the decision meant for his own career. Privately, he was totally convinced that only Senator Kent Conrad could replace Senator Quentin Burdick and he said so in the most unmistakable terms. "I was convinced that in the person of Kent Conrad, who was totally an astonishing person in pubic service, a brilliant mind, great public conscience, great understanding of the Constitution and what American democracy is about ... that there wasn't any question of who should be there."[8]

Sinner's support for Conrad convinced him to make an interim appointment. The first two points of Sinner's plan logically led him to the third. In short, an interim appointment would allow Conrad time to step back and to be true to his word, but still be available should another opportunity present itself. "You had a few issues that could be helped by one person, Senator Burdick's wife," said a relieved Sinner. "When I realized that's who it should be, it took me all of about two hours to put it together. I called Judge Myron Bright and he said, "'I think it's a great idea. Let me talk to Jocie for you.' He called back and said she would do it."[9]

Judge Bright downplayed his role in the appointment. "This was Sinner's choice. As a close friend of Jocie's, George Sinner asked me to inquire as to whether Jocie would accept an appointment. She said she would and I told that to George."[10] Jocie accepted the appointment primarily because, as she put it: "I felt I wanted to carry on the traditions that Quentin had been interested in."[11] At the same time, she leaned on Bright quite heavily before she accepted. She was not sure she could accept the appointment and be in Washington so soon after the death of her husband.[12]

Sinner's appointment brought immediate approval. From the Burdick family, Eugene and May Bright heaped praise on the governor. "I thought that was a neat way to solve the problem," reasoned Judge Burdick. May was more euphoric. "I think it was the smartest thing the governor ever did."[13] North Dakota historian D. Jerome Tweton recalled watching news of the appointment on television with his wife, Paula. When he expressed surprise with Jocelyn's appointment, his wife exclaimed: "You chauvinists! If I were George Sinner, I would appoint Mrs. Burdick. This would be a harmless appointment and it would leave it open, but yet give her some honor."[14] Charles Fleming, Sinner's chief of staff, said he had little or no involvement in the decision, but he doubted whether the idea originated with the governor.[15]

Was Kent Conrad the source of Jocelyn's appointment? In Governor Sinner's big picture, he certainly was. Eugene Burdick also spoke to Kent at Quentin's funeral and told him, "I hope you decide to run. I want you to know that you're off the hook on your promise because you're not running for that term."[16] Conrad said straight up that he was not involved in the decision. "I was informed of his decision before he announced it publicly; but no, I had no role in it." He added, however, "It was brilliant on so many different levels. First, of all, Jocie is an exceptional person, and just did a beautiful job as a senator. It was also a fitting tribute to Quentin to have his wife serve out until the required special election was held. I thought it was also a tribute to women because that's the first woman serving in the U.S. Senate from North Dakota."[17]

What seemed so dark for North Dakota Democrats in September of 1992 turned into a white Christmas by December. There was much to celebrate. Governor Sinner appointed a woman to serve in the U.S. Senate, a first for women, and a first for the state of North Dakota. His appointment protected the hegemony of the state's congressional delegation in several ways. First, his choice caused no fracas within the party and deflected any public criticism. Second, it favored no serious contender to the office by favoring no single Democrat, and in doing so gave no advantage to a Republican challenger, either. In the end, Jocelyn Birch Burdick graciously served her state and the memory of Quentin Burdick in the U.S. Senate.

Congressman Byron Dorgan was elected Senator Byron Dorgan in November. Also elected was Insurance Commissioner Earl Pomeroy, who replaced him. In a special election held in December, retiring Senator Kent Conrad became a new senator, winning the two years remaining on Senator Burdick's term. Finally, Governor George Sinner slept well on Christmas Eve knowing that his decision was a great present for his party and penance for his earlier sin.

Shades of Pink

The provenance to the *Roll Call* article was uncomplicated. The existence of the Burdick file appeared on a general list of federal files, and Glenn Simpson, a *Roll Call* reporter, wisely pursued it. He filed a request to examine the Burdick file under the Freedom of Information Act and was permitted partial access. The remainder of the file, which was substantial, remained closed. Simpson noted at the close of his story that "Large portions of the Burdick file were censored to protect the privacy of others, to protect informants, and for national security."[18] This, of course, was bureaucratic baloney. To this day, restricting portions of government files requested under the Freedom of Information Act is standard procedure, although Simpson bemoaned the government's decision. In addition, repeated attempts to convince Jocelyn Burdick, who by then had been senator in her own right, to obtain a copy of the entire file for historical importance met with no success. Her reasons remain private, as do the total contents of Burdick's FBI file.

So what was released?

The file on Burdick was created in 1944. It was based on information that Burdick was then a subscriber to an American communist periodical. The file added information about Burdick's work with the North Dakota Farmers Union, his involvement with the North Dakota chapter of the Progressive Party, and his support for Henry Wallace for president at the national Progressive Party convention in 1948. Bits and pieces were added to the file in subsequent years, but the meat of the opened portions of the file centered on the 1940s. That was it.

The Burdick file languished for many years and apparently no one in the federal government paid any attention to its contents. It was not until January of 1959 that Hoover ordered his staff to re-examine the file and summarize its contents. The reason for the renewed interest in the file, according to Simpson, was the presence in Washington of Burdick as a newly elected member of the U.S. House of Representatives. A portion of the memo prepared for Hoover contained the following summary of Burdick's alleged communist activities: "Burdick was an attorney, supported by the Farmers Union, had good relations with the American Federation of Labor, was a big Mason and cooperated with the communists one hundred percent."[19] Hoover then forwarded the memo to U.S. Attorney General William P. Rogers. The file label read: "Quentin Burdick Information Regarding Internal Security." Hoover added that "Burdick has not been the subject of a security investigation by the Bureau and our files do not reflect that he is a member of the CP."[20]

In June 1960, shortly before the Burdick-Davis Senate election, someone unidentified in North Dakota requested information from the FBI on Burdick. The bureau, however, refused to release contents of the file or the 1959 memo to Hoover. An internal FBI memo found in the Burdick file noted in part "that the FBI will not become involved in this political campaign."[21] Simpson did not discover who requested the information but speculated that it probably came from only two sources — either someone from the Davis campaign or the press. Burdick, of course, went on to defeat Davis by a slim margin and his FBI file remained closed until Simpson obtained portions of it for his article.

Simpson tackled two major themes in his *Roll Call* piece. First he questioned the evidence that supported the file's contentions that Burdick had communist ties. Second, he discussed the possible political fallout in North Dakota if the FBI had released information about Burdick's communist activities prior to the 1960 special Senate election. The primary headline in bold black print introduced Simpson's first theme: "Was Senator Burdick a Communist Sympathizer?" A smaller subheading entitled "FBI Files Obtained by Roll Call Reveal Late North Dakota Senator Was Found To Have Ties to CP. Had it Gone Public in 1960, He May Never Have Been Elected," supported the reporter's second theme.[22]

Simpson supplemented the FBI file on Burdick with two key interviews. He interviewed Lloyd Omdahl, of Grand Forks, the veteran authority on North Dakota politics, and Burdick's longtime Fargo friend and associate, senior federal judge Myron Bright. Both men told the reporter "they had never heard these allegations against Burdick."[23] The quote is from Simpson's article and it is not a direct quote from either Omdahl or Bright. The article is unclear about what allegations these men did not know about. If the reference is only to the FBI file, then the statement makes perfect sense. If on the other hand, it refers to them not knowing about the charges being made against Burdick by North Dakotans, their statement makes no sense. North Dakota Republicans used these same communist alleged activities against Burdick repeatedly, especially in Burdick's humiliating beating by Senator Milton R. Young in the 1956 Senate race. None of this was new news for anyone familiar with North Dakota politics in the two decades following World War II.

The main focus of Simpson's interviews centered on one *what-if* historical question: Would the outcome of the Burdick-Davis race have been different if the FBI had released its investigation prior to the election? Bright, who played a key role in the Burdick birthday bash and the appearance of Democratic presidential candidate Senator John F. Kennedy, downplayed the consequences. "John F. Kennedy came to Fargo 10 days before the election and in essence put his arm around Quentin and said, 'Here's a good American,' said Bright."[24] Omdahl took a less traveled road. "If they had done that in 1960, it could have been damaging because the election was so close."[25]

If others can speculate about the effect of the FBI file on the outcome of the 1960 election, one might inject another hypothetical question as well. What would have been Quentin Burdick's reaction to the FBI file? This is, after all, the key question about Burdick's historical legacy. At first blush, Burdick probably would have exploded with anger. His face would have turned red and anyone present in the office probably would have received an earful. A second wind, however, would have produced a much different response. His face would beam with pride. The FBI file was, when all is said and done, a reaffirmation of who Quentin Burdick really was and what he stood for. It was not a blight on his political obituary, but a badge of courage to support those who he believed needed to be protected the most. The FBI file, like his old Minnesota Gopher jersey, spoke loud and clear. "Yes, I ran with the North Dakota farmers who wanted cooperatives and I blocked for the Fargo Teamsters who wanted the right to collective bargaining."

A Justice Building Named Burdick

In comparison to the controversy that surrounded the surprise release of the Burdick FBI file, the new wing of the Fargo federal courthouse spelled relief. It was properly presented as an honor to Senator Burdick, his family and the entire Fargo community. It perpetuated his name and solidified the presence of the growing federal judicial system in North Dakota. The *Fargo Forum*'s editorial boosted the building's architectural significance and the contribution it would make to the city's downtown revitalization efforts. At the same time, the editorial snubbed Senator Burdick entirely. Not one word was written about him. The building's importance to Fargo was the key point, not Burdick's political career.[26]

In other ways, the Burdick building represented an embarrassment of riches. At some juncture in the life or death of a long-serving U.S. senator, a federal building will pop up someday in his or her home state adorned with his or her name on it. It happens all the time in state after state. The Burdick building was a Senate perk awarded in this instance to a deceased member of the club by living members of the same club who someday will be recipients of the same practice. There is little doubt Senator Burdick would have relished the occasion. It is a privilege of age and of public service. Forget his grousing over the purchase of a new suit or his anger that his worn-out shoes were missing. Those Depression scars never left him. Fargo was his home and fighting for justice one of his greatest legacies. One can only guess, however, whether the FBI file spoke louder to his fight for justice than the new wing of the federal courthouse and the historical artifacts of his life displayed in it.

In the final analysis, Senator Quentin Burdick was a people's person. Buildings paled in comparison to the needs of farmers and the rights of union workers. The Burdick building honors his long service to the federal government, but the FBI file honors his unabashed support for his constituents.

FBI File

The FBI file was a tribute to Burdick's compassion for the common people of North Dakota, not a condemnation of his loyalty to the United States. Contemporaries, even in North Dakota, neither understood the struggle or the political tradition. They viewed the commie charge as outrageous, maybe even a taint to their own political careers, a generation later. They did not understand at all how real it was to Burdick's experience in life and North Dakota's years of drought, Depression and despair.

By reacting outrageously, they ruffled their own feathers, not the deceased senator's. He would understand the issue and the accusation. He was there. The younger generation showed with its whining that it did not understood the issue, only the accusation. It was not there.

Endnotes

1. *Fargo (N.D.) Forum*, July 30, 1998.
2. Jocelyn Birch Burdick, interview by author, Feb. 6, 1995.
3. Lloyd Omdahl, interview by author, Jan. 18, 1995.
4. Ibid.
5. George Sinner, interview by author, Jan. 19, 1995.
6. Ibid.
7. Ibid.
8. Ibid.
9. Ibid.
10. Myron Bright, interview by author, March 26, 1996.
11. Jocelyn Birch Burdick interview.
12. Ibid.
13. Eugene and May Burdick, interview by author, Feb. 28, 1995.
14. D. Jerome Tweton, interview by author, April 1, 1995.
15. Charles Fleming, interview by author, April 25, 1995.
16. Eugene Burdick interview.
17. Senator Kent Conrad, interview by author, March 27, 1995.
18. Glenn R. Simpson, "Was Sen. Burdick a Communist Sympathizer?" Roll Call 23 (September 1993): 13.
19. Ibid.
20. Ibid.
21. Ibid.
22. Ibid.
23. Ibid., 14.
24. Bright interview.
25. Omdahl interview.
26. *Fargo Forum*, July 30, 1998.

- thirteen -

Stories

Stories are marvelous vehicles for understanding more about events and people. They yield nuggets of personal information not found in published sources or even primary material. Stories add color, humor and pathos to historical events and biography. Many stories become exaggerated through time, yet most stories harvest grains of historical truth.

Stories about American politicians appear particularly ripe. Politicians remain a living legend of our political culture. All politicians love to tell stories and in turn relish having stories told about them. The most popular stories, of course, get repeated again and again, some so often that they actually take on an existence of their own. Political stories make legends and legends create heroes. Heroes become popular, and popular heroes win more elections than those candidates who are less popular. Politicians in America who do not tell stories and do not have stories told about them are not very successful.

Nowhere is the juxtaposition between stories and historical fact greater than in the case of Abraham Lincoln. A recent review of the works of Lincoln suggests that there are more stories about Lincoln than facts; after time it is impossible to separate the two.[1] Which are the true stories about the 16th president? There is no easy answer because there are so many stories that have been repeated so many times. Yet, without *any* reliance on these stories, we would know very little about his early life. Lincoln stories embellish what we know about the historical man; the stories season his personal life.

Quentin Burdick was by no historical measurement Abraham Lincoln. He was, however, a popular politician who served North Dakota for more than 30 years. Like Lincoln, stories about Burdick abound. In fact, what many North Dakotans remember most about Quentin Burdick is simply a story or two. People do not recall how he voted on a particular bill or whether he gave a speech or said nothing at all. North Dakotans remember Burdick in less dynamic ways. For example, riding a horse in a local parade; wearing an old, green polyester suit; or freezing in the open stands watching an NDSU-UND football game. Many Burdick stories get recycled. They are stories repeated from firsthand experience or heard from someone else. In either instance, these stories — like those told about Lincoln — have been repeated so often that they have become part of the Burdick legacy. As a result, there are usually several versions to the same original story. Burdick stories, like Lincoln stories, add to our understanding of his character and to our knowledge of North Dakota history.

In almost all of the interviews I conducted for this book, I solicited and received an abundance of Burdick stories. Some fit more appropriately in other places within this work. However, since the majority of them focus on some aspect of Burdick's frugality, I decided to separate the best of these stories and include them in this Appendix — a sort of Top 10 list, if you like. Editorially, I also decided to put the stories in some sort of order and to identify themes based on different aspects of his frugality.

Following Quentin's stories are a few stories about Usher, too. Usher Burdick's wit and acumen adorn the pages of the *Congressional Record*. When he spoke, House members listened. What he said, more than bills or committee work, explain best who he was. Some of these Burdick quotables, identified here with subject headings, provide a taste of his spoken word and his homespun philosophy.

Quentin Burdick Stories

The Well-dressed Man

▌ That shirt *(Tom Burgum)*

See, what he wore really didn't matter a lot. He used to come out to my house, and in those days, you changed your own oil. He had this 1965 Pontiac and he would drive out on Saturday mornings. He would change the oil in his car and I would change the oil in mine. We would have lunch and then watch a college football game on television, or if it was late in the afternoon, Mary, my wife, would make dinner and then Burdick would go home.

He would always bring this old shirt. There was enough plastic in that shirt to hold off the OPEC oil boycott! It had oil stains all over it. Jocie, his wife, referred to it as "that shirt." So you can appreciate the shirt's status. One Saturday, he left it at our home and Mary washed it, which is kinda dangerous. But fortunately it survived. Burdick called Sunday morning.

"Did I leave my shirt out there?"

Yes, I replied, "Mary just washed it."

"Oh, my God! Is it all right?"

"Yeah. What do you mean, is it all right? Sure, it is all right."

"Good. I like that shirt!"[2]

▌ New shirts *(Bruce McKay)*

One time, I believe in 1988, Senator Burdick was filming political spots in Fargo. I don't know if something spilled on his white shirt or if he showed up at the television station without one because I was not there at the time. But I understood that he chased his staff around Fargo for quite awhile until they could find a white shirt for $10 or less. He wasn't going to spend more than $10 for a white shirt. He probably never did.[3]

■ New Suits *(Tom Burgum)*

Burdick earned the cheap thing image because he would always wear these old suits. I will tell you a story about that, and Mary, my wife, was also involved. She was working downtown and she would go over to Burdick's office to wait for me, and we would have dinner after 7. One night while she was waiting, Burdick called me into his office and said, "I'm going down to William Bard's. They have suits on sale."

By the way, this is 1975. Suits there cost anywhere from $1,200 to $800 a suit. Mary said, "Senator, you won't like it there. You should go to such and such a place."

He replied, "Oh, no."

Well, he went down to the store and they wouldn't even wait on him. He was wearing this old, green polyester suit. They said, "This isn't one of our customers." They were right. He wasn't one of their customers. He wasn't going to buy one of those expensive suits.

So the next morning, Burdick comes into his office. He is furious because they would not even wait on him. "Get your wife on the phone," he told me. "What's the name of that other store?"

So he went over to this other store. They had good suits there, but it is a discount store and their slogan was, "An informed customer is our best customer." So if you know something about suits, you can actually get a good deal. Burdick bought two suits and they were actually quite nice. Thursday he comes into the office and he is all dressed up, and he even has a vest on. I mean, he received more comments than if someone would have run over to him and asked, "Quentin, why aren't there any gravy stains on your tie?"

Later that afternoon, Marybelle, one of his staff people, was getting ready to drive him to the airport. "Wait," Burdick said. "I've got to change."

Marybelle turned to him and said, "What do you mean?"

Minutes later, the senator comes out wearing his familiar green suit.

"Senator, why are you wearing that?"

"I'm not going home in my best!"

So he flew back to Fargo in his old green suit![4]

■ *(Birch Burdick)*

My mother had a tremendous task every time it was time for him to get a new suit because his last one was threadbare. She would call the Sterns, good friends, down at the Straus store in Fargo and explain to them she was about to make the odyssey again. They would be prepared. So between the Sterns and my mother, they were able to coax my father, with a great deal of effort, into buying a new suit every several years.

I think it was a bit of a game. I think my father knew that when my mother decided it was time for a new suit that he wasn't going to get out of it, but he wasn't going to make it easy, either. It would be the game again and he would incorporate others into the game, like the Sterns.[5]

(Jocelyn Birch Burdick)

I did try to make him look better. He didn't want to spend a nickel on himself. Not a nickel! So it was very hard to explain to him that you couldn't buy a suit for what you used to. So I used many devious means. I bought him an ultrasuede jacket one year and would not tell him how much it cost. I told Eddy Stern, at the Straus store, that I would have his throat if he told him, and I didn't even tell Quentin what it was.

I just said, "This is a nice jacket."

"What is this?" he said.

"Oh, I don't know," I replied.

I wasn't going to say because if I said "ultra," he would think right away that it was expensive. He was so funny![6]

Black tie (Tom Burgum)

On one occasion, Burdick was invited to attend a formal dinner for five Western senators. The dinner was sponsored by some Native American group, and Burdick was one of the guests of honor. It was strictly a black-tie event. I was working as a lobbyist then and Burdick called me up.

"I want you to meet me downtown," he said. "I want you to go to this with me."

So here comes Burdick walking into the event wearing a sport coat and a black tie! I said to him:

"Black tie, Senator!"

He replied, "What color does it look like?"

About this time, one of the other senators, I think from Idaho, arrived wearing his tux and black tie. He greeted us.

"God, Quentin. I wasn't real worried that you would disappoint me because I knew you would not dress up."[7]

■ New ties *(Bruce McKay)*

I used to think that my own dad was frugal, but he looked like a free spender compared to Senator Burdick. Geri Gaginas, the senator's longtime executive secretary, went out and bought some new ties for him a couple of years before he passed away because she had just had enough of the old soup-stained neckties that he wore. He wore them a day or two and then suddenly showed up again with his old ties on again. She asked him what in the world he had done with them and he said he'd put them in the drawer because they were too good to wear. He told her he was saving them. You know, what are you saving ties for when you are 82 years old?[8]

■ Old Pants *(Birch Burdick)*

This story has to do with a pair of paint pants. He was not one who liked to part with any clothes, nor did he want to buy new clothes. He had a pair of paint pants he wore around the house in Fargo. They were in the worst possible shape. They had a split down the leg. The zipper didn't work. There was paint all over them, and my mother wanted to get rid of them because she thought they were just atrocious. So she threw them in the garbage can. Apparently, about the same time, my father decided he wanted to put that pair of pants on and do some work around the house, but they weren't to be found. Somehow he thought to look in the garbage can and he found them and rescued them.

My mother, however, undaunted, later repossessed the pants when he was not watching and marched down the alley and threw them in the neighbor's garbage can. My father soon discovered that his pants were gone again. So he retraced his steps and looked in the trash can. But this time he didn't find any pants.

Seeing some of the neighbor kids playing in the alley, he questioned them, "Have you seen Mrs. Burdick in the alley?"

With little fingers pointed to the garbage can, one replied, "Yes, she went over there."

So he rescued those paint pants once again from the neighbor's trash can![9]

■ Brown shoes *(Helen Pepple)*

I think one of the funniest things I remember is [when] I went out for Bud Sinner's inauguration as governor. The ball was beautiful. Bud in his tails and his wife, Jane, and all of those children in dress clothes. Here is Quentin with brown shoes, which struck me as terribly funny.

The other funny part of that evening was the color guard. They couldn't keep in step and I thought out of all of North Dakota, they ought to have been able to find enough people that knew right from left.[10]

The Fan

■ *(Thomas Clifford)*

I thought he was impervious to pain because in all kinds of weather, he just hung in there. He was, of course, tenacious, proud and macho. We talked about doing judo together and he was telling me how he would break boards.

Anyway, we were down at NDSU at homecoming. He had a small booth up there where the dignitaries could sit. [The booth] was nice and warm [even though] it was a cold, cold day.

We also had a roped-off area in front that we were sitting in. I sat down beside Quentin, and it was cold. He had his black hat on and his wooly coat, but with no collar on it. I looked down because our feet were in the snow and he had those little oxfords on and thin cotton socks. It was cold and the snow was piling up around his shoes like an ice cream maker. But we sat there and finally I said:

"Senator, will you let me get you a blanket?"

"No. No. I don't need any blanket," he said.

After a bit, I said, "Would you like me to get you a cup of coffee?"

"No. No. I don't need any coffee."

"Would you like to go up in the booth for a little bit and warm up?"

"No. Are you trying to move me out of here?"

"Well, aren't your feet cold?"

"I'm all right. I'm doing fine."

Well, I'll tell you, if he was doing fine, I'm the Queen of the May because my feet were ice and I was wearing boots. He had to be frozen, but he didn't want to show any signs of physical weakness. He was very, very set on that.[11]

■ *(Henry Tomasek)*

Senator Burdick always came, as most politicians did, to the football games at UND and NDSU for homecoming. As usual, we would tell the announcer at the game that certain people would be there, [give] him their names and instruct him to introduce them when the time came. At one game, for whatever reason, the announcer didn't read Quentin's name for a while, or anybody's name for that matter. They were too busy announcing the game. Quentin got pretty angry and I think he walked out before they finally got to introducing him.

He said, "It has nothing to do with me."

People may have thought that his ego was too big.

But he repeated, "It has nothing to do with me. It is the prestige of the Senate."

He wanted to be introduced ahead of the governor. There is a regular chain of protocol. Our football announcers don't know what the protocol is and they fit introductions in when the game is lagging or when the teams are changing sides for the quarter or at half time. When he walked out, the fans thought he was being rude, but he explained his reason later and he was serious about it. He demanded that the Senate be respected as an institution and that the position of senator be respected in the proper hierarchy. He believed in order and procedure, which is a lot different than what you might expect from his action of getting up and walking out.[12]

■ (Henry Tomasek)

He was one of the most loyal football fans you'll ever find. Many other politicians always left the game after they were introduced. They had other people to visit in town, but not Quentin.

There was one UND homecoming game when we had a downpour. Rain, rain, rain. I thought every underpass in town would be flooded, and Jocie, his wife, was getting wet. I offered to take her to the sorority house, where she could watch the game on television. I should have probably said that normally I was assigned to Senator Burdick whenever he visited UND. I always made sure that I had extra blankets in the car for the football games. But I left this game and did not come back. I tell you it was the worst rain I'd ever seen.

The next morning, the Grand Forks Herald published a photograph of the football stands with one lone figure. One person. Now, I don't know if that was a photograph of the whole stands or just one section because a good cameraman can do some of that. But it was Quentin! He wore what today is called a storm coat, but in those days, it looked more like a buffalo coat. It had a water-resistant shell and I'm sure it had a liner of 2 to 3 inches. He never got cold. He never wanted a blanket, and he sat there alone in that rain for the entire game.[13]

The Hitchhiker

■ *(Lloyd Omdahl)*

He was known as the hitchhiker among the Democratic inside circle because he was so cheap that he would figure out ways to catch rides with other people rather than drive his own car. If he did come back with a car to North Dakota, it was an old car. He had an old Chevy that he used to drive around with. It was one of the most economical versions that the Chevrolet company ever produced, and if he wasn't using it, he was getting rides with other people.

Another thing that Scott Anderson told me was that when they were riding together and had to stop for gas, Quentin would get out of the car and say, "I'll pay for the gas."

At first, this gesture simply astonished Anderson because he knew of Burdick's frugality. After the gas station attendant filled up the tank, Quentin wrote this guy a check from the U.S. House of Representatives bank. As they drove away, Burdick turned to Scott and said, "He will never cash that check. He will keep it for a souvenir." So Quentin figured whenever he wrote out a personal check, he was actually getting free gas.[14]

■ *(Arvin Kvasager)*

I think we were in Cavalier, North Dakota, and pulled into a gas station. Jay Graba, of the North Dakota AFL-CIO, was driving and we filled up with gas. At that time, I think gas was probably 29 or 30 cents a gallon, so filling up the tank amounted to only three or four dollars.

Quentin said, "I'll pay."

If you ever [traveled] with Quentin Burdick, he didn't offer very often to pick up the tab. He was tight as a drum. But this time he said, "I'll pick up the tab."

Jay and I both looked at each other and thought, "Geez, this is a first."

Burdick went in, opened his checkbook and wrote out a check to this Farmers Union gas station in that big scrawl of his and signed it, "United States Senator Quentin N. Burdick," and handed the guy the check.

When he got back in the car we turned to him and said, "Quentin, you wouldn't have had to do that. We have taken you out and should pay for the gas."

"Don't worry about it, fellows," he replied. "They'll never cash that check. They'll hang it above the office."

Invariably, that's what they did with the check. Here was Senator Quentin Burdick in Cavalier, North Dakota, buying gas at the Farmers Union gas station, and no way would they cash that check. It was a souvenir.[15]

■ (Mary Wakefield)

When Senator Burdick was out doing fundraising in California, David Strauss was to meet him at the airport and give him a ride into town that evening for dinner. Somehow they missed each other at the gate. There was a car waiting for him, but David could not find him. It turns out that they did not make contact with each other for several hours. They finally discovered that the senator took a bus from the airport. I mean a bus. It's going to stop at every single hotel, but that did not matter to him. He didn't have to do that to show anything. It was coming out of his own pocket, and he wasn't going to use campaign funds willingly, either.[16]

■ (Ardell Tharaldson)

I was Senator Burdick's chauffer for two weeks during the 1970 campaign. What I remember about it was that he started to use my toothbrush. I remember after the second day, I said to myself, "God, I gotta buy my own toothbrush. I'm not going to share a toothbrush with the senator!" I had to have my own toothbrush.[17]

■ (Wayne Sanstead)

Well, I had always heard the American Legion stories about how it never cost Quentin Burdick anything to travel across North Dakota. He would sit down and write a small check to somebody for whatever, and the check was always small enough that people would keep the check for a souvenir. Never cash it.

So I had heard all these stories. Boy, if anybody is tight-fisted, Quentin is the guy. So wouldn't you believe that very next night when we got to Gackle, North Dakota, for a fundraiser when the thing is kind of grinding down, he turns to me and says, "Hey, can you step outside for a minute?"

I said, "Sure. Why?"

"Have you got any money?" he replied. "I have to get to Fargo and take the bus and would you believe that I don't have any money in my wallet."

I quickly looked in my wallet and said, "Oh, yes, senator. I have a couple of tens here."

"Oh, no. It isn't going to cost me more than ten," he said. "Could you give me a ten and I will write you out a check?"

"No problem," I said. I gave him the ten and he gave me his check.

The bus came about 9:15 p.m. and I got in my car and drove all the way back to Minot and got home at about midnight.

"You won't believe it," I said to Mary Jane, my wife. "I was with Senator Burdick tonight and boy, did we have a good time."

After I dumped everything out of my pocket in the bedroom, she comes walking back into the kitchen. "You got a check from Senator Burdick?"

Smiling, I replied, "Oh, yes, I did. A ten dollar check!"

"Tell you what, Wayne. We aren't going to cash it. We will put it into the boys' scrapbook."

"No," I said. "We are not going to put it in the boys' scrapbook. We are going to do what he doesn't expect us to do. We are going to cash the check."

I never heard anything from him, but I always thought somewhere along the way he might ask me about it.[18]

■ *(Larry Erickson)*

I remember one time when I was state chairman of the North Dakota Democratic Party, Burdick flew into Bismarck. He called up the Democratic headquarters and said, "I'm at the airport. Come and pick me up." So I drove out right away to pick him up.

"God, I was lucky," Burdick said when I greeted him. "I didn't have a dime on me and I had to borrow a dime from some guy to call you to come and get me."[19]

■ *(Dick Backus)*

One time Quentin called me up and said he and his family were coming into Minot on the train later that night from Yellowstone, and asked me if I would drive him to Bismarck so he could catch an early plane to Washington the next morning. The train came in about 10 p.m. and Larry Erickson and I were there waiting at the station to drive him to Bismarck. Burdick got off the train wearing his familiar suit — the one he had probably worn straight for a year. It was all rumpled, dirty, and looked like hell.

"Where do you want to go, Quentin?" said Larry as we approached Bismarck.

"Let's go to the governor's mansion. They got a free room there."

So we arrived in Bismarck about midnight and Burdick got out of the car and pounded on the door.

Jean Guy finally came to the door in her robe.

"Hi, Quentin," she said. "It's good to see you."

We went in and started to visit. Governor Bill Guy got up and visited with us while Jean made us some sandwiches. I don't think Quentin had eaten since he left Yellowstone Park because he ate all the sandwiches. Everything was free. He was that way.[20]

■ (Larry Erickson)

I remember I was in Burdick's office in Washington. He was rushing to catch an airplane to Sweden. One of the girls on his staff, who was worried he might miss his flight, said, "Senator, where is your suitcase?" He turned to her and said, "Right here." But all he had was an attaché case. "What can you put in there?" she asked. Somewhat irritated by the question, he opened it for her. There were the papers he needed for the conference, one white shirt and one large can of Right Guard! He was ready to go and that is what he went with. That is kind of the way he traveled.[21]

■ (Lucy Calautti)

I was on the road a lot in politics in North Dakota during the 1970s and 1980s. The Democratic Party would send me on the road, so I'd find myself on the road with Quentin Burdick from time to time. I'd always get my own hotel room, but Tommy Stallman and Quentin always shared a room, at least when I was around. I just wanted my own privacy. Quentin didn't pay for his own room and yet he was insistent that he share the room with somebody. I always [thought] that was so funny. He'd always stay at different motels than I stayed at. I'd stay at a more expensive place because I just wanted to be comfortable. Not him. He'd find the cheapest motel and that's where he'd stay. I'd heard that about him, but by heaven, it was true.[22]

■ (Charles Mertens)

The Great Northern Hotel in Devils Lake at the time had deteriorated to the point where there were very few occupants in the upper hotel. They were just closing off floor after floor. This was a very beautiful hotel built by the Great Northern Railroad right across [from] the depot with red French brick, I think shipped in from France. It was never an expensive hotel, though. It was a railroad hotel.

At the time, Tommy Stallman was Burdick's lead man to take him around the state. We had scheduled a meeting with Burdick in Devils Lake and arranged to meet him ahead of time. We asked where he was staying and he said, "the Great Northern Hotel." Stunned, I said, "You've got to be kidding." So we went to the Great Northern and climbed up the grand steps to the second floor. I honestly believe he was the only occupant in the entire hotel. Tommy Stallman greeted us first, almost with tears in his eyes.

"Chuck, can you talk to the boss? Nobody should have to live in these conditions."

Quentin, overhearing the conservation, interrupted, "It was good enough for my dad and it is good enough for me."

Burdick was never a highflier and he didn't go to the very best hotels.[23]

The Fixer

■ *(Jon Lindgren)*

One morning, Elaine, my wife, and I wanted to see Burdick when he was back in Fargo. This particular incident occurred in the late '70s or early '80s when he was quite an elderly fellow. We called the house and he answered the telephone. "Come on over. Jocie's not here, but come on over." We went over and there he was in his grubbies. He had to show us that he was fixing the dishwasher. He laid down on his back and was pointing with a flashlight up into the pipes and explaining to us what he had replaced. He was so proud of his work, especially that he had jerry-rigged something else up there. "If you go to the hardware story and buy one of these pieces of pipe, it's several bucks, you know." So he spent his entire morning saving $2 and getting greasy. It was kind of a typical day for the senator."[24]

■ *(Leslie Burdick)*

I can't imagine a more wonderful way to grow up than in North Dakota, but also including that Minnesota part where you can grow up around lakes and sort of swim and paddle around. It's just a fantastic thing for a kid to do.

Quentin liked it, too. He used to love to come back on the weekends. One of the first things he would wonder about is what was broke. This is something that he actually looked forward to. What could he fix? The dock? The boats? I mean, he wanted to, and he wanted no help.

When the summer ended — I don't know if anybody has told you this, but Mother (Jocie) will just have horror stories about this. He didn't want — I mean, most people would either hire this work out or call on people all up and down the beach to come and help them bring in the dock or do this or do that, but not Quentin. He wanted to be the real he-man and do all this himself or do it with us. We were his little deputies and he would issue the orders. We would help him do these various things. We're talking heavy boats, heavy dock section, and a heavy, heavy raft to pull up. He would devise these winches and all this special equipment to pull things in and out and to do this or that so he would be beholden to no one. He could do it himself and we, his little deputies, would help him. He loved it.[25]

■ *(Leslie Burdick)*

As you know, this man who grew up, I mean, who came of age during the Depression, started his family all during that time. How tight he was with a dollar or even a penny!

One other story, small story, is just the way we would go from hardware store to hardware store even pricing nails. He wanted to get the best deal on nails and he would go to all the hardware stores in town until we found the best price on nails and anything else. I really don't know too many people who price nails.[26]

■ *(Jocelyn Birch Burdick)*

One year, Quentin built a canoe. This was when Leslie was in college and her college friend came to visit. We got this canoe ready, and when she wrote and thanked me for the week she spent with us, she said the most fun of all was riding in the homemade canoe.

It was a fiberglass canoe that was made from a kit. They have a million screws in them. If you think we had some kind of an electric screwdriver, we didn't. Quentin ran out of screws one day and he sent me into Detroit Lakes to buy some more screws. I went in with one screw to the hardware store and asked if they had some more screws like the one I did.

The man looked at me and said, "You must be Mrs. Burdick."

"Well, yes, I am," I said. "How did you know?"

"Your husband bought every screw like that we had in the store."

I just laughed. I thought that was so funny when he said you must be Mrs. Burdick, a man I had never seen before.[27]

■ (Lois Casavant)

I knew him somewhat through Campfire Girls. I was president of the Lake Agassiz Campfire Board for more years than I wanted to be. Jocie was on the board and so was Mary Andrews, so I had a little clout in Washington. Quentin was always ready to help. We would have roofing days at the camp, which is by Fergus Falls, Minnesota, and Quentin was always there on top of the roof.

Some distance from the camp was a small island in the lake, and for some of the activities of the camp, the older girls would row to the island and make a fire and so on. Evidently, this island came up on some government surplus list and someone from Detroit Lakes wanted to buy it. That would not have been a good thing for the camp. We seemed to be getting nowhere with the people we were dealing with, so finally we talked Jocie into talking with Quentin to do something. Lo and behold, Quentin got the island for us. We almost put up a plaque for him![28]

■ (Jocelyn Birch Burdick)

We have a tree house at the lake, too. My grandfather built it for me when I was a little girl because I started building a tree house myself and he thought I would fall down and kill myself, so he built it for me. Well, then Quentin came along and he built a roof on this tree house. He was always building something. He built a fence behind the bunkhouse to hide our gas tanks. He built posts for the dock, and also the dolly for the boat. He would tackle anything.

Someone said to me once, "You're so lucky that your husband can do all those things."

"Sometimes," I replied, "it's a blessing not to know how to do them."[29]

■ (Sara Garland)

We renovated our house on Capitol Hill, so we had lots of tools. I remember one Saturday morning when Senator Burdick was doing something in his apartment, he called and asked if we had a certain type of tool. We did. He would never pay to have anybody do anything for him. He said he'd be over in about 20 minutes. I stood out on the porch so that he wouldn't miss me. I waited and waited. I was looking southeast and I could see this big, black

Cadillac going up and down the street, so he had clearly gotten northeast and southeast confused.

Finally I get a phone call. It was Senator Burdick.

"I can't find your house."

"Well, I can see your car going back and forth."

"Well, you gave me the wrong address."

"There's no way I would give you the wrong address to my house."

In a few minutes he found the house and picked up the tool. He was just very funny and very endearing.[30]

■ (Jennifer Burdick)

My father loved puttering around the house. He got great delight in finding very inexpensive ways to either build or repair something. He took a great deal of pride in saving money. As it turns out, he was saving money and squirreling it away so that when the four of us got to college age, there was money available to go to any school we wanted. I think he was also very concerned about retirement or if something happened to him that my mother would be taken care of. [A] lot of the frugality had to do with saving. The money was there, but he was saving it. He wasn't spending it.[31]

The Race Driver

■ (Leslie Burdick)

He was an absolute terror! He scared the dickens out of all of us. He scared me because he didn't usually take the opportunity to look to see if anybody was coming whether he was changing lanes or whatever. We would all be madly looking about us when he was driving, trying to make sure we wouldn't run into anything. He thought, of course, that was crazy, and was not particularly pleased when we would warn him of some oncoming traffic as if he didn't see it. I didn't think he did see it, but he usually didn't appreciate my feedback on the topic. I kind of thought he had the feeling that was where he wanted to be and there should not be anybody else in the way. He was a terror.[32]

■ (Kevin Carvell)

I guess one ride to the airport is a classic one. I was out in Washington and David Strauss and I were staying at a place together. David, of course, was working for Senator Burdick then. The senator, David and I all had to return to North Dakota. Burdick was going to give David a ride to the airport and I was looking for a ride, too. "The senator is giving me a ride," said Strauss. "You should ride along with us." The senator and Jocie both picked us up and we drove off to the airport. We were a little late. Burdick made a wrong turn and we had to hurry even faster. I remember it was sort of a wild ride. He said it would have made the Iranian cab drivers in Washington look slow.[33]

■ (Gary Holm)

I remember talking with one guy who was on the weekend commute between Washington and North Dakota, pretty much the same as Burdick. He used to accept rides with Burdick because he would always have his car in the parking lot.

"Now it's gotten to the point," he told me, "where I really try to avoid him because he'll have me driving back with him. There's been a good number of times when we haven't made it back very quickly. He'll go to the parking lot and the car won't start and he'll just stay there and try and fix it himself."[34]

■ (Mark Andrews)

He was a pretty bad driver. I didn't drive with him very often because generally he would want to go with me in my car. Out in North Dakota, if the two of us were ever seen driving together in a car, we would make everybody suspicious.[35]

Quaker State

■ (Mark Andrews)

You know when you are a farmer you are always looking at the price of oil. I would have breakfast with Quentin when we would discuss something, and at the end of the discussion, he would turn to me with a broad smile and say: "By God, I bought some Quaker State oil for 47 cents a quart."

Here Quentin is down in Washington and he's going around scouting where he can buy some motor oil cheaper. He might have saved two bits over what he could have gotten someplace else, but he was just as happy as can be that he could do that.[36]

■ *(Sara Garland)*

I lived about 12 blocks from the Senate office building. This was probably in the early 1980s. My desk was right outside of Senator Burdick's doorway. When he walked out of his door, he looked right into my desk (That's not the way I wanted it, by the way).

I remember one day he walked out of his office. He also lived on Capitol Hill, maybe seven or eight blocks from me.

"Do you know where I can get the oil changed on my car?"

"No," I replied. "I really don't."

"Well, I actually have the oil in the trunk of my car," he said. "So do you know where I can change my oil?"

I knew exactly what he was hinting.

I said to him, "We can go to my house, and if you want to change it there, that's fine."

We drove over to my house in that awful Cadillac of his. Actually, I liked it. It was like this big, black ship in the night. He had to be in his early 70s at this point in his life. He parked in the back of the alley by our house, and I remember him opening up the trunk and there was a case of Kmart oil and an old pair of coveralls. He put the overalls over his suit, got underneath his car, and in about a half an hour, had changed the oil on his car in my alley on Capitol Hill. I remember him coming into the house with all those dirty rags. He wanted to know how to dispose of them. He wanted me to know that he was environmentally correct, I assume.[37]

■ *(Hank Weber)*

I recall as we were driving along in this old car of his campaigning, it seemed like he changed his own oil. He was asking me what kind of oil I was using in my car or pickup. I thought this was really something, that a guy of his stature would be changing oil in his car, crawling under there and draining it and all this and that. I've always thought of that as something where he was being quite thrifty, frugal or just stingy, or whatever you want to call it.[38]

The Car Salesman

■ (Geri Gaginis)

I had a lot of shopping trips for Senator Burdick. I think one of the funny ones is when he bought the old car. First of all, he took me along simply because I had a Pontiac LeMans. This was the same car that was for sale somewhere in Virginia. I think he paid $275 for it. We drove out there and looked at this blue Pontiac. It was a LeMans. The owners were sort of hippies. They were chart readers and astrological people.

So I am test-driving the car. Right! Senator Burdick isn't.

We're going along and finally he says, "I'm going to buy this little car."

"Why," I asked. "New tires?"

"It isn't just for the tires," he said. "It's for everything else."

So he wrote this guy a check. You could always sort of tell Senator Burdick was important, but you didn't know why. These people, of course, had no clue who he was.

They kept asking him and finally I said, "Senator, can I tell them you're a senator because they might think that it's kind of strange."

"No, no, no. Don't tell them anything. Just give them the check. Give them the check and we'll get the car."

In the end, the senator gave the car away [Democratic Party for an auction] and the guys in the Senate cloakroom [Senate employees] sort of knew Senator Burdick, too. The day after he gave the car away, we put a check for $750 on his desk just for the heck of it.

"Oh, do you believe that?" he said after looking at the check.

"I just gave that car away and here I could have had $750."

He was fun to kid.[39]

The Great Entertainer

■ (Gorman King)

It was about 10:30 p.m. at night.

I said, "Quentin, I haven't eaten. I came all the way to Washington on my own and the least you can do is buy us dinner."

"Okay," he replied. "There is a hamburger joint across the street."

"No, Quentin. We're going to order a real dinner."

"God, Gorman. It's expensive!"

Scott Anderson was scared. I told him to relax because I would pay for it, but I didn't want Quentin to know. We went to the restaurant and I ordered the most expensive item on the menu. I think Quentin ordered a cheese sandwich. Scott also ordered some meager bill. I paid for the bill and Quentin was very relieved.[40]

▪ *(Mary Wakefield)*

I just knew that if I would be with him over at the Senate dining room and he was going to pick up the tab, I would never, ever think of ordering more than the bowl of soup — the same thing he ordered. You just wouldn't do it because you would be in serious trouble if you did. He would often say, "I'm a product of growing up during the Depression." He would attribute it to that. And I would counsel incoming staff who we would hire, "Hey, if you end up being out for dinner with him or if you're in the dining room, don't cross him that way because you're going to look like you're taking advantage."[41]

▪ *(Chub Ulmer)*

I cussed Senator Burdick out a few times. We tried to break him down a little bit. One night three or four of us jumped all over him.

"Why the hell don't you relax down here and be a little better to your staff," we told him. "You know, you are going to die someday and you will want the people to think well of you. So just relax."

"What should I do?"

"Why the hell don't you get a little booze in your office so we can have a drink instead of having to go to some smoky bar."

I didn't see it, but I heard that about three months later, somebody went into his office and he actually offered him a drink. Some labor guys had been in earlier and had left Burdick some crème de menthe or some awful damn stuff and he had gotten out some paper cups and some cheap scotch. He made a grand thing out of doing it. When we went around the horn, we traced it back to the time we had chewed him out.

"Don't ever make any suggestions like that to Burdick again," we decided. But, he was really very royal and graceful about serving him a drink.[42]

Family Hurts

■ *(Jan Mary Burdick Hill)*

Every day was frugality. How can I choose one? I think the stories grew as he became a senator. The stories have grown since.

My frugality stories are not happy. They hurt.

They hurt. They hurt my mother a lot. I remember buying a prom dress and having to lie to him about the money, where it came from. She had to use the grocery money to buy me a prom dress. So for me to say they were fun [stories], no, not at all.

No. We would have to hide things from him. It was very hard on my mother. "Now, don't tell your dad," she would say to me. You know, it's kind of hard to take your grocery money to buy your daughter a prom dress.

If you want to call him frugal or cheap, fine, but no, I would say they were more unhappy times because I think it was very hard for my mother to live so poorly.[43]

■ *(Jennifer Burdick)*

Dad resisted getting a television for a long time. We didn't have a television in the house way past when everyone else did. The only reason we got a television was for Friday night fights. He really liked the fights. Really, that's why he got the television.[44]

■ *(May Burdick)*

Well, I'll tell you a story that first comes to mind. The first Christmas after Quentin and Jocie were married [1960], she started to get ready for the Christmas season. She made a big deal out of Christmas, just like we did at our house. "You can tell everybody in the family," Quentin told her, "not to pay over a dollar for any Christmas gifts for me."

The poor girl was crushed.[45]

■ *(Jerome Lamb)*

We'd see Burdick at the Fargo Public Library almost every year right before Christmas. He'd come in to get the Consumer Report, November issue, which had the best buys of the year. Sometimes his wife was with him, but frequently she was not. I suppose she got electric knives and who knows what else for Christmas.[46]

■ *(Margaret Scott)*

It was true. He was frugal and he carried it to extremes. He really did. I would tell Quentin, "Come on and give a $5 donation." It would hurt him to do that. He worked hard for that $5 and he knew it. I think his biggest fault, not a fault [really], he just couldn't understand that people couldn't remember how hard it was to make $5. I don't think he ever got over that. Oddly enough, a lot of us got over it and went overboard. We don't even remember it anymore and it was rough, really rough.[47]

■ *(Ethel Werner)*

Senator Burdick had this little apartment in Washington. It was above a restaurant and there was a long flight of stairs to climb to get up there. Jocie came down and furnished it with drapes and stuff. He had just a fit about the cost of all this. I'm sure she paid for it. On weekends he would go home to Fargo. But before he left, he would take all the stuff out of the refrigerator, unhook it and bring it down to the office. He thought his light bill would be less.[48]

Senate Kindnesses

■ *(Jessica Burdick)*

I remember following Dad around the Capitol during that last year when I was helping him. I was absolutely fascinated with how he interacted with people. The guards in the Capitol building, the train operator, the elevator person and the maid who cleaned the floors. He was always having chit-chats with everybody, with these normal people. He'd just sit down and chit chat. "Well, what is happening in your life today?" He was a friendly person and everybody knew him on Capitol Hill. I mean not the important people in life but just these ordinary workers on Capitol Hill. They all knew Senator Burdick because he was so friendly with everybody.

It was a good experience to go with him and to see how he would interact with people and how people interacted with him. How the common, ordinary person had respect for him as a person and treated him with dignity, not because he was a senator, but because he was a human being. They treated him with respect because he was a person who treated them with respect. It was a mutual relationship.[49]

Usher Burdick Stories
Excerpts from the *Congressional Record*

Usher on Usher

Every time I am speaking in this House and I get interested in the subject myself, the time runs out.[50]

I am a good deal like a preacher we had in our western country who was a good preacher, but was a little bit too liberal for the conservative element that ran the affairs of the church. No one came to church except on Easter Sunday, when the conservatives all came out to exhibit their Easter purchases. At the conclusion of the sermon, the preacher said: "My friends, I am very grateful for your coming out this morning. In case I do not see you again until another Easter I want to take the occasion to wish you a Merry Christmas and a Happy New Year.[51]

I never had anybody with me in North Dakota except for the voters.[52]

Many Republicans have said to me, "Why don't you leave the Republican Party if you don't like the way we operate?" My reply has always been that when I am in a party and it is right, my desire is to stay in the party and keep it right; if I am in a party and it is wrong, my desire is to stay in the party and make it right. I have not left the original Republican Party of Lincoln — I refuse to be legislated out of office by my own party.[53]

The Depression

We have asked for relief for the first time in 53 years ... a family of nine in our state is getting $2.50 per week for the entire family.[54]

The interest shark is more of an outlaw than Jesse James ever was. Jesse James robbed railroad trains but he never broke a railroad; he robbed banks but he never closed one.[55]

I think we know just about as much about handling relief as an inmate of a foolish asylum knows about the hereafter.[56]

I think I am perfectly safe in asserting that there are not 10 members of this House who know what the word communism means. ... Many good people would have us believe that every strike, every demonstration against a foreclosure of a home is communist-led. This unrest is not communist at all. Do you wonder that farmers gather in huge masses to protest farm foreclosures?[57]

I understand what some of the eastern members think if we cannot live out there in the West, we ought to move out. We are not moving out, however.[58]

On Agriculture

Do not get too excited about the Farm Bureau Federation. That organization is much like a bumble bee — it is biggest when first born.[59]

The farmer is not yet getting cost of production. He is selling his normal output at a loss, and this subsidy is an attempt and probably the only attempt that can be made in this Congress to even up the loss.[60]

When Brother Benson gets out in the Wheat Belt and the farmers find out that Benson soil-bank acres will be taken out of the already meager allotted acres for wheat, there will be a roar group that will probably last until Election Day.[61]

World War II

Those who are doing most to work up a war fever in this country will not be included in the draft; and if some may come within the draft provisions, they will enter a safe branch of the service or hide behind conscientious scruples against war.[62]

If war comes to the U.S,. it will not come across the Atlantic but across the Pacific. Yet we hear very little about this threat.[63]

Foreign Affairs

This Congress is getting more like the Zo-Zu bird of South America every day. Nature equipped the bird with eyes in the back of its head instead of the front. It cannot see where it is going, but it does know where it has been.[64]

The reporter who took out after Senator Langer for charging up an expense of $2,400 for trips to North Dakota really started something. Langer is the luckiest politician I know of. He gets more publicity than anyone here, and invariably the charges against him are trivial. ... While we are in a frenzy over Langer's expense account, I am going to attempt to place before the people all the bills of the members of the Senate and the House who thought it necessary to look after the people of foreign countries. If I can do this, Langer's expense account will look like a fly speck on the map of North Dakota.[65]

I have always considered that our efforts in the United Nations would not produce a deterrent to war. The only contribution made by the United Nations as such is to present a U.N. flag to our command in the Korean battle front.[66]

The Indians

I do not want to be listed as one of those who is mentally lopsided. I am not anymore interested or should not be any more interested in the Indians than any other member of the House. I probably know a few more of them a little better because I have lived among them for 60 years, but as between man and and man, it should not make any difference.[67]

Communists

Congress is treading on dangerous ground by making unlawful what a man may think.

I am speaking from experience. In the dark [D]epression days in North Dakota, when foreclosures and dispossession were rampant and whole families were being ejected out on highways because they were helpless; when wheat was selling for 26 cents per bushel and good steers selling for less than 2 cents per pound, and the purchasing power of the farmers had disappeared, men were caught in this dilemma and had families to support and would embrace any kind of ism that they thought might relieve them from this dire need, want and suffering. In that period, communists had a state ticket in the field and attracted many good people to it.[68]

Endnotes

1. McPherson, "Lincoln Speaks," *The Atlantic Monthly* 278 (December 1996): 119-24.
2. Tom Burgum, interview with author, March 24, 1995.
3. Bruck McKay, interview with author, March 28, 1995.
4. Burgum interview.
5. Birch Burdick, interview with author, April 18, 1995.
6. Jocelyn Birch Burdick, interview with author, April 18, 1995.
7. Burgum interview.
8. McKay interview.
9. Birch Burdick interview.
10. Helen Pepple, interview with author, April 13, 1995.
11. Thomas Clifford, interview with author, April 14, 1995.
12. Henry Tomasek, interview with author, Jan. 3, 1995.
13. Ibid.
14. Lloyd Omdahl, interview with author, Jan. 18, 1995.

15. Arvin Kvasager, interview with author, Jan. 26, 1995.
16. Mary Wakefield, interview with author, March 30, 1995.
17. Ardell Tharaldson, interview with author, Jan. 25, 1995.
18. Wayne Sanstead interview with author, Jan. 26, 1995.
19. Larry Erickson, interview with author, Jan. 9, 1995.
20. Dick Bakus, interview with author, April 27, 1995.
21. Erickson interview.
22. Lucy Calautti, interview with author, March 24, 1995.
23. Charles Merten, interview with author, Feb. 8, 1995.
24. Jon Lindgren, interview with author, Jan. 21, 1995.
25. Leslie Burdick, interview with author, March 28, 1995.
26. Ibid.
27. Jocelyn Birch Burdick interview.
28. Lois Casavant, interview with author, Jan. 23, 1995.
29. Jocelyn Birch Burdick interview.
30. Sara Garland, interview with author, March 22, 1995.
31. Jennifer Burdick, interview with author, March 26, 1995.
32. Leslie Burdick interview.
33. Kevin Carvell, interview with author, Jan. 23, 1995.
34. Gary Holm, interview with author, Jan. 27, 1995.
35. Mark Andrews, interview with author, April 19, 1995.
36. Ibid.
37. Garland interview.
38. Hank Weber, interview with author, April 20, 1995.
39. Geri Gaginis, interview with author, March 30,1995.
40. Gorman King, interview with author, April 25, 1995.
41. Wakefield interview.
42. Chub Ulmer, interview with author, April 25, 1995.
43. Jan Mary Burdick Hill, interview with author, April 18, 1995.
44. Jennifer Burdick interview.
45. May Burdick, interview with author, Feb. 28, 1995.
46. Jerome Lamb, interview with author, Jan. 20, 1995.
47. Margaret Scott, interview with author, Jan. 22, 1995.
48. Ethel Werner, interview with author, April 17, 1995.
49. Jessica Burdick, interview with author, Jan. 28, 1995.
50. *Congressional Record*, 76th Congress, 3rd sess.,1940, vol. 86, pt. 4, p. 4044.
51. Ibid., 76th Congress, 1st sess., 1939, vol. 84, pt. 2, p. 2187.
52. Ibid., 75th Congress, 2nd sess., 1937, vol. 83, pt. 5, p. 5660.
53. Ibid., 84th Congress, 1st sess., 1955, vol. 101, pt. 5, p. 5773.
54. Ibid., 74th Congress, 1st sess., 1935, vol. 79, pt. 1, p. 720-721.
55. Ibid., 76th Congress, 1st sess., 1939, vol. 84, pt. 4, p. 3580.
56. Ibid., 76th Congress, 1st sess., 1939, vol. 84, pt. 7, p. 7339.
57. Ibid., 77th Congress, 2nd sess., 1942, vol. 88, pt. 7, p. 9661.
58. Ibid., 75th Congress, 2nd sess., 1937, vol. 83, pt.5, p. 5658.
59. Ibid., 77th Congress, 2nd sess., 1942, vol. 88, pt. 7, p. 9661.
60. Ibid., 78th Congress, 1st sess., 1943, vol. 89, pt. 7, p. 9716.
61. Ibid., 84th Congress, 2nd sess., 1956, vol. 102, pt. 4, p. 4519.
62. Ibid., 76th Congress, 3rd sess., 1940, vol. 86, pt. 10, p. 11379.
63. Ibid., 77th Congress, 1st sess., 1941, vol. 87, pt. 14, p. A5059.
64. Ibid., 81st Congress, 1st sess., 1949, vol. 95, pt. 16, p. A6007.
65. Ibid., 84th Congress, 2nd sess., 1956, vol. 103, pt. 3, p. 3072.
66. Ibid., 81st Congress, 2nd sess., 1950, vol. 96, pt. 9, p. 11611.
67. Ibid., 77th Congress, 2nd sess., 1942, vol. 88, pt. 7, p. 9661.
68. Ibid., 83rd Congress, 2nd sess., 1954, vol. 100, pt. 11, p. 14644.

Bibliography

NEWSPAPERS

Bismarck Daily Tribune. June 19, 1908.

Bismarck Tribune. Aug. 20, 1960, 1-2.

Bonham, Kevin. "Decline of the House of Usher." Grand Forks Herald. Dec. 10, 1995.

Cassel, Andrew. "Buffalo Commons Thesis Angers North Dakotans." St. Paul Pioneer Press. Nov. 15, 1989.

Clymer, Adam. "Congress Stumbles on Honors for Welk." New York Times. March 12, 1991, sec. A, 18:1.

Dobson, Dick. "Rep. Usher Burdick: Salty Wit His Trademark." The Fargo Forum. June 20, 1964.

The Fargo Forum. Aug. 20, 1960, 1.

The Fargo Forum and Daily Republican. June 19, 1908,

Farney, Dennis. "On the Great Plains, Life Becomes a Fight for Water and Survival." Wall Street Journal. Aug. 16, 1989.

"Jocelyn Speaks." Grand Forks Herald. Oct. 2, 1993.

Jacobs, Mike. "A Senator Comes Home." Grand Forks Herald. July 15, 1984.

Grand Forks Herald. Sept. 27, 1983.

Grand Forks Herald. Feb. 6, 1978.

Grand Forks Herald. Feb. 26, 1987.

Grand Forks Herald. Oct. 25, 1988.

Grand Forks Herald. Oct. 28, 1988.

Grand Forks Herald. Oct. 29, 1988.

Lawrence, W.H. "Wallace Accepts Calling on Allies to Give up Berlin." New York Times. July 25, 1948, 1.

McLauchlan, Alden. "Usher Burdick will be Remembered for His Fine Mind, Rapier-like Wit." The Fargo Forum. Aug. 20, 1960.

Minneapolis Morning Tribune. Aug. 20, 1960, 1.

Minot Daily News. Aug. 20, 1960, 1.

New York Times. June 30, 1960.

New York Times. Feb. 10, 1991, sec. IV, 16:1.

New York Times. March 8, 1991, sec. A, 11:3.

New York Times. Feb. 10, 1991, sec. IV, 16:1.

New York Times. May 25, 1978, sec. A, 19.

New York Times. Nov. 16, 1956.

New York Times. Oct. 10, 1958.

New York Times. Oct. 31, 1958, 31.

New York Times. June 19, 1908, 1.

New York Times. June 19, 1908, 10.

New York Times. June 20, 1908, 7.

New York Times. Aug, 20, 1960, 19.

New York Times. Aug. 23, 1960, 29.

Rylance, Dan. "Quentin Burdick's 1931 Hospital Escape is Hard to Beat." Grand Forks Herald, July 30, 1992, 4.

Simpson, Glenn R. "Was Senator Burdick a Communist Sympathizer?" Roll Call, Sept. 23, 1993, p. 13.

Shabecoff, Philip. "Now the Environment According to North Dakota." New York Times, Jan. 9, 1987, sec. I, 16:3.

The Fargo Forum. Dec. 30, 1930, 1.

The Fargo Forum. March 29, 1932, 18.

The Fargo Forum. Nov. 11, 1932, 1.

The Fargo Forum. Aug. 29, 1933, 1.

The Fargo Forum. Oct. 16, 1932, 3-1.

The Fargo Forum. Nov. 30, 1933, 1.

The Fargo Forum. Jan. 22, 1935, 1.

The Fargo Forum. Jan. 23, 1935, 1.

The Fargo Forum. Jan. 24, 1935, 1.

The Fargo Forum. Jan. 25, 1935, 1-7.

The Fargo Forum. Jan. 26, 1935, 7.

The Fargo Forum. Jan. 28, 1935, 1-8.
The Fargo Forum. Jan. 30. ,1935, 9.
The Fargo Forum. Feb. 1, 1935, 1.
The Fargo Forum. Feb. 2, 1935, No 1.
The Fargo Forum. Feb. 9, 1935, 1.
The Fargo Forum. Feb. 13, 1935, 2.
The Fargo Forum. Feb. 16, 1935, 2.
The Fargo Forum. Feb. 17,. 1935, 1-4.
The Fargo Forum. Feb. 19, 1935, 10.
The Fargo Forum. Feb. 20, 1935, 9.
The Fargo Forum. Feb. 21, 1935, 9.
The Fargo Forum. Feb. 24, 1935, 1.
The Fargo Forum. Feb. 27, 1935, 1.
The Fargo Forum. March 3, 1935, 1.
The Fargo Forum. April 24, 1935, 10.
The Fargo Forum. Oct. 2, 1935, 1.
The Fargo Forum. Oct. 5, 1935, 1.
The Fargo Forum. June 16, 1939, 1.
The Fargo Forum. March 15, 1942.
The Fargo Forum. May 11, 1945.
The Fargo Forum. July 20, 1948.
The Fargo Forum. Aug. 3, 1955.
The Fargo Forum. Sept. 19, 1956.
The Fargo Forum. March 27, 1958.
The Fargo Forum. April 7, 1958.
The Fargo Forum. June 26, 1958.
The Fargo Forum. Oct. 25, 1958.
The Fargo Forum. Nov. 20, 1959.
The Fargo Forum. May 22, 1960.
The Fargo Forum. June 7, 1960.
The Fargo Forum. June 26, 1960.
The Fargo Forum. July 13,1960.
The Fargo Forum. July 30,1998.
The Fargo Forum. Nov. 5, 1958, sec. E.
The Minnesota Daily, Sept. 28, 1926, 1,6.
The Minnesota Daily. Oct. 1, 1926. 1.
The Minnesota Daily. Jan. 4, 1930, 1.
The Minnesota Daily. Jan. 24, 1930, 1.
The Minnesota Daily. Sept. 28, 1926, 9.
The Minnesota Daily. Sept. 29, 1926, 5.
The Minnesota Daily. Oct. 10, 1926, 6.
The Minnesota Daily. Dec. 3, 1926, 4.
The Minnesota Daily. March 29, 1927, 1.
The Minnesota Daily. April 26, 1927, 4.
The Minnesota Daily. May 14, 1927, 4.
The Minnesota Daily. Sept. 27, 1927, 4.
The Minnesota Daily. Nov. 26, 1927, 1.
The Minnesota Daily. March 31, 1928, 6.

The Minnesota Daily. April 4, 1928, 6.
The Minnesota Daily. May 24, 1928, 6.
The Minnesota Daily . Dec. 4, 1928, 1.
The Minnesota Daily. Feb. 15, 1929, 4.
The Minnesota Daily. March 9, 1929, 4.
The Minnesota Daily. April 30, 1929, 4.
The Minnesota Daily. May 4, 1929, 4.
The Minnesota Daily, Oct. 20, 1931, 4.
The Minnesota Daily. Oct. 20, 1930, 4.
The Munich Herald. May 5, 1910.
The Munich Herald. Dec. 29, 1910.
The Munich Herald. Aug. 31, 1911.
The Munich Herald. Oct. 12, 1911.
The New Prague Times. March 23, 1933, 1.
Special Strikers Bulletin (Fargo) Feb. 2, 1935, No. 1.
Special Strikers Bulletin (Fargo) Feb. 9, 1935, No. 7.
Special Strikers Bulletin. (Fargo) Feb. 15, 1935, No. 11.
The Spectrum (North Dakota State University). Feb. 1, 1945.
The Washington Post. Jan. 8, 1950.
The Williston Herald, Feb. 14, 1924.
The Williston Herald, Oct. 29, 1925.
The Williston Herald, Dec. 17, 1925.

JOURNALS

Anderson, A.H. "Space as Social Cost." Journal of Farm Economics 32 (1950): 411.

Blantz, Thomas. "Father Haas and the Minneapolis Truckers Strike of 1934." Minnesota History 42 (Spring 1970): 14.

Dibbern, John. "Who were the Populatist? A study of Grass-Roots Alliancemen in Dakota." Agricultural History 56 (October 1982): 681.

Dodd, James W. "Resolutions, Programs and Policies of the North Dakota Farmer's Holiday Association, 1932-1937." North Dakota History 28 (April-July 1961): 117.

"Farmers Educational and Cooperative Union of America, North Dakota Division v. WDAY, Inc." North Western Reporter 89, 2d Series. (North Dakota, 1958): 104.

Fite, Gilbert C. "Peter Norbeck and the Defeat of the Nonpartisan League in South Dakota." Mississippi Valley Historical Review 33 (September 1946): 217.

"Heuer v. Heuer." North Western Reporter 253. (North Dakota, 1934): 858.

Kramer, Dale. "The Dunne Boys of Minneapolis" Harpers 184 (March 1942): 389.

"National Farmers Union Life Ass'n v. Krueger." Northwestern Reporter 38. (North Dakota, 1949): 565.

Pratt, William C. "The Farmers Union and the 1948 Henry Wallace Campaign." Annals of Iowa. 49 (Summer 1988): 351.

Rylance, Dan. "William Langer and the Themes of North Dakota History." South Dakota History 3, (Winter 1972): 47.

"State v. Russell et al." North Western Reporter 264. (North Dakota, 1935): 534.

Talbott, Ross B. "The North Dakota Farmers Union and North Dakota Politics." The Western Political Quarterly 10 (December 1957): 877.

Wallace, Henry. "Report of Farmers." New Republic 116 (June 30, 1947): 12.

Tweton, D. Jerome. "Considering Why Populists Succeeded in South Dakota and Failed in North Dakota." South Dakota History 23 (Winter 1992): 331.

BOOKS

A Century Together: A History of Fargo, North Dakota, and Moorhead, Minnesota. Fargo-Moorhead Centennial Corporation, 1975.

Amer, Mildred. Members of the U.S. Congress Who Have Served Thirty Years or More. Washington: Library of Congress, 1991.

Blegen, Theodore C. Minnesota: A History of the State. Minneapolis: University of Minnesota Press, 1963.

Boorstin, Daniel. The Americans: The National Experience. New York: Random House, 1965.

Burdick, Usher Lloyd. A Short History of Munich Western Cavalier County North Dakota. Langdon: Cavalier County Republican, 1953.

Burdick, Usher Lloyd. Reminiscences of Mayville: The State Normal School North Dakota. Williston: Williams Plains Reporter, 1955.

Conlin, Joseph R. The American Past: A Survey of American History. New York: Harcourt Brace, 1997.

Connell, Evan S. Son of the Morning Star. San Francisco: North Point Press, 1984.

Conrad, Charles and Joyce. 50 Years: The North Dakota Farmers Union. Privately printed: 1976.

Danbom, David B. "A Part of the Nation and Apart from the Nation: North Dakota Politics Since 1945." in Politics in the Postwar American West, ed. Richard Lowitt, 175. Norman: University of Oklahoma Press, 1995.

Elkin, David. The Hurried Child. Reading MA: Addison and Wesley Publisher, 1981.

Frazier, Ian. Great Plains. New York: Penguin Books, 1989.

Gray, John C. The University of Minnesota: 1851-1951. Minneapolis: University of Minnesota Press, 1951.

Guy, William L. Where Seldom Was Heard a Discouraging Word ... Bill Guy Remembers. Fargo, N.D.: The North Dakota Institute of Regional Studies, 1992.

Innis, Ben. "Brief History of Williams Country, North Dakota: 1805-1910." In Vol. 1 of The Wonder of Williams: A History of Williams County North Dakota. Williston: The Williams County Historical Society, 1975.

Leuchtenberg, William. Franklin Roosevelt and the New Deal. New York: Harper and Row, 1963.

MacDougall, Curtis. The Components of the Decision, Vol I, Gideon's Army. (New York: Marzani and Munsell, 1955.

MacDougall, Curtis. The Decision and the Organization. Vol II Gideon's Army. New York: Marzani and Munsell, 1955.

Matusow, Allen J. Farm Policies in the Truman Years. New York: Atheneum, 1970.

McCullough, David. Truman. New York: Simon and Schuster, 1992.

Martinson, Henry. History of North Dakota Labor. Fargo: Labor Temple, 1970

Meachum, Henry M. The Closed Panther: Ezra Pound at Saint Elizabeths. New York: Trayner Publishers, Inc., 1967.

Miller, Nathan. Theodore Roosevelt: A Life. New York: William Morrow and Company, Inc., 1979.

Moon, William Least Heat. Blue Highways: A Journey Through America. New York: Fawcett Crest, 1982.

Morlan, Robert. L. ed. Political Prairie Fire: The Nonpartisan League 1915-1922. St. Paul: Minnesota Historical Society Press, 1985.

Morris, Edmund. The Rise of Theodore Roosevelt. New York: Coward, McCann and Geoghegan, Inc., 1979.

Neihardt, John G. The River and I. Lincoln: University of Nebraska Press, 1968.

North Dakota Centennial Blue Book. Bismarck: 1989.

North Dakota Votes. Grand Forks: UND Bureau of Governmental Affairs. No Date.

North Dakota, Secretary of State, Compilation of State and National Election Returns. 1946-1964. Bismarck: 1965.

North Dakota Votes. Grand Forks, N.D.: University of North Dakota Bureau of Governmental Affairs, no date, 161.

Omdahl, Lloyd. Insurgents. Brainerd: Lakeland Color Press. 1961, 9.

Peterson, Frank Ross. Prophet with Honor: Glen H. Taylor and the Fight for American Liberalism. Lexington: University of Kentucky Press, 1974.

Pringle, Henry. Theodore Roosevelt: A Biography. New York: Harcourt, Brace and Company, 1931.

Remele, Larry. "Introduction to the Reprint Edition." In Political Prairie Fire: The Nonpartisan League 1915-1922, ed. Robert L. Morlan. St Paul: Minnesota Historical Society Press, 1985.

Remele, Larry. "Power to the People: The Nonpartison League." In North Dakota Political Traditions, ed. Thomas W.

Howard. Ames: Iowa State University Press, 1981.

Robinson, Elyn B. History of North Dakota. Lincoln: University of Nebraska Press, 1966.

Register of North Dakota Veterans, World War II, 1941-1945 and Korean Conflict, 1950-1953. Bismarck: North Dakota. No Date.

Rylance, Dan. "Fred G. Aandahl and the ROC Movement." In North Dakota Political Traditions, ed. Thomas W. Howard. Ames: Iowa State University Press, 1981.

Schell, Herbert. History of South Dakota. Lincoln: University of Nebraska Press, 1961.

Schlesinger, Arthur Jr. The Coming of the New Deal. Boston: Houghton Mifflin, 1958.

Sevareid, Eric. Not So Wild A Dream. New York: Atheneum, 1976.

Smith, Glenn. "William Langer and the Art of Personal Politics." In North Dakota Political Traditions, ed. Thomas W. Howard. Ames: Iowa State University Press, 1981.

Stegner, Wallace and Page. American Places. Moscow: University of Idaho Press, 1983.

Stegner, Wallace. Wolf Willow: A History, a Story, and a Memoir of the Last Plains Frontier. New York: Penguin Books, 1990.

Steinbeck, John. Travels with Charlie: In Search of America. New York: Viking Press, 1962.

The Almanac of American Politics 1982. New York: E.P. Dutton, 1982.

The Almanac of American Politics 1984. New York: E.P. Dutton, 1984.

The Almanac of American Politics 1986. New York: E.P. Dutton, 1986.

The Almanac of American Politics 1988. New York: E.P. Dutton, 1988.

The Damon Runyon Omnibus. New York: Blue Ribbon Books., 1960.

Tweton, D. Jerome. In Union There is Strength. Grand Forks: The North Dakota Carpenter (Craftsman Heritage Society, 1982), 58.

Tweton, D. Jerome. "The Anti-League Movement: The IVA." In The North Dakota Political Traditions, ed. Thomas W. Howard. Ames: Iowa State University Press, 1981.

Walton, Richard. Henry Wallace, Harry Truman and the Cold War. New York: Viking Press, 1976.

Webb, Walter Prescott. The Great Plains. New York: Grosset and Dunlap, 1931.

Who's Who in North Dakota. Mandan: North Dakota. John Maher Publisher, 1984.

Wick, Douglas. North Dakota Place Names. Fargo: Prairie House, 1988.

Wilhelm, John. Ezra Pound: The Tragic Years. University Park: Pennsylvania State University Press, 1994.

Wilkins, Robert P. "Alexander McKenzie and the Politics of Bossism." In The North Dakota Political Traditions, ed. Thomas W. Howard. Ames: Iowa State University Press, 1981.

PUBLIC DOCUMENTS

Congressional Record, 74th Cong., 1st sess., 1935. Vol. 79, pt. 1, pp. 720-721.

Congressional Record, 75th Cong., 2nd sess., 1937. Vol. 83, pt. 5, p. 5660.

Congressional Record, 75th Cong., 2nd sess., 1937. Vol. 83, pt. 5, p. 5658.

Congressional Record, 76th Cong., 1st sess., 1939. Vol. 84, pt. 4, p. 3580.

Congressional Record, 76th Cong., 1st sess., 1939. Vol. 84, pt. 7, p. 7339.

Congressional Record, 76th Cong., 3rd sess., 1940. Vol. 86, pt. 4, p. 4044.

Congressional Record, 76th Cong., 1st sess., 1939. Vol. 84, pt. 2, p. 2187.

Congressional Record, 76th Cong., 3rd sess., 1940. Vol. 86, pt. 10, p. 11379.

Congressional Record, 77th Cong., 1st sess., 1941. Vol. 87, pt. 14, p. A5059.

Congressional Record, 77th Cong., 2nd sess., 1942. Vol. 88, pt. 7, p. 9661.

Congressional Record, 78th Cong., 1st sess., 1943. Vol. 889, pt. 7, p. 9716.

Congressional Record, 81st Cong., 1st sess., 1949. Vol. 95, pt. 16, p. A6007.

Congressional Record, 81st Cong., 2nd sess., 1950. Vol. 96, pt. 9, p. 11611.

Congressional Record, 83rd Cong., 2nd sess., 1954. Vol. 100, pt. 11, p. 14644.

Congressional Record, 83rd Cong., 2nd sess., 1954. Vol. 100, pt. 1, p. 765.

Congressional Record, 84th Cong., 1st sess., 1955. Vol. 101, pt. 5, p. 5773.

Congressional Record, 84th Cong., 2nd sess., 1956. Vol. 102, pt. 4, p. 4519.

Congressional Record, 84th Cong., 2nd sess., 1956. Vol. 103, pt. 3, p. 3072.

Congressional Record, 86th Cong., 2nd sess., 1960. Vol. 106, pt. 13, p. 17030-17033.

The Future of the Great Plains. Report to U.S. House of Representative, 75th Cong., 1st sess., 1947. Washington: GPO, 1947.

"Farm Bureau Fed v. National F.U.S. Corp." 198 F2d20, 33ALR2d, 1193.

Laws of North Dakota. 24th sess., 1935. 459-460

MAGAZINES

Binford, Howard. "The Senator and His Lady." Howard Binford's Guide , 13 (July 1980), 30.

"Cancer in the Air." Newsweek, 47, Nov. 26, 1956, 102.

"Cancer and Women Smokers." Time, 67, March 5, 1957, 71.

"Great Humiliation." Time, 64, Aug. 9, 1954, 65-66.

"Hoxsey and His Cure." Newsweek, 47 April 1956, 89.

McPherson, James M. "Lincoln Speaks." Atlantic Monthly, December 1996, 119-124.

"Smoking and Health." Time, 67, June 7, 1957, 40.

"Things Get Hotter for Hoxsey." Life, April 16, 1956, 125.

UNPUBLISHED SOURCES

Burdick, Quentin. Letter to Usher Burdick. Dec. 21, 1958. Box 34, Folder 4. Usher L. Burdick Manuscript Collection, University of North Dakota, Grand Forks, N.D.

Burdick, Quentin. Letter to Usher Burdick. Jan. 18, 1958. Box 34, Folder 4. Usher L. Burdick Manuscript Collection, University of North Dakota, Grand Forks, N.D.

Burdick, Quentin. Letter to Usher Budick. May 17, 1947. In possession of Jennifer Burdick. Baltimore, Md..

Burdick, Quentin. Memo to Glenn Talbott. July 22, 1948. Box 8, Folder 23, Talbott Family Collection, University of North Dakota, Grand Forks, N.D.

Burdick, Quentin. Letter to Emma Burdick. Nov. 11, 1933. In possession of Jennifer Burdick, Baltimore, Md.

Burdick, Usher. Autobiographical Notes. 1932. Box 36, Folder 12. Usher L. Burdick Manuscript Collection, University of North Dakota, Grand Forks, N.D.

Burdick, Usher. Autobiographical Notes. 1951. Box 36, Folder 2. Usher L. Burdick Manuscript Collection, University of North Dakota, Grand Forks, N.D.

Burdick, Usher. Letter to John Burke. Jan. 12, 1934. Box 35, Folder 7. Usher L. Burdick Manuscript Collection, University of North Dakota, Grand Forks, N.D.

Burdick, Usher. Letter to Eileen Burdick. Sept. 25, 1940. Box 16, Folder 14. Usher L. Burdick Manuscript Collection, University of North Dakota, Grand Forks, N.D.

Burdick, Usher. Letter to Eileen Burdick. Oct. 7, 1940. Box 16, Folder 14. Usher L. Burdick Manuscript Collection, University of North Dakota, Grand Forks, N.D.

Burdick, Usher. Letter to Dick Gordon. Feb. 18, 1957. In possession of Jennifer Burdick, Baltimore, Md.

Burdick, Usher. Letter to John Burke. July 18, 1935. Box 35, Folder 7. Usher L. Burdick Manuscript Collection, University of North Dakota, Grand Forks, N.D.

Burdick, Usher. Letter to L.C. Connell. Jan. 27, 1955. Box 33, Folder 7. Usher L. Burdick Manuscript Collection, University of North Dakota, Grand Forks, N.D.

Burdick, Usher. Letter to Mrs. H.C. Williams. June 22, 1958. Box 17, Folder 24. Usher L. Burdick Manuscript Collection, University of North Dakota, Grand Forks, N.D.

Burdick, Usher. Letter to A.J. Biewer. November 1958. Box 36, Folder 14. Usher L. Burdick Manuscript Collection, University of North Dakota, Grand Forks, N.D.

Burdick, Usher. Letter to Judge Eugene Worley. Nov. 20, 1958. Box 34, Folder 20. Usher L. Burdick Manuscript Collection, University of North Dakota, Grand Forks, N.D.

Burdick, Usher. Letter to O.J. de Lendrecie Company. Dec. 26, 1951. Box 16, Folder 14. Usher L. Burdick Manuscript Collection, University of North Dakota, Grand Forks, N.D.

Burdick, Usher. Letter to Harold Shaft. July 7, 1960. Usher L. Burdick Manuscript Collection, University of North Dakota, Grand Forks, N.D.

Burke, John. Letter to Usher Burdick. Jan. 15, 1934. Box 35, Folder 7. Usher Burdick Manuscript Collection, University of North Dakota, Grand Forks, N.D.

Janeck, Mrs. Telegram to Usher Burdick. Jan.30, 1958. Box 31, Folder 4. Usher Burdick Manuscript Collection, University of North Dakota, Grand Forks, N.D.

Kelly, David. Letter to Harry S. Truman. Dec. 11, 1958. Box 2, Folder 10. David Kelly Collection, University of North Dakota, Grand Forks, N.D.

Lanier, Bill Jr. Letter to John P. Moore. Dec. 11, 1956. Box 2, Folder 16. David Kelly Collection, University of North Dakota, Grand Forks, N.D.

Miller, John. "A State that Forgot Time." Chapter 5. Unpublished Manuscript. 1960.

Moore, V.C. Telegram to Glenn Talbott. Jan. 6, 1947. Talbott Family Collection, University of North Dakota, Grand Forks, N.D.

Nygaard, Daphna. Letter to Katie Louchb-
beim, Dec. 10, 1958. Box 3, Folder 3.
Dapha Nygaard Collection, University
of North Dakota, Grand Forks, N.D.

Shaft, Harold. Letter to Usher L. Burdick.
July 1, 1960. Box 16, Folder 14. Usher
L. Burdick Manuscript Collection,
University of North Dakota, Grand
Forks, N.D.

Sylvester, Chris. Inteview with D. Jerome
Tweton. Box 796, Folder 10. Milton R.
Young Collection, University of North
Dakota, Grand Forks, N.D.

Talbott, Glenn. Letter to V.C. Moore. Jan.
23, 1947. Box 8, Folder 23. Talbott
Family Collection, University of North
Dakota, Grand Forks, N.D.

Talbott, Glenn. Letter to Quentin Burdick.
July 28, 1948. Box 8, Folder 23. Talbott
Family Collection, University of North
Dakota, Grand Forks, N.D.

Young, Milton R. Interview with D.
Jerome Tweton. Box 794, Folder 19.
Milton R. Young Collection, University
of North Dakota, Grand Forks, N.D.

Young, Milton R. Interview with D.
Jerome Tweton. Box 794, Folder 29.
Milton R. Young Collection, University
of North Dakota, Grand Forks, N.D.

DISSERTATIONS

Thorson, Herbert A. "The Campaign and
Election of Quentin Burdick 1958."
M.A. thesis, University of North Da-
kota, 1963, 57.

Remele, Larry. "The Public Reaction to
the North Dakota Farmers Holiday
Association." M.A. thesis, University of
North Dakota 1969, 82.

Young, Allan. "Race of the Century: Guy
vs. Young 1974 U.S. Senate Election."
M.A. thesis, University of North Dakota, 1989, 45.

NONPRINT SOURCES

Andrews, Mark. Interview by author. May
19, 1995.

Backus, Dick. Interview by author. April
27, 1995.

Bergland, Bob. Interview by author. Jan.
27, 1995.

Bieri, Suezette. Interview by author. Jan.
17, 1995.

Bright, Myron. Interview by author. March
26, 1996.

Burdick, Birch. Interview by author. April
18, 1995.

Burdick, Jennifer. Interview by author.
April 26, 1995.

Burdick, Jessica. Interview by author. Jan.
28, 1996.

Burdick, Jocelyn Birch. Interview by
author. April 18, 1995.

Burdick, Leslie. Interview by author.
March 28, 1995.

Burdick, Quentin. Interview by author.
Jan. 6, 1992.

Burdick, Eugene and May. Interview by
author. Feb. 28, 1995.

Burgum, Tom. Interview by author. March
24, 1995.

Byerly, Ken. Interview by author. April 21,
1995.

Calautti, Lucy. Interview by author. March
24, 1995.

Carvell, Kevin. Interview by author. Jan.
23, 1995.

Casavant, Lois. Interview by author. Jan.
23, 1995.

Clifford, Tom. Interview by author. April
14, 1995.

Conrad, Charles. Interview by author.
March 25, 1995.

Conrad, Senator Kent. Interview by author. March 27, 1995.

Conrad, Joyce. Interview by author. March
25, 1995.

Dewing, Ralph. Interview by author. Feb.
9, 1995.

Dorgan, Senator Byron. Interview by
author. March 27, 1995.

Engel, Austin. Interview by author. Feb.
9, 1995.

Erdman, Walter. Interview by author. Jan.
17, 1995.

Erickson, Larry. Interview by author. Feb.
29, 1995.

Fargo WDAY Television Video. In possession of author. Sept. 11, 1992.

Fleming, Charles. Interview by author. April 25, 1995.

Fuglie, Jim. Interview by author. Feb. 2, 1995.

Gaginis, Geraldine. Interview by author. March 30, 1995.

Garland, Sara. Interview by author. March 22, 1995.

Glassheim, Eliot. Interview by author. Jan. 29, 1995.

Guy, Jean Mason. Interview by author. Jan. 20, 1995.

Guy, William. Interview by author. Jan. 20, 1995.

Hefflin, Senator Howell. Interview by author. March 31, 1995.

Hagen, Bruce. Interview by author. April 25, 1995.

Hill, Jan Mary Burdick. Interview by author. May 2, 1995.

Heitkamp, Heidi. Interview by author. Jan. 27, 1995.

Holm, Gary. Interview by author. Jan. 29, 1995.

Inouye, Senator Daniel. Interview by author. March 22,1995.

Jungroth, James. Interview by author. Feb. 5, 1995.

Karaim, Reed. Letter to author. Oct. 26, 1995.

Kelly, John. Interview by author. Jan. 22, 1995.

Kelly, Tish. Interview by author. Jan. 22, 1995.

Kemnitz, David. Interview by author. April 26, 1995.

King, Gorman Sr. Interview by author. April 25, 1995.

Kvasager, Arvin. Interview by author. Jan. 26, 1995.

Lamb, Jerome. Interview by author. Jan. 20, 1995.

Leonhard, Terry. Interview by author. Sept. 19, 1996.

Limvere, Karl. Interview by author. Jan. 24, 1995.

Lindgren, Jon. Interview by author. Jan. 21, 1995.

Link, Arthur. Interview by author. Jan. 25, 1995.

Long, Senator Russell. Interview by author. March 22, 1995.

McKay, Bruce. Interview by author. March 28, 1995.

Maher, John and Betty. Interview by author. April 26, 1995.

Matchie, Tom. Interview by author. April 17, 1995.

Mansfield, Senator Mike. Interview by author. March 28, 1995.

Mertens, Charles. Interview by author. Feb. 8, 1995.

Meschke, Herb. Interview by author. Feb. 10, 1995.

Miller, Penny. Letter to author. June 6, 1994.

Moore, Stanley. Interview by author. Jan. 24, 1995.

Mushik, Corliss. Interview by author. Feb. 9, 1995.

Omdahl, Lloyd. Interview by author. Jan. 18, 1995.

Pearson, Gary. Letter to author. Feb. 15, 1998.

Pepple, Helen. Interview by author. April 13, 1995.

Pomeroy, Representative Earl. Interview by author. March 24, 1995.

Sanstead, Wayne. Interview by author. Jan. 26, 1995.

Scott, Marge. Interview by author. Jan. 22, 1995.

Serkland, Chester. Interview by author. Feb. 13, 1995.

Sinner, George. Interview by author. Jan. 19, 1995.

Skewes, Morteer. Interview by author. April 15, 1995.

Stallman, Tom. Letter to author. fall 1996.

Strinden, Earl. Interview by author. Feb. 3, 1995.

Strauss, David. Interview by author. March 30, 1995.

Tharaldson, Ardell. Interview by author. Jan. 25, 1995.

Tomasek, Henry. Interview by author. Jan. 3, 1995.

Tweton, D. Jerome. Interview by author. April 1, 1995.

Ulmer, Chub. Interview by author. April 25, 1995.

Vogel, Bob. Interview by author. Jan. 16, 1995.

Vogel, Lois. Interview by author. Jan. 21, 1995.

Vogel, Mart. Interview by author. Jan. 19, 1995.

Vogel, Sarah. Interview by author. Feb. 7, 1995.

Wakefield, Mary. Interview by author. March 30, 1995.

Werner, Ethel. Interview by author. April 17, 1995.

Zaleski, Jack. Interview by author. Jan. 23, 1995.

Index